ORANGE AND STUART

Pieter Geyl, who was born in Dordrecht in 1887 and educated at the University of Leyden, was the greatest Dutch historian of his time, and a scholar of European renown. In 1913 he came to London as the correspondent for a Dutch newspaper, and in 1919 he was appointed Professor of Dutch Studies at London University. He later returned to the Netherlands as Professor of Modern History at the University of Utrecht, where he remained until his retirement in 1958. During the Second World War, he was imprisoned in a German concentration camp, and wrote *Napoleon: For and Against* (1944). He produced many books on Dutch history, including *The Netherlands Divided, 1609–1648* (1936), and several volumes of essays of which *Debates with Historians* (1962) and *Encounters in History* (1963) are the best known. He died in 1966.

ORANGE AND STUART
1641–1672

Pieter Geyl

Translated by Arnold Pomerans

PHOENIX
PRESS

5 UPPER SAINT MARTIN'S LANE
LONDON
WC2H 9EA

A PHOENIX PRESS PAPERBACK

First published in Great Britain
by Weidenfeld & Nicolson in 1969
This paperback edition published in 2001
by Phoenix Press,
a division of The Orion Publishing Group Ltd,
Orion House, 5 Upper St Martin's Lane,
London WC2H 9EA

A CIP catalogue record for this book
is available from the British Library.

Printed and bound in Great Britain by
Butler & Tanner Ltd, Frome and London

ISBN 1 84212 226 6

Contents

CONTENTS

prepares; Sole Bay (7 June); Defective land defences;
The French–Münster attack – Distress of Holland; Attempted
assassination of De Witt; Jacob van der Graeff – De Groot's
mission to Louis XIV (26 June); Amsterdam's bravery – The
people act; Events in Dort and Rotterdam; The Perpetual
Edict dissolved; William III Stadholder of Holland (4 July
1672) – Van Beuningen persuades the States of Holland to
break off the negotiations with France (7 July) – Arlington
and Buckingham cheered by the people (4 July); The prince
resists their bait (5 July) – England looks to Zeeland;
The negotiations continued; Treaty of Heeswijk; The envoys
return (25 July 1672) – Campaign of slander; Rotterdam
council in difficulties; William's intervention (7–10 July) –
Change in the prince's attitude towards the regents;
Charges against De Groot (20–23); Letter to De Witt (22);
Cornelis de Witt accused (26 July); Developments in Zeeland;
The popular movement – William's secret negotiations; The
seven-points (end of July); Charles's letters (22 July and 10
August) – Opposition moves; Differences of opinion about the
fleet (5–14 August); Anti-Orangist pamphlets; De Witt's
resignation – Charles II's letter to the prince published (15);
Massacre of the De Witts (20 August) – Intimidation;
The resolution of 27 August; The 'change of the law'; Pieter
de Groot's mission examined.

REFERENCES

Preface to the first edition

The subject matter of this book has been engaging my attention for many years. It was in 1923 that I first published an article on Frederick Henry of Orange and Charles I, in the *English Historical Review*, adding that it was the first chapter of a book. The article was, in fact, continued in various journals during the next few years,[1] but the promised work remained uncompleted – I had meanwhile been drawn into related studies covering a later period, of which the published result was my *Willem IV en Engeland tot 1748*. (*William IV and England to 1748*). In 1927, moreover, I was busily engaged on my *Geschiedenis van de Nederlandse Stam* (*History of the Dutch People*), and *Orange and Stuart* had to wait once again. And when I eventually returned to it, it had become clear that my original plan would have to be extended to cover the revolution of 1672.

As a result, the last part of this book was written some ten years after the first. However, throughout the interval, I kept reverting to the subject, the more so as it kept forcing itself on my attention even during my study of later periods, and particularly of the party struggle in the eighteenth century, when the English links of Frederick Henry, William II and William III continued to supply the enemies of Orange with a great deal of political ammunition.

I know, of course, that modern historians have dealt with the main consequences of those links both at home and abroad at some length, yet their full importance has never been brought out. That this applies to the policies of Frederick Henry and William II, few people familiar with Dutch history will deny; but I believe that the same is true of the period dominated by De Witt.

To begin with, De Witt's attitude to Orange cannot be fully understood unless his memories of Frederick Henry and William II are borne in mind. Secondly, the man who, in our day, has delved

most deeply into the political history of De Witt's reign, completely changing the prevailing ideas, Dr Japikse, not only played
down but perhaps even obscured the links between England on
the one hand and Orange and Orangists on the other (the two were
quite distinct, particularly during the minority of William III).
I referred to this point in 1931, when reviewing the first part of
Japikse's *Prins Willem III*,[2] and would merely like to add that my
respect for Dr Japikse's detailed knowledge of the period, which
despite our difference in approach I acknowledged at the time, has
only grown deeper with my closer perusal of his work.

But our difference of opinion remains, and I am now more
convinced than ever before that, to gain a true picture of that
crucial event in our history – the struggle between the Loevestein
and Orangist parties – we must view the events against the background of the Orange involvement with Stuart.

My attempt to provide that background, and to make it the
central thread running through my entire book, by following every
twist and turn in the relations between the two families and between their supporters, may open me to the accusation that I have
leaned too far in the other direction. All I can plead in mitigation
is that I have been fully aware of the danger, which I have tried to
minimize by paying attention to all the accompanying circumstances.
In so doing, I hope that I have achieved yet another aim: to make
my book acceptable to a wide circle of readers.

My published sources are fully acknowledged in the footnotes at
the end of every chapter. As for unpublished material, I have
drawn freely on the Public Records Office,[3] the British Museum,
The Bodleian Library, the Dutch State Archives, and the Amsterdam Municipal Archives. I am most grateful to the staff of all
these institutions, and also to that of the Royal Netherlands and
the Utrecht University Libraries, for the extremely helpful way
in which they have supported me at all times.

Last but not least, my thanks are due to R. R. Goodison, of the
University of London, who rendered me services of a very special
kind.

In 1935, Mr Goodison obtained his MA degree with a thesis,
written under my direction, entitled *England and the Orange Party,
1664-72*. His thesis was meant to pave the way for the conclusion
of my own work on Orange and Stuart and, as such, stood me in

PREFACE TO THE FIRST EDITION

excellent stead. I must confess that without Goodison's spade work I should never have been able to continue from Utrecht.

As the attentive reader will gather from my notes, I have simply lifted large sections straight out of his paper. But Goodison's thesis was more than a mere storehouse of unpublished material; he also perused a host of printed sources – including De Witt's correspondence, Aitzema, etc. – with deep understanding and scrupulous attention to detail, thus greatly easing my own task. Had his thesis covered the entire period of this book, I should gladly have coupled his name to mine on the title page.

Utrecht, Spring 1939   P. GEYL

REFERENCES

1. *Scottish Historical Review*, April 1923; *Bijdr. Vad. Gesch.*, 1925; *De Gids*, 1927 and 1928.
2. Reprinted in *Kernproblemen van onze geschiedenis*, 1937, pp. 116 ff.
3. State Papers Foreign, Holland; State Papers Foreign, Flanders; Newsletters, Holland.

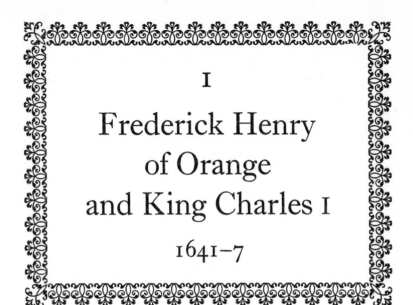

I

Frederick Henry
of Orange
and King Charles I

1641–7

The Stadholder's Position

The interest of Orange and Stuart first became joined when the
marriage of Frederick Henry's only son, William, to Mary, the
eldest daughter of Charles I, was solemnized in May 1641 in the
chapel of the palace at Whitehall. It is not difficult to show what
reasons led Frederick Henry to seek this alliance: he was swayed
by purely dynastic considerations, and hoped that by linking the
name of Orange with a royal line he would lend greater prestige
and power to the Republic. The prerogatives of the Stadholder
were ill-defined, and in the struggle with the burgher-oligarchy
of Holland, high titles, military fame and the splendour of court
life were valuable assets.

In 1625, when Frederick Henry succeeded his brother Maurice,
he had been forced to be cautious. It was a serious time for the
Republic. From its resumption in 1621, the war with Spain had
gone very badly, and had added fresh dangers to the aftermath
of the bitter quarrels between strict Calvinists and Arminians,
which marked the Twelve Years' Truce. The new Stadholder,
whose sympathies had been with the vanquished party rather

1

than with his brother, was careful not to make his bias public. At one time it even seemed as if the Stadholder would bow to the States. Frederick Henry was not only courteous and affable, he was subservient. He adopted a genial tone towards the patricians, declaring that he had 'no taste for German pomp', but that he was a Hollander like themselves, 'born at Delft'.[1]

With the first successes on the battlefield, however, his attitude changed, and it soon became apparent that he was far more intent on making his power felt than Maurice had been before him. Maurice had seized power when his passions had been aroused by a violent political crisis, only to let it slip almost heedlessly from his grasp as soon as he had gained his end.

It was not so with Frederick Henry. He worked consciously and steadily, patiently and cautiously, towards the strengthening of his position. Moreover, he had a son, so that unlike Maurice he worked not for himself alone, but also for his House. He made use of all the advantages accruing from the peculiar constitution of the Republic. The distribution of offices gained him partisans in every quarter. The permanent committees that played such an important part in the administration of the Dutch Republic were devoted to his interests, and in more than one province his confidants and protégées were able to sway their respective provincial States' assemblies to do his bidding.

Frederick Henry turned his particular attention to the composition of the States-General. The deputies were usually appointed for long periods, and it was an easy matter for him to exercise considerable influence, at least upon the representatives of the inland provinces, most of whom were nobles and depended on him to advance the military careers of their sons and relatives. Far removed from their principals who, moreover, were in session for only a few weeks in the year, they were able to follow their own, or rather the prince's, will much more easily than could the Hollanders who, as the States-General met in the Hague, were always under the eyes of their masters, the States of Holland. When in the course of time, for the sake of speed and secrecy, it became customary to allow the Stadholder to decide important questions of foreign policy with a committee of the States-General meeting in his 'cabinet', Frederick Henry had little difficulty in selecting men ready to follow his lead. In this way he came near to holding supreme power.

In June 1643, this Secret Committee (*Secreet Besogne*), which had until then been a purely informal body, was set on a somewhat firmer basis. A resolution was passed authorizing the prince to have all the decisions of the Committee recorded by the greffier of the States-General and laying it down that these decisions would be as valid as if they had been taken in full assembly. While the States-General did not completely relinquish their control of foreign policy, they were now reduced to deciding whether or not questions should be 'deferred' to the Committee. It must have been difficult, however, for them to re-open a question once it had been so 'deferred' because the Committee's deliberations continued to be secret – indeed that was what mattered to the prince.[2] So far did his influence extend by then that the States often allowed him to select (to 'assume' was the current term) members of the Committee.[3]

For a number of years, there had been a few differences of opinion on national policy, and the Stadholder came to be regarded as a natural leader. This helped him to pave the way towards a position of real power. Curiously enough, at the very time when the Secret Committee was established more firmly than ever before and had fallen so largely under the prince's sway, there was growing dissension over the plan to form an alliance with France with a view to the final conquest of the Spanish Netherlands and their division between the two powers. But Frederick Henry managed to get the military alliance with France adopted: the Secret Committee, just established, proved an efficient tool in his hands, and the decision to wage war on Spain further strengthened his hand – at least for a time. Richelieu's gratitude was such that he began addressing Frederick Henry as 'Your Highness', whereas hitherto, like his brother and father, Frederick had had to be content with a mere 'Your Excellency'. This, too, was an important step, and without it the next one, the royal marriage, might never have taken place. Moreover, his confidential understanding with the French ambassadors greatly enhanced the prince's foreign standing.

Thus, from the moment when the French alliance was mooted there was a renewal of opposition to the Stadholder, but it was of an entirely different nature from the opposition encountered by

Maurice. This time, it was not merely a protest against a particular policy, but also against the growth in the Stadholder's powers. All over Europe, sovereigns were struggling to wrest absolute power from assemblies that held fast to their ancient privileges. In France, Richelieu furthered the cause of his king with marked success, and it was Richelieu, who in 1635 had entered into close relations with Frederick Henry, and who, doubtless, did all in his power to reinforce the monarchical principle in the Republic as well. In England, Charles I had been ruling without a parliament, and when at length he was obliged to summon one, the only result was bitter conflict. It was Charles I who was such a fervent monarchist that, speaking to a Dutch ambassador, he described the Dutch government, quite calmly and without a thought of discourtesy, as 'a populace without discretion'.[4] It was with Charles that Frederick Henry was now seeking an intimate connection, one that would further increase the prestige of Orange; many people at the English court even regarded it as a preliminary to a *coup d'état* by which the Stadholder would be transformed from servant of the States to sovereign ruler of his country.[5]

No wonder, therefore, that the regent class of the Netherlands, and especially of the wealthy trading province of Holland, did not favour the prince's marriage plan. More so even than the French alliance, the royal connection caused a storm of opposition against the Stadholder in his later years. Indeed, what was held particularly against him was that his intimacy with the Stuarts was palpably at variance with the national interest: it was so obviously a purely dynastic move. In pursuing this type of policy, Frederick Henry, and William II after him, could no longer count on that popularity with the Calvinist middle-class which had stood the Princes of Orange in such good stead in their struggles with the States of Holland. The army, of course, never failed to support them, nor the nobility, especially the poor gentry of the inland provinces who looked to the Stadholder for help against the ambitions of the towns, represented in their States assemblies.

It was thanks to them that Frederick Henry had so great a hold over the States-General. However, the fact that the smaller provinces generally stood by the Stadholder's policy, while the main opposition invariably came from Holland, is no proof that the interests of these provinces were best served by the Stadholder's policy, which meant first, war with Spain, and soon afterwards,

4

war with England. It was simply that Holland, the wealthiest province by far, with the strongest and most self-confident burgher-class, represented the element in the Republic that was sufficiently independent to stand up to the Stadholder's encroachments.

The offer of marriage (1639); The advantages to Charles (May 1641); Civil War in England

At the time when Frederick Henry, on behalf of his son, approached Charles for the hand of one of his daughters, Charles was much more inclined to side with Spain than with her enemies, France and the United Netherlands. In 1635, the English court heard with displeasure of the plan to share out the southern Netherlands, and in 1637, the king told the Count d'Estrades that he would do everything in his power to oppose the conquest of the Flemish coast. True, as a result of growing internal dissension and the impending Scottish revolt, Charles's power was extremely limited. By levying ship-money, he had been able to equip a fleet, but in 1639 he was unable to prevent the Dutch admiral Tromp from attacking the Spanish expeditionary fleet in English waters. The attitude of the English government to this affair was so ambiguous that Holland at first suspected, and afterwards generally believed, that England had promised support for the Spanish enterprise.[6] The suspicion was in fact groundless, but Charles I was certainly anxious to curry favour with Spain. His dearest aim in those days – it had been his father's before him – was to negotiate Spanish marriages for his children. His wife, Henrietta Maria, sister of the reigning King of France, strengthened him greatly in this resolve, and her friend, the Duchesse de Chevreuse, who was a sworn enemy of Richelieu, acted as go-between. In these circumstances, the French government could hardly regard the English court as anything but hostile. There is no conclusive proof that Richelieu actually supported the Scottish rising of 1639, but he certainly did maintain friendly relations[7] with the English parliamentary opposition when, in the following year, it was able to make itself felt again and increasingly paralysed Charles's capacity for action.

It was then that the subject of the marriage between Frederick Henry's son and one of the daughters of Charles I was broached once again. It was first raised with the Queen's mother, Marie de

Médici,[8] the Queen Mother of France (and no friend of Richelieu's) during her stay in Holland in 1638. In the following year Jan van der Kerckhoven, Lord of Heenvliet, who had earlier been presented to Marie de Médici, was sent to England as the prince's private envoy, with secret instructions[9] to start marriage negotiations. He made little progress and, in February 1640, Frederick Henry, on behalf of the States-General, requested that Aerssens van Sommelsdijk, who was then in England, approach Heenvliet and take over from him.[10]

It was Sommelsdijk's official task to explain the motives that had led the States-General to order Tromp's attack on the Spanish fleet; at the same time he was to study the possibilities of signing a treaty with England. But the attitude of the English court was not very encouraging, and when Frederick Henry's appeal reached him, Sommelsdijk had just sent an urgent request for his recall, suspecting as he did that his presence in England was merely being used to force Spain to support the English against the Scots. Sommelsdijk was enough of a statesman to protest vigorously to Frederick Henry, when he gathered that Charles had been told (apparently by Heenvliet in his zeal for the matrimonial plan)[11] that he had instructions not merely to justify Tromp's action, but also to apologize for it. At the same time, he was too much of a courtier not to accede with zeal, even with gratitude, to the request to take charge of the marriage negotiations. (The regular ambassador from the States-General, Joachimi, who had been in England for many years and was by now a very old man, barely took part in these negotiations. He was a refugee from Flanders and a supporter of the States of Holland rather than of the House of Orange.)

It can be imagined that a Dutch statesman, especially one who belonged to the Orange party, which believed in war to the death with Spain, would try his utmost to couple the marriage plan with an attempt to divorce England from Spain.[12] Sommelsdijk did in fact take this line on a number of occasions.[13] But could he seriously have supposed that with the prevailing temper at the English court, he would have any chance of success? After all, the proposed marriage was no favour to the English king, and hence no bargaining counter.[14] As early as January, Sommelsdijk, although not yet charged with furthering Frederick Henry's plea, made just that point, when he tried to win Charles over with the following argument:

6

By this marriage you will gain for yourself a first claim on the affections and interests of His Highness and the United Provinces, while if you seek kinship with a house of greater power than your own [Spain], you can expect nothing from their ambitions, but will only lose your daughter, whom you will force into wedding interests opposed to your own.[15]

The doubtful character of a dynastic relationship between Stuart and Orange could not have been better expressed. In generations to come, this relationship repeatedly threatened to place the lesser of the two houses in a position of dependence. Heenvliet, in fact, had been instructed to assure the king in the most respectful manner that the prince, his consort and his son would never forget the great favour of this connection, but that he, Frederick Henry, would on the contrary 'acknowledge it by his services whenever it might please His Majesty to let him know his commands'.[16]

But Sommelsdijk at least tried to make one stipulation, namely that only the eldest daughter would be acceptable. That ought at any rate to have ruled out the possibility of a Spanish marriage, for Spain would certainly not condescend to take the second daughter if the eldest had been allotted to the Prince of Orange. But, no doubt for the same reasons, the English court was only prepared to consider offering the second daughter. Sommelsdijk blamed this design on the two queens.[17] He even feared that, like the political treaty, the marriage negotiations were merely a means of putting pressure on Spain.[18] If it was possible to get only a younger daughter, he said finally, then he preferred a marriage to a French princess.[19] Certainly a French connection was much more in keeping with the policy of Orange at that juncture, but Frederick Henry had set his heart so much on a marriage with one of Charles's daughters that he decided to make do with the second.

Thus when the matter was settled in principle at the end of 1640, it was Elizabeth, a child of five, who was designated as the future bride of William II. The final negotiations were carried on by a formal embassy of the States-General, who were officially informed by Frederick Henry in December 1640 – the position of the Stadholder was such that the marriage of his son was regarded as a matter of state. Sommelsdijk, who was appointed to the new mission as well, could now give even more positive assurances that the friendship of the Prince of Orange meant the friendship of the

7

Republic. At the same time, Frederick Henry sent Beverweert to France, where the English marriage project was causing great uneasiness, to explain that it was a private matter and in no way affected the policy of the Republic.

The fact that, in January 1641, the ambassadors should have listened to English proposals for a treaty between the two countries, in no way detracted from the sincerity of the view expressed to France. The ambassadors were expressly instructed to do what they could to separate England from Spain, and it was the popular interpretation of the marriage plan that it would serve that very purpose. The only questions were, how far the royal negotiators actually represented the king's views or even how sincere the king himself was when he informed Parliament of his intentions.[20] The House clearly favoured a treaty. But was it not Charles's design to use the name of Orange as a mere sop to Protestant irritation, and to do so without loosening his ties with Spain?

Domestic difficulties were beginning to overwhelm the king. After ruling without a parliament for eleven years (except for the so-called Short Parliament of April and May 1640), he was forced to summon one shortly before the arrival of the Dutch ambassadors; this assembly (the Long Parliament as it was later called), aware of the king's impotence against the Scottish Covenant army in the north of England, at once launched into an open attack on the monarchy. Charles's advisers, Strafford and Laud had already been arrested; Windebank and Finch had fled. Yet Charles did not for a moment think of adopting a Protestant, anti-Spanish policy, which would have gone a long way towards pacifying his new parliamentary advisers. Instead he continued to look upon the marriage through Sommelsdijk's eyes: as a way to gain the good offices of the Prince of Orange. And as things then were, this was a prospect not to be despised.

Charles 1 had an exaggerated idea of the power of the Stad-holder, although that power was undoubtedly great.[21] He thought, and Somelsdijk did nothing to disabuse him, that the prince could dictate the Republic's foreign policy, and that he could effectively intervene in England's domestic troubles. No wonder that Charles was now willing to give his eldest daughter to the young Prince of Orange.[22]

Thus, even before it took place, the significance of the marriage was entirely changed, but this in no way deterred Frederick Henry.

8

At the very moment when Sommelsdijk was beginning to realize that the upheavals and divisions in England militated against the signing of a political treaty, he gave his consent to a marriage linking the Stadholder's power, not to England as a whole, but to one of the parties contending for supremacy. Moreover, it was given to the one that was for a long time to remain the weaker. On 12 February, the contract was signed.[23]

When young William of Orange came to England for his marriage to Mary (early in May 1641), the royal family was feeling the deep humiliation of Strafford's trial. Mary, despite her youth, had been present to witness the tragic proceedings in Parliament.[24] A few days before the marriage ceremony, the Lower House had passed the bill of attainder against Strafford; a few days later, the Upper House concurred. Even before William (who had to leave his bride behind for a time) had set sail from England, the king had given his assent to the bill. It was indeed a most unpropitious moment for a union with the Stuarts. The English people who, not so long before would have welcomed the Protestant marriage as a sign that the king was at last turning away from Spain, now regarded it with suspicion, fearing that Charles had given his consent against a promise of help in subduing his own subjects.[25]

Sommelsdijk had strong suspicions that the marriage might be annulled later by the English, who put up an obstinate resistance to all suggestions that the nine-year-old Mary accompany her husband to Holland. Others, too, thought this a bad augury. Before the bride had 'actually gone on board',[26] ran the opinion of Van Reigersberch, the brother-in-law of Grotius, it was useless to hope for anything from the marriage; the suspense, he went on to argue, was entirely to the advantage of the English, who would be able to extort still further concessions. When, in October, the question of a new embassy to England arose, ostensibly to negotiate an alliance but in reality to bring about the *domiductio*, Reigersberch feared that the English would want to 'make use of this goad a little longer';[27] he expressed anxiety that negotiations carried on in such circumstances would not be very favourable to the interests of his country. But the choice of his daughter's place of residence was soon afterwards taken out of Charles's hands. In 1641, his fortunes went from bad to worse. Finally, at the beginning of 1642, came civil war. Charles had to leave London, and sent his wife,

Henrietta Maria, with the Princess Royal to their new friends in Holland.

In announcing the intended journey to the States-General, Charles's resident, Sir William Boswell, said that Charles was sending his daughter over as a token of his friendship to the Netherlands, and that her mother was merely going along to keep her company. As a matter of fact, fear for the safety of his wife, a Roman Catholic whose strong personality had made her the heart and soul of the anti-parliamentary party, was the main motive of Charles's decision. The sea journey was in the nature of a flight. Yet, as we shall see, Henrietta Maria meant to turn it to good advantage by enlisting help in the Netherlands.

Instead of the dowry stipulated in the marriage contract, Henrietta Maria brought along the crown jewels, which she hoped to pawn in Holland. In addition, she tried to obtain war materials, and permission for English officers and men then serving the States to rejoin the king's standard.

The two royal ladies who landed in the Netherlands under such unhappy circumstances were received with great pomp. Yet all they now brought the House of Orange was their royal blood. All the more anxious was Frederick Henry that they should receive due homage. If we are to believe a royalist writer of the period, the prince never entered the presence of his daughter-in-law, then a child of ten, 'but with a reverence more like a subject towards his sovereign than the freedom of a father towards his son's wife'.[28] In fact, he made detailed dispositions as to the formalities with which the Princess Royal was to be treated, now that she was delivered into the hands of the Orange family, and these were all calculated to lay stress on her rank.[29] On the English side, too, great care was taken to maintain her rank.

It was by no means a small household that was deemed befitting to the king's daughter. According to the marriage contract, she had to be allowed forty English servants, in whose appointment the House of Orange had no say, although it had to bear the entire cost. At the head of her household, it is true, Charles I placed a Dutchman,[30] the self-same Heenvliet whom Frederick Henry had charged to negotiate the marriage. But the ambitious Heenvliet – he was the son of a Leyden professor of theology and had merely bought the manor of Heenvliet – had meanwhile given a pledge of loyalty to the English royal family. Shortly before – his first wife having died in March 1640[31] – he had married an English widow of position, Lady Stanhope, and his ambitions were now centred in English titles and English property. Lady Stanhope (she continued to use that name after her second marriage) was appointed governess to the young bride.

The retinue of eighty persons which Mary brought with her from England was modest compared with the three hundred followers who, according to Aitzema, attended her mother. Frederick Henry resigned himself to bear most of the costs. The States occasionally complained at their share, especially when the queen 'for her amusement' travelled through the province 'at the country's expense, with a retinue of 600 persons'.[32] (Such is the number given, but this probably included the Stadholder's court.)

The people were dazzled by the splendour of it all, and especially by the ceremonial reception in Amsterdam, to which the princess, accompanied by the Stadholder and his son, paid a visit in May. In the allegorical scenes that formed part of the celebrations, reference was made to marriages between Counts of Holland and Gelderland and English princesses, thus likening the Prince of Orange to sovereigns of former times. Vondel's voice, too, was heard in heartfelt jubilation; to him the children of princes, like the children of kings, were

> . . . those who by God as helmsmen are ordained
> To serve the common weal.[33]

Even Hooft – the scion of an Amsterdam regent family – who in that year dedicated his *Historiën* to the prince (not, of course, omitting a reference to the 'royal bridegroom') referred to himself as the prince's 'subject', conveniently overlooking the sovereignty of the States.

All this was just what Frederick Henry intended. But the situation was not without its ugly aspects. The royal child was far from being docile. Before the year 1642 was out, there were reports of a violent scene in which she showed her mother-in-law 'contempt, hatred and dissatisfaction',[34] and her effect on the public, too, was anything but reassuring. The people might revel in their display of pomp, but that did not alter the fact that they had little love for a papist queen. Events in England were followed with interest,[35] and sympathies were almost universally on the side of Parliament.

Thus even Dr Rivet, young William's tutor, had been unable, during his stay in England, to disguise his sympathy for the parliamentary party.[36] True, he never dared to express it openly,[37] but others, and particularly clerics less closely connected with the court, were not nearly so scrupulous. In particular, the Synod of Zeeland made its attitude known on more than one occasion, and its letters were used by the Presbyterian party in the struggle with Episcopalians and Independents alike. These letters were in fact inspired by the minister of the Scottish Staple at Middelburg (Spang by name),[38] through whom Scottish Presbyterians kept in touch with the Dutch Reformed Church. And indeed the Synod of South Holland, too, learned 'with joy' that the Synod of Westminster had put before Parliament 'a certain project of church government that agreed on most points with the government of the Reformed churches in this country'.[39] Nor did the Dutch Reformed Church in 1644 and 1645 confine its support to mere words. It sanctioned a collection for 'the oppressed Protestants in Ireland', which brought in 300,000 guilders.[40] By 1652 enthusiasm had cooled under the influence of the rise of the Independents and because of the war with the English Commonwealth; one pamphleteer recalled with bitterness that 'we prayed for them in the churches', and reproached the rebels for diverting 'moneys collected for them in our country to the struggle against their lawful sovereign'.[41] Whether the generous donors of 1644 and 1645 would have minded is an open question.

In any event it was natural that the bishops with their rites should have appalled the Dutch Calvinists, and the papist, Henrietta Maria, was not the best ambassador to make them change their minds. No wonder, therefore, that the clergy, who in other respects were the most loyal adherents of the House of Orange,[42] were the first to shake their heads at the Stuart connection. In England the religious struggle was bound up with political issues, much as it had been in the Netherlands during the Dutch war of liberation. Reference to this fact was one of the favourite pieces of propaganda of the parliamentary party in the Netherlands,[43] and was certainly more effective in that it was known that Charles had looked to Spain before his hands became tied.

But this traditional Calvinist and democratic hatred of despotism was now linked to the republican feelings of the regent class, which before long expressed itself in an unwillingness to make the kind of liberal donations to the young couple on which the Orangists had counted.[44] It was an unwillingness that was clearly reflected in Aitzema's caustic remarks on the pretensions of the English, their avarice, etc. The honourable members bowed down to the queen, and kissed the hem of her garment,[45] but none the less they felt uneasy about the royalist encroachment, and this feeling was intensified by the suspicion, soon to be confirmed, that the whole thing was not merely a harmless, if annoying, exhibition, but a calculated move by the Prince of Orange.[46]

On the very day the royal personages arrived, a dispute is said to have arisen; the story is too telling to omit from our account.[47] During a supper attended by a number of English visitors as well as by officers of the States and regents of Holland, the prince's health was drunk before that of the States-General, to the dismay of the assembled regents; the prince, they said, was their servant and stood in their pay. A French captain of horse retorted that a prince who had just married his son to 'a daughter of England, granddaughter of France' should be ashamed to pass for the servant of brewers, bakers and feltmakers. Clearly, the conflict between the House of Orange and the oligarchy was growing sharper all the time.

The royal alliance certainly gave rise to the universal suspicion that the Stadholder was ambitious for sovereign power.[48] His foreign policy was watched all the more closely. And here the oligarchy and the Calvinist commonalty found themselves at one – a rare occurrence in Dutch history. Under the prevailing conditions of government, only the States of Holland could offer any effective resistance, and for once they could count on popular support in their struggle with the Princes of Orange. Thus one of the first fruits of Frederick Henry's dynastic triumph was the infusion of new life into the opposition which the States of Holland put up against the stadholderate in the name of the national cause.[49]

The issue was one of great importance: it was whether, in the struggle between the King of England and Parliament (which broke out openly in August 1642) the Netherlands should remain neutral or should side with the king, at least to the extent of supporting him in secret. Holland was powerful enough to secure a declaration of neutrality as the official policy of the States;[50] but Frederick

Henry, for his part, supported as he was by most of the smaller provinces and by some officials and even some colleges of the Generality, was able to obstruct or ignore the official policy. As a result, while Charles did not receive the aid on which he had counted, and which might have averted his ruin,[51] Parliament was nevertheless given abundant cause for violent resentment.[52]

The main concern of Henrietta Maria and her advisers during their stay in the Netherlands was to provide the king with money, troops and munitions. In this, they were fully supported by Frederick Henry, He was the only man of any power on the continent prepared to exert himself on behalf of the king – Henrietta Maria knew full well that she could expect nothing from her brother, the King of France, or his government. Without the Stadholder's help, Charles I could not have held out as long as he did. Indeed, Frederick Henry's services to him were considerable. Not only did he bear the burden of Henrietta Maria's retinue, but he stood personal surety for a loan to her of 300,000 guilders, and this at a time when his own income was no longer sufficient to meet his own expenses.[53] As Captain-General in the States' army, moreover, he was able to aid the king by permitting English officers serving under him to rejoin the royalist standard.[54] Thus it came about that in August 1642, Charles's nephew, Prince Rupert, left the Republic with his brother Maurice and a following of some hundred officers. Frederick Henry even placed a Dutch warship at their disposal when it proved difficult to find alternative means of transport.[55] Moreover, in spite of the scruples of the official concerned,[56] he allowed guns from the arsenal to be sold to the royalists.

This was clearly not enough. One of the first things the queen meant to do in the Netherlands was to raise a loan on her crown jewels, which were valued[57] at 1,265,300 guilders. She did not find this an easy task. The bankers thought the stones too large, and they did not much care to do business with princes; to make things worse Parliament had lodged a strong protest with Joachimi, claiming that the queen had no authority to dispose of the jewels. Heenvliet, who represented the prince and the queen in Holland (the prince himself had been with the army in the field since June), did all he could by interceding with men of experience and influence; but it soon became obvious that unless the prince was willing to ignore Parliament and raise a loan on the jewels in

Amsterdam in his own name, the jewels would remain unpawned. Heenvliet had once told the queen[58] that it would not do to provide arms openly from the Dutch arsenals, while there were plans for mediation between the contending parties in England; to do so would be *'procéder contre la foy publique et tout honneur'*. Whether it was any more loyal or honourable to provide the arms in an under-hand way is a moot point; in any case, the raising of a loan on the crown jewels in Amsterdam in the prince's name, was done more or less in public – for Frederick Henry succumbed to the entreaties of the queen, faithfully reported to him by Heenvliet.

Was Frederick Henry won over by her pathetic entreaties, or was he rather worn down by her proud and passionate reproaches? The promise of fresh favours carried more persuasive power than reference to those already granted, now that the little princess had been delivered up irrevocably to the house of Orange;[59] and un-doubtedly it also carried more power than the pleas the child was forced to make repeatedly at the instance of her despairing parents.[60] If the prince and his consort, Amalia of Solms (there are many references to the zeal[61] of this ambitious woman) took so much trouble to satisfy the queen, if they suffered her vehemence and her threats, if they led the Republic again and again to the brink of a breach with Parliament and were ready to bear the brunt of a bitter contest with the States of Holland, it was above all because of the prospects of a second marriage, a marriage between the Prince of Wales and their daughter, Louise Henrietta.

To have their daughter crowned Queen of England – even in the perilous circumstances in which the Stuarts found themselves – seemed well worth a great deal of unpleasantness, and even a loss of prestige among Calvinists at home. While still in England, Henrietta Maria had discussed the idea with Heenvliet. Now, with the help of the queen's counsellors, Goring and Jermyn, they worked together continuously to win the prince over. Heenvliet reports that Jermyn kept referring to the affair of the jewels and the transfer of officers and men: *'il mesle tousjours parmy son dis-cours l'affaire que V.A. sçait.'*[62] He did not do it very delicately either, but said quite bluntly, as Heenvliet records 'that the one thing would be done in return for the other and not for nothing'. This was the chief reason (there were personal ones as well[63]) why Heenvliet was so anxious about the queen's possible displeasure, why he 'made excuses' for the States of Holland[64] and why he

spoke so highly of the good disposition of the prince. And this
was why the prince, as he himself put it, did 'the impossible in
order to please her'.[65]

The most important question during the queen's stay in Holland
(she returned to England in March 1643, after raising the loan
on her jewels) – the question, too, that led to the first serious clash
between the Prince of Orange and the States of Holland – was
the export of the arms and munitions bought for Charles in the
Netherlands; and bound up with it, was the question of what
attitude should be adopted to Strickland, an envoy Parliament had
sent to the Netherlands in September 1642 with express instructions to prevail upon the States to forbid the traffic. Heenvliet was
taken aback by the queen's excitement at the appearance of 'this
person', and the excitement grew to fever pitch when the States-
General received him, not, it is true, in full assembly, but at a
meeting attended by delegates from all the provinces, and listened
to his message. Its crux was a complaint that a number of ships
with munitions for the king's army had been equipped in Dutch
harbours; several were at that very moment making ready for
departure. The majority of the States-General had been reluctant
to receive the envoy. Now that he had been received, they tried to
sugar the pill by giving a ceremonious reception to one of the king's
ambassadors who was passing through the country.[66]

It is not surprising that the States-General was afraid to affront
Parliament. Its dominance over the greater, or at least the most
important, part of England was now assured, and above all, it was
powerful at sea – and Parliament was at least as anxious as the king
had been to watch over the trading and colonial interests of England. Though Joachimi did his utmost to avoid contact with
Parliament, his correspondence is full of complaints and threats
by the new office holders about Dutch encroachments. The prince
and his supporters, who were not ordinarily interested in trading
matters, now missed no opportunity to point out how detrimental
it would be to Holland, were the English Parliament to come out
on top. The Hollanders retorted that Parliament's irritability over
such issues was in reality due to the unfair and offensive treatment
it had received at the hands of the Orangist States-General. They
insisted, therefore, that heed be paid to Strickland's complaints,
and knowing perfectly well that no decisive action on the part of the
States-General could be expected, the States of Holland took

matters into their own hands and themselves ordered the detention of the ships then making ready to sail for England.

This roused the queen to fury, and she was in no way soothed by the assurance that the Hollanders, having once embarked on their investigations, also discovered ships destined for Parliament and ordered that these should be detained with the others, because they said they wished to observe strict neutrality.[67] It was precisely this equality of treatment which she felt to be insulting. She called Frederick Henry to her assistance with the loudest complaints and reproaches. 'The States [she declared to Heenvliet] had promised that the marriage alliance should not be the concern merely of His Highness but also of the state; but they are not acting up to this.'[68]

The prince, reminded in this way of the ambiguous assurances of Sommelsdijk, could hardly do less than admit that the Hollanders had been mistaken in their action,[69] but all the same, he could do little to change their policy of neutrality. Theoretically there might be something in the view that the Republic was bound to the English king by treaties,[70] but it was no longer possible to identify the king with England now that the power of Parliament had become so great and tangible.

Small wonder, then, that throughout this affair Holland enjoyed the support of Zeeland, although the Stadholder, in his capacity of First Noble and Lord of Veere and Flushing, had an exceptionally strong position in the States of that province. So great was resentment of the way in which the States-General allowed themselves to be manipulated by the prince, that there was some talk of a closer association between the two seaboard provinces, and even of secession. The Grand Pensionary of Zeeland and De Knuyt, the prince's representative, exchanged acrimonious words in the provincial States assembly. But in the end, the prince's policy was so impossible that he had to abandon it.

On 1 November 1642, Their High Mightinesses the States-General issued a proclamation forbidding the export of arms to either of the contending parties. Thus the principle maintained by Holland was definitely accepted as an article of federal policy, and Strickland had scored an important success.[71]

Yet the prince continued to work against the policy in an underhand way, and as several of the smaller provinces and some of the administrative colleges of the Generality were devoted to him, he was able to do so with considerable effect. The greffier of the

States-General, the notorious Cornelis Musch, was a great friend of Heenvliet according to the latter's own statement,[72] and was invaluable when it came to invalidating orders for the detention of ammunition-carrying ships. Strickland felt greatly aggrieved by this attitude,[73] and even more so by the treatment he received in early December at the hands of Renswoude, a man who had recently been made a member of a mediatory embassy (about which more below).[74] On one occasion Strickland called on Renswoude when the latter happened to be 'President of the Week' (of the States-General) to protest about ships in Medemblik then making ready to carry a number of officers, two or three hundred men and twenty guns to England. Without even looking at the note that Strickland handed to him, Renswoude declared that Strickland had no facts to support his complaint, and demanded the name of his informant. But, writes Strickland, no English or Dutch merchant would have cared to be mentioned as informant for fear of incurring the displeasure of the 'great ones'. So angry was he that he told his government he could be of no use in the Netherlands unless he received assurances that such incidents would not recur. Probably with a view to pacifying him, the prince himself received Strickland when he came to present a letter from Parliament soon after the incident.[75] But this so aroused the anger of Henrietta Maria that the prince instructed his confidants to declare that Strickland had taken him by surprise and that he would not be received in future.

A little while later, there was a far more serious clash between the envoy of Parliament and the States-General. The queen had at last taken her leave of the Netherlands – to the relief of the States-General, says the Venetian ambassador in England, and we can well believe him! But even her departure was accompanied by dissonance and friction. The ship in which she crossed to England on 28 February 1643, was joined by another, packed with arms and soldiers. Parliament intended to intercept this ship at the mouth of the river Maas. But she was escorted by a Dutch fleet under Tromp, who had orders to defend her and did so, even after she had landed and came under bombardment by an English squadron.[76] Shortly afterwards, Strickland approached the States-General with the complaint that there were twenty-four ships lying at Dunkirk (in the Spanish Netherlands) all ready to sail out against Parliament, and that the Prince of Orange had already issued orders for two of them to pass through the Dutch blockade without let or hindrance. The prince's indifference to the threat that Spain might use Dunkirk as a base of support of the Catholic revolt in Ireland, had for long given rise to grave suspicions in England. But the prince strongly denied the truth of Strickland's latest imputation, and the States-General, packed with his supporters, were so incensed at this insult to the Stadholder that there was every reason to fear a rupture between the Republic and Parliament. Once more, however, matters were smoothed over. Parliament greeted with scepticism Tromp's statement that he had let the town ships pass on the strength of a letter from the queen and remained in the firm belief that he must have received instructions from the prince as well. However, Parliament allowed itself to be pacified by 'letters from Holland'. Soon afterwards the Orange party tried to bring about a breach in a different way.

Orange attempts to provoke war with Parliament (1644–5)

Attempts to 'mediate' between the two contending parties seemed to offer them a golden opportunity. As early as January 1642, Joachimi, the ambassador of the Republic in England, had been instructed to make an offer of such mediation. But Joachimi was not the man to suit the royalists. The States-General would have liked to include Heenvliet in this mission, (he was still at the English court as envoy of the Prince of Orange). Holland, however, refused to agree, because choosing Heenvliet as mediator would have been tantamount to choosing sides. The Prince of Orange nevertheless tried to induce Joachimi to accept Heenvliet's co-operation 'either in my name or otherwise'[77] but the States of Holland had taken the precaution of informing Joachimi of their objection,[78] and so nothing came of the prince's efforts. And in fact, when one learns what Heenvliet thought of the mediator's task one cannot but applaud the Hollanders' stand. Heenvliet objected to Joachimi's method of open negotiations. He considered it would be much better, with the King's connivance, to lure supporters of the parliamentary party away with offers of titles, offices and other favours.[79] In the event, Joachimi had no chance of trying either approach, for soon afterwards he had to report that the parliamentary party would not hear of mediation.

All this happened before Henrietta Maria arrived in the Hague, and when she did it was decided to send an embassy all the same. Holland alone, basing her policy on reports from Joachimi 'that no mediator from this country would be pleasing to Parliament',[80] held up the proposal in the States-General until May, when she had to fall into line – not, however, without reservations.[81] One of these, namely, that the ambassadors should not attempt to spread dissension among members of Parliament, shows that there were apprehensions that Heenvliet's methods might yet be adopted. In fact, the gentlemen chosen for the embassy, William Boreel and Reede van Renswoude, both Orangists, were vociferous supporters of the royalist cause.[82]

But it was a long time before they set out. At first the English royalists in Holland, much to the annoyance of the Prince of Orange, would have nothing to do with the peace mission.[83] Later the opposition was once again led by Holland. It was hinted in the States-General that Holland looked upon the continuation of the civil war as advantageous to her trade;[84] and Boswell, Charles's resident at the Hague, made the same galling observation.[85] But it seems unlikely that it was this conviction which led the States of Holland to sabotage the mission. Their principal objection was, without doubt, the fear that an embassy so strongly influenced by the Prince of Orange would inevitably side with the royalist party, thus leading the Netherlands into a clash with Parliament.

These were questions of great consequence. The English marriage and the resulting complications had brought the Stadholder into sharp conflict with public opinion on issues of vital interest to the state as a whole. As always, it was the States of Holland who had enough political power to change from disapproval to opposition, and inevitably they directed their attack against the personal control over foreign policy, which the prince had been consolidating at a time when he was not yet discredited by his dynastic ambitions. Holland could no longer afford to leave the solution of the fiercely contested English problem to the Secret Committee, in which her deputy could be voted down by the prince's own men while having to preserve strict secrecy about the proceedings. We saw earlier that, in 1642, the province had already ventured to issue a private warning to Joachimi, the ambassador of the States-General, against accepting Heenvliet as joint mediator. This was a very strong step for any province. But in view of the English entanglement it was inevitable that Holland should try her utmost to wrest the lead in national affairs from the Stadholder. His abuse of the powers vested in him by the Generality – 'abuse' because of his dynastic aims and also because of the methods of pressure and corruption he applied to the deputies of the smaller provinces – was most effectively countered by a stress of the principle of provincial sovereignty. This is what the States of Holland now did, with shattering effects on the prince's policy. Their private warning to Joachimi had been applauded by that staunch republican, Van Reigersberch, as a welcome 'sign of public vigour'. Yet he had gone on to speak slightingly of 'particular views' as the motive force behind their action and to deplore that this vigour 'was nowhere to be found in matters of greater importance and weight'.[86] A year later he had nothing to complain of in that respect.

In August 1643, in fact, the States of Holland drew up a new instruction on which their deputies in the States-General had to swear an oath. It was intended to tie them more strictly than before to the directives of their own States. In particular they were instructed, in the assembly of Their High Mightinesses *or elsewhere*, not to act without directives on such points as: 'Peace or truce, war, negotiations with other potentates about alliances or aid, lands or cities . . . also the sending abroad of ambassadors or any notable deputations.' All the eighteen towns voted in favour of this resolution; only the 'member of the nobility' (a committee of some five or six men representing the entire order and casting one vote out of a total of nineteen) entered reservations. Aitzema took care to point out, in passing, that the 'member' – meaning the entire delegation – of the nobility 'depended entirely upon the prince'. In any case the States of Holland overrode this opposition, and by voting for the instruction they clearly killed the Secret Committee instituted nine years before, which was precisely what they meant to do. The Lord of Mathenes, the noble member of the Holland contingent in the States-General, had objected that 'it was sometimes necessary to keep matters secret among a few'. 'But that [Aitzema commented] was the very reason why Holland had passed the instruction, knowing that secrecy was the pretext under which the most important questions were settled by the prince and a few men "assumed" by him.'[87]

It is idle to accuse the Holland States party of sacrificing a national institution to provincial particularism. Far too often the States-General, and especially the Secret Committee, had struck the Hollanders not as true upholders of Union interests, but as tools of an ambitious Stadholder. How general the concern felt over Frederick Henry's policy really was is shown by the fact that nearly all the provinces now tried to follow the example of Holland, though only in Gelderland was a similar set of instructions issued; everywhere else the Orange party managed to block the way.[88] This does not necessarily mean (to repeat the caution) that these provinces had any real sympathy with Frederick Henry's foreign policy. Thus Aitzema tells us that when a man carrying letters of recommendation from the prince applied for the office of Bailiff of Salland in October 1643, he discovered,

that the Overijsel towns, both on account of the English marriage and because they did not like His Highness's favouring the King of England more than Parliament, would not be much impressed by this recommendation, and that it might do him harm rather than advance his cause. For which reasons he kept the letters by him.[89]

The fact remained, however, that the prince could still count on the deputies of most of the provinces in the States-General, and the struggle therefore continued with increasing bitterness. To begin with, Holland could not prevent the appointment of Boreel and Renswoude to the English embassy. The province endeavoured to add a third man of less pronounced Orangist leanings,[90] but nothing came of this, and it was difficult for Holland to persist in her opposition when, in 1643, the situation in England seemed to have altered so much to the disadvantage of Parliament that Joachimi declared that the embassy might well be able to accomplish something, while Strickland refused to say anything at all. Thus in October 1643, Holland agreed to the departure of the envoys, and early in the following year they at last set out.

It was only natural that the leaders of the parliamentary party should have received the envoys with suspicion. The war had quite suddenly taken a fresh turn in their favour: they had concluded an alliance with Scotland, and Charles was now in grave danger. At the beginning of December 1643 a letter was intercepted, in which one of Charles's councillors wrote to a royalist at the Hague urging the dispatch of the mediators.[91] Even before this, however, it was well known in England that the idea of mediation had come from the Orangist States-General, and that both envoys were outspoken supporters of the Prince of Orange and had already shown themselves inimical to Parliament. Nor could it have been a secret that Renswoude kept up a regular correspondence with the Stadholder's court.[92] Thus, when the ambassadors arrived at Oxford, where the king held his court, Baillie expressed the view that they would be able to accomplish nothing, 'for they are taken here [in London] for the Prince of Orange's creatures'.[93]

Even so, the envoys met with a better reception in Oxford than in London, where the parliamentary leaders had done their best to isolate them.[94] Baillie complained loudly that, taking advantage of a moment of discouragement after the disaster of Newark, Renswoude and Boreel created dissension in Parliament and between England and Scotland.[95] In fact, the ambassadors themselves admitted in their report – which, since Holland was certain to examine it closely, must have been anything but frank – that they were persuaded to stay a little longer in London so that the 'good' people, i.e. the peace lovers, might not lose hope of some arrangement.[96] After another journey to Oxford, they returned to London and during their stay lasting many months, received nothing but worthless compliments, mixed with a good deal of impatience. There were so many wild rumours about the evil intentions of the so-called mediators, that they eventually asked to be recalled. But the States-General instructed them to make one more attempt. Without doubt, the Prince of Orange and his royalist friends had come to think that they might yet be able to further the king's cause.[97] So they travelled once more to Oxford and back again to London. On that occasion – it was now 1645 – the suspicions of the parliamentary party[98] gave rise to an unpleasant incident, which was highly resented by the ambassadors. Hence it was in a very bad humour that, in April 1645, they delivered their farewell speech to Parliament, adding more fuel to the flames. The ambassadors made it perfectly clear that they blamed the parliamentary party for their failure, and London came to the conclusion that the States-General had at last decided to side openly with the king.

And, indeed, the report the ambassadors submitted to the States-General on their return seemed to point that way,[99] and it is difficult to escape the impression that this was precisely what the Orange party had intended all along. At any rate, we know from letters preserved by chance[100] that in April, while the envoys were still in England, the Prince of Orange was already discussing with Dr Goffe, the king's emissary, how best to use their return as a means of persuading the States to side with the king.[101] Also considered was the possibility that, after their return, they would work hard and in close collaboration with the Stadholder's court and the same Dr Goffe, to overcome Holland's opposition to their war policy. Goffe was delighted at their zeal. The Prince of Orange himself praised them to the Englishman in the highest terms: '*Ils se crèveront*', said he, if they do not succeed in accomplishing some good.[102] And Goffe declared that their report was so clearly in favour of the king, that no better plea could have been made for Charles's cause by one of his own subjects.[103] As for Boreel, his 'mind was set on serving the king', and he was determined to do something in the States 'which shall be very great and bold'.[104]

But the bold plan came to nothing. Frederick Henry's action was paralysed because he could not, as he would have done only a few years earlier, deal with the report in his 'cabinet', and with 'assumed gentlemen'. Everything now came before 'the full assembly' of the States-General, where it was not so easy to interfere with Holland's policy of neutrality, a policy with which most of the deputies sympathized. The prince, however, had not yet given up hope of reaching his goal by devious ways. As late as June he was still assuring Goffe that everything would be settled satisfactorily:

Hee [Goffe wrote] had given Sir William Boswell his taske, to propose the liberty of their Havens and hiring of ships, and the Ambassadors theirs to urge the necessity of granting of Letters of Reprisall to the many complaints received in England from their owne people, and had added: *Croyés-moy, par ce moyen ils seront menés insensiblement dans une guerre*.[105] [The word '*insensiblement*' speaks volumes.]

However this proved of no avail. The former mediators had already tried to draw attention to the harm caused to trade by Parliament's supremacy at sea.[106] But the Hollanders, who must have smiled at the Stadholder's sudden concern for their trading interests, managed to get the States-General to refer these matters, too, to the provinces and thus to postpone them. All the Orangist deputies in the States-General succeeded in doing was to inflict a few pin-pricks on Parliament. Thus when Strickland tried to clear his masters from any blame for the lack of respect shown to the ambassadors during their stay in London (a great deal was made of the 'insults' offered them by Parliament) he was, at the instance of Boswell, denied a hearing. However, the States of Holland did receive him, and he was able to speak freely about the partiality with which the ambassadors had conducted themselves in England. Holland was not as easily intimidated as Dr Goffe and the prince had anticipated, and still less so since several other provinces, somewhat hesitatingly to be sure, ventured to join in their opposition to the unpopular pro-Stuart policy of the court.[107]

Plans for a second marriage (1647); Great schemes (1645-6); The collapse (1646)

When the question of war or peace with Spain became acute again in 1645, it was not the only point of foreign policy on which the prince and the States differed. In 1644 and 1645 a war was raging in the Baltic, in which Holland, almost dragging the States-General along, threw the weight of her powerful influence behind Sweden. Holland's trade interests clearly demanded such a policy. Denmark controlled the Sound and exacted tolls that fell more heavily on the Netherlands than they did on any other country. Added to this was the fact that in her wider European policy Denmark had for a long time been siding with the Habsburg party. But the King of Denmark was an uncle of Charles I, and Charles's friends looked to Denmark for tangible support.

The outbreak of the Baltic war was a blow to the royalists, who had all through 1643 and 1644 been counting on help from Danish troops.[108] Then, when the war turned to Sweden's advantage, Frederick Henry made plans to come to the aid of Denmark, but the States of Holland would not hear of it. The prince's warning that his plans against Antwerp would be endangered by a new war – and this was the only argument he could use openly[109] – had little or no weight with Holland, which had no particular ambition to subdue her great commercial sister town on the Scheldt. On the contrary, at the beginning of 1645, Holland threatened to withhold all contributions to the campaign in the southern Netherlands if she were not allowed to pursue her northern policy unhampered. Frederick Henry, burdened as he already was with the odium of his dynastic policy, was thwarted once again, the more so as public opinion was on the side of the States of Holland. However, with the help of Zeeland, which was more dependent on him than any other province, he obstructed Holland's policy wherever he could, and his attitude so embittered the Hollanders that one of their party felt impelled to warn him 'not to strain this rope too much lest greater ill arise therefrom'.[110]

The public had its suspicions as to the causes of this new outburst of zeal for the Stuart cause, and these suspicions were fully confirmed in the following year.[111] At the beginning of 1644, when the two mediators were on the point of crossing to England, a French diplomat in the Hague had written[112] that many people thought that Renswoude had instructions to re-open the subject of the marriage between the Prince of Wales and Louise Henrietta of Orange. There is no direct evidence that this was so: no trace of such an instruction can be found in the archives of the House of Orange; Renswoude's own letters make no reference to the subject, nor does his name occur in letters to the English court. But then we have no letters from Renswoude before April,[113] and from what he wrote to Huygens on more than one occasion, it is quite obvious that he had other means of keeping in touch with the prince while he was in England. In any case, it is a fact that he and his colleagues had hardly arrived in Oxford, when the subject of the marriage, which had been allowed to lapse[114] in 1643, i.e. at a time when the king's prospects seemed healthier, was again broached in a letter from Jermyn to Heenvliet.[115] And so while the envoys were 'mediating' under an instruction which expressly forbade them to listen to proposals for an alliance until the contending parties were reconciled,[116] Charles I and Frederick Henry were busily negotiating not only a second marriage, but a political alliance as well. In 1641, the English court had been content with a marriage alone, relying on the assurances of Sommelsdijk that it would earn the royalists the friendship of the States. Now, with the wisdom of experience, the English stipulated a formal alliance as their price for the marriage.

The plan as presented to Frederick Henry in June 1644 by Dr Goffe contained two alternatives:[117] if France came in, it was to be a triple alliance, in which the Republic would provide ships for the transport of French troops to England; if France was not willing to participate, the Republic was to conclude a truce with Spain, and then send English troops in the Dutch service over to England by the regiment. Frederick Henry replied immediately that he could only sign a truce with Spain if France agreed – his hands were tied by the treaty of 1635. But then peace negotiations between Spain and the two allied powers, France and the Dutch Republic, had already been opened at Münster. Indeed, a month or two earlier, the French plenipotentiaries to the congress at Münster had written from the Hague that the Prince of Orange was too conscious of the unpopularity the English connection had earned him to risk a peace that would make it easier to dispense with the services of a Captain-General.[118] A peace that would alienate France and whose only purpose was to forge still closer bonds with the Stuarts, would be too hazardous. However, France might well be persuaded to agree to a truce. Since the death of Richelieu in 1642, the French attitude to the Stuarts had grown softer, and Charles had great hopes in his negotiations with Mazarin.[119] This was the climate of opinion which, in 1645, persuaded the Prince of Orange to accept the English royalists' demand that he induce the States to declare formally against Parliament, and that he should raise a force of three thousand fighting men for England; but only in conjunction with France.[120]

But we have seen that the dangers of this plan were effectively resisted by the States of Holland. The triple alliance between France, the Republic and Charles I, on which the English royalists had set their hopes, came to nothing. Moreover, another member of the Stuart combination, Denmark, was put out of action by Holland, and this despite the endeavours of Frederick Henry. Other circumstances, too, favoured the cause of Holland. French support for the prince was often lukewarm, so much so that the former English mediators blamed Frederick Henry's poor showing in his struggle with the States of Holland in May and June 1645 on the 'private discouragements' he had suffered at the hands of France. They accordingly advised the Queen of England to use her influence with the Queen Regent and Cardinal Mazarin.[121] But fate was against them, for the Stuart cause itself went into a sharp decline. On 24 June 1645, Charles's army was routed at Naseby. From Lord Digby's papers captured on that occasion, Parliament was able to prove, as it had indeed suspected for a long time, that the king had been negotiating with the Catholic rebels in Ireland – thus completely discrediting him in Protestant eyes.[122] While Charles roamed about before his final surrender to the Scottish army in May 1646, his own army was reduced to irregular bands, of which the strongest was commanded by Montrose, the most romantic of the Cavaliers.

As Charles's fortunes waned, Frederick Henry grew the more anxious to come to his aid, albeit his help could only take the form of unauthorized actions and obstructions.[123] The prince was in a curious position. Not only had he felt entitled to use the Dutch envoys, whose ostensible task it was to mediate in England in the name of the States, for royalist intrigues, and to hatch plots with the ambassadors of Charles I and with France, behind the back of the States, but he had even taken it upon himself to withdraw ships from the blockade of the Flemish coast and to place them at the disposal of the Queen of England.[124] At the end of 1645 and the beginning of 1646 he turned his attention to the equipment in Holland or Zeeland of a considerable fleet for the transport of French or such other troops as the Duke of Lorraine[125] was prepared to provide. At first he was hopeful that the Baltic peace (September 1645), and the subsequent return of a host of ships to Dutch harbours, would give him his opportunity. Particularly in Zeeland, where the prince's representative and First Noble, De Knuyt, was ready to lend help, the English agents felt certain of being able to assemble a large fleet.[126] Again, nothing came of these and similar efforts. In the early months of 1646, some ten ships were being equipped in Amsterdam at French expense and were doubtless intended for the English adventure. The States of Holland, acting upon complaints from England, induced the States-General, which had long been inactive, to put an end to this enterprise.

All Frederick Henry's plans were part of one great scheme. Support for Charles I must be based on an alliance with France. France in her turn would help Frederick Henry to gain a share of the southern Netherlands, either by war or by signing a peace with Spain – early in 1646 there was talk of a reconciliation between France and Spain, with the latter ceding the southern Netherlands and the former evacuating Catalonia. The French obtained the prince's agreement not only by holding out the prospect of an independent position outside the dominion of the States[127] (preferably in Antwerp), but also by hinting that, if only their hands were freed from the Spanish involvement, they might prove more co-operative in the restoration of Charles I.[128] To the States these plans were not only objectionable in themselves, but also because they tended to increase the power of the Stadholder very considerably. Once he was allied to two great monarchs, one of whom, the French King, would have become an immediate neighbour of the Republic, and once he was master of a new and important territory, the States could no longer have stood up to Frederick Henry.

But the Spanish-French peace plan was abandoned when it suddenly became clear that it had never been more than a ruse by which the Spaniards intended to create dissension between the States and France. The States were greatly alarmed when the Spaniards leaked news about the negotiations, while the prince, once he discovered that he had been duped, could do nothing but hurry to the States-General and deny all knowledge of the entire transaction. His explanations did not really take them in.[129]

This proved the final straw, and Frederick Henry had to abandon his old policy. In April 1646, negotiations for a marriage between the Prince of Wales and the Stadholder's daughter were definitely broken off.[130] In May, Charles I surrendered to the Scots. At about the same time the Netherlands learned the details of Frederick Henry's secret negotiations with the Stuarts, which had fallen into the hands of Parliament with the papers of Lord Digby. Dr Goffe's reports on his conversations with the Stadholder – from which I have quoted earlier – appeared in Dutch translation.

When the regents of Holland studied his highly confidential comments on their Stadholder's foreign intrigues, they must have said, 'Amen' to the prayer of thanks with which the English Puritans introduced this publication: 'God's blessings appear in the discovery of the enemy's counsels as well as in the dispersal of his hosts.' To begin with, their self-assurance was greatly strengthened. Henceforth it became difficult to persuade the leading provinces to subscribe even a meagre sum for the new campaign in the southern Netherlands. This great scheme, so much was clear to them, was doomed to utter failure. The prince, discouraged and old before his time, felt his authority totter.

The storm of opposition against his dynastic policy had been gaining momentum during all the years that had gone before. His unfortunate involvement with the Stuart family, a settled suspicion that every suggestion made by Frederick Henry was inspired by his determination to acquire sovereign power – these were the sentiments that gave impetus to the anti-Stadholder movement. In 1646, things had come so much to a head that three members of the States of Holland dared to tell the Stadholder to his face that all his dealings with France were aimed at the subjugation of Holland, and when the prince refused to take them seriously, their principals came forward to repeat the accusation.[131] The French plenipotentiaries at Münster, who were trying to keep the Republic from engaging in serious negotiations with Spain, for which the Hollanders believed the time was ripe, and who in 1646 were continually travelling back and forth between Münster and the Hague, noticed with great dismay that the reality of power now rested with the States of Holland.[132] As early as April,[133] they expressed the fear that Frederick Henry, anxious for the future of his House, would prefer to give way and allow the States to conclude a separate peace with Spain, thus breaking the treaty of alliance with France (of 1635), by which the contracting parties had undertaken not to make peace separately.

And their fears were only too well-founded. Amalia of Solms saw greater advantage[134] in accepting the proposals of Spain, which, according to the French ambassadors, would bring the family '*3 ou 400,000 livres de rente*'. Considering how little chance there was of retrieving the vast sums advanced to the Stuarts, the temptation must have been very great. The increasing helplessness of the old prince goes a long way towards explaining Amalia's choice as well as his. Young William, his son and soon afterwards his successor, did not think all was lost, and resisted the change in policy to the utmost of his ability; he was furious with De Knuyt who had negotiated the treaty with Spain (on the authority of the princess, but taking good care to line his own pockets in the process).

The truth of the matter was that Frederick Henry's dynastic policy had called into being forces beyond his control. At the end of his life, the whole edifice of his great scheme stood in ruins, with the States of Holland looking on in triumph.

REFERENCES

1. *Brieven van N. van Reigersberch aan Hugo de Groot* (Utrecht: Hist. Gen., 1901), p. 51.
2. Vreede, *Geschiedenis der Nederl. Diplomatie (1858–61)*, I, p. 58.
3. In August 1634, for instance, the Groningen member of the Secret Committee, on being told that he must not give any information about the current negotiations to the States of his province, replied that he would abstain from taking any part in further proceedings except in so far as directed by those States (L. Aitzema, *Saken van staet en oorlogh* (1658), III, p. 267). Opposition by Groningen did not have to be taken too seriously, but we shall see that this was the very point on which Holland, in 1643, was to aim a deadly blow at the Secret Committee. Under William III, the Secret Committee was revived (*Recueil des instructions données aux ambassadeurs de France, Hollande*, II, p. 168) and again caused friction; see Sylvius *Historien onzes tijds* (1684), p. 41. The history of the Secret Committee deserves a systematic study. Vreede, *op. cit.*, Van Riemsdijk, *Griffie van H.H.M.*, p. 21, and Fruin-Colenbrander, *Staatsinstellingen*, p. 187 merely deal with the subject in passing.
4. Arend, *Algemeene Geschiedenis* (1868), III, v. 261
5. Vreede, *op. cit.*, I, p. 212, n. 2.
6. See the evidence in *Archives de la maison d'Orange-Nassau* and in Van der Capellen cited by Ising in *Bijdragen*, New Series, IV, p. 255. Fruin has shown, by a reference to the *Clarendon State Papers*, that the suspicion was unfounded. In May, Sir William Boswell was already reporting similar rumours from Holland (*State Papers, For., Holland*, CLV).
7. Ranke, *Französische Geschichte*, II, pp. 506 ff.; Lavisse, *Histoire de France*, VI, ii, p. 350.
8. I do not think that Marie de Medicis could really have favoured the match. Sommelsdijk tells us that, in January, she and her daughter were keen on a Spanish marriage (*Archives*, II, iii, p. 161)
9. Arend, *op. cit.*, III, v. p. 248; cf. Aitzema, *op. cit.* IV, b, p. 75. The instructions, 6 December 1639, are given as an appendix in T. J. Geest, *Amalia van Solms en de Nederl. politiek van 1625 tot 1648* (1909).
10. *Archives*, II, iii, p. 197.
11. All we know about this incident is based on a letter from Sommelsdijk to Frederick Henry of 2 February (*ibid.* p. 198). Sommelsdijk's emphatic tone suggests that he thought the prince needed persuasion.
12. *Venetian Calendar* (1640–2), p. 110.

13. Cf. *Archives*, II, iii, pp. 161, 206.
14. The inequality of the marriage may be illustrated by contrasting the forms of address used by Frederick Henry in his letters to Charles II with those used by the king. The prince of Orange writes: 'Sire, la gracieuse lettre dont il a plu à V.M. m'onorer . . . Je lue témoigneray tousjours par mes devoirs et très-humbles services que je suis avec passion, Sire, de V.M. très-humble et très-obeissant serviteur . . .' The king writes: 'Mon cousin, Vous verrez . . . Je suis, mon cousin, votre très-affectionné cousin . . .'
15. *Archives*, II, iii, p. 161.
16. Geest, *op. cit.*, p. 91.
17. *Archives*, II, iii, p. 217.
18. *Ibid*, p. 220.
19. To Mademoiselle, later known as 'la grande Mademoiselle' (*ibid*. p. 218).
20. See *Venetian Calendar*, p. 124.
21. L. Aitzema, *Saken van staet en oorlogh*, V, p. 336 (quarto edition), in relating the visit of the Queen to Holland, remarks that she 'seemed to have been informed of the prince's great authority and power' and believed that 'he did as he willed with this state'. Indeed, that is how the position was regarded at the English court: early in 1639, Secretary Coke had this to say to Boswell, the resident at The Hague: 'The building of the fort at Breda, as it secureth that place, so it showeth what great power the Prince of Aurenge hath among them' (*State Papers, For., Holland*, CLV).
22. *Venetian Calendar*, p. 119.
23. It stipulated, among other things, that the bride should remain in England until she had reached her twelfth year; that the marriage portion should be £40,000 payable in four half-yearly sums of £10,000.
24. *Archives*, II, iii, p. 430.
25. By March, the suspicions of Parliament had so increased, that the king's commissioners insisted, at the last moment, that the envoys of the Prince of Orange should be content with an informal and secret ratification of the contract (*ibid*. p. 400; see also p. 460). This is what Baillie, the Scottish Covenanter, must have had in mind when on 7 May 1641 OS (17 May, NS) he wrote from London: 'The precipitation of this marriage is feared by manie' (*Letters and Journals*, I, p. 351; cf. also *Venetian Calendar*, p. 115).
26. 'De bruid neit in de schuit' (*Brieven*, p. 649). What especially made R. suspicious was 'the care with which the princess had been kept *intactam*, in fact and in the opinion of the world, which will know what happened for half an hour in the presence of the king, queen, ambassadors and some bishops, the princess being put to

bed in a double shirt, sown fast below and above, between two sheets, over which two more were spread in which the prince was lying'.

27. *Ibid*, p. 674: 'Die praem wat langer zullen willen gebruycken.'

28. May, *Life of Duke of Gloucester and Princess Mary* (1661); quoted in Green, *Lives of the Princesses of England*, VI, p. 128.

29. Agnes Strickland, *Lives of the Last Four Princesses of the Royal House of Stuart*, p. 28. Miss Strickland's historical appreciations are, if possible, even more amusing than Miss Green's. Cf. also Clarendon, *Rebellion*, p. 819 and P. C. Hooft, *Brieven*, IV, p. 344.

30. By an act of 10–20 February 1641–2, *Rawlinson Letters* (Bodleian Library), A, cxv. This volume contains letters written by the Orange and Stuart families to Heenvliet and his wife, together with a few official documents of personal interest to them both.

31. Reigersberch, *Brieven*, p. 605.

32. *Ibid*, p. 719.

33. '. . . Hen die van Godt tot Godheid zijn gewijt Ten dienst van 't algemeen.'

34. *Venetian Calendar*, p. 158.

35. For the year 1642 alone, Knuttel, *Catalogus*, mentions some seventy pamphlets dealing with disputes between the King of England and Parliament, mostly translations of declarations, proclamations and justifications of the two parties.

36. 'We have met at length sometimes with Dr Rivett: he is one fullie in our minds and against the bishops' (Baillie, *Letters and Journals*, I, p. 181).

37. Although Bailie later encouraged him to do so (*ibid*, pp. 169, 181).

38. William Spang, cousin of Robert Baillie and one of his most regular correspondents (see Baillie, *op. cit.* II, pp. 75, 115, 180).

39. Knuttel, *Acta der . . . Synoden van Zuid-Holland*, II, p. 505.

40. *Ibid*, pp. 466–504.

41. *Ernstig gesprek . . . tusschen drie personen* (1652 [Knuttel, *Catalogus*, No. 7256]), p. 35. Cf. *De Nederlandsche Nijptang* (1652 [*ibid*., No. 7251]), p. 13.

42. It is true that they were often offended at the worldliness of Frederick Henry and his protégée, the refugee Queen of Bohemia (another Stuart!). Thus *State Papers, For., Holland*, CLV, contain a letter by Samson Johnson, 'from Her My's Court at The Hague' (i.e. from the court of the Queen of Bohemia), to Archbishop Laud, dated 5 December 1639, in which he says: 'The consistorye in this towne have done all they could for suppressing of the French players licenced by the magistrate and protected by the P[rince] of Orange as his servants, but their invectives for

condemning of all stage-players or the like shews have bin soe intemperate in theyr pulpitts, that they are gone backward rather than forward; all the preachers were with the P[rince] of Orange to represent the unlawfullness, but it seemes used noe argument that could worke on him, his counsell was that they should preach better and the playes would be less frequented. They came also to her Matye and desired shee would forbeare going; her Matye told them that shee conceaved 'twas a pastime that might be lawfully used and shee would use her discretion; and wondred at their incivilitye. I had nothing to doe in the business, they came not to me but formerly they desired me to preach against bare-necks, by reason her Matie uses to goe toe, which I refusing as being not sent to tell her Matie how to dress herself, they let me pass in this business. Beside there has been a proposition made to the consistorye here by the persons of best qualitye that they might have organs for to play with the psalms as in some townes of these countryes, but they plainly denyed it'. The celebrations in honour of Henrietta Maria gave offence in much the same way (see Knuttel, *Catalogus*, No. 4869). Charles never ceased to demand that the stipulations of the marriage contract, guaranteeing the observance of the Episcopalian form of worship at his daughter's court, should be adhered to. (*Rawlinson Letters*, A. cxv).

43. Knuttel, *Catalogus*, No. 4870; *Lettres inédites de Henriette – Marie*, ed. Baillon, p. 66.

44. According to Reigersberch, *op. cit.* p. 707, the ambassadors in England 'had been generous in promising as much as 50,000 guilders a year, but this without the knowledge or authority of those who would have to pay. . . . The States of Holland, seeing many provinces anxious to appear generous but at no cost to them-selves, resolved to give what they wished to give apart and of them-selves, leaving the others to carry out their own liberality.' See also Aitzema, *op. cit.* V, 343; *Venetian Calendar* (1642–3), pp, 21, 28.

45. Aitzema, *op. cit.* V. p. 335.

46. 'Many are only just seeing the results of this alliance,' Reigers-berch wrote on 24 March 1642 (*op. cit.* p. 708), 'and some do not see it yet.'

47. Green, *op. cit.* VI, p. 129.

48. Aitzema, *op. cit.* V, p. 467; *Archives*, II, iv. p. 166.

49, In November, 1643, Reigersberch (*op. cit.*, p. 740) wrote to Grotius that 'the present vigour of many has its origin more in resentment of English affairs and religious ideas than in steadfast principles of state policy and freedom'.

50. See the dispatch by the States-General to Joachimi, 26 July 1642, in Müller, *Mare Clausum*, p. 318, n. 3.

51. 'Il ne faut pas que le Prince laisse périr le Roy', was what Henrietta Maria told Heenvliet in January 1642 (*Archives*).
52. Joachimi (correspondence in nineteenth century copies at Br. Mus.) constantly reported bitter complaints. His reply, that his country was following a policy of declared neutrality, gave no satisfaction, because the States-General still held that the export of arms was consistent with that policy.
53. See the letters of his treasurer, Vosbergen, in Worp *Briefwisseling van Constantijn Huygens* (Rijks Geschiedkungdige Publicatiën), III, *passim*.
54. Cf. my 'Toepenlichten en schepenhuren in de dagen van Frederik Hindrik', in *Bijdragen*, 1918.
55. Eva Scott, *Rupert, Prince Palatine*, p. 59, gives 'Coulster' as the name of the captain of the Dutch ship. Reigersberch (*op. cit.* p. 728) wrote on 30 June 1642, that Rupert and Maurice, 'with a following of some hundred officers', left for England 'yesterday'. That must have been the first, unsuccessful, attempt to cross, which according to Miss Scott took place in August.
56. *Archives*, II, iv, p. 40.
57. *Ibid.*, p. 42.
58. *Ibid.*, p. 39.
59. Reigersberch (*op. cit.*, p. 701) wrote immediately: 'The state will profit to this extent: the bride being brought home, they will not have to court England's favour so much [*men minder schoon op sal hebben te dienen*].' The queen herself wrote to the king (17 March 1642): 'Je travaille avec le Prince d'Orange et espère en avoir contentement, quoyque ce soit une personne malaysée à engager; mais les intérests ont de grands pouvoirs' (*Lettres inédites de Henriette-Marie*. p. 25).
60. 'Dearest Daughter, I desyre you to assist me to procure from your Father in Law the loane of a good ship to be sent higher to attend my commands. It is that I may safely send and receive Expresses to and from your Mother' (Charles to Mary, Newcastle, 16 September 1646, OS [26 September NS], *Rawlinson Letters*, A, cxv). The date 1646 is obviously wrong; it must have been 1642.
61. See, for instance, *Archives*, II, iv, p. 43.
62. *Ibid.*, p. 49.
63. In April 1645, Charles I made him Baron de Kerckhove. Whereupon Jermyn wrote to Digby that this was not enough, in view of the fact that the queen in Holland 'upon the important services she received from Heenvliet' had promised a title for his son by Lady Stanhope. On 7 June 1649, Charles II fulfilled this promise by creating the son himself Baron Wotton of Marley (*Rawlinson Letters*, A, cxv).

64. *Archives*, II, iv, p. 43.
65. *Lettres inédites de Henriette-Marie*, p. 402.
66. Arend, *op. cit.*, III, v, p. 383.
67. *Archives*, II, iv, p. 71. The Hollanders were particularly moved by the report that there were *canons d'état* on board these ships. They found none, but this does not mean that the report had no foundation in fact.
68. *Ibid.*, p. 69.
69. Letter to Heenvliet, *ibid.*, p. 75.
70. Reigersberch, *op. cit.*, p. 727, writes: 'The alliance is made with the king, so that it cannot rightly be argued that arms may be denied him.' He went on to say that Amsterdam and Rotterdam were against an arms embargo 'under the pretext that trade must be free'.
71. A year later, Boswell still censured this resolution in a letter to his government, which happens to have been preserved because it was intercepted by the parliamentary party (*State Papers, For., Holland*, CLVII).
72. *Archives*, II, iv, p. 73. 'Notorious' for his corruption.
73. On 11 November 1642, Strickland wrote to Pym that he had given information about one such ship to the States-General, 'but there is so much form in their resolutions as to make the work fruitless. When I sought to hasten it, the Greffier, who is to dispatch the order, told me that he cared not whether she were gone or not. I find him harsh in all that concerns the Parliament' (*Hist. MSS. Comm., Xth Report*, vi, p. 91). See also *Archives*, II, iv, p. 43. The Council of State allowed itself to be used by Frederick Henry, and so, up to a certain point, did the Admiralty College of Amsterdam. Concerning Musch, Dr Goffe wrote to Jermyn as late as 16 April 1645 (*Digby's Cabinet* [see below, n. 100]): 'He is a very serious servant of her Majesties, and ought to be gratified, whatsoever becomes of other businesse.' And, as a matter of fact, at the end of May 1645, he received a gift of 3,000 guilders (*ibid.*, p. 39).
74. *Hist. MSS. Comm., Xth Report*, vi, 93. Renswoude, like Musch, was a confidant of the Prince of Orange (*Archives*, II, iv, p. 97).
75. Reigersberch, *op. cit.*, pp. 730 ff.
76. *Lettres inedites de Henriette-Marie*.
77. *Archives*, II, iv, p. 9.
78. *Ibid.*, p. 17.
79. *Ibid.*, p. 18.
80. Reigersberch, *op. cit.*, p. 707.
81. Arend, *op. cit.*, p. 707.
82. William Boreel (Elias, *Vroedschap van Amesterdam*, I, p. 540), a member of a well-known Zeeland family, had settled in Amster-

dam and had become pensionary of the town in 1627. Heenvliet took him into his confidence over the question of the crown jewels (*Archives*, II, iv, p. 43). One of Heenvliet's sons became a gentleman at the court of Frederick Henry, and Boreel took a warm interest in the career of this young man (see Worp, *op. cit.*, V, p. 55). He himself owed his appointment as ambassador to Paris to William II. According to a note, the source of which I cannot trace, he was paid 1,000 livres a year by the Prince over and above his normal salary.

Renswoude, the well-known Orangist deputy for Utrecht in the States-General, was a brother of Reede van Nederhorst, a member of his Highness's council (Waddington, *La République des Provinces-Unies*, II, pp. 257, 260). In December 1642, Strickland wrote, with great annoyance, that Renswoude was a notorious anti-parliamentarian (*Hist. MSS. Comm., Xth Report*, v. p. 93). Henrietta Maria received a visit from one of the two which very much pleased her (*Lettres*, p. 31).

83. *Archives*, II, iv, p. 39. See also Reigersberch, *op. cit.*, p. 726.

84. The French ambassador, Harcourt, too, writes in the same spirit (*Archives*, II, iv, p. 97).

85. *State Papers, For., Holland*, CLVII.

86. Reigersberch, *op. cit.*, p. 699.

87. Observations on the wrecking of the Secret Committee by means of this new instruction are to be found in Van der Capellen's *Gedenkschriften*, II, p. 173; Waddington, *La Republique des Provinces-Unies*, II, p. 35 (d'Estrades to Mazarin); and in a French memorandum of 1647 published in *Bijdragen en Mededelingen* (Hist. Gen.), XV, p. 134. The instruction: Aitzema, *op. cit.*, V. pp. 552 ff.

88. Aitzema, *op. cit.*, V, p. 619.

89. *Ibid.*, p. 563. See also Duanne Lon in *Venetian Calendar (1642–1643)*, p. 220: 'The Prince knows how much his authority has suffered since the alliance of his son with the Princess Mary of England, because of what he has had to do in the interests of the Crown' (31 December 1642).

90. Reigersberch, *op. cit.*, p. 734.

91. Baillie, *op. cit.*, II, p. 113.

92. See his letters to Huygens, the Prince's secretary, in Worp, *op. cit.* IV, *passim*; Worp calls Renswoude by his family name, Reede. In these letters Renswoude makes no secret of his anti-parliamentary leanings, e.g. when he alleges that 'the government of the Parliament means ruin to our state' (4 November 1644, p. 95) and 'I understand that Joachimi is working secretly in Holland that he may come with us, which will be to the disadvantage of His

Highness and the King; it must therefore be prevented' (10 March 1645, p. 131).

93. Baillie, *op. cit.*, II, p. 143. Shortly afterwards, he said simply that they were 'sent by the Prince of Orange to serve the King's ends'.

94. Arend gives a detailed résumé of the report handed to the States-General by the ambassadors on their return.

95. Baillie, *op. cit.*, II, pp. 155, 167.

96. Arend, *op. cit.*, II, v, p. 501.

97. See Huygens to Joachimi, 6 February 1645 (*Archives*, II, iv, p. 128): 'Il a esté procuré que nos ambassadeurs n'auront à bouger d'Angleterre pour quelque temps, vers où donc, si la France se résoult d'en envoyer de son costé durant leur séjour par dela, ils pourront entrer dans les communications que vous sçavez et veoir à quelle sorte de concert les affaires se pourront conduire entre leurs mains.'

98. More particularly of the Independents.

99. Arend, *op. cit.*, II, v, p. 518. See also the bellicose tone of a letter from Renswoude to Huygens of 14 August 1645 (Worp, *op. cit.*, IV, p. 192).

100. On 6 March 1646 OS (16 March NS), the House of Commons issued an order for the publication of Digby's papers, which had fallen into their hands during a battle at Sherburn in Yorkshire. They were published under the title *The Lord George Digby's Cabinet . . .*

101. *Digby's Cabinet*, Goffe to Jermyn, 17 April 1645 OS (27 April NS). 'When the ambassadors are returned, all endeavours shall be used to induce the States to a League defensive and offensive.'

102. *Ibid.*, Goffe to Jermyn, 8–18 May 1645.

103. *Ibid.*, Goffe to Jermyn, 15–25 May 1645.

104. *Ibid.*, Goffe to Jermyn, 1–11 May 1645.

105. *Ibid.*, Goffe to Jermyn, 29 May–8 June 1645.

106. Aitzema, *op. cit.*, VI, p. 75.

107. Gelderland and Friesland joined Holland in voting to hear Strickland. (Aitzema, *op. cit.*, VI, p. 77).

108. See Kernkamp, *De Sleutels van de Sond*, p. 44.

109. The suspicion that he was far more concerned about 'the marriage alliance between himself, the King of England, and Denmark', is expressed in Van der Capellen, *Gedenkschriften*, II, p. 98, and Van der Capellen was by no means inimical to the prince.

110. *Ibid.*, p. 98: 'om deze coorde niet te stijf te trecken, opdat daeruyt niet erger kome te ontstaan'.

111. By the revelations in *Lord Digby's Cabinet*; see below, p. 28.

112. *Archives*, II, iv, p. 97.

113. Worp, *op. cit.*, IV, p. 473.
114. See Gardiner, *History of the Civil War*, I, pp. 328–9.
115. *Archives*, II, iv, p. 98.
116. Arend, *op. cit.*, II, v, p. 493.
117. *Archives*, II, v, p. 103.
118. *Ibid.*, II, iv, p. 97.
119. The French attitude to English domestic differences was no more honest than that of the Orangist majority in the States-General, but it was certainly more cautious. In the British Museum there is a bulky volume comprising *Négociations de M. de Sabran en Angleterre en 1644* (Add. MS. 5460). The instructions, dated 19 April 1644, state that the attempts of Grécy to mediate between King and Parliament were not acceptable to Parliament because he showed himself too keen an adherent of the King. Sabran was to 'appuyer les justes prétentions du Roy et le favoriser en tout et par tout', but 'avec tant d'adresse qu'on ne puysse luy imputer qu'il soit son partisan'. 'La raison d'état' required this, not only because he was to appear as an impartial mediator but also because 'la raison d'état exige qu'en une chose incertaine on ne se déclare pas si ouvertement que, s'il arrivoit un changement qu'on n'eust peu prévoir, l'on ne se trouve pas hors termes de s'accorder avec celluy que sera resté le Maistre.'
120. *Archives*, II, iv, 134.
121. *Digby's Cabinet*, Goffe to Jermyn, 29 May–8 June 1645.
122. See Gardiner, *op. cit.*, II, p. 258.
123. In February 1645, Huygens had put it all quite frankly to Lord Jermyn: there were two distinct groups in the Republic, the one dependent on the will of His Highness, the other on the States; as for the first, there would never be cause for complaint; as for the second, His Highness could only do his best (*Archives*, II, iv, p. 128).
124. Arend, *op. cit.*, III, v, p. 560; *Archives*, II, iv, p. 128; *Digby's Cabinet, passim*, particularly pp. 37 ff. These ships were used for the export of tin from the west of England – the only source of income for the Queen – and to maintain communications between the royalists on the continent and the king. Captain Colster, or Coulster, who is mentioned in nearly all these reports, took Prince Rupert and his company over to England, on the instructions of the Prince of Orange. See note 55, above.
125. Charles IV of Lorraine who, after having been driven out of his country by France, fought with the Spaniards, mostly as a leader of irregular bands.
126. *Archives*, II, iv, pp. 142, 144; Worp, *op. cit.*, IV, p. 226. It was intended to appoint Dorp, Huygens' brother-in-law, admiral.

127. Le Clerc, *Négociations secrètes touchant la paix de Münster et et d'Osnabrug* (1724), III, 52, 107, 112.
128. *Ibid.*, pp. 56, 57.
129. I have described this incident more fully in 'De Oranjes en Antwerpen, 1646–50', *Tijdschrift voor Geschiedenis*, 1925; reprinted in *Kernproblemen van onze geschiedenis*, 1936.
130. *Archives*, II, iv, p. 152.
131. *Ibid.*, p. 151.
132. *Ibid.*, p. 166.
133. *Ibid.*, p. 152.
134. *Ibid.*, p. 162.

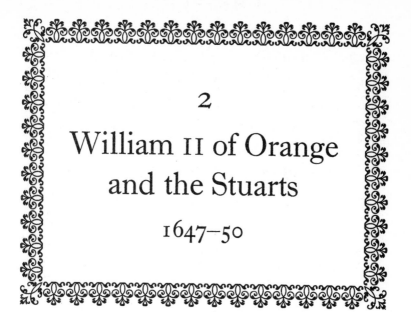

2

William II of Orange and the Stuarts

1647–50

The Prince of Wales in exile; The execution of Charles I (30 January 1649)

William II had not wanted to give way as his parents had, and when his father died, in March 1647, it might have been supposed that he would still have his way, for the peace with Spain had not yet been concluded. While his father was still alive, William had in fact been in close touch with the French ambassadors, who gave him to understand that his greatness depended on France, and that France was prepared to do everything to maintain, indeed even to advance, his interests.[1] When he became Stadholder, his French ties became more intimate still, and the French vigorously urged him to prevent a breach of the treaty of 1635.[2]

But although the young prince made a few attempts to show that he still cherished the plans his father had been forced to abandon in despair, and though he was anxious to avert a peace that would spell their final collapse, his French friends soon afterwards expressed their bitter disappointment in him. It was clear that '*ce bon petit prince*', as De la Thuillerie scornfully called the twenty-one year old youth,[3] could not stand up to the States of Holland.

'Neither determination nor prudence' – was the phrase Servien used to characterize William's conduct in the critical conflict with the States during the first phase of his Stadholdership. In May 1648, the Count d'Estrades wrote bluntly that he had gained a most unfavourable impression of the young prince: William did not seem to care about the inroads made on his authority by the States, lost as he was in frivolity and debauchery; advice was wasted on him, for all his time was spent on hunting and playing ball. And so the peace was made with Spain.

But strangely enough, no sooner was the separate peace an accomplished fact, than William II seemed to throw off his indifference. On 13 July 1648, Brasset recorded the prince's firm resolution, expressed two days earlier, to apply himself seriously to matters of state from that day on,[4] and although one may feel inclined to smile at resolutions expressed with so much emphasis, it is certain that during the two years of life that still remained to him, William II cut a much more determined figure. Thus while reports of wine and women continued even during this period, no one now accused him of indifference, lack of ambition or lack of courage. On the contrary, from that time onward, William II threw himself with youthful impetuosity into the task of undoing the peace and rejoining France, into plans not only for partitioning the southern Netherlands, but also for the restoration of the Stuarts.

In 1648, the position of the Stuarts looked far more hopeful than it had in earlier years. The increasing power of the Independents, who enjoyed the support of the army under Cromwell and Fairfax, and who opposed the imposition of an unbending and intolerant Calvinist theocracy by the Presbyterian Parliament, seemed to hold out excellent prospects for the captive Charles I. But after making sudden overtures to the Independents, Charles unexpectedly made common cause with the Presbyterians, and thus precipitated a new civil war. His main hopes were centred in a Scottish army under the Duke of Hamilton, but there were serious disturbances in the south of England as well. At the beginning of June, a number of ships in the parliamentary navy declared for the king, and took refuge in the roadstead of Helvoetsluis. At first, the young Duke of York, who had lately fled from England, tried to secure the command of this fleet, but the lack of unity among his counsellors was such that the Prince of Wales had to be called to the rescue. He arrived at Helvoetsluis on 21 July, and to his brother's great indignation, stripped him of his command.

The Prince of Wales had spent two years in France, where his mother was continuing her vain efforts to obtain tangible aid from Mazarin's government. Mazarin's chief purpose was to prevent any party in England from achieving a complete victory which, by restoring unity, might renew England's power; hence he encouraged resistance to the Independent army which was then the stronger. But at the time, owing partly to the defection of the Dutch Republic and partly to domestic troubles with the *Fronde*, France was in no position to spare money or troops for an English expedition. Once more all the hopes of the royalists were centred on the Prince of Orange.

An envoy from the Scottish Committee of Estates, then dominated by the royalist Presbyterian party of Hamilton, had just sent a report from Amsterdam that the States would not hear of an alliance with Scotland against the English Independents – no wonder since even loyal adherents of the Prince of Orange placed no faith in the power of the Hamilton party or, for that matter in the power of the prince himself.[5] It was at about this time that William II made his resolve to turn over a new leaf, and it soon became clear that, in spite of Scottish pessimism, he was prepared to render what help he could. True, he could not carry the States of Holland with him, and he even warned his brother-in-law not to expect any action that ran too obviously counter to the declaration of neutrality, nor to count on financial support from the States.[6] All that could be expected was the kind of help his father had always given – almost ruining himself in the process and yet unable to avert the fall of the luckless Stuart family. Together with the unpredictable Duke of Lorraine, in whom Frederick Henry, too, had reposed such high expectations, the prince raised troops which he encamped at Borcum, while he chartered and equipped a few ships in Amsterdam. This transaction took place in consultation with the English royalists.[7] At the same time, the prince arranged to spend up to 30,000 francs on the purchase of munitions for the Scottish army.[8]

This was the first business into which William II threw himself after his new resolve, and his servants observed it with profound concern. A man like Heenvliet, to be sure, served without offering criticism and was content with the gratitude of the Stuarts.[9] But the letters in which De Wilhem, a member of 'His Highness's Council', who was put in charge of the purchases, described these activities to his brother-in-law, Huygens, were one long series of lamentations. De Wilhem ventured to warn his master against 'getting more deeply involved in the English labyrinth', but the prince paid him no heed.

In particular, De Wilhem complained most bitterly about the incapacity and intractability of the servants of the Prince of Wales and about the infinite confusion prevailing among his councillors.[10] In those days, Culpepper had more influence on the Prince of Wales than anyone else, and, in general, the predominant party among his retinue followed the lead of the queen and her confidant, Jermyn, placing all their hopes in the Presbyterians. True, the king had attached such Episcopalians as Sir Edward Hyde and Sir Edward Nicholas to his son, but they had not yet begun to make their influence felt. It is certainly remarkable that De Wilhem, as strict a Calvinist as any among the Prince of Orange's followers, should have been so lukewarm about the policy of co-operation with the Presbyterians. In any case, his judgement was right. He realized that no reliance could be placed in the Hamilton party, which was losing ground even in Scotland, and he shook his head at the imprudence of exposing the Prince of Wales to this hopeless enterprise. Meanwhile, after fruitlessly cruising off the English coast for a week or two with his ill-disciplined fleet,[11] young Charles – he was eighteen at the time – was making plans to place himself at the head of the Scottish army. He was still in the Hague when the news came that this army no longer existed; Cromwell had beaten it decisively at Preston (late August 1648). According to De Wilhem, the 30,000 francs worth of munitions, which had just been dispatched, would probably fall into the enemy's hands as well; the troops at Borcum were disbanded, and the Prince of Wales with his ill-assorted retinue – Catholics, Episcopalians and Presbyterians; English, Irish and Scots – lingered on at the Hague as a guest of his Orange brother-in-law,[12] his ships blockaded at Brill by a parliamentary fleet under Warwick, and gradually disintegrating through lack of funds.

William II was too active a man not to be impatient at the ease with which the English prince accommodated himself to idleness.[13] As for the States of Holland, they would not have been sorry to see the parliamentary admiral seize the opportunity of destroying the weaker royalist fleet at one fell swoop,[14] but when he missed his chance, they could hardly do otherwise than observe neutrality. Soon afterwards, Rupert, Prince Palatine, was placed at the head of this fleet, and such was his energy that he succeeded in preventing its further disintegration, even though he had the greatest difficulty in finding enough money to render the fleet seaworthy. All sorts of ambitious plans were built on this force – which was all the royalists had left – but the only end for which Prince Rupert was ever able to use it, after he set course for Ireland early in 1649, was for privateering missions against English merchantmen, and these missions soon became the only source of income that reached young Charles in his exile.

The disaster at Preston had sealed the fate of Charles I. Scotland still maintained her independence: now that those Presbyterians who had followed Hamilton in supporting the Stuart cause were beaten, power was in the hands of the implacable Presbyterians under Argyll. For a time, this party worked with the Independents although it had little more in common with them than had Hamilton's. But in England there was no one left to challenge Cromwell's power. In December 'Pride's Purge' removed all traces of opposition from Parliament, and in January the king appeared before his judges.

The Prince of Wales, who had forgotten his political troubles at the pleasure-loving court at the Hague, where he enjoyed the company of his brilliant Palatine-Bohemian cousins and the beautiful sisters of his brother-in-law, the Prince of Orange, now had a rude awakening. On 22 January 1649, he received reports which made it clear that his father's life was in jeopardy. Next day, he appeared in the States-General, where Boswell spoke up for him, saying: *'J'ai horreur de dire, qu'un prince d'Angleterre vient requérir intercession pour la vie du Roi son père.'* At the proposal of Holland it was resolved to send two emissaries to England without delay: Joachimi, who was on home leave, and Pauw van Heemstede. Everybody realized by now that supporters of the House of Orange were not the best men to soften the hearts of the Independents; even so when, ignoring storm and ice, the envoys had sped to London, they were received with courtesy, but it needed some insistence before they were granted access to Parliament. Their plea for the king's life was heard in complete silence. Next day, on 30 January 1649 (9 February NS), Charles I was beheaded at Whitehall. A few hours later Parliament issued a solemn warning that no man was to presume to claim the title of King of England.

The execution made a profound impression in the Netherlands. The nation, its own revolution by now a memory stored in the glorified annals of the past, watched with horror as 'the hosts of hell' built 'their throne in England's realm', as Vondel put it. Even those who had previously sided with Parliament, be it on grounds of freedom or of religion, now expressed their detestation. Such is the testimony of Aitzema,[15] the chronicler, and there is no doubt but that he was a faithful reporter. Strickland, so it is said, dared not show his face in the streets.[16] Ministers of religion were vehement in their condemnation of 'the atrocious deed'. No doubt they had little sympathy with the Episcopalian doctrines, and even Catholic leanings, of the Prince of Wales and his councillors, but for a long time past they had looked on the looming spectre of Independentism with great uneasiness. The Zeeland ministry, under the influence of Spang, and Voetius himself, the 'Pope of the Dutch Reformed Church' as he was sometimes called, were no less loud in their protests against Independentism, that is against freedom of worship (for Protestants), than in their attacks on Episcopalianism. The religious sympathies of Dutch Calvinists were entirely with the Presbyterians, who had now suffered defeat in England. The *odium theologicum* is clearly reflected in an address by four Hague clerics who felt it their duty to offer condolence and comfort to the son of the dead king. After vigorous manifestations of horror at 'this unheard-of parricide, that accursed destruction of the holy, anointed head, and that utterly deplorable murder of this one king of the Reformed Faith', the reverend gentlemen declared that it all went to show 'what it means to be an Independent'.[17] But they were sharply reprimanded by the States of Holland for their meddling in politics. The States told them in unmistakable terms that they were not in future to address foreign potentates as a body, that they were not to discuss the affairs of Great Britain from the pulpit, and that they were not to carry on correspondence across the sea.

For even in the midst of the general excitement, the States of Holland were unyielding in their adherence to their guiding principle, that it was essential to keep on friendly terms with the parliamentary party, all the more now that this party had the whole country under its control. Aitzema remarked caustically that the

States party was determined at all costs to keep in with the winning side. Indeed this was a worldly-wise maxim, one that the French government had established as the unshakeable *raison d'état*,[18] and one, moreover, that was so obviously in the interest of the Netherlands that the other commercial province, Zeeland, felt impelled to support Holland in spite of William's great influence over them. All the other European powers – with the exception of Sweden, where the somewhat unbalanced Queen Christina indulged in a short-lived outburst of noble indignation – took it as their guiding principle as well. As for France, with which the Prince of Orange would so gladly have allied himself in order to set things right in England, she had her hands full then with the *Fronde*.

However, it was by no means only their love of *Realpolitik* that swayed the States. These men, who did not really sympathize with the religious aims of the Presbyterians any more than with those of their own Calvinist clergy, must have had a great deal of secret admiration for the bold republicanism of the Independents. Aitzema himself could not refrain from remarking on the folly of the public, who were now all 'full of compassion at the death of *one* man, but had looked on with dry eyes while *thousands* had lost their lives in England, Ireland and Scotland, during the English disturbances'.[19] And he mentioned the feeling of 'Libertinists' that Calvinist ministers had little cause to be indignant now, when their own sixteenth-century predecessors had offered armed resistance to a lawful king. People objected that the English republic was only established by a small section of the House of Commons. But as Aitzema went on to remark, the revolution in the United Netherlands had been the work of the rabble of Flushing and Enkhuizen, and not of parliamentarians . . .

That there were men who dared to say such things, and not under their breath either, we know from other sources as well. A student in the University of Utrecht published a refutation of Professor Boxhorn's *Dissertatio de successione et jure primogenitorum*, whose author had argued that the innocent sons of kings possess a right to succeed to the throne which cannot be invalidated by the deposition of their fathers, whether guilty or not. How did the professor – the student wanted to know – reconcile this with his loyalty to the state from which he drew his salary and which would not be an independent state if Philip III's right had not been invalidated by the 'abjuration' (or deposition) of his father? He went on to state as a general proposition that kings do not rule by the grace of God, a phrase without meaning, but by the grace of the people. And he was not a little surprised to see men living in free states and republics and yet thinking so highly of royal authority.[20]

When the well-known lawyer, Dirk Graswinckel, published a little book, or rather, when an older book of his was specially reprinted, the ultra-royalist views expressed in it drew further opposition. In a well-written pamphlet, an educated citizen pleaded in temperate terms for the principle – indeed a typically Dutch principle, as he did not fail to remind his readers – of royal power limited by the interests of the people. And he concluded very sensibly that those who meant well by the king ought now to wish that he had listened more to his people and less to his court.[21] And that, in fact, was also the view of most of the regent class.

William urges Charles to come to an understanding with the Scottish Presbyterians (1649–50)

All this does not alter the fact that the rise of the Independents and their treatment of the king caused a great revulsion of public feeling in the Netherlands. Calvinists, who had all along been in sympathy with Parliament in its struggle with the king, were now distinctly hostile to the English Commonwealth. William II therefore had good reason to believe that a policy of interference with the domestic affairs of Great Britain, although not actively desired, would be less unpopular now than it had been in the days of his father, particularly since even the Scottish Calvinists, or Presbyterians, had begun to feel more favourably inclined to the monarchy.

Yet there was an unexpected hitch. For even while the Presbyterians, frightened by the danger of Independentism, were anxious to return to the monarchy, Charles II was by no means eager to meet them. He would no doubt have liked to make common cause with Hamilton's party, although even that was not at all to the taste of the majority of his English advisers. But the Marquis of Argyle's party, which had come into power after the fall of Hamilton, was considerably more obnoxious to him. It consisted of the most rigid Presbyterians, unwilling to make the slightest concession to the policy of the Stuarts, or even to put an end to the persecution of those who had formerly served them, or were tainted with Episcopalian leanings. There was no doubt that the execution of Charles I had aroused great and universal indignation in Scotland also. The Scottish Parliament, moreover, immediately after the receipt of the news from London, had proclaimed his son King of Scotland. It did, however, attach conditions to this proclamation, which in the main came down to a demand for personal assurances from Charles II in the matter of religion, and that he was to swear adherence to both the National Covenant of 1638, which established the Presbyterian church order in Scotland and required severe persecution of men of different persuasions, and the Solemn League and Covenant of 1643, which was intended to introduce Presbyterianism into the king's other realms as well. In other words, Charles II was expected to embrace a policy so unacceptable to his father and his father's faithful followers that they had preferred to face civil war. Small wonder the king's English council was so strongly opposed to acceptance of the Scottish demands. The failure of the previous year's naval expedition had considerably weakened the influence of Culpepper and other Presbyterians. It was now the turn of the strict Episcopalians, such as Hyde and Cottington. Charles II indeed, who, as far as his nature allowed him to believe in anything, believed in the full royalist programme and in the Episcopalian Church, did not relish the prospect of submitting to the Presbyterian yoke and entrusting himself to people who, as party feelings put it, had sold his father to his executioners. Hence he looked for an alternative.

In Ireland the Lord-Lieutenant, the Marquis of Ormonde, had not only managed to stand his ground, but had concluded a peace with the Catholic insurgents; he was confident that he would soon be able to restore to their allegiance to the king all the towns now in the hands of Parliament, and that he would then be able to assemble an army large enough to make an attempt on England herself. In February he sent an envoy to the Hague, inviting Charles to Ireland, and one can imagine how greatly tempted the young king must have been to accept. Here, in new guise, was the old plan of Charles I and Strafford to establish the royal power in England with the aid of Catholic Ireland. In case of success, young Charles, instead of being bound in religion and in politics by Covenants, would become the autocrat his father had always dreamed of being. The greatest obstacle was that Ireland's position seemed weak, in spite of Ormonde's assurances to the contrary, and that several English councillors preferred an alliance with Scotland. There were, moreover, in the Hague, Scots of various shades of opinion who advised acceptance of the Scottish conditions, among them several nobles of the Hamilton party who had been banished by the present government. Of the Scots it was only Montrose – the representative of absolute royalism, the man who had fainted on hearing of the execution of his king – who unhesitatingly urged the choice of Ireland, and there was no one to whose urgings Charles gave a readier ear, no matter how fiercely the Presbyterians might hate the man. Then, in April, the envoys of the Scottish government arrived to negotiate with 'the proclaimed King'.

One cannot wonder that, in these circumstances, the Prince of Orange greatly preferred to see his brother-in-law in Scotland rather than in Ireland. For anyone anxious to gain the support of the people of the Netherlands, the Scottish plan had all the advantages. It was one thing to recommend an alliance with the free Presbyterian kingdom of Scotland, but a very different matter to plead for the support of an Episcopalian Stuart, dependent on Catholic Ireland and aiming at autocracy. The chaplains whom the Scots wanted Charles II to dismiss were equally repugnant to the Dutch; one of them, for instance, used to preach vigorously against Calvinists in general.[22] The Scots themselves expected William II to press their cause with the king, and used all their influence with him.

The fullest and most authentic account of the negotiations is that of the Scottish minister, Spang, whom we have met before.[23] He left Veere for the Hague in March, at the request of his friends in Scotland, and had a personal audience of the prince lasting over an hour.[24] From Spang's detailed report it appears that the prince was very well informed about the confused state of affairs in England and Scotland, and that, although he gave a sympathetic hearing to the Presbyterian emissary, he was familiar with the arguments of Charles's English councillors and put them forward forcefully. Above all, he was fully aware of the dangers posed by the fierce intolerance of the party in power, and he was afraid – and with good reason – that to embrace the Solemn League and Covenant would alienate the Catholics and Episcopalians in England from the king. Yet he concluded the audience with the promise that he would advise the king to accept both covenants, and he assured Spang on the following day that he had done so.[25] When the envoys of the Scottish government themselves arrived at the beginning of April, they were able to report immediately that they hoped to get their demands accepted with the help of the Prince of Orange.[26]

In the view of Lord Byron, Ormonde's envoy, the Scottish sympathies of the Prince of Orange and his mother were chiefly due to the renewed hope of a marriage between the king and one of Frederick Henry's daughters.[27] While there is no positive evidence to corroborate this view, there is no doubt that Amalia of Solms gave open support to the Scottish envoys;[28] moreover, Sophia of Bohemia, afterwards Electress of Hanover, declared in her *Mémoires* that the old princess later (in 1650) threw suspicions on her, Sophia's, orthodoxy, the better to press the claim of her own daughter to the dignity of Queen of Scotland.[29] And of course we know only too well how very largely Amalia's policy was dictated by the matrimonial prospects of her children. Byron, however, somewhat later, commits himself to the rather surprising statement[30] that William II, far from allowing himself to be talked round by the Scottish lords, had a higher opinion of his, Byron's principal, Ormonde, and desired to maintain friendly relations with him. This probably meant no more than that the prince, who wanted to take up a conciliatory attitude, thought it worth his while to cultivate the Irish party as he did the others, and was prodigal in his protestations of friendship.

In any case, William does not seem to have followed a consistent course in this difficult matter. Even Henrietta Maria and Jermyn, of whose advice William II thought very highly, considered that the Scots were too exacting. And the Queen of Bohemia and her daughters, too, were utterly opposed to the acceptance of the Covenants, the more so as the most famous of her sons, Rupert, was at sea with the royalist fleet. How much more attractive to chivalrous minds was the idealistic royalism of Montrose or even the unbending Episcopalianism of Hyde. In November, the Queen of Bohemia wrote to Montrose informing him that her niece, the Princess Royal, 'still keeps steadfastly to our side'. All the English personages in his cosmopolitan court and in his cosmopolitan family brought their influence to bear on the prince, to the detriment of the Scots. Nevertheless it is certain that in June, when Charles was already at Breda and on the point of setting out for

Ireland, the prince once more brought serious pressure to bear on him in a final attempt to induce him to accept the Scottish demands.

And indeed, however much one may sympathize with the English royalists, who not only felt deeply wronged by the negotiations with the Presbyterians, but considered any alliance with them both insincere and humiliating, it must be agreed that by putting Dutch before English considerations, the prince only acted rightly and, incidentally, proved his independence. That the States-General wanted an arrangement between the king and Scotland is most positively asserted in all the contemporary sources.[31] Strickland summed it all up when he observed that the prince was doing his best to bring the king and Scotland together, 'hopeing by that means to carrie all heere'.[32]

In 1649, however, when there was still a possibility of a choice between Scotland and Ireland, William II, for all the obligations under which he had laid the king, did not succeed in keeping him back from Ireland. Nor did the Scots make things easy for Charles. Compliance with their demands to introduce the Presbyterian religion into England and Ireland would have cost him the only true friends he had left. In Scotland, moreover, the persecution of true royalists continued unabated; the execution of the Marquis of Huntly in the beginning of April was particularly painful and galling to the king. It was at about the same time that the Scottish envoys arrived in the Hague, and the first demand they made (and in the most offensive manner at that) was that the king banish Montrose from his retinue.

It seems unlikely that the States of Holland could have been prevailed upon to give any practical help, even if Charles had chosen the Presbyterian path. *They* were no admirers of that particular ecclesiastical system. In any event, they were not put to the test, but when the king applied to the States-General for transport and a loan of £200,000 to further his expedition to Ireland,[33] at the same time explaining in detail why he could not pay heed to Scotland's call, the request fell on completely deaf ears.[34] The Prince of Orange, though in favour of the alternative course, had supported the king's request, and in June, when the king at last set sail for Ireland, William had once more to put his hand in his own pocket, lest Charles be detained by his creditors.[35]

Yet all his trouble was of no avail. Charles's cause in Ireland went badly from the moment Cromwell set about subduing the island. The king himself, after a long delay in France, never got any farther than Jersey, where he waited for months in the most straitened circumstances, and where eventually in September and October, the news of Cromwell's complete triumph reached him. 'It is obvious [wrote De Wilhem to Huygens][36] that God wishes to make him understand that Scotland is the only way to his restoration.' In fact there was nothing else left for him to do. But the Scots had not become more tractable. True, they were ready to resume talks – they had even sent envoys to the king in Jersey – but always on the same conditions. They now proposed a meeting at Breda, where the Prince of Orange could act as mediator.[37]

The king accepted this proposal on 21 January 1650 (NS). Next day he nevertheless wrote to his trusted Montrose asking him to proceed with the proposed expedition against the Scottish government. Montrose, the faithful royalist, had become Charles's only alternative, but the way in which he deployed him against the Scottish Presbyterians at the very moment he was entering into negotiations with them is a striking example of Charles's duplicity.

The mediator's position was extremely delicate. After consulting his mother in France, Charles and his destitute retinue arrived in Breda early in April. Feelings between his English supporters and the Scots had not improved since 1649. The English were suspicious even of the Prince of Orange. They knew that the Scots were counting on his support and that some of their spokesmen had spent the whole winter in the Hague trying to bring their influence to bear upon him.[38] According to an English Republican, who had wormed his way into Charles's retinue and thence sent vivid reports to the government in London,[39] the king's followers comforted themselves with the thought that Charles could feel fairly independent of William, who had so completely ruined himself in the service of the Stuarts that little further financial support could be expected of him, and who faced serious domestic difficulties, as well.[40]

There is no doubt that, just as he had done in 1649, the prince again did his best to induce the Scots to become more reasonable. Even the English royalists, for all their malicious talk, recognized that fact. According to the Republican spy, William made particular use of the services of Dutch Calvinists – of Dr Rivet (who was at that time rector of the university founded by Frederick Henry in

Breda), and even of Voetius[41] himself. Dutch Calvinists, as the spy put it, were 'nothing so rigid' as their Scottish counterparts, and the prince's overriding desire was to get the two parties to agree, he cared not on what terms. The English Republican, who watched the proceedings at Breda with a keen eye for their humorous aspects, kept reiterating that the prince's main interest was to get rid of Charles and his retinue who were straining his already lean purse beyond endurance.[42] Quite possibly, the prince may have been partly swayed by such considerations (although he had just obtained the use of a very large sum of money).[43] But as we have shown, an agreement between Charles and the Scots was in line with his general policy, in which the alliance between the States-General and the Stuarts against the English Commonwealth played so important a part. In any case, it is certain that the prince urged his brother-in-law to accept the Scots' most pressing demands: from a few of the documents that have been preserved[44] we learn that he urged Charles not only to take his oath upon the National Covenant and the Solemn League and Covenant, but also to observe the Presbyterian form of worship all the time he was in Scotland.

And so, to the bitter disappointment of Charles's English followers, the negotiations ended in victory for the Scots. Charles made a few reservations but, in the main, he accepted all their demands. Montrose and Ormonde were repudiated and with them Episcopalianism as well. Charles signed the agreement in early May. Dr Rivet, who consulted with the Scottish ministers on the best way of removing the Anglican chaplains from the king's entourage in accordance with the treaty, was present at the signature.[45] Staunch royalists learned with indescribable bitterness that the king had adopted a religion for himself and his subjects, in which he had no faith, and that he had agreed to cast off all those who had ruined themselves for him and the Episcopalian cause – and all this merely to be received as sham king to the hated Scottish rebels. His mother herself repudiated the allegation that she had 'urged him to sacrifice his honour and his conscience'. Royalists in England were bitterly disappointed.

Even before he left the Netherlands, Charles received news that drove home to him the false position in which he had placed himself. Montrose had fallen into the hands of the Scottish government. Quite possibly his expedition might have succeeded better had not Charles, by his negotiations with the Covenanters, smothered the desire of wavering Scots to join Montrose's ranks. At any rate, no mercy was shown to the captured hero who, despite the king's commission, was hanged and quartered as a traitor. No greater disrespect could have been shown to Charles. The news reached him while he was staying with his sister and brother-in-law at Honselaarsdijk,[46] in readiness for his embarkation. For one moment it caused him to waver.[47] What would his own life be worth if he put himself into the power of these inexorable fanatics? But it was too late to turn back. Towards the middle of June, he set sail on a Dutch man-of-war, commandeered by his brother-in-law. With him sailed a party of English Presbyterians and moderate Scots, whom ardent Presbyterians regarded as nothing short of 'prophane', and whom on arrival (still further concessions having been wrung from him *en route*) he was forced to dismiss. Charles was now irretrievably delivered into the hands of the unbending clerical party, and they were to spare him no humiliation.

Nor were the Scots the only people Charles had to reckon with. There was also the English Commonwealth. The English spy informed his government that now the agreement was signed, the royalists would move heaven and earth to get foreign troops into Scotland with a view to mounting a full-scale attack on England. 'Therefore if you be wise, shut the back door this summer, and then you will be safer next'[48] – advice that Cromwell was to follow in less time than Charles needed to get hold of foreign auxiliaries. For although William, in whom, as ever, Charles's main hopes remained centred, had provided him with fresh funds,[49] he had to overcome considerable Dutch opposition before he could even think of mobilizing the resources of the Netherlands on behalf of the Stuarts.

Struggle between William and Holland; Schaep's mission (May 1650); William's secret proposal to France (February); Crisis (July); William's death (November 1650)

The history of the last year or two had proved that the opposition of Holland was enough to cripple all political action on the part of the Stadholder. In order to grasp that fact, we must go back to the middle of February 1649, when the news of the execution of Charles I reached the Hague. From that moment, there was as

55

violent an onslaught on the policy of neutrality as there had been
in 1645, with the States of Holland putting up a particularly fierce
resistance. The Hollanders refused to be swayed by the general
clamour against 'the regicide', and never wavered in their determination to keep on good terms with the new rulers of England.
It was not so much a feeling of spiritual kinship with the Republican party that prompted their attitude, as a dispassionate appreciation of the interests of their own province. Certainly, it could
be argued that those interests might be threatened by a revolutionary conquest of Scotland. The French, as we saw, were quick
to realize that a disunited island kingdom suited their own purposes best, and events were soon to prove to the Dutch, as well,
how dangerous a strong and united Great Britain could be, be it
under Cromwell or under the Stuarts. However, the policy of
Holland, then as always, was largely swayed by her commercial
interest, and that, of course, meant keeping in with the Commonwealth, so powerful at sea. In addition, the States of Holland,
realists though they were, must have found it exceedingly hard to
take an unprejudiced view of a policy which, as a result of Orangist
dynastic machinations, had become so intimately bound up with
party feeling. Had the States of Holland and the House of Orange
been of one mind, they might well have played off the Stuarts
against the Commonwealth – dangerous though that policy would
have been – but as things stood, Holland was far more afraid of
Orange playing off Stuart against her.[50]

The Orange party, meanwhile, tried to make the proclamation
of the Commonwealth a pretext for an immediate break, hoping
to carry the States-General with them in their dangerous policy.
The Lord of Renswoude, an Orangist from Utrecht whose role as
'mediator' the reader will remember, happened to be 'President'
of the States-General for that week, while the Greffier Musch,
whose duty it was to 'extend' – that is, to sum up and formulate –
'resolutions', could always be counted on to side with Orange.
These two men now tried to steam-roller the States into passing
a resolution whereby Charles II was formally acknowledged as the
King of Great Britain. Holland and Zeeland – the latter once again
opposing Orange control on purely commercial grounds – fought
this resolution tooth and nail, and succeeded at last in having it
amended: Charles would merely be acknowledged as king, an
appellation to which his proclamation by the Scottish Parliament

unquestionably entitled him. The two provinces also succeeded in preventing the ostentatious recall from England of the special ambassadors who had vainly tried to save the king's life. Pauw van Heemstede, who returned for private reasons, deeply offended the Orange party when he reported that the new rulers of England had treated him with the utmost consideration. But van Heemstede had been merely an envoy extraordinary; the important thing was that, Joachimi, too, should remain at his post. And, in fact, there was no reason for his recall. After all, the ambassadors of France, Portugal and Spain had remained in England, even though the English Commonwealth was not then recognized by these countries or, for that matter, by anyone else.

However, the Dutch Republic was a house divided against itself. Each party succeeded in thwarting the other, and the result was a sad lack of purpose in the conduct of foreign affairs. The States-General could not recall Joachimi against the wish of Holland, but could prevent his being accredited to the new government. All the ambassador's urgent requests for more definite instructions elicited no other reply than orders to keep his ears and eyes open but not to enter into negotiations. This attitude naturally irritated the new rulers of England.

Then a sensational event took place in the Hague. In May, Parliament appointed Doreslaer, a Hollander in the English service, as joint ambassador to the States (with Strickland). A few days after his arrival in Holland, Doreslaer was murdered in cold blood by Scottish royalists. The States of Holland did what they could to bring the criminals to justice, but without success, and the murder naturally caused a great stir in England. Parliament addressed a very sharp note to Joachimi, who expressed his regrets and revulsion at the deed in writing. This incensed the States-General, because in writing his letter he had implicitly recognized the Republican government. The States-General, moreover, persisted in their refusal to receive Strickland, the English ambassador, who tried in vain to present his new credentials. Here again national division resulted in a negative policy, which, however, suited the Orange party. So long as the Netherlands did nothing at all, relations with England were bound to get worse and worse, and eventually result in open conflict.

In fact the problem of recognition was to become the thorniest of all. Holland, as has been said, found it easy to prevent Dutch embroilment in Charles's Irish expedition. But although she could obstruct, she could not compel. And so Strickland, in spite of all his pleas and even the threat that he would have to leave the country, could not gain admittance to the States-General. This failure was taken very much amiss in England. Strickland, for his part, if we can believe his letters in the *Thurloe State Papers*,[51] consoled himself with the fact that the States of Holland showed him due deference and received him as Resident of the Commonwealth of England as soon as he approached them.[52] He was perpetually urging his masters, the Council of State, to encourage Holland by meeting her demands on the subject of the blockade. The English government was quite willing to comply, but their threat to recall Strickland and thus to break off all diplomatic relations was seriously meant nevertheless. To avert it, the States of Holland, no doubt impressed by Cromwell's current victories in Ireland, now embarked on a course of action that bitterly offended the Orange party, but was all the more enthusiastically welcomed by Strickland.

Until then, the Hollanders had been trying to bring the States-General round to their own view with long arguments presented by countless delegations, but now the deputies requested the 'recording' of a formal and vigorous protest. What makes this document so interesting is that it contains an accusation against the deputies of the other provinces (with the exception of Zeeland which was siding with Holland once again) couched in the most undiplomatic of terms. These deputies were accused of holding up the admission of Strickland '*under pretext* of having no instructions',[53] and were further described as 'agents who, knowing the wishes of their honourable principals in these important matters of state would delay their implementation, instead of reporting and acting upon them in due time and place'. Possibly the Hollanders had gone further than they really intended, for as Strickland pointed out, all they meant to do was to direct the attention of the provincial States assemblies to the cavalier treatment of the English ambassador. Those States, he explained, 'who live remote and know noe more then their deputyes informe them', did not see through 'the mystery of iniquitye' that was being enacted in the Hague. No doubt he was right, for assuredly, the deputies of the inland provinces allowed the Stadholder to use them for his own purposes, perhaps not against the express intentions of their respective States' assemblies, but in the comfortable knowledge that these provinces were too 'remote' to keep a close check on what happened at the Hague. And clearly that was the view of the Hollanders as well, and the reason why they expected their protest to result in a censure of the deputies by their principals. As a matter of fact, both Aitzema and Strickland testify that the protest created a good deal of uneasiness among the accused deputies. But the power of the prince, as dispenser of countless jobs, was still such that no reprimands were uttered,[54] and that Holland's protest remained unheeded. There was little to stop the prince from forcing the States-General into a policy that served no single Dutch interest, but one that ran directly counter to them all.

In these circumstances, the States of Holland decided to embark on a step of extreme gravity. At the beginning of December 1649, the Holland assembly[55] proposed to send a 'commissioner' to England on behalf of the province, and in fact, on 21 May 1650, Gerard Schaep of Amsterdam crossed to England in that capacity, with an instruction dated 5 May.[56] The aims of this mission, which were quite clearly stated in the instruction, must have been twofold. In the first place, Holland, whose inhabitants had so many interests in England, felt the need for a representative more forceful than Joachimi, the regular Union envoy, who was nearly ninety years old, and who, as we saw, had incurred the displeasure of the States-General. Moreover, in view of the fact that there was the very real danger of Strickland's recall, Holland was afraid of being left powerless to undo the harm caused by the Orange party. If Holland was not meekly to submit to the dynastic folly of the Stadholder's policy, which threatened to plunge the country into senseless war, the dispatch of an ambassador, to which Holland was, in any case, entitled by the Union of Utrecht,[57] was an essential step, albeit one that seriously undermined the unity of the Dutch Republic. The Prince of Orange expressed his dismay to the French ambassador, describing the whole episode as a manœuvre that would have to be thwarted, lest it lead to the complete disruption of the Union.[58]

Solicitude for the Union was always the fine-sounding shibboleth with which the Princes of Orange tried to impress public opinion. In reality, William II was far more concerned with the pursuit of his English policy than with the national interest. True, the Union had begun to totter on its very foundations – the conflict between Holland and the Orange party was almost as much as the makeshift constitution could bear – but, as the reader will have gathered from preceding remarks, the main causes of the crisis were the prince's dynastic pursuits coupled with the unrepresentative, even corrupt, character of the States-General; Holland's basic attitude was one of self-defence. Constitutional slogans were not the real issues of the struggle; they were the weapons with which it was fought.

At that juncture, the conflict was beginning to focus on the question of the disbanding of troops. Now that there was peace, Holland wanted to reduce military expenditure, and to start clearing the public debt. Although important in itself, this question became a lynchpin in the great argument over foreign policy and its ultimate control.

Here the English question, which had already been the chief factor in reviving opposition by the States to the Stadholder under Frederick Henry, continued to be the chief bone of contention. Aitzema, after referring to the problem of Strickland's poor reception, went on to say: 'This in time caused a difference between Holland and the Prince, which was increased by economic questions and the reduction of the army.' It should be noted that Aitzema, too, regarded the English question as the main cause of the breach. An even more outspoken comment was that of Brun, the Spanish ambassador, who was anxiously watching a struggle whose outcome might well draw his own King into a war. 'It appears [he wrote a few weeks after the attack on Amsterdam to be mentioned below] that events in Holland were a direct reaction to the appointment of a resident in England, and in no way connected with the troops.'[59]

While the English question was not the only foreign problem at the time, it is true to say that it was indissolubly bound up with all the others. For the prince it was part and parcel of the peace with Spain and of his attitude towards France. As we saw, he was planning to undo the work of Münster, and to renew the alliance with France, with a view to partitioning the southern Netherlands and restoring the Stuarts to the throne of England.[60] In this policy he followed in his father's footsteps, albeit his father trod far more cautiously. Thus William's scheming with France to break the recent truce was much rasher than anything Frederick Henry had ever done. To make things worse, William's secret negotiations had the highly objectionable purpose of drawing France into the Dutch domestic quarrel.

In October 1648, he made the first approach through Aerssens van Sommelsdijk, the younger, but, as we saw, Mazarin had his hands full with the *Fronde* and the whole year of 1649 went by without any progress being made. Then things began to look brighter – though not for long – and William put forward a number of concrete proposals. Probably no document in its archives redounds so little to the credit of the House of Orange as William's instruction of February 1649[61] to his private envoy in France. It was written in imperfect French, and dealt with the subject of mutual co-operation. France was assured that William had sufficient influence over the six small provinces to count on their support in a war against Spain. Without mincing his words, he called on France to help him suppress all opposition from Holland. He spoke of a possible split within the Republic, with the six provinces ranged by his side against Holland – and a disunited Holland at that. If only France were prepared to recognize the six provinces as a state and come to their financial assistance, he would be able to overcome Holland with his army and lead the whole Republic into the war.

Of course the States of Holland had no knowledge of this startling document, but the Hollanders must nevertheless have had a fair suspicion of what was going on. In December 1649, for instance, the prince managed to prevail upon France not to call back her troops in the service of the Republic, as she was entitled to do under the treaty of 1630. Why was he so anxious to retain them? Clearly because the French troops could be deployed more readily against Holland than could the Dutch.[62] And when the States of Holland pressed for a recall of the French troops, the French government demurred.

Compared with William's near-treasonable relations with France, the Schaep mission, the boldest step that the States of Holland ever took, was innocent enough. If this act more than anything else persuaded William II to launch his *coup d'état* of July and August 1650, it was due not so much to its constitutional impropriety as to its political import. Naturally the Orange party pounced upon Holland's excursion into diplomacy as a justification of the prince's recourse to force, but to do so, they had first to misrepresent Holland's motives. Although, upon hearing the news, the French ambassador immediately declared[63] that the 'commissary' had obviously been charged to forge an alliance between the province of Holland and the Commonwealth of England, there is no shred of proof that this was actually so. In fact, when Van der Capellen, an Orangist from Gelderland, reported the rumour[64] that 'Bicker, De Witt, and others' had, through the medium of Schaep, carried on 'a secret correspondence with the English Parliament', he was forced to add that there was 'no evidence of it'. As a matter of fact, such stories were circulated quite deliberately. At about the time that the attack on Amsterdam was being launched, there appeared a pamphlet containing an alleged letter from Schaep, dated 14 July 1650, with a complete draft-treaty for a military alliance between Amsterdam (not even Holland!) and the English Commonwealth. This was a bare-faced fabrication, part of the plot against the great city. The charge caused quite a stir at first,[65] though soon afterwards people began wondering why the prince could produce no proof in support of these accusations.

Needless to say, in view of their opponents' machinations, a working alliance between the Republican parties in England and the Netherlands was by no means out of the question. Nor is there any doubt that Holland wished Cromwell every success in his military ventures against both the Scots and the Irish.[66] The desire to keep in with England went so far that the States of Holland did their best to suppress the attacks of Salmasius and Graswinckel on Milton's *Pro populo Anglicano defensio*.[67] The reporter of the *Briefe Relation*[68] even reported hearing such rash utterances as: 'If the rest of the provinces will be slaves, they will not. If the bundle of arrows must be unbound, they of Holland know into what quiver to put their arrows with safety and advantage.'[69] Remarkable language certainly, but obviously more the expression of irritation and fear than the reflection of a responsible political idea. Indeed, caution was one of the chief characteristics of the regents of Holland. Their tactics had all the weakness that usually goes with a defensive attitude of mind. Before they could go over to the offensive, they had first to be organized under a universally respected leader. Men like the Bickers of Amsterdam and De Witt of Dort certainly made their weight felt in the States of Holland, but the only position from which a true leader could emerge – that of grand-pensionary – was held by the timid and compliant Cats.[70]

The States generally left the initiative to their opponents who, whatever else they may have lacked, had the advantage of being led with a firm hand.

Hence, when the prince launched his attack at the end of July 1650, the States party was taken completely by surprise, the more so as William acted without French support – the *Fronde* was still troubling his prospective ally. Here we need not enter into such familiar details as the capture of the six members of the States of Holland, or the attack on Amsterdam – it is enough to observe that in none of the struggles between the House of Orange and the regent party did the former enjoy so little popular support. The German captain of horse who snapped at one of the arrested men that 'whoever has the army on his side is master',[71] hit the nail on the head. It was sheer military might that eventually decided the issue.

It is true that most of the Calvinist clergy supported the prince,[72] no doubt because they were grateful to him for making peace between Charles II and Presbyterian Scotland at Breda. The Reverend Maximilian Teellinck, for instance, a Zeelander, waxed quite eloquent when he dedicated his father's *Den Polityken Christen* to the prince. After glorifying Maurice and Frederick Henry and reviling their adversaries, he extolled William for having *the wisdom of God* (I Kings 3:28) and for opposing the peace (of Münster), *a girdle marred, profitable for nothing* (Jer. 13:7).

It cannot be denied [he continued] that there are many *sons of Belial* [Judg. 19:22], Papists, Arminians, enemies of religion and of the state, in our midst, who dare *bring a railing accusation against* [Jude 9] Your Highness ... as if Your Highness, who has in all this proved yourself to be *wise in heart, and mighty in strength* [Job 9:4], would have had no other aim than to make your own authority *increase* and the authority of the state *decrease* [John 3:30] ... *The Lord God of Gods, he knoweth and Israel he shall know* [Josh. 22:22], with all true patriots [that] your *witness is in heaven*, your *record is on high* [Job 16:19], and that suchlike never occurred to your princely heart.[73]

No less instructive than the praise is the defensive tone of his effusion.

The merchant class could hardly have looked forward with anything but the greatest uneasiness to the Prince of Orange's military plans. We have seen how Zeeland, a province over which the prince had great personal sway but which shared most of Holland's commercial concerns, ventured to make a stand against his English policy in 1649. That was no longer so in 1650, when Zeeland once again deferred to his dictates. As Aitzema put it, so unflatteringly: some of the 'chiefest' of the Zeeland delegates 'tried as ever to comply with the prince's wishes, so as to further their private interests and intrigues.'[74] The people of Amsterdam, on the other hand, staunchly supported their regents throughout the siege.[75]

One might have thought that the prince's failure to subdue Amsterdam would have offered the States party a splendid opportunity for squaring accounts with the ambitious Stadholder once and for all. But here the party's lack of organization told against them. Van der Capellen wrote scornfully that he 'had expected more wisdom and courage from these gallant spirits'.[76] Indeed, the lack of unity among Amsterdam magistrates in particular, some of whom used to opportunity for ousting the Bickers from power,[77] was pitiable to behold.

Thus, in spite of his initial defeat, William II managed not only to come out of the débâcle unscathed, but even to strengthen his position decisively. Moreover, he now showed far greater political skill than ever before. There are many signs that his opponents were so cowed by the *coup d'état* that they left him a free hand for quite some time. The small provinces swallowed their objections[78] and vied with one another in offering him resolutions of gratitude. Aitzema relates that, although the States of Groningen had passed a resolution asking the States-General to accept the credentials of the envoy of the English Commonwealth, their delegates were afraid to table this demand.[79] The English Republican from whom I have been quoting so freely, noted it all with rising annoyance. Writing at the beginning of September,[80] he referred to

the miserable base business of Amsterdam, whereby hath been discovered the baseness of som Provinces, and the weakness of other, and by both their ripeness for slaverie, and readiness to succumb. Certainly that gallant spirit, which possest those people when they bravely (to their hitherto lasting honour) vindicated that libertie from the oppressions of the most potent Prince of Europe, which they have now tamely given up into the hands of their own servants, hath made a transmigration into our Nation.

Indeed, what records we have of the conduct even of Hollanders in their hour of crisis, do not leave one with much respect for their strength of character. The six captives were left to their fate, and some of them addressed the prince in letters that were as abject as any.[81] Gerard Schaep, writing from London, asked the Secretary to the Frisian Stadholder, who happened to be William's cousin; to dispute what 'sinistre opinies' the court might still have of him.[82]

Nevertheless it would be quite wrong to believe that the crisis had placed William II in an unassailable position. There is no doubt that he was preparing to pursue his foreign plans with even greater vigour before death took him by surprise. But it is equally true that Holland thwarted him again when, as early as August, the question of war was brought up once more.[83] The States had bent under the force of the storm, but they were by no means bowed. They were probably as impotent as ever to take the initiative against the prince, but their new leaders were at least as adept in the tactics of parrying and checking[84] as the old ones, whom the prince had removed by force. The English Republican, writing from Leyden, held that the prince would succeed in persuading the States-General to declare war on the Commonwealth, should Cromwell prove unsuccessful in Scotland.[85] There was a close link between developments in that country and in the Netherlands. The Scots themselves expected a great deal from William II.[86] MacDowell, as resident of the King of Scotland, put tremendous pressure on the prince, and it was as much as the Hollanders could bring themselves to do, to make vague protests against the vehemence with which he expressed himself against the English Republic in official documents.[87]

The battle of Dunbar, however, at which the Scottish army suffered a crushing defeat (13 September, NS), also dealt a fresh blow to William's English policy. In October, the English government felt strong enough to expel Joachimi, as a reprisal against the Dutch refusal to receive Strickland. Diplomatic relations between the two countries was now broken. Moreover, Dunbar greatly strengthened the hands and courage of the prince's opponents in Holland herself. On 24 September, Sir Edward Nicholas, one of the most eminent of royalist exiles, wrote from the Hague that party feeling against the Stadholder was increasing daily.[88] Opposition to William was far from dead, and was ready to do battle the moment he pressed for a decision on the all-important matter of foreign policy.

Nobody can tell what the outcome of that battle would have been. On 6 November, the prince, but twenty-four years old, died of smallpox, and the States of Holland, led by the staunchest Republicans, suddenly found themselves masters not only of their own province, but of the entire Republic.

REFERENCES

1. *Archives*, II, iv, p. 180.
2. The treaty, as we saw, stipulated that neither of the contracting parties would conclude a separate peace.
3. *Archives*, II, iv, p. 235, 5 August 1647.
4. *Ibid.*, p. 262.
5. *Hamilton Papers* (Gardiner, 1880), p. 228, letter by Sir W. Bellenden from Amsterdam, 9 July 1648 (presumably OS): 'At all time of my acces to the P. of Orange I did moue him what was to be doin be ws for the conjunction with the Staits, but the trewth is that he is not so ripe and painfull in and for business as his condition doeth requiet.'
6. Memorandum from William II to the Prince of Wales, September (?) 1648, *Archives*, II, iv, p. 267.
7. As we know from the letters of De Wilhem to Huygens in *Archives*, II, iv, pp. 263 ff.; published more fully by Worp, *op. cit.*, IV, pp. 491 ff., and also from a letter by Sir Edward Hyde in *Clarendon State Papers*, II, pp. 455 ff. He gives the number of men as 900; De Wilhem as 500.
8. De Wilhem received a receipt from Bellenden.
9. At a later date, the Prince of Wales expressed their gratitude most emphatically (letter from St Johnston, 21 January 1651, *Rawlinson Letters*). He explained that, from the moment that they had first met in Helvoetsluis, Heenvliet's services had been inestimable.
10. 'Pleust à Dieu que nostre maistre ne s'engageast plus avant avec ces gens sine luce, sine cruce, sine deo; jamais de ma vie je vis un tel désordre et confusion' (18 September); in Worp, *op. cit.*
11. According to Eva Scott (*The King in Exile*, p. 51) it was the generosity of the Prince of Orange which enabled this fleet to set sail; he supplied it with provisions for three months. Miss Scott, however, lists no sources.
12. The Prince of Wales was received in state and entertained for the customary ten days at the expense of the States-General; the States of Holland refused to allow this term to be prolonged at the

pleasure of the Prince of Orange (De Wilhem to Huygens). The young Duke of York, too, was still living at the expense of his brother-in-law. In order to relieve William of this burden, the Duke of York went to France in December, while the Prince of Wales's court was curtailed as much as possible (Aitzema, *op. cit.*, VI, p. 575). According to Aitzema (*op. cit.*, VI, p. 782), in 1649, William II was paying the lords of Charles II's court pensions of 2,000 guilders each. Cf. also Carte's *Ormonde Papers*, I, pp. 199, 209.

13. At the time these decisions were taken, William was in Groningen, whence he informed Heenvliet on 15 September that he had sent a letter to the Princess Royal for the Admiralty of Rotterdam, in case the Prince of Wales might like to have a ship to go to Scotland. On 20 September – by which time Heenvliet had apparently told him about the disaster at Preston – he wrote the following characteristic words: 'J'ay receu vos lettres. Je voy que les affaires sont bien incertaines et qu'ils ne savent de quel bois faire flèce. Me semble qu'il vaut toujours mieux un Royaume [Scotland] que rien, mais le temps perdu est beaucoup' (*Rawlinson Letters*).

14. Aitzema tells us that, at the time, most people's sympathies were still with Parliament.

15. Aitzema, *op. cit.*, VI, p. 682.

16. Eva Scott, *op. cit.*, p. 73.

17. Aitzema, *op. cit.*, VI, p. 694.

18. See Chapter 1, note 119.

19. Aitzema, *op. cit.*, VI, p. 685.

20. The Latin dissertations, both translated into Dutch, were followed by two more pamphlets. See Knuttel, *Catalogus*, Nos. 6377-83.

21. Graswinckel, *Korte onderrechtinge raeckende de fundamentale Regeeringhe van Engelandt* (Knuttel, *Catalogus*, No. 6375). *Beduncken op de onderrechtinghe*, etc. (Knuttel, No. 6376).

22. Aitzema, *op. cit.*, VI, p. 688.

23. See Chapter 1, note 38.

24. Baillie, *op. cit.*, IV, pp. 73 ff. Spang wanted to speak in English or Latin, but William II preferred Dutch. Lord Byron, the envoy, or Ormonde, explained: 'He understands English very well, though he speak it not, so that your Exc. shall not need trouble to write in French' (Carte, *Ormonde Papers*, I, p. 269).

25. Spang, as one might imagine, was very well disposed towards William II: 'Ye will find our young Prince of Orange one of the hopefullest youths that ever Europe brought forth, and willing to doe all good offices for the cause' (Carte, *op. cit.*, I, p. 83).

26. *Ibid.*, pp. 88, 90.

27. *Ibid.*, p. 239.

28. Sophia of Bohemia, for one, said so in a letter to her brother,

Rupert, on 13 April 1649 (*Cal. St. P. Dom.* [1649-50], p. 85).
Baillie, one of the Scottish envoys, wrote home to the same effect.

29. The Queen of Bohemia hoped to win Charles for Sophia. The Bohemian family was Calvinist, but most of its members were far from faultless in doctrine. Sophia herself was blamed for accompanying Charles to common prayer. Cf. Sophia's *Mémoires*.

30. Carte, *op. cit.*, I, p. 264.

31. Byron, for instance, after mentioning the Scottish demands, added: 'But the King being now unfortunately in a Presbyterian country cannot resent these indignities so as otherwise he would' (Carte, *op. cit.*, I, p. 268).

32. *Thurloe State Papers*, I, 115; 19 September 1649.

33. *Clarendon State Papers*, II, p. 482.

34. *Archives*, II, iv, p. 309. The assertion in *Nicholas Papers*, I, p. 127, that the money procured for the King by William II, was 'underhand provided by the States', is most improbable. A similar account is found in 1650 (Gardiner, *Letters and Papers Illustrating the Relations Between Charles II and Scotland in 1650* [1894], p. 77). Strickland wrote in September 1649: 'Pray, sir, doe but gratifie the States of Holland, and my life for it, P.C., who hopes only to retrieve his game from hence, shall doe nothing, notwithstanding the greatness of the greatest heere' (*Thurloe State Papers*, I, p. 119).

35. Aitzema.

36. *Archives*, II, p. iv, 315; 19 October 1649.

37. Gardiner, *op. cit.* The Princes of Orange had a special connection with Breda where they had a residence.

38. *Ibid.*, p. 60.

39. His reports appeared in *A Briefe Relation*, the official organ of the English Council of State, and are reprinted in Gardiner's book.

40. *Ibid.*, p. 30.

41. *Ibid.*, p. 51.

42. Gardiner, *op. cit.*, p. 76 *et passim*.

43. He had just raised a large loan in Amsterdam.

44. Wynne, *Geschillen over de afdanking van het krijgsvolk*, p. 93. Reprinted in Gardiner. Unfortunately these documents are not dated.

45. Gardiner, *op. cit.*, pp. 81, 85.

46. Not far from Delft. According to the English spy, he spent a further month in Breda after the conclusion of the treaty, because he did not want to face the displeasure of the States of Holland at the Hague (Gardiner, *op. cit.*, p. 119). The *Rawlinson Letters* contain an undated letter by the Princess Royal to Heenvliet, written in Breda, apparently during May 1650. She asked him to show this

letter to her husband, and continued: 'afin que nous puissions vennir à La Haye. Le Roy est en grande impassiance et ne fait que demander quand vous viendrés icy.'

47. On 13 June, William II wrote from Schoonhoven: 'Je croy qu'il sera bien périllieux aprés avoir attendu cy longtemps de s'embarquer, et il vaudroit mieux remettre l'affaire à une autre fois' (Rawlinson Letters). By that time the king was on board ship.

48. Gardiner, *op. cit.*, p. 90.

49. Cf. p. 43.

50. Cf. *Br. Rel.*, 9 September 1650 (Br. Mus.; not in Gardiner, *op. cit.*; published by me in *Bijdr. en Meded.*, 1924): 'They [the Hollanders] wish verie well to your affaires in Scotland.'

51. *Thurloe State Papers*, I, 113 ff.

52. *Ibid.*, p. 118.

53. Aitzema, *op. cit.*, VI, 831.

54. In 1649, for instance, William granted a lieutenancy to the six-year-old son of Jonkheer Boldewijn Jacob Mulert, deputy in the States-General for Overijsel. The towns of that province (each province was responsible for the pay of particular regiments assigned to it) were so indignant that they decided to refuse payment (Bussemaker, *Geschiedenis van Overijsel, 1650–72*, I, 25). After William's death, Mulert was criticized in the States of Overijsel because, without authority, he had voted in the States-General for the resolution of 5 June 1650, which the prince used as an excuse for his *coup d'état* (*Brieven aan De Witt, W.H.G.*, I, 33).

55. *Archives*, II, iv, p. 317.

56. Aitzema, *op. cit.*, VII, p. 23.

57. Article X of the Union merely prohibited the members from entering into separate 'alliances or treaties' with other states.

58. *Archives*, II, iv, p. 317.

59. 16 August 1659: P. L. Muller, 'Spanje en de partijen in Nederland in 1650', in *Nijhoff's Bijdragen* (Nieuwe Reeks), VII (1899), 149. In my opinion Müller is quite wrong in calling this 'a rather curious utterance'. His incredulity merely proves how completely neglected have been the aspects of the foreign policy of Frederick Henry and William II which are being presented in this study.

60. According to the writer of *Openhertig Discours . . . rakende de subite dood van Z.H.* (Knuttel, *Catalogus*, No. 1651), William II would have liked to subdue all the provinces, dismissing the independent magistrates everywhere and replacing them with 'servile' officers, 'whereupon we should have been plunged into two wars at the same time; to wit, against the Parliament of England to please the King of Scotland, and against Spain to please the frivolous French, in whom he places all his faith.'

61. *Archives*, II, iv, p. 298. The document is not dated, but Groen suggests it was written in late February 1649.
62. See *Archives*, II, iv, p. 318.
63. *Archives*, II, iv, p. 317.
64. *Gedenkschriften*, II, p. 281.
65. See, for instance, the pamphlet *Ernstig gesprek tusschen drie personen* (Knuttel, *Catalogus*, No. 7256). *State Papers, For.*, *Holland*, CLIX, contains a letter of 11 August 1650, from Utrecht, signed Cha. Ledison (one of the pseudonyms of Sir E. Nicholas), dealing with the attack on Amsterdam: 'Its reported that in order to render themselves soveraigns and to curbe the rest of the provinces a factious party in that city hath by their Agent Monsr Scape now in England, and other underhand intruments, treated with the Rebells there to send them to Amsterdam by the Tassell [Texel] 10,000 men, whereof 5000 were to have come very speedily being (some say) alreddy levyed and reddy to be shipped under pretence of being sent for Irland, and the other 5000 were to be sent a monthe or 6 weeks after. By their complices in England its easy to make judgment of their designe and intentions; but I believe untill the English rebells see the success of their forces now marched into the Northe, they will be wary how they sent many men into any foreigne partes.' But on 15 August, Nicholas wrote: 'Methinkes those who are of the Prince of Orange's counsell should use all possible industry to get proofe of the truth of what is printed concerning the agreement between Scape and the Rebells of England, which is a business of very great importance to these States to knowe.'
66. See Chapter 1, note 96.
67. See Wicquefort, I, p. 522, and 'Briefe Relation' in Gardiner, *Charles II and Scotland in 1650*.
68. Who had left the court of Charles II for Leyden (Gardiner, *op. cit.*, p. 115).
69. *Ibid.*, p. 114.
70. 'Be pliant, friend, whoe'er thou be, A virtue 'tis will profit thee.' From *The Reed and the Oaktree*.
71. Pelnits to Nanning Keyser; *Bijdragen en Mededeelingen Historisch Genootschap*, XVIII, p. 356.
72. Aitzema, *op. cit.*, VII, p. 53; *Briefe Relation*, 9 September 1650.
73. *Zeeuwsche vreugde* . . . (Knuttel, *Catalogus*, No. 9675). It was against this dedication that Vondel wrote an impassioned poem entitled: 'On the Rebelliousness of the Godless Zeelander Max. Teellinck.'
74. Aitzema, *op. cit.*, VII, p. 11.
75. See Fabio Chigi to the Cardinal-Secretary of State, *Bijdragen en Mededeelingen Historisch Genootschap*, XXXV, p. 121.
76. *Gedenkschriften*, II, p. 281.

77. Elias, *Vroedschap van Amsterdam*, I, p. XCIX.
78. How strong these objections were may be gathered from a letter to Van der Capellen by his son, published in Wicquefort, *op. cit.*, I, p. 448.
79. Aitzema, *op. cit.*, VII, p. 155.
80. *Briefe Relation*, 9 September 1650.
81. Wynne, *op. cit.*, p. 156 (Duyst van Voorhout), p. 166 (Nanning Keyser); Ruyl's performance was even worse.
82. *Ibid.*, p. 179.
83. Fruin, *Verspreide Geschriften*, IV, pp. 166 ff.
84. On 28 August, Brun wrote (Müller, *op. cit.*, p. 166): 'My confidants in the province of Holland say . . . that despite all this their province is not overthrown, as people think, but that she is still as powerful as before and watches her interests and safety more closely than she formerly used to do.' It is true that he did not place much faith in these professions.
85. *Briefe Relation*, 9 September 1650.
86. A republican correspondent in London wrote on 18 November 1650: 'La mort de Son Altesse d'Orange fauche les espérances de nos ennemis et nous fera sans doute voir quelque grand changement aux affaires d'Escosse.' *Bijdragen en Mededeelingen Historisch Genootschap*, IV (1880), p. 239.
87. Aitzema, *op. cit.*, VIII, p. 155.
88. 'The party in these parts increases every day in faction against the Prince of Orange' (Nicholas Papers, I, p. 198).

3

The Princess Royal

1650–61

The guardianship dispute

William II's death brought a radical change in the Republic's political condition. The Orange party became disorganized, and there was no one to take William's place or to wield his authority.

William Frederick, the Stadholder of Friesland, the only possible candidate, was opposed by the Holland States party with particular vehemence – during the life of William II, he had been one of the chief firebrands[1] in the prince's party. His opponents now sought to frighten him with the threat of a prosecution for his share in the events of July and August. Nor was he the only one to tremble. A few hours after the prince's death, Heenvliet had given orders for all the relevant State papers to be sealed, and many people's anxious thoughts hovered round the iron chest in the Stadholder's palace[2] in which these secrets were kept. As far as William Frederick was concerned, the threats were so effective that, for a few months after his cousin's death, he did not so much as dare to show his face in the Hague – no wonder when even the Orange party was by no means unanimous in sponsoring his cause. In particular, the champions of the little prince, born a few

72

days after William II's death, suspected the Frisian Stadholder of wishing to oust the legitimate contender for good. Their suspicions grew even stronger when, early in December, William Frederick succeeded in getting himself appointed Stadholder of the province of Groningen.[3]

But the infant William III still enjoyed considerable social and political esteem. Not only could he count on the devotion of the people of Holland, who greeted his birth with the kind of public jubilation normally reserved for a new sovereign prince, but he also was master of Breda, Geertruidenberg, Turnhout, Meurs and Lingen which, though heavily encumbered with debt, nevertheless ensured their owner of a great position. Moreover, his hereditary right to have a say in the appointment of the magistrates of Veere and Flushing gave the young boy a firm foothold in the States of Zeeland and hence in the government of the country as a whole. This widespread influence, temporarily vested in the Council of His Highness and in the two princesses, i.e. in the mother and widow of the deceased prince, might have served to keep the Orange party firmly united, had the two princesses not been bitterly divided by a quarrel over the guardianship of William III.

There had never been any affection between Mary Stuart and Amalia of Solms, two determined women with opposed ambitions. 'The old Princess' naturally had a great advantage not only in age and experience, but in actual power as well. Even after Frederick Henry's death, she continued to exercise considerable influence over her son, and she was known as a born politician.[4] No wonder that the young princess clung all the more stubbornly to her rank, for rank was her only advantage. We saw how much importance Frederick Henry himself attached to it, and the girl, educated in accordance with his precepts and further encouraged by her ubiquitous English attendants (in particular by Lady Stanhope, Heenvliet's wife) had grown up with a royal pride so intense that it often embittered her relations with the prince's family. One such conflict took place in 1646, and is mentioned by an English reporter.[5]

In December of that year, after plans for her marriage to the Prince of Wales had been finally dropped, Louise Henrietta of Orange was married to the Elector of Brandenburg. It was laid down that, as Electress, she would have precedence over Mary, a mere Princess of Orange. But Mary, unwilling to forget her royal birth, refused to attend the ceremony and the subsequent festivities.[6] This incident must have increased the animosity between the young princess and Amalia, who had always thought highly of the Brandenburg connection and who undoubtedly had less patience with her daughter-in-law's royal pride now that the royal family found itself in so precarious a situation.

But misfortune never made the Stuarts and their supporters hang their heads. When the princess's exiled brothers had been enjoying the hospitality of the Stadholder's court, they sat at a special table with the princess, while her husband was relegated to another table where he presided over members of the States, senior officers and so on, all men who could not be permitted to share a table at which a king's sons were seated. When the solemn day of William II's funeral was approaching (on which occasion, incidentally, the Princes of Portugal, though descendants of William I, had to give way to the Duke of York, who stood firm on his precedence), Sir Edward Nicholas, Charles I's old Secretary of State, then staying at the Hague, wrote an indignant letter to a friend, protesting against the declared intention of Charles II to be represented (the young king was unable to tear himself away from Scotland, where his position had grown desperate). Sir Edward deemed it most unfitting that his Majesty should do honour 'to the body of a petty Prince not of royal blood'[7] – conveniently forgetting that the dead man was the king's brother-in-law and one, moreover, who had nearly ruined himself to save the king's house from collapse! Even earlier, in November 1650, immediately after Mary's confinement, the question arose whether the young mother could properly invite the Princess of Hohenzollern,[8] who was expected to pay her a visit, to take a seat by her bedside. The old princess approached Heenvliet, the intendant. He was afraid she could not, whereupon (as he himself noted in his journal) Her Highness 'flew off in such a rage that I shall rather forget what passed than describe it'.[9] Questions of precedence, so important in the eyes of the generation, kept cropping up time and again. Thus when the Elector of Brandenburg and his wife were staying in the Hague in June 1651, they purposely neglected to pay a visit to the Princess Royal and, as if to draw even greater attention to the omission, called on their little nephew on a Sunday morning, when they were sure his mother had gone to church.[10] By themselves, such incidents would have had little effect on the course of political events, but it was a serious matter for the Orange party when the antipathy between the two women gave rise to the great guardianship quarrel, a quarrel that did so much harm to the prestige of the House of Orange and, moreover, compelled both princesses to enlist the services of the States of Holland.

The Princess Royal based her claim on her late husband's last will – in the form of a draft and not even signed. By it, the guardianship of a son, should one be born to him after his death, would fall to the Princess Royal assisted by members of the States-General to be named in due course – an event that never took place.[11] Nothing was more natural than that the old princess should have objected to an arrangement by which her husband's family was to be totally excluded from any direct say in the education of the little prince or in the administration of his landed possessions and the patronage attached to them. Mary, for her part, was encouraged to stand up to the old princess by the Heenvliets, whose influence over her was very great and who, as Heenvliet himself testified, were afraid their own position might be undermined should the old princess ever decide to exert her authority.[12] They looked for support to Charles II, who had renewed their appointment in 1649 (the original appointment was made by his father in 1642) and to whom Heenvliet now wrote asking to be confirmed in his office.[13] At the same time, Heenvliet also sought allies among the regents of Holland who, now that William II was dead, had grown much more powerful. His excuse was that the Princess Royal could only hope to have her fatherless son appointed Stadholder by keeping on friendly terms with the States of Holland.[14] This policy was not really in line with Charles's interests, but far away in Scotland as he was, he could hardly keep a close watch on what was happening at the Hague.[15] The old princess, for her part, relied on the support of her son-in-law of Brandenburg, so much so that Mary felt impelled to tell Heenvliet she 'wanted no dealings with the Elector, despite persuasions by Her Highness'.

The whole affair was a web of intrigue and personal ambition, in which the secret chest played a considerable part as well. Sommelsdijk, for instance, was afraid the old princess might ruin him by having the chest smuggled into the hands of the States of Holland, and he accordingly pressed the Princess Royal to have it opened and the compromising documents burned. In the end, the chest, unsealed and sealed again, found a new hiding-place in the office of His Highness's Council. Even then Heenvliet kept alluding to it from time to time, for his own dark purposes.

It has been suggested[16] that Amalia of Solms represented the national point of view and defended the true interests of Orange, which were in danger of being sacrificed to the Stuarts by the Princess Royal and her hangers-on. But this view presupposes that Amalia had far nobler motives than the whole unedifying business suggests, or at least that there was a vast gulf between her motives and her public actions.[17]

As to the latter, there is no doubt that Amalia showed the Orange flag when she thwarted Mary's plans to name the new-born prince 'Charles', and had him baptized 'William' instead. However, this does not entitle one to infer that her policy was, in fact, different from her daughter-in-law's. True, in the matter of the guardianship she asked that the House of Orange be treated as 'an illustrious house' whose interests were to be handled as a matter of state, whereas Mary wanted to subject them to common law. But both had to look to the States of Holland for support, and did what they could to curry favour with what were, in fact, the great antagonists of the House of Orange. This helped to turn the tables on William Frederick when the States of Holland directed their first attack against him. As for help to the Stuarts, no one in the Orange party dreamt of severing the connection with the English throne; but though Mary, the living symbol of that link, naturally made the most of it, she was not prepared to support her brother by making further inroads into her son's heavily encumbered fortune. This, in any case, was the position during the first years of her widowhood, when she was still completely under the sway of the Heenvliets – she was only nineteen when she gave birth to the prince – who had personal reasons for urging moderation in this sphere. English royalists bitterly resented the princesses' steward not only because he was obviously out to please the States of Holland, but also because he was careful not to queer his pitch with the ruling party in England, mindful as he was of his wife's landed possessions there.[18]

In later years, however, Mary often risked a great deal for her brothers. And, as far as the national interest was concerned, it was in any case undesirable that the power and influence of the House of Orange should be vested in a young woman with no personal abilities, but liberally endowed with the Stuart obstinacy and frivolity – a young woman who recognized an English king, about to be exiled, as the head of her house and awaited his 'commands', and who never bothered to learn Dutch, speaking English by preference or, if need be, French. Moreover, as the years went by, she nurtured a growing hatred of her son's country and people, putting her family's friends to a severe test by her indifference and chilly haughtiness. This was why a man like Huygens could sincerely hold that he was serving both Orange and the country by lending his support to Amalia of Solms's claims. When one remembers the obstinate and narrow ambition with which she arranged her children's marriages, one feels inclined to wonder whether Amalia was worthy of his devotion – for which she made Huygens a very poor return.

The political implications apart, it was only reasonable to expect that the claims of the paternal family should receive some recognition; no wonder, therefore, that they were taken into account when the final settlement, after great arguments first in the Court of Holland then in the High Council, was reached in August 1651. Mary accepted her mother-in-law and the Elector of Brandenburg as co-guardians – with one vote between them. The magistratures of the Zeeland vassal towns were shared out: the Princess Royal was given Flushing, and the old princess received Veere.

Perhaps they were satisfied. As for the nation, it was heartily sickened by the squabble within the Orange party so soon after the death of William II, with the result that the party not only lost influence, but its power to act into the bargain.

The Great Assembly; The English diplomatic mission; Orange obstruction of the negotiations (1651); War (1652)

The States of Holland, on the other hand, showed an admirable presence of mind in face of the rift between the princesses. Now that the autocratic sway of the House had been broken so opportunely, it must never again be allowed to resume its former power: no Stadholder must ever again be appointed in the province of Holland and no Captain-General in the Union; above all, no single person must ever again be allowed to hold two such important offices at once.[19] Nor was that all. If Holland's policy, however triumphant in the province itself, was not to be wrecked in the

Generality, she must give the entire federation the kind of leadership and singleness of purpose which had formerly come from the Princes of Orange.

A good many observers felt that Holland's chances of success were extremely slender. There had been veritable explosions of pessimism before: at the conclusion of the Truce in 1609 and above all upon the signing of the peace of 1648. On both occasions the same argument was heard: that this loose amalgamation of provinces, with its impossible constitution, would collapse the moment the external threat receded. The religious quarrels that shook the state during the entire twelve years of the Truce had been foreseen by Lipsius in 1595, and were, in fact, the grounds on which he had advised the Spanish king to agree to the truce. When the disturbances eventually broke out, they merely supplied the sceptics with fresh ammunition. French diplomats were gravely perturbed and Chigi, the Papal Nuncio, who visited Holland in 1650, was of the opinion that a split had become unavoidable after the attack on Amsterdam – so bitter were the divisions and so bad the constitution that a return to Spanish rule seemed to be the only possible solution.[20] Yet the proud republicans maintained that all the disturbances of the past were but the price the country had been forced to pay for vesting excessive powers in a single person; now that this failing had been remedied, there was every reason to believe that the situation would become stabilized.[21] French observers, on the other hand, inspired by the monarchical ideas which France had begun to champion, asserted confidently (as early as 1647) that the Republic could not possibly survive in the absence of 'an eminent leader'. What all these prophets of ruin failed to appreciate was first of all the strength of national sentiment in the northern Netherlands, and secondly, the great political ability of the regent class of Holland.

And yet these regents had shown their mettle in the past, for instance when they ran the country under Oldenbarneveldt, and ran it well until, in the end, their differences with Maurice became insuperable. Until that happened, the Prince of Orange had lent his personal prestige to add further weight and lustre to the preeminence of Holland and of Holland's 'Advocate'. If Holland now opposed his successors, it was only because the political gulf that had opened in Maurice's later years continued to divide the province from the House. Nothing was more natural than that the

States of Holland, after their recent experiences at the hands of William II, should have wished to assume direct control over the Generality, whose whip they had been made to feel so painfully.

In their discussions of these events, contemporary witnesses and later historians alike generally pay far too exclusive attention to the purely constitutional aspects of the struggle, treating the Orange party as upholders of the principle of unity, and the States party as advocates of particularism or even of separatism. The debate hinges on the problem of William II's constitutional right to oppose the demands of Holland. Most historians seem to take an exaggerated view of the extent to which Holland's leading position among the seven provinces menaced the federal constitution, once there was no prince to make his authority felt over them. It is too often forgotten that the constitutional issue was not really the crux of the struggle, but merely the weapon with which it was being conducted. In reality, the conflict revolved round quite other considerations, and particularly round the question of whether or not the Princes of Orange should be allowed to drag the Republic into their own wars and whether, after having curbed the power of the oligarchy, they would not try to assume autocratic powers like so many other European rulers of the day. In order to achieve that very aim, the House, after getting a stranglehold on the States of the smaller provinces, found it convenient to raise the Generality cry, thus exploiting the prevalent jealousy of Holland's predominance. In order to defend herself against the Stadholder's policy and the corrupt States-General, Holland, for her part, found it convenient to entrench herself behind the particularist rights and functions guaranteed by the Union of Utrecht. No doubt these rights impeded the smooth running of the Republic, the more so as, in the heat of the struggle, the province often gave them too wide an interpretation. Even now that the prince's authority had lapsed, Holland, albeit she developed a keen sense of responsibility towards the Generality soon afterwards, continued to look upon her provincial sovereignty as the best guarantee against a revival of the old threat – and no one could argue that it had been dispelled once and for all.

For disorganized though it was by the death of William II, the Orange party was still very much alive. In particular, the state colleges were still packed with supporters of the old régime and the States-General had much the same composition as before, although it should be added that some of the members now ran into trouble with their provincial States who disapproved of actions they had taken in deference to the late prince.[22] While several of these delegates now recognized Holland's power and adhered to it as readily as they had served Orange before, others persisted in their antagonistic attitude, and merely bided their time.

From the start, Holland tried her utmost to convince the other provinces that she posed no threat to their interests or those of the Union. Solemn declarations were issued, envoys sent to several provincial States. In that way, Holland quickly succeeded in convening a Great Assembly, to which the provinces appointed men of more independent mind than the regular deputies, and which helped to neutralize the influence of the Orangist States-General. When the new delegates arrived at the Hague, they were treated with great cordiality by the deputies of Holland, who arranged a host of private conferences to expound their policy to the guests and eventually won them round. Province after province came out against the appointment of a Captain-General. The provinces also agreed to assume powers of control over the troops in their pay ('at their repartition') and to make use of the right to supervise their deployment ('patents') in the territory under the province's jurisdiction – two safeguards against a repetition of last year's dangerous game of using the entire army against one of their members. The result, needless to say, was to render the army a far less efficient instrument of war. The towns were confirmed in their unfettered right to choose councillors and magistrates: suspicions of the Reformed Church ministers were quickly lulled by a re-affirmation of the decisions taken at Dort. Before the Assembly disbanded it passed an act of amnesty for 'the Amsterdam affair'; it was extended to Aerssens van Sommelsdijk only after he made a 'humble' request to that effect. The act included an explicit and sharp condemnation of the guilty party, and declared the resolution of 5 June 1650 unlawful and void.

The States of Holland were thus well on the way to consolidating their leading position in the Republic, and had already succeeded in pushing through measures to ward off what they considered as the main threat: the establishment of a military autocracy. But what of the other great issue which was involved in the change of régime, the issue of foreign affairs? Here, few questions were as important as relations with England; and Holland, as we know, had always been the champion of peace and friendship with her great neighbour. How then are we to explain that before the Holland party had been in power for two years, they found themselves at war with the English Commonwealth?

At first, Holland had prevailed in foreign affairs as well. The provinces had promptly dropped their opposition to the admission of Strickland and were quick to recognize the English Commonwealth, no doubt appreciating that to do otherwise had always been against their own best interests. Other factors were at play as well; thus the Royalists were rapidly losing what goodwill they had with the Dutch public as a result of the Duke of York's privateering attacks on the Dutch merchant service.[23] Moreover, Spain herself had taken the initiative of giving formal recognition to the English Revolution. Still, it was the elimination of the prince's over-riding influence above all that caused the provinces' change of heart. Take the case of Zeeland. Towards the end of William II's life, it was this province, more openly anti-Commonwealth and at the same time more dependent for its trade upon England than any other province, which had given the English Republicans the greatest offence. Now Zeeland was the first to join Holland in recommending recognition of the Commonwealth to the States-General[24] which, on 28 January 1651, agreed to receive the envoys of the English Republic, and instructed Joachimi to return to England.

Needless to say, these developments made a profound impression in England. The English Republicans were still swayed by the ideas that had inspired their revolution, namely Republicanism and Protestantism. True, more materialistic considerations were coming to the fore and were beginning to affect the formulation of foreign policies, but for the time being the idealists retained the upper hand. For them the Revolution in the Netherlands – they called it by no less a name – had a very special significance. As early as September 1650, two months before William II's death, the correspondent of the *Briefe Relation* had reported that whereas it looked very much as if no human power would save the States Party, 'there seems to be a providence moving to the extirpation of Tyrannie, under the power of which hee [the Prince of Orange] is likelie to fall in due time'.[25]

And how miraculously that prophecy had now been fulfilled! God's own hand had liberated the United Netherlands, a Protestant Republic, from the yoke of the tyrant, the Orange prince, a relative and ally of the Stuarts. No other country the whole world over was more beloved to the English, who now felt that friendship with the Netherlands should become the corner-stone of their entire Continental policy. In March 1651, England dispatched a solemn embassy to the Hague with instructions to effect a close association between the two Republics.

It was at about this time, when the king's collapse in Scotland and Ireland was unmistakably drawing near, that the need for a more specific foreign policy first presented itself to England's new rulers. So far they had only been looking for allies in their struggle with the Stuarts, but now, almost for the first time since the reign of Elizabeth, the English were once again rulers of the sea, and as such in a position to take a leading part in European politics. France and Spain were still at war, the former, moreover, weakened by the *Fronde*, and the latter by a general decline. Spain was clearly trying to woo the new English régime, and France, too, despite her championship of the Stuarts, was gradually coming round. But friendship with one could only be gained by declaring war on the other. The Dutch Republic, on the other hand, was flourishing and prosperous, and though her trade monopoly might arouse envy, there were many in England who felt that the two Protestant sea powers could form an invincible combination.

But to what end? Peace was not really what the English Republicans wanted. When they looked at Europe, it was only to wonder which country to attack, once the army could be withdrawn from vanquished Ireland and Scotland – for England must attack either in the cause of her ideals or for the sake of her power or trade. The English outlook was typical of revolutionaries – a mixture of idealism and violence. The Dutch States party on the other hand had left its revolutionary period far behind. Both Republicanism and Protestantism had long ago outstripped the heroic stage. Hollanders 'prefer gain to godliness', as Cromwell put it[26] and Cromwell knew what he was talking about, for he was an adept at combining the two. Moreover, when it came to furthering their trade interests, the Dutch preferred different methods from those of their English rivals. While the English, aware that they had still a long way to go, called for protection, for action, the Dutch, with their enormous lead, wanted nothing more than peace and the general adoption of a maritime law under which peaceful trade might be carried on freely even in the midst of war. Hence a good deal of compromise between the Netherlands (or rather Holland) and the English was needed before the two views could be reconciled. Moreover, as the English negotiators were to discover before long, the point of view expressed by Holland was by no means the dominant one in the Republic, for the Orange party still had a very large say.

That such fundamental facts came to them as so many unpleasant surprises, merely proves the lack of experience of these revolutionary diplomats. No less characteristic was their crude method of presenting a host of sweeping proposals. They arrived at the conference in large numbers – the solemn entry of no less than 246 people[27] on 7 March 1651 was meant to reflect the greatness of the new England, the more so as they were led by Oliver St John, the Chief Justice, a man, incidentally, who had never before been involved in international politics.[28] One might have expected Strickland, who returned to the Hague with the embassy, to have had a clearer appreciation of the impending difficulties. No doubt, he imagined that the changes that had taken place during his absence were far more radical than they turned out to be.

The English instructions to the envoys have not been preserved, so that we cannot tell what precise plans were put forward for the alliance of the two countries. However, judging by earlier pronouncements[29] and from Cromwell's unmistakable attitude in 1653, we can safely assume that when the English envoys opened the negotiations by declaring that they had come to forge the closest possible bond between the two nations, they were thinking of nothing less than union within a single state. Protestantism and Republicanism – the sons of the English revolution could think of no firmer bases for national unity. But whatever they may have thought, it is hardly necessary to state that no group of any importance in the Netherlands would have subscribed to a plan of this nature.

There was not only the aversion which the Orangist masses felt towards the English nation. The regent class, too, would never have considered sacrificing their newly-won liberty for a union in which England was bound to prove the stronger partner. True, in 1585, during the early stages of the revolt against Spain, when things had looked black indeed, it was decided to offer sovereign power to the Queen of England, but after the unhappy experience of Leicester's governorship the dominant desire was to free the country from all English control. True also that in 1650, in the prevailing bitterness against the Prince of Orange, as English reporter was able to write that voices were clamouring for closer union with England.[30] But voices raised in opposition far too often fall silent in office. And the English envoys must have appreciated this when, instead of coming forward with a clear-cut proposal for union, they left the Dutch commissioners to make the first move. Far from achieving this objective, they merely succeeded in rousing Dutch suspicions, with the result that a month was spent on idle manœuvres. In the end, the envoys dropped all ideas of union, and instead broached the possibility of an offensive and defensive alliance. However, the long preliminaries had put a severe strain on English goodwill, and a series of untoward incidents hardened their attitude even further.

From the day of their arrival, the envoys were continuously shocked by the attitude of the people of the Hague. The town swarmed with English Royalists, who now greeted the brilliant cortège to the Great Assembly with hoots and threats; nor was there any doubt that popular sentiment was on the side of the trouble-makers, in whom they saw staunch friends and defenders of the young Princess of Orange. One of the princess's pages reportedly distributed money and incited the populace to heap abuse on the envoys.[31] So hostile, in fact, was public opinion, that the Englishmen, not all of whom could be accommodated in the house made available by the States, were afraid to split up into groups of less than five or six, both in taking up lodgings and also in venturing into the streets. The States of Holland had to issue special edicts against disturbances of the peace, and some of the trouble-makers were brought before the Court of Justice, but the effects were barely noticeable. Servants of the embassy were molested,[32] and had the windows of their lodging-house smashed. Towards the end of April, the English complained to the States-General that they were living as in a beleaguered fortress and could not show themselves outdoors. A special guard was detailed to protect them, but even that did not put a stop to their humiliations.

In fact, the rioters enjoyed the protection of the Princess Royal and the States were afraid to reprimand her or even to take strong measures against her more vociferous relatives, Prince Edward of the Palatinate[33] and the Duke of York among them. Prince Edward, it is true, went too far – and this despite the fact that his mother was living on the bounty of the States – and proceedings were eventually taken against him, but only after the envoys had lodged repeated protests. In the end, he was simply allowed to depart from the Hague. At first, the leading Royalists had deemed it best and most dignified to give the 'regicides' a wide berth. Thus the Duke of York left the Hague the day the envoys made their entry, and Sir Edward Nicholas even deplored the fact that lack of money had prevented the duke from going a few days earlier.[34] But the Princess Royal stayed on and this was taken as a rallying call to the Royalists. In May, the Duke of York returned, and Sir Edward Nicholas expressed the hope that he would remain. The envoys now complained that the duke and his sister made it a point to drive daily past their lodgings in great ostentation and that the Orange servants committed all sorts of mischief against them. Obviously the leading spirits among the Orange-Stuart party had realized that they could do as they pleased, and, moreover, that they could provoke the envoys to the point of endangering the success of their mission. In the States of Holland it was suggested that the princess and her brother might be invited to move from the Hague for the duration of the parleys, but when the nobility and several towns opposed the motion, it was simply resolved to ask them to keep their 'domestics' in order. Clearly the States of Holland did not yet feel sufficiently strong to offend the House of Orange. The upshot of it all was that St John and Strickland were profoundly hurt, and that they drew a political lesson from the discourtesy of their treatment, with all the dire consequences this implied.

The lesson was only reinforced when the negotiations with the commissioners of the Great Assembly showed clearly that the Holland party was by no means master in its own house. The mere fact that the commission included a man like Renswoude, must have convinced Strickland that the Orange party was far from silenced, the more so as the negotiations were drawn out unnecessarily by the underhand opposition of some of the small provinces, and quite particularly by Friesland,[35] Gelderland and Overijsel.

One of the chief arguments of the Orange party was that, before any final decision was made, it would be best to await the outcome of the war in Scotland.[36] After the defeat of Dunbar, Charles II was holding out in the north of Scotland, and there was reason to hope he might yet carry the day, particularly as dissatisfaction with the republican régime seemed to be growing even in England. But when the King's army was annihilated at Worcester (2 September 1651), even the most hopeful voices were silenced. The reasons for keeping on the right side of the Stuarts existed no longer.

Meanwhile a month had been wasted, and when the envoys at last realized that their scheme of full union was doomed to failure, they came forward with more specific proposals for a loose alliance. Another month went by before the Great Assembly could agree on a basis for discussion, and yet another for the seven provinces to draw up a set of detailed counter-proposals, consisting of thirty-six articles. It was now 24 June 1651.

The inland provinces were much less interested in an association with England than were Holland and Zeeland, and hence the Orange party found them much more fertile soil for their anti-English machinations. In Zeeland, on the other hand, their activities caused as much irritation as they did in Holland. On 26 June, the Secretary of Zierikzee, Justus de Huybert, told Johan de Witt that he felt Holland and Zeeland, 'the two mother provinces and, to all intents and purposes, the only ones to take an interest in this business', ought to bring the other provinces into line with the threat of signing a separate agreement: 'We know well enough that it is only by an appeal to their private passions and interests that the other provinces can be moved.'[37] While it never came to that, it was undoubtedly true that Holland and Zeeland were the only provinces concerned with bringing the negotiations to a successful conclusion. This must have become obvious to England as early as April, when the envoys were instructed to return home. The English government was quite naturally indignant at the treatment meted out to the envoys, and preferred to continue the discussions in London, where, if nothing else (so ran the comment) at least the safety of the negotiators could be ensured. And now instructions went out, not to Joachimi, the ambassador of the States-General, but to Schaep, the agent of the States of Holland, then still in England, to do his utmost to mollify the English government and to obtain some respite. He succeeded in doing so, and when his report arrived in the Hague, the deputies of Holland and Zeeland went in a body to pay their compliments to the departing English envoys.

It goes without saying that Holland had her hands tied in drafting her offer to England or the thirty-six articles of 24 June would certainly have had quite a different look. The actual policy of Holland must be read between the lines of the official documents, which are explicit neither on that subject nor on the particular attitudes of the various factions. At the time, no leading statesman stood out from the general anonymity of the colleges and committees, and there was a dearth of political correspondence, or rather, if there was not, few letters have been preserved. The *Archives de la maison d'Orange* contain little more than the impotent grumblings of the opposition. Soon afterwards, the extensive correspondence of De Witt was to provide historians with an intimate account of the secret intentions of the real makers of policy, but not so in 1651. Yet the main trends can be inferred with certainty, and there seems very little doubt that Holland would have wished to meet England more liberally than she did in the thirty-six articles.

True, there were differences between England and Holland as well. Thus Holland tried to use the negotiations as a lever to consolidate her commercial supremacy. It was to that purpose that she proposed unrestricted residence rights in both countries, freedom of fishing, and freedom of trading in each other's colonies – all demands which, as things stood, would benefit Holland, economically more developed as she was, far more than they would England. But although these proposals aroused strong opposition in England, it is by no means certain that the opposition would have carried the day. Modern historians have an exaggerated tendency to explain all historical events in economic terms alone, and thus to oversimplify matters. It has been pointed out already that in the policy of the English Commonwealth, economic motives were opposed by ideological considerations. There is no doubt that the English were quite sincere in proposing union to the Dutch, even though many English merchants had strong misgivings about the implicit economic concessions. Even when the union idea had to be dropped in favour of a loose alliance, the English were still more than willing to make economic concessions in order to achieve their political purpose. Holland, for her part, was prepared to make political concessions to further her economic ends, although, as we saw, she was not ready to go the whole hog. Thus she succeeded in overcoming the scruples of the other provinces when she had mutual assistance in the event of war written into the thirty-six articles. How reluctant the States-General were to accept this clause may be inferred from their explicit stipulation that it did not apply to the war still raging in Scotland.

It was only natural that each side should have tried to make the smallest number of concessions against the greatest number of advantages. Thus the economic demands embodied in the thirty-six articles were by no means meant to be final;[38] they were deliberately pitched too high and were intended to serve as bargaining counters. But the time for economic bargaining had not yet come; attention had been almost totally focused on the political issues, and the chief reasons why these had become bogged down was English resentment of the States' incapacity to protect them against the violence of the Orange party. As a result, undue attention was paid to the relationship between the States and the Stuarts or their relatives, the Orange family. The proposals submitted by the envoys on 20 May dwelt on that subject at very great length. They did not leave it at the suggestion that rebels or fugitives from either Republic would have to be expelled on request, but drew up a special clause by which the Princess Royal and her infant son were expressly forbidden to give shelter to enemies of the English Republic or to lend them help or assistance of whatsoever kind, on penalty of having their property confiscated. Seeing that the States of Holland had not even dared to beg the Princess Royal to leave the Hague for a short while, they could not have been very happy about so radical a proposal. As for the other provinces, it was only with the utmost difficulty that they could be persuaded to accept even the relatively inoffensive clause that neither country should permit its inhabitants to assist 'the other's rebels'.

Indeed, what with having to wrest economic concessions from the English and political concessions from the other provinces, the States of Holland were waging an uphill struggle that taxed their strength to the utmost. To make things worse, obstruction by Royalists and pro-Orange street mobs in the Hague and Orange deputies in the States of all the provinces, thoroughly spoiled the atmosphere in which the negotiations took place. It was probably sheer ill temper which caused the envoys to include their impossible strictures on the Princess Royal and the Prince of Orange, and to offer far stronger opposition to the economic demands of Holland and Zeeland than heretofore. The troubles of 1651 were clearly rooted in the marriage of 1641 by which the House of Orange, the Orangist party and popular feeling had become disastrously entangled with the Stuart family, whose ideas were completely alien to the Dutch spirit and whose misfortunes the Dutch ought never to have been expected to share. It was this very involvement which also lay at the heart of the ensuing war, from which the Netherlands had nothing to gain, but a great deal to lose.

Immediately after submitting their thirty-six articles, the envoys broke off their three months' stay and departed for England. In the Netherlands there were high hopes that the negotiations might continue abroad, perhaps even more smoothly than they had at home.[39] But the mood in which St John and Strickland returned was one of profound disappointment at the poor results they had achieved and of bitter resentment at the reception they had been accorded. Their report boiled down to the fact that the importance of the political change in the Netherlands had been exaggerated; that their Protestant neighbour could no more be trusted now than during the lifetime of William II; that the Orange party was still as pro-Stuart as ever before and its obstruction in the States-General still a factor of great importance; and that Holland's chief concern was to consolidate her economic supremacy.[40] Now that St John and Strickland had had their chance, it was inevitable that English commercial interests should raise their voices in loud protest – if the Netherlands could not be trusted politically, there was no reason at all to acquiesce in their trading monopoly.

The new policy was pursued with the fervour so characteristic of all new régimes. Moreover, when Cromwell soon afterwards rid the country of internal enemies, there was even less reason for fearing the Dutch. Charles II, defeated at Worcester in September, once again took refuge on the continent; Scotland and Ireland lay at Cromwell's feet. By October, Parliament felt free to pass the contentious Navigation Act, which provided that all imports should be brought into England in English vessels or in vessels of the country producing the goods. The Act was clearly directed against the Dutch traders; it denied them the freedom of the seas on which they had insisted throughout the negotiations at the Hague. Soon afterwards, the English government gave an even stronger proof of its hostility to the United Netherlands, when it issued letters of reprisal to the heirs of an English merchant, who was said to have suffered damage by the Dutch. These letters not only caused the Netherlands an unexpected financial loss, but involved recourse to a maritime law that had always been resented by the Dutch and had been the subject of long and tedious negotiations with the kings of England. To top it all, English men-of-war began to search Dutch ships quite arbitrarily for 'contraband'.

Needless to say, all these steps caused considerable uneasiness in Holland, the more so as it looked as if Sweden, aggrieved at Dutch expansion in the Baltic, was now using an agreement with Denmark as a pretext for siding with England.[41] The greatest possible speed was therefore used in dispatching an embassy to London, though it was not until the end of the year that all the problems had been ironed out and the envoys could at last depart, with orders to use the thirty-six articles as their instructions. But by then these articles were completely out of date – the time that the English might have agreed to compromise with Holland's commercial interests was long past, and the Navigation Act would not easily be undone.

Now that she realized that her economic objectives were no longer attainable, Holland would have been more than content simply to preserve the peace. But with the prevailing mood even that had become unlikely. A strong English party was out for blood, and, moreover, saw in war a means of strengthening the navy *vis-à-vis* Cromwell and the army (the main exponents of the radical views that had flowered into the idea of a union between the two Republics). The Dutch envoys now found that all attempts at conciliation fell on deaf ears. Their declaration, at the start of their mission, that the States were equipping a fleet for the protection of Dutch merchantmen, was treated as a threat by a hateful combination of trade monopolists and Orangists. This view was reflected in the demands that were now handed to the envoys and, though the States were desperately anxious to preserve the peace, they felt unable to swallow such humiliating conditions. Not only the English but the Dutch, too, were showing a mounting irritation, and the angry mood was not confined to the Orangist gentry and the common people. The merchant class, constantly exposed as it was to the arrogance of the English, was beginning to remember that England was not the only country to boast a navy. War with England ran counter to the entire political system of Holland, but there were higher considerations, and no Dutch government could stand by while the interest and honour of the country were being trampled underfoot. Even so, a last-minute compromise might still have been arrived at, had Blake's fateful meeting with Tromp not provoked the English to further steps.

There were many Hollanders who blamed Tromp's Orangist inclinations for his refusal to salute the English admiral at sea, and for the ensuing exchange of shots. In point of fact, the demand that Dutch men-of-war should strike the flag upon meeting an English ship in the North Sea implied recognition of English supremacy. Tempers were by then so frayed on both sides, and the flag issue so much a matter of dispute, that Tromp's political bias could not have been the only cause of the incident. Be that as it may, even at this late stage no less a personage than Pauw, the Grand Pensionary of Holland, was hastily sent to England in an attempt to patch the matter up, but in vain. On 31 June 1652, the States-General recalled their envoys. The two republics were at war.

The first Anglo-Dutch war; Holland's Peace Policy (1652-3)

It was easy to foresee that war with England would have violent repercussions on internal affairs in the Dutch Republic. The Orange party was jubilant. They had followed the negotiations in London with alternate hope and fear. In February 1652, in a letter to Count William Frederick, Aerssens van Sommelsdijk had expressed his confident belief that a rupture was imminent and that it was bound to lead to the restoration of the old régime in the Netherlands.[42] In March, he wrote sadly that it looked as if the whole business would end in a treaty.[43] Given the solidarity of Orange and Stuart, it was natural that the Stadholder's party as well as the Royalists should have been pleased to see their respective adversaries fall out among themselves. Indeed, as far as English Royalists were concerned, it was a matter of complete indifference which side would prove victorious in the war. As Sir Edward Hyde, Charles II's principal counsellor, who had taken refuge in Paris, put it: 'I am not wise enough to judge which would be best for us, that the Dutch should beat the English or the English the Dutch...'[44] The Orange party had not yet reached that degree of impartiality, but the fact remains that a luckless war (and the war was just that) offered them chances which they seized with both hands.

To begin with, the declaration of war caused an upsurge of pro-Orange sentiment. The enemies of Stuart-Orange were now the enemies of the state as well and war seemed to require the appointment of 'an eminent leader'. In March, Aerssens had already crowed with pleasure at the thought of the difficulties the leadership problem would cause the States.[45] And in fact, the month of July saw the birth in Zeeland of a movement calling for the revival of the Captain-Generalship, which was to cause a great deal of anxiety in Holland. In the council of Middelburg a voice was heard to say (and apparently without any contradiction) 'that there is hardly any group of people, be it of the lower or of the more respectable citizenry, but speak longingly of a military leader'.[46] In Zeeland, as elsewhere, the movement drew its strength from the common people, led by the ministers of religion.[47] Meanwhile, most of the regents of Zeeland remained unshaken in their desire to co-operate in the republican policy of Holland, even though one of their number was so outraged by the conduct of the English and so imbued with solicitude for the country's future that he had a complete change of heart.[48]

The Zeeland regent class was by no means as firmly entrenched as its counterpart in Holland. As a result, it was unable to follow a consistent political line, or to resist pressure from below.[49] Compared with the wealthy Holland regents, who could rely on the support of powerful Amsterdam and who, in 1650, had little difficulty in getting the nobles to toe their line, the Zeeland regents were a somewhat provincial body. To make things worse, Veere and Flushing acted as disrupting influences, refusing to avail themselves of the free election of magistrates when this was offered to them by the States of the province, after the Stadholder's death. They invariably lent their ears to whatever Orangist plans or plots were being hatched, and the pro-States representatives of the four other towns went in constant fear of having the tables turned on them.

In August 1652, a number of Orangist members of the Middelburg town council, relying on the support of the commonalty and of Veere and Flushing,[50] suggested that the town should instruct the States of Zeeland to propose to the States-General, through a special delegation, the appointment of young William III as Captain-General, and the nomination of William Frederick as his acting deputy. And so great was the pressure that the majority was forced to comply. Yet in the previous year, the council of Middelburg had dismissed the Orangist burgomaster Thibaut, following riotous protests against the personal corruption of the Orangist regents, though not against the Orange party as such. Johan de Witt, a rising star in the States of Holland, described that minor revolution as 'a visible miracle and a work of God's hand'.[51]

However, before the Middelburg resolution was voted on by the States of Zeeland, a deputation from Holland arrived and tried to dissuade their 'ally' from proceeding with the matter. The party included De Witt who, in his capacity of Pensionary of Dort (the senior town in the province), had often stood in for the ageing Pauw as Grand Pensionary of Holland. In his letters he expressed his utter contempt for those Zeeland regents who allowed themselves to be ordered about by the Orangist mob and who even shrank from taking steps to protect the Holland visitors when their lives were threatened.[52] In spite of Holland's admonitions, the States of Zeeland adopted the Middelburg proposal on 21 September.

What happened next was sheer comedy. Weeks were allowed to pass before 'a few minor objections' by Zierikzee and Goes (two Zeeland towns) to the form of the resolution were ironed out; meanwhile, no special delegation could, of course, take the proposal to the States-General.[53] Soon afterwards, it transpired that Tholen (another of the six towns represented in the States of Zeeland) still had objections, and when at long last – it was now the middle of November – the Zeelanders showed up in the Hague, it appeared that the resolution of 21 September contained no instructions to lay the matter before the Generality, but rather to confer on it separately with the other 'allies'. Now one of these was Holland which now succeeded in convincing the Zeelanders – if convincing they needed – that the proposed elevation of Orange and Nassau would militate severely against peace with England.[54] Only three of the twelve deputies – including those from Veere and Flushing, the two vassal towns – felt it incumbent upon them to obey the letter of their instructions and to consult with the other provinces as well. But though the attitude of Gelderland was still uncertain,[55] and though it was known that Friesland would uphold the interests of its Stadholders, the Hollanders now felt content to let things take their course. The consultations were matters of pure formality and when the delegates returned to Zeeland they had not raised the

question in the States-General. Popular feeling had by then subsided, and William Frederick was still as far as ever from the
coveted Lieutenant-Captain-Generalship.

Yet the Holland States party could not feel secure as long as
the war was on. No doubt, this fact played a large part in their
efforts to restore peace, much as the hope to see the Holland party
overthrown caused the Orange party to favour war. The war, unfortunate product of English revolutionary imperialism and pro-
Stuart intrigues at home, could, in any case, not bring any political
advantages to the Netherlands, and was proving highly detrimental
to Dutch commerce and shipping. The war at sea was straining
the finances of Holland, already depleted by the Eighty Years War,
to breaking-point, the more so as little help could be expected from
the inland provinces which bore the chief responsibility for the
outbreak of hostilities. Though Holland had scored a great diplomatic success in the north, when the King of Denmark had closed
the Sound to enemy ships, the English navy was known to be much
more up-to-date than the Dutch. Even Tromp's reputation as a
fighting admiral was no guarantee against misadventure, and
England had so great a strategic advantage that the slightest mishap
could easily turn into disaster.[56] However, once the English recovered from the unreasonable mood which had made a break inevitable, they, too, saw no good reason for continuing the struggle,
which now pleased no one except Orangists in the inland provinces. To circumvent obstruction from that quarter, Holland decided to by-pass the other provinces when she put out the first
peace feelers.

And the English reaction was favourable, now that resentment
at the treatment of St John and Strickland had subsided. The war
was unpopular, not only because it clashed with the Protestant
sentiments of the army and of the Puritans in general, but also
because it caused considerable inconvenience all round. So in
November 1652, when a new Council of State was elected, the
peace party headed by Cromwell carried the day. Cromwell did not
delay in making it known in the Hague that he favoured a settlement, and Holland responded as he expected. Early in February
1653, Pauw, the Grand Pensionary, was authorized to put his name
to a letter by which Holland's desire for peace was to be made
known in England. It was endorsed by all the States with the exception of Leyden (*more solito*, as De Witt explained).[57] But in

December, the English fleet had been driven off by Tromp, and the 'reputation' of the English allowed of no negotiations, at least before their fleet had put to sea again. When that happened, in February 1653, luck was so much with the English (who worsted Tromp in the Three Days' Battle) that victory rather than peace became once more the dominant English theme.

Pauw had meanwhile died and, in his capacity as acting Grand Pensionary, De Witt now persuaded the States of Holland to send another letter to England – while Pauw had ostensibly written on his own behalf only, the new letter came officially from the States. The danger inherent in this procedure came to light the moment the letter (dated 18 March) was published in England by way of a pamphlet entitled *Humble prayer of the States of Holland for Peace.* The English government was not apparently responsible for this embellishment, which, needless to say, played into the hands of the Dutch war party. When Parliament sent its reply on 11 April (NS), it became quite obvious that the English had no intention of making things too easy for the embarrassed Republic: the demands submitted to Pauw in June, after the unfortunate flag incident at sea, the very demands, in other words, that had been the immediate cause of the outbreak of war, were now presented as a minimum basis for negotiation. Still the English reply showed willingness at least to re-open peace discussions, and that is all De Witt needed for the moment. On 30 April 1653, he got the States-General to send a reply to Parliament, in which the subject of the English demands was neatly skirted with the suggestion that envoys be sent to a neutral country, there to discuss peace, and even an alliance. True, only four provinces voted for the proposal, while the deputies of three others refused to commit themselves without further instruction from their respective States, but the letter was sent all the same.

Meanwhile, political conditions in England had been radically changed by Cromwell's *coup d'état.* Parliament had been forcibly dissolved and Cromwell, as yet without a title, was firmly in the saddle. The changes boded well for the outcome of the peace negotiations, but in his reply, which arrived at the Hague on 23 May, Cromwell insisted on the conditions laid down by Parliament on 11 April. He also demanded that envoys should be sent, not to a neutral country, but to London. The Orange party quite naturally used the occasion to complain of English intractability.

Most of the provinces favoured the dispatch of a further letter insisting that the English demands were no more acceptable now than they had been in June 1652. But Holland, contending that 'a letter cannot reply', succeeded in persuading the assembly to send 'certain adroit persons' to London 'without any qualifications [i.e. restrictive instructions], but supplied with due credentials and authorization', there to lay the Dutch point of view before the new ruler of England. What De Witt wanted above all – and one can readily sympathize with him – was to avoid the certainty of loss of time and the possibility of misunderstandings and friction inherent in the continued exchange of letters. A trusted representative in England was bound to iron out all the outstanding problems. After a good deal of discussion, the States-General agreed to the proposal and passed a resolution to that effect on 5 June. But there was still a good deal of bickering about the selection of the envoys. Thus when it was decided to allow Friesland and Zeeland, both trading provinces, to appoint one envoy each, Holland demanded two for herself. In the end, Van Beverning and Nieuwpoort were nominated for Holland, Van der Perre for Zeeland, and Jongestal for Friesland. Van Beverning crossed on 21 June, the other three followed a week later.

Throughout these proceedings, Holland, under the firm and able leadership of her youthful Grand Pensionary, had taken a clear and constant line. In March, when the contents of Holland's letter to Parliament was made known, Friesland and Stad en Lande (i.e. Groningen)[58] protested in caustic terms in the States-General against a line of conduct that struck them as being incompatible with the spirit of the Union of Utrecht. But a month later, when it was proposed to take note of Parliament's reply, it was Friesland and Groningen which voted for the resolution, while Zeeland, Overijsel and Gelderland insisted that they were not 'authorized' to commit themselves. For a brief spell, Zeeland even acted as leader of the opposition, stipulating an alliance with France as a prerequisite of peace negotiations with England. Then, before the month was out, Zeeland, to the great indignation of Gelderland,[59] allowed herself to be brought round by private discussions with Holland, with the result that the important resolution of 5 June, bitterly but vainly contested by Friesland, Groningen and Gelderland, was finally adopted, and unity between Holland and Zeeland restored.

Policy of the Orange party; Collaboration with the Stuarts (1652–3)

The great driving force behind the Orange party was the vehement anti-English sentiment of the Dutch people, an attitude intimately bound up with their love for the House of Orange. Without giving a thought to the precarious situation of their country, Orangist pamphleteers kept inveighing against the treacherous English rebels, with whom there could be no firm peace. Ministers of religion railed at the States of Holland, who in their letter of 18 March had spoken of a community of faith: community of faith, indeed, with sectarian Independents![60] But the chief Orangist argument was the inherent untrustworthiness of regicides and wild revolutionaries.[61] It is difficult to believe that many of the regents, however pro-Orange they may have been, were really convinced of the soundness of that argument.[62] Some must simply have allowed themselves to be moved by party passion; others were afraid of the threatening mood of the people, stirred up as they were by Orange agitators.[63] In any case, the policy with which the Orange party had allowed itself to be identified was so unreasonable that no experienced regent could have felt happy about it. 'Throughout Holland,' wrote Aitzema,[64] 'the poorer and more miserable the lot of the people became, the louder and more ardent became the shouts of "Vive le Prince!" and "No peace with England!".' In fact, the chief causes of the war with England must be sought in the widespread English opinion that most Dutchmen sided with the prince and the king (Charles II). Inside the Republic itself, however, the Orange allegation that Dutch governmental neglect or even treachery was responsible for the unfortunate course of the war; the abuse Orange pamphleteers kept showering upon the English;[65] the boast that it was the English who were suing for peace lest Tromp might pounce on them again, and that it was foolish to meet them half-way[66] – all that and similar idle talk could not soften the blow struck by the revelation that the Dutch navy had failed and that the Dutch exchequer was exhausted.

After William Frederick had 'generously' (Aitzema's term[67]) permitted his provinces (Friesland and Groningen) to vote for the dispatch of the letter to England (30 April) – and no one had any doubts that it was only on his express instructions that they did so – he offered the following explanation: 'I understand that peace is both desirable and necessary for the state; and I must put the service of the state before all private considerations, before the King of England, before everything.' Even he, therefore, could not always delude himself into believing that the country's interest demanded war. And yet, six weeks earlier, in a confidential letter to the French ambassador,[68] he had written that the resumption of negotiations with the English Republic seemed to run counter to all the principles of his state. Small wonder that the vote cast by his provinces on 30 April completely startled public opinion, and that Hollanders should have been particularly suspicious of his motives. As far as they were concerned, all the count wanted was to have a voice in the negotiations now that these had become inevitable. They accordingly treated Jongestal, the Frisian nominee to the embassy, with ill-concealed distrust, in the certain belief that he was out to undermine the success of their endeavours.[69]

Indeed, one cannot but seek less 'generous' motives behind William Frederick's attitude than Aitzema did – and who can say that Aitzema did not have his tongue in his cheek? A few months later, Sir Edward Nicholas wrote the following confidential note from the Hague to one of his political friends:

... I continue sometimes on occasion to correspond with Count William, albeit I have no great confidence in him, having heard and observed him to be so avaricious and ambitious as that he will for his own ends and advantage do that which I cannot understand to become a person of his quality to do. His former permitting the two provinces whereof he is Governor to comply with the States of Holland in sending first of all commissioners into England was certainly a great assurance of his great inclination to hold fair with that party here (which without all question will never confide in him) ...[70]

A tireless intriguer, at one moment the fiercest zealot of his party, at the next wooing the favours of his adversaries, in the end trusted by no one – this indeed is the unattractive picture that the entire career of William Frederick conjures up. That a man like him should have held an office that singled him out for leadership of the Orange party was, in itself, sufficient reason why the six provinces were never able to combine against the influence of Holland.

Special circumstances, moreover, weakened their position still further. How could they, who suffered far less directly from the disasters of the war, blame Holland for seeking peace, and yet fail to pay their share towards the cost of the campaign?[71] Thus Gelderland, the most vigorous opponent of the mission to England, was effectively silenced in the States-General when Holland (perhaps represented by De Witt himself?) reminded them of the arrears, and even threatened them with 'due punishment' in accordance with the terms of the Union of Utrecht – an insult the province was long to remember.[72]

In all fairness, it must be admitted, however, that Orange opposition to negotiations with England was not wholly negative. They did put forward an alternative. Unfortunately this was so far-fetched that all it could do was to exacerbate party strife, and that it did in full measure. The Orange alternative was to embrace the cause of the exiled Stuart King, and to use his name and personal intervention for creating a division in the enemy ranks, and quite particularly in the English navy. Moreover, the alliance with France, broken in 1648, was to be renewed. In other words, they were asking for a large-scale war with republican England, and probably with Spain as well, but in concert with France and Stuart – thus reviving the old policy of Frederick Henry and William II. This plan was as futile as it was foolhardy.

When war was declared, English Royalists had rejoiced at what they thought was their great opportunity. Hyde's expressed indifference about the outcome of the war (see p. 91) showed that he, for one, was shrewd enough to realize that the Dutch meant to wage the war in their own best interests. Now these were clearly not served by making common cause with the House of Stuart, which would have meant turning the war into a struggle to the end, rather than trying to bring it to a speedy close. Even a pro-Stuart victory would not have served Holland's cause – in its wake would have come a wave of royalist reaction against the States party. Such a victory was not even a remote possibility, what with Charles exiled to France, a country shaken by internal dissent, and unable to offer anything more than his name. No, an alliance with the Stuarts would merely have served to embitter England's rulers.

In 1649, Charles's fleet had been driven from English waters and soon afterwards it was to be sent scurrying from Europe. In 1653, when Rupert returned from his long privateering expedition to America, all he could boast of were a few ramshackle ships which he sold to France. Yet Charles felt free to declare[73] that his name alone would help the Dutch to conquer harbours in Ireland and Scotland, Guernsey, the Scilly Isles and the Orkneys, and, moreover, cause the defection of many English ships. The navy's loyalty to the revolution was never unwavering, and even at a later stage of the war, a Zeelander reported that many 'sensible people' in England believed that if only the king had been with the Dutch fleet during 'the latest battle' (13 June) quite a few English men-of-war would have changed sides.[74] The regents of Holland, however, refused to pay heed to all such speculations.[75] And it must be admitted that great faith would have been needed to base the war on the expectation of English disloyalty. Tromp himself, who never made a secret of his preference for Orange and Stuart, told a Royalist in March 1653 that the failure of the English to come to their king's aid during his (Tromp's) invasion two years earlier, made it seem doubtful that they would take more positive action now.[76]

In any event, the States of Holland could not be persuaded to espouse the king's cause. For a time, the Royalists kept deluding themselves with the hope that they might be able to attain their purpose with the help of influential friends in the other provinces. Through Sir Edward Nicholas, the king had kept in touch with several members of the Dutch government though, needless to say, not with members of the Holland States party – Sir Edward's relations with them remained purely formal. Even Heenvliet, whom Charles, and especially his mother and Jermyn, had so trusted in the past, was given a wide berth. Sir Edward, as has been noted,[77] could not forgive Heenvliet's wish to remain on good terms with the enemies of Orange and Stuart and, in the circumstances, felt no reliance could be placed in him. A year earlier, he had written that: '. . . Heenflete, who has neither brains nor credit to do anything among the leading men here, who hold him a covetous wretch, if not worse'.[78] The regents to whom Sir Edward went for information and advice were Renswoude, from Utrecht, a staunch Royalist, and Van der Capellen, from Gelderland. Aerssens, too, the leading Orangist in Holland, and who was now kept out of all public affairs, remained in touch with the Stuarts. On the other hand, Sir Edward had to be most circumspect in his contacts with William Frederick whom the Princess Royal regarded with great suspicion if not with hatred. Thus, in September 1652, Hyde[79] reported that, in the view of 'most men' Count William of Nassau was 'the most considerable in all the provinces, and the king believes him to be a person of very good affection towards him, yet (though advised to it by many friends from those parts) forbears to write to him least his sister might take it ill'.[80]

These dissensions within the Orangist party caused Charles and his ministers great anguish. Every so often, Hyde would beg Nicholas to tell him the exact circumstances of these quarrels, and although he could read the answers in their entirety,[81] he does not seem ever to have understood the situation in all its complexity.[82] What worried English Royalists above all was that the discord among their friends did immense harm to the Stuart cause in the Dutch Republic. They left no stone unturned in their attempts to stop the bickering.[83] More than once the king urged his sister to be 'at least polite' to William Frederick,[84] whose friendship had become the more important as he had married Amalia of Solms' daughter in May 1652, and thus became the brother-in-law of the Elector of Brandenburg (who, the reader will remember, had married another daughter of the old princess). Charles II had learnt by his misfortunes and had at last become wise enough to make amends to Amalia's relatives for what his sister's pride had inflicted upon them. It was mainly of the old princess and of William Frederick that he was thinking when he flattered the Elector of Brandenburg by addressing him familiarly as 'brother' – which, by the way, was greatly taken amiss by the other German princes who had to content themselves with a mere 'cousin'.[85] For Charles was now seeking support in whatever quarters he could get it, and readily took Van der Capellen's advice to enlist the help of France and the German principalities in commending the Stuart cause to the States-General.[86]

France, was by far the more important of the two, and for a time it looked as if more than mere recommendations might come from that side. The Dutchman with whom English Royalists were most wont to discuss the French prospects was none other than the Netherlands Ambassador in Paris, Willem Boreel, who had been sent to Oxford in 1644 with Renswoude. In 1649 it was thanks to William II that he was appointed ambassador to France. Even under the new régime at home, he remained loyal to his old protectors,[87] and this despite the ingratitude of the Princess Royal who, ignoring her brother's pressing requests, refused in 1653 to promote Willem Boreel's son to the office of intendant at her court. This action had incensed Boreel to the point of declaring that he intended to relinquish the king's service,[88] but he relented almost at once. The princess changed her mind as well – before long young Boreel obtained the office he had sought.[89] By 1652, at any rate, the ambassador was once again full of zeal for the Stuart cause, though at first he could do little more than transmit Charles's offers to the States. He kept up a regular correspondence with Hyde, who trusted his opinions on Dutch affairs and who assured Sir Edward Nicholas that Charles II invariably heeded Boreel's advice.[90] Sometimes though, Boreel struck him as being a little 'fearfull',[91] – and indeed even Renswoude had begun to exercise greater caution at the Hague. It goes without saying that the ruling party in Holland did not look with favour upon their ambassador's intimate contacts with a royalist minister.[92]

But all the discussions with Charles were bound to be fruitless in the absence of an agreement with France. According to Aerssens, 'Holland's policy is so much dependent on France that there is no hope for us except through a French alliance'.[93] And that was something Boreel could do nothing about just then. Ambiguous though Cromwell's attitude might have been – he even flirted with the French rebels – the French government was so weak that it had willy-nilly to persist in attempts to woo him.[94] Meanwhile the English felt nothing but distrust for a country that, unlike Spain, had not yet recognized their Republic and was extending hospitality to the son of their late king. In September the English fleet under Blake even made a surprise attack on a French squadron before Dunkirk, which was thereupon reoccupied by Spanish forces. The English were clearly intent on an alliance with Spain, and Mazarin had little choice but to turn to England's enemies, thus encouraging the Orange party to persist in their dream in a possible alliance between the Netherlands, France and the Stuarts. Boreel was busily engaged in conferences with the Cardinal and wrote enraptured reports to the Hague. Both Mazarin and the ambassador kept Charles II fully informed,[95] and the Orange party at home was in ecstasies of hope. Yet many Dutchmen were deterred by the realization that a French alliance was not only likely to exacerbate the conflict with the English Republic, but was also likely to lead to a new breach with Spain,[96] a break in which enfeebled France was unlikely to render assistance of any great value. Holland, for one, remained opposed to the entire scheme, unlike the other provinces: according to Nicholas, all six of these were anxious to co-operate with France.[97]

But by then (December 1652), it had become clear that Mazarin was not taking the negotiations too seriously. As early as October, he expressed the fear that more definite French offers would merely be used by Holland as levers against the English; and in December the French themselves sent an envoy to London, thus showing that they, too, were merely intent upon using the Dutch negotiations as bargaining counters against England. France, as has been repeatedly stressed, was so exhausted by her long war with Spain and by her own *Fronde* troubles, that she was quite unable to revenge the attack on Dunkirk, and had but the one desire to split England from Spain and to gain her as an ally. Mazarin's mission to London was tantamount to recognition of the Commonwealth. Although Mazarin was full of fine phrases for them, the Stuarts in Paris felt their last friend had deserted them and trembled at the prospect of prolonged exile in yet another country. According to Hyde[98] Boreel, too, was 'hugely troubled' when he learned the news, 'being so contrary to what they always assured him'. It was, indeed, the final collapse of the policy he had been recommending to his principals.

No doubt, France and the English Republicans were still far from united, and Cromwell was still forging plans to fall upon France in alliance with Spain, and thus to come to the aid of the Protestants in the south (who held out until July 1653). But it was plain to everybody that France would avoid war at all costs, and that, in these circumstances, the hard-pressed Netherlands had few expectations from that quarter. The call for a French alliance had become a mere party slogan, and a senseless one at that. Zeeland, in particular, raised it every time she wanted to block Holland's policy, and only gave her consent to the resolution of 5 June 1653 when Holland agreed to simultaneous negotiations with France. But when these negotiations eventually took place, they were no more than a sham. An alliance against England was no longer on the cards, since all the French government now aimed for was inclusion in the peace treaty between England and the United Provinces.[99] The English Royalists were no longer under any illusions. 'If France by its domestic divisions and ill managery make its friendship inconsiderable what can they (the Dutch) do?' Hyde commented in February 1653.[100] And at the beginning of July, he wrote:[101] 'The Cardinal advises urgently that the king shall go to Holland, that being the best method to promote the

alliance', – 'and much stuff to that purpose', he added indignantly, fully realizing that the intention was simply to get rid of
the king.

The Cardinal might talk as he pleased, but Holland gave Charles
clearly to understand that he would not be welcome. France's
defection from the Stuart cause had put an end to any chance that
the Dutch Republic might compromise herself by treating with the
exile. Many of Charles's friends continued to place hope in his
possible journey to the Netherlands, but even they realized that he
could not set out against the express wishes of the States of Holland.
And Holland's opposition to his reception was soon to be made
clear beyond the least doubt. Charles was longing to get away
from France and to prove his mettle in some field of action. After
the Three Days' Battle of February 1653, which ended so badly
for Tromp, he wrote a letter to Boreel in which, after expressing
his regrets, he offered to sail in person with whatever fleet the States
might care to place under his command.[102] All Charles's advisers,
Boreel included, were opposed to this proposal,[103] and indeed,
nothing could have been further from the mind of Holland's leading statesmen who were about to take the decisive step of addressing an official letter to Parliament.[104] The king himself realized
how low his star had sunk in the Dutch Republic when Beverweert, his sister's great confidant, felt compelled to exonerate himself by disclosing the contents of a letter Charles had sent him, to
the States of Holland, the better 'to show his great ingenuity and
dependence on them'.[105] Charles therefore thought it best to assure
his friends in the Netherlands that he was not planning an unexpected arrival. The way to peace negotiations with the Commonwealth seemed clear at long last.

Defeat off the Flemish coast (12–13 June 1653); Orangist riots

However, just when this policy was about to be implemented and
the envoys were making ready to leave, violent riots threatened to
upset all Holland's plans. On 12 and 13 June, Tromp suffered a
new and serious defeat off the Flemish coast and was compelled
to retire to the Wielingen. His fleet had proved too weak and too
badly equipped to stand up to the English. Tromp declared that
before it could put to sea again with any chance of success it would

have to be 'notably strengthened'. His vice-admiral, Witte de With, told the States of Holland quite openly that the English would remain complete masters of the sea until they could be met with stronger naval forces. The States now bent all their energies on building and equipping new men-of-war with the result that, when the two navies met again, in August, off Terheide, the Dutch were able to put up a far better show. But Tromp himself was killed, and his loss was deeply felt.

By then, the commonalty had ceased to place any trust in the States. In a letter of 18 July, De Witt described the situation as follows:[106] 'The present position of our dear fatherland, as I see it, presents a highly distressing, nay almost desperate picture, it being as if occupied and besieged.' Merchantmen were afraid to set sail, unemployment was rising, and so was the price of food. To quote De Witt again:

Since men must always assign a cause to all their misfortunes, they generally blame them on the evil intent of their regents; . . . and as always, there are now many who fish in troubled water, filling the minds of the commonalty with the notion that things will go from bad to worse unless they appoint a head over them. And this notion has gained so much ground that hardly one commoner in a thousand but does not hold that opinion.

Panic was so rife among the population that they fell easy prey to every demagogue. The crudest Orange calumnies against the States found ready credence among them. The story went round that the States had sold out to the Parliament of England and were supplying the enemy with men-of-war.[107] The States of Holland were forced to issue a public denial of the slander that the lord of Obdam, their representative to the fleet, had orders to persuade Tromp 'to deal leniently with the English'.[108] These and similar accusations of treason, which were laid against the States during most crises, were now seized upon by the Orange party. Their efforts to have a Captain-General appointed had come to nothing a year previously because of resistance from the States of Holland – now they were confident they would break that resistance with the wrath of the people.

A 'frenzy' (the word was used by a friend of De Witt's from Overijsel)[109] of pro-Orange feeling had gripped the people, both of Holland and of the other provinces as well. 'It will seem unbelievable some day,' a pro-States pamphleteer exclaimed, 'that a warlike people should, in its distress, have sought salvation from a little boy still in his swaddling clothes.'[110] Reason was, indeed, no part of the people's temper that summer, when symbols, catch-words and demonstrations were the order of the day. Civic guards paraded the streets adorned with Orange ribbons; drummers charged with the recruiting of men in the name of the States-General were urged to mention the name of the Prince of Orange as well. All this was bound to lead to outbursts of rowdyism and rioting. The local authories,[111] always impotent in the face of public violence, simply closed their eyes to much that was happening, though the Commissioned Councillors did insist that the prince's name be dropped from the recruiting campaign. The Amsterdam municipality alone felt strong enough to prevent all excesses.[112] In the Hague, under the very eyes of the States, civic guardsmen riddled their 'States standards', from which the prince's arms had been removed, with bullets. The Fiscal Boey, who had incurred the wrath of the mob by his severe handling of a children's demonstration in honour of the little prince's home-coming from Breda, had his windows smashed. Jacob de Witt (Johan's father) was molested in the streets of the Hague.

At Enkhuizen, where English command of the sea had led to severe unemployment among the fishermen,[113] the riots assumed a far more serious aspect. Here, too, recruitment in the name of the States was the direct cause of the troubles. A burgomaster's house was ransacked, and when the States of Holland, at the request of the local magistracy, sent troops to restore order, the citizens closed the gates, pointed cannons at them, and dissolved the town government. On the tower they raised the Orange flag. The States of Holland were now faced with the threat that Enkhuizen, situated as it was on the Zuider Zee, might help the Stadholder of Friesland, whose ambitions had been made quite plain in 1650, to invade their territory. While it is not clear what grounds there were for the rumour that he had reached an understanding with the Enkhuizen rebels, there is no doubt that the States of Holland heeded it sufficiently to divert from Enkhuizen to Texel those Frisian troops whose dispatch had been requested by the Commissioned Councillors of the Northern Quarter of the province (in preparation against a possible English landing). Soon afterwards, William Frederick, accompanied by a large court following, paid a visit to

Texel where the civic guard received him 'as though he were the Stadholder of Holland'.[114] But he did not take further advantage of the situation, and the Enkhuizen rebellion dragged on until September, when delegates of the States of Holland managed to smuggle a garrison into the town and to restore the old government.

One cannot help but admire the energy with which the States of Holland tackled the storms of that perilous summer of 1653. On 23 July, at a time when De Witt, as we saw, described the situation as 'almost desperate', the States found the courage to confirm him in the office of Grand Pensionary. His acceptance, too, was an act of courage. But this young man (he was then twenty-eight) never wavered in what he considered his line of duty, and in particular, refused steadfastly to bow before the mob. He accordingly resolved to suppress all disturbances with an iron hand and at the same time to do his utmost to preserve the accord of the States of Holland. This last was the more necessary as many members had become intimidated, and this at a time when Zeeland felt the time was ripe for renewing their proposal of the previous September before the States-General: that William III be appointed Captain-General of the Union with William Frederick as his Lieutenant.

Popular agitation in Zeeland had been greater even than in Holland. In June, while the battle off the Flemish coast was still fresh in everyone's mind, the popular party in the town of Goes had, by underhand methods, been able to replace a number of pro-States councillors with supporters of the prince during the annual election of magistrates.[115] While Goes, whose representatives were rather uninfluential men, was unable to exert any great pressure in the States,[116] their voice strengthened the pro-Orange faction of Veere and Flushing, and the rest of Zeeland, including particularly Middelburg,[117] mindful of the fate of the deposed regents of Goes, bowed before the storm. Thus when the question of the Captain-Generalcy was laid before the States-General on 28 July, it was Veth, the Grand-Pensionary of Zeeland and himself a staunch States supporter, who took it there.

Yet the States of Holland never flinched. De Witt[118] observed with heartfelt satisfaction that even Leyden, traditionally an Orange stronghold, voted with the rest. Holland once again stood as a firm bulwark in the States-General, and infused States supporters in Gelderland, Utrecht and Overijsel with renewed courage.

How can we explain the unanimity of the nineteen 'members' of Holland? To begin with, the States party had the advantage of a divided opposition. There was one group in the royalist camp whose advice the king systematically ignored, else the riots might well have shaken the States of Holland far more than they actually did. These were the Presbyterian exiles in Holland. Their obvious leader was MacDowell, the Scottish resident, but the driving spirits behind them were General Massey, who lived in Rotterdam, and 'Alderman' Bunce.[119] These men had never shared Nicholas's belief in intrigues with well-disposed regents, and wanted the king to send an ambassador, preferably one sympathetic to Presbyterianism, with instructions to stir up the masses. Massey himself put it like this:[120]

As for what I wrote of my thoughts of a necessity of His Majesty's sending of an ambassador hither, I must beg leave to continue of the same opinion till I find reason to convince me, or a better success to follow private actings with this State, for the Louvestein Lords' States, enemies of the House of Orange, are resolved of their way that no arguments can move them, and only the rage of the people may enforce them to a compliance with the rest of the States, His Majesty's and the House of Orange's friends. And this I conceive, a public person or ambassador's demands or offers he may make in public, when private persons have neither the power nor authority either to debate His Majesty's business with them nor can justify the setting or giving out anything as offers or proposals that the whole generality of the land may come to know and consider it as they would what were acted and offered by an ambassador; this is only, my Lord, my conception, and I hope I shall not incur a displeasure for writing thus freely to your Excellency my thoughts.

The advisers who had the king's ear – and Sir Edward Hyde in particular – had always been opposed to this type of appeal to the people, and Charles himself had no wish to heed the Presbyterian counsel that he make common cause with Dutch Calvinists – for such was their plan. He had left Scotland with a profound grudge against the Presbyterians, who had caused him so much anguish, and the Covenant, which he had signed in order to gain Scotland, was as nothing to him now that Scotland was lost. This attitude did not endear him to Dutch Calvinists. According to Massey,[121] the popular objection to siding with His Majesty was that, since the king had broken the promises he made by the treaty of Breda and in Scotland, no one could place any real trust in him. It was even rumoured that the king had gone over to Catholicism, and while that might be no more than loose talk, it was a well-known fact that the Princess Royal had shed bitter tears[122] when she could not prevent her youngest brother, Henry, Duke of Gloucester, but recently freed from imprisonment in England, from visiting their mother – she felt sure that he would be coerced into accepting a cardinalship. Moreover, Charles was known to have started negotiations with the Pope, and this so disturbed the exiled Presbyterians that they kept urging him to join the Huguenots at prayers in Charenton, if only for the sake of the excellent impression it would make on his many Dutch friends.[123] But this was about the last thing Charles could bring himself to do; constant references to the subject were unlikely to make the letters of Massey and the Presbyterians more palatable to him. Hyde, a faithful Anglican and the most influential counsellor at the king's court in Paris, referred to MacDowell as 'Your foolish resident'[124] and never mentioned Massey's reports but with impatience and scorn. Even Lord Culpepper, who was staying in the Hague, where he exerted himself greatly for the cause, did not have the king's full confidence. Charles never forgot that he was of the party of Henrietta Maria and Jermyn and inclined to Presbyterianism. Advice was welcome from no one but Sir Edward Nicholas.

The Orange cause suffered further by the Princess Royal's reluctance to channel popular discontent into a systematic onslaught on the States of Holland. Charles, on the other hand, was now quite willing to rely on the populace if only as a final resort. Early in July, he informed his sister that he was intent on coming to the Netherlands, regardless of how the States of Holland felt about it. When Mary, probably prompted by Heenvliet, warned the States they urged her to dissuade Charles with all the powers at her command, and so in fact she already had done of her own accord.[125] What is more, the States made it known publicly that no high-born persons would in future be allowed to enter the province without their fore-knowledge, a decision that Van Beverning immediately communicated to the English government.[126] The Princess Royal could hardly have chosen a more propitious moment to show the States of Holland that they had nothing to fear from her.

Quite apart from Heenvliet's advice, which was so clearly inspired by personal motives, her attitude must have been prompted
by the fear that William Frederick would use his office to the detriment of her son, the true heir of Orange. De Huybert might write
to De Witt[127] that the people 'wanted to live and die with Orange
and Nassau', but Orange and Nassau could quite obviously not live
with one another! 'The Princess Royal,' wrote Nicholas,[128] is 'passionately against the having of Count William to be Lieut.-
General.' And the people wanted to see William in just that office.
To make things worse, the 'old princess', too, opposed the appointment of Count William, charging the Count of Dohna to inform
De Witt[129] that she thought her son-in-law 'incapable of serving in
the offices which he seemingly covets and that, in case he might at
any time come to be appointed, she would the next day leave the
country'. The old princess went on to say that she would consider
the appointment of her grandson 'highly inopportune' – clearly,
like the Princess Royal and William Frederick before her, she was
anxious to keep in with the regents of Holland. The people, of
course, knew nothing of all these intrigues, which played so large
a part in strengthening the States' resolution in the face of so much
public commotion.

Worst of all for the Orange prospects was the fact that a restoration of Orange or Nassau was so intimately bound up with foreign
politics, and that few regents could have been blind to the dangers
to which a victory of the Orange party would expose the country.
The people, driven into the streets by the hardships of war, were
clamouring for a policy that could only perpetuate the war without
improving the chances of success. Wiser men even in the Orange
party were fully aware of that. 'These sea-warriors,' De Kuyt
wrote to Huygens in June 1653,[130] 'are hitting us harder than any
land army in the past. The sooner this war is over the better and
more bearable its outcome.' According to De Witt, the Zeeland
deputies were loath to lay their province's proposal (i.e. the prince's
appointment) before the States-General, once they realized that it
would merely serve to impede the current peace negotiations.[131]

It so happened that on the very day De Witt made that comment,[132] the two Hollanders in the delegation to England, Van
Beverning and Nieuwpoort, wrote to inform him that the most
serious obstacle to their negotiations was the growing feeling in
England,

that they can count on the mutinies and disorders they see sweeping over our state, that they feel virtually certain that, the menace of their attacks being added thereto, we shall fall into the most extreme confusion and quite particularly [this is of especial interest to our argument] that the factions and dissensions concerning the position of the Prince of Orange are so great, that those good patriots who care most truly for the well-being and liberty of their fatherland may not suffice to prevent that he shall be from now on designated for the offices of his forefathers. .... We must ... admit that all these matters are causing us the gravest concern, and feel obliged to affirm quite frankly that, knowing as we do the composition of the government and the opinions of its members here in England, there is no chance whatsoever of our being admitted not only to negotiations but even to any further audience, if any public proposals as to that point are made in our Republic.

The two envoys exaggerated their case, for as we saw, Zeeland did make just such a proposal on 28 July, and England made no move to break off the negotiations. But it seems certain that they would have done just that, had not the envoys from Holland been able to assure them that their province would stand firm against the proposal, and, moreover, to back up their claim soon afterwards when the Zeeland motion was opposed by a unanimous resolution by the States of Holland, and this despite all popular pressure. Clearly, Holland was in full control of the Republic's internal affairs, and the English accordingly paid greatest heed to the Hollanders in the Dutch delegation. Jongestal, who represented a province under the Nassau Stadholder, and Van der Perre, who represented a province that had proposed Nassau for the post of Deputy-Captain-General, quite naturally enjoyed a far smaller measure of English confidence than did Van Beverning and Nieuwpoort. This greatly strengthened the hand of the Grand Pensionary, with whom both delegates kept up a confidential correspondence. Henceforth, he never relaxed his iron hold on the Republic's foreign policy.

Cromwell's policy; The peace (8 May 1654) and the Act of Seclusion; De Witt's apology

Even so, the atmosphere was not nearly as propitious as it might have been. As in 1651, the Dutch view differed radically from that of the English Republicans. There is no need to go into details; suffice it to say that the disastrous story of the 1651 negotiations

was about to be repeated in full. While the Dutch were as determined as ever to make the thirty-six articles the basis of negotiations, the English again put forward their hybrid plan for a union
between the two countries.[133] In 1651, they had merely hinted at
it; now under Cromwell's bold and imaginative leadership, they
became quite open. The war had not, however, so broken the spirit
of the Dutch as to make them accept a proposal that threatened
their independence and one, moreover, that was likely to drag
them along the treacherous path of Cromwell's grandiose dreams
of imperial conquest. Van Beverning himself indignantly denounced the proposal in a letter to De Witt,[134] contending that
salvation now depended on resistance, with God's blessing, to
England's 'exorbitant conduct'.[135] When the proposal was brought
to Holland by two of the four envoys in the middle of August, many
Dutch voices clamoured for the immediate ending of the negotiations. Reports of the battle of Terheide (Van Beverning wrote his
letter while awaiting the outcome) was overshadowed by the news
of Tromp's death – and this despite the fact that the Dutch Fleet
had shown itself a better match for the English than ever before.
In any case, there was no reason now to succumb to English pressure or, as De Witt himself put it,[136] to turn an almost desperate
position into a completely desperate one by way of proclamation.
Far better, he argued, to bide one's time and, like the patient
angler, wait for the fish to bite.[137]

No wonder then that he was utterly opposed to the many proposed Royalist expeditions, all of which he felt, were more likely
to incense Cromwell than to overthrow him. One such expedition,
in aid of the Highland rebels, was just being made ready by Sir
Thomas Middleton on Charles's instructions. For months, Sir
Thomas had stayed on in Holland, moving heaven and earth to
obtain a subsidy from the States. The Princess Royal, pressed by
her brother, presented him with a small sum (£100 at most), and
later – in January 1654 – agreed to stand surety for a further 20,000
rix-dollars.[138] Afraid of arousing opposition, she made her grants
in great secrecy, but the Orange party quite blatantly associated
itself with the affair. In September, Van der Capellen wrote a
jubilant letter to Huygens asking him to inform the princesses[139]
that the party had succeeded in doing something 'for the House of
Orange and its Allies': Gelderland would refuse to contribute its
levy to the Generality unless the other provinces were admonished

'to assist the Scots and the Irish, thus openly embracing the interests of Charles II, to be described as ruler of Great Britain'. And this at a time when Charles's own inactivity was calling forth bitter criticism from those of his adherents who were planning the latest expedition![140] Van der Capellen's further reference to the desirability of a military alliance with France also suggests that the Gelderland party was hopelessly out of touch with reality. All their plans could have delayed matters at best. Yet even after the resumption of negotiations, the pro-Orange provinces continued to take an interest in Middleton's expedition, so much so that Holland was unable to prevent the departure of the troops which, in the end, proved unable to stem the collapse of the Scottish rebellion.

It was not until 21 October that the States-General were able to agree on an answer to England, rejecting the proposed union, but leaving the door wide open to further negotiations. In England, meanwhile, the leading protagonists had tempered their more radical demands. The two envoys were handed new proposals, in which (echoes of 1651!) the call for union was replaced by one for a military alliance. Cromwell was hatching plans for a grand coalition of Protestants, and for the seizure of colonies from Spain with whom he was still allied. To that end, he went out of his way to tempt the Dutch Republic, the pivot of his entire system. Not only would the Republic share in the rich colonial spoils with England – Spanish America going to the latter and Brazil, Africa and Asia to the former – but he even promised to repel the Navigation Act.[141] Unfortunately, the price he demanded – a world-wide war of religion – was too high; no Dutch party, no Dutch statesman could have afforded to pay it.[142] On 21 October, the two envoys were accordingly sent back with instructions to do no more than repeat the earlier Dutch proposals.

Cromwell now realized that it was idle to count on co-operation by the States in his grandiose plans. This in no way lessened his desire to live at peace with his Protestant neighbour. If the worst came to the worst, England would crush Spain by herself; meanwhile a stop must be put to the fratricidal struggle. Clearly though, since the Dutch Republic was unwilling to share in the great work, it had no right to expect economic concessions. This was an attitude wholly similar to that following the failure of St John's mission, except that now there was an unmistakable desire for reconciliation. All the same, in November, when negotiations were finally resumed, though the demand for union had been dropped, the remaining English terms were exceedingly stiff. Their twenty-seven articles, submitted on 27 November, contained everything on which the 1652 negotiations had foundered, and much more besides. Even De Witt was disconsolate. He felt the new situation was no longer 'almost' but 'completely' desperate,[143] and we know from Aitzema[144] that he made a bitter speech before the States of Holland, in which he asserted that a military alliance with France was the best the country could now hope for.

Had the Orange party won the day after all? In the event, the French alliance never came to anything, for France had very little to offer. On the very day that De Witt made his gloomy pronouncement, the French government drafted an instruction to Chanut,[145] who, a few weeks earlier had replaced Brasset as French ambassador to the Hague. In it there was an anxious desire to spare the susceptibilities and allay the suspicions of the English Commonwealth. The ambassador was, moreover, instructed that, while trying not to effect a break with the House of Orange, to which France was linked by old and close ties, he must refrain from espousing its cause in a manner that might offend the States. Yet if France sought the friendship of the new Dutch rulers, it was not in order to make common cause with them against the English, but rather to arrive with them at a durable peace with the Commonwealth. Luckily, it did not take De Witt long to regain hope in a satisfactory settlement. As early as 17 December, Van Beverning and Nieuwpoort reported that they saw a new gleam of light.[146] The English had made a number of concessions, though a repeal of the Navigation Act was now out of the question. On 26 December, the envoys wrote that even the delicate problem of including Denmark (which Holland refused to desert) in the peace settlement no longer presented an insuperable obstacle. The chief stumbling block now was English insistence on excluding the Prince of Orange from high office.

This was stipulated in the twelfth of the twenty-seven articles, handed to the envoys in late November.[147] For the rest, that article was a repetition of the excessive demands that had caused so much friction in 1651: the exclusion of all Royalists and the prevention of possible Royalist plots, with the help of the Prince of Orange, in the territory of the States. The new stipulation, debarring 'William, Prince of Orange, grandson of the late King of England,

and all members of his family' from the offices of Stadholder, Captain-General, or Fortress-Commander, had clearly been inspired by the events of the preceding summer, when the prince's return to power had suddenly become a very real possibility. English disquiet at this turn of events was only too natural. If the United Netherlands were not prepared to do what a Protestant Republic should have been only too glad to do – to link their fate to that of the English Commonwealth – then the Commonwealth had every right to demand guarantees against the resuscitation of the unholy Orange-Stuart alliance, the more so as their party could still count on so much support in Holland.

Alas, the States-General could not possibly accept such conditions. Not only because now – as in 1651 – so many supporters of the Orange party still represented the smaller provinces in the States, but also because, lying inland, these provinces were not particularly afraid of what English naval power might do to them or to their country. Van Beverning and De Witt[148] therefore had good reason to fear that 'the Prince of Orange might yet prove the fly in the ointment'.

Soon afterwards, however, the States-General were informed that the whole problem might be skirted by the ingenious solution to the 'temperament', a compromise by which it was hoped to allay English fears without sacrificing national honour. No longer was the prince expressly excluded from holding high office but, like any other servant of the state, he would merely be expected to swear his allegiance to the peace treaty. The twelfth article, and quite especially the crucial stipulation that the two contracting parties would undertake not to aid rebels in the other's camp, remained in the treaty, but the prince and his mother were no longer referred to by name. An acceptable formula had at last been found. Still, the thorny problem of Denmark remained. This was a subject with which many Dutchmen felt their prestige and entire standing in the Baltic to be bound up, and on which they were not prepared to compromise. In the end, they got their way. By January, the negotiations had made so much progress that the envoys returned to the Hague with a draft treaty to which they felt they could give their approval.

Months passed before all the objections were finally overcome. To the great disappointment of the Orange party,[149] all the provinces including Zeeland, agreed to the terms, though some, and particularly William Frederick's provinces, still pressed for the inclusion of France. The Hollanders, on the other hand, saw no reason for endangering the peace with such a stipulation,[150] and William Frederick was quite unable to overrule their attitude to a power that had such long associations with his family.[151] His spokesman, Jongestal, proved no match for Van Beverning,[152] and while Holland succeeded in getting the peace treaty adopted, France had to engage in long and arduous negotiations before reaching her own objective in November 1655. Holland was able to follow her own line without alienating the French – France's interest in keeping on good terms with the most powerful party in the Republic outweighed any feeling of gratitude for William Frederick's efforts on her behalf.

On 22 April 1654, when the States-General endorsed the peace treaty, it accordingly agreed to include the 'temperament' regarding the position of the Prince of Orange. A ratification by the Lord Protector (for such was now Cromwell's official title) duly followed, on 8 May the peace was solemnly proclaimed. But the States-General were kept in the dark on a number of points. Thus the position of the House of Orange had not really been settled by the temperament but by a secret agreement between Cromwell and Holland.

The story has often been told. The temperament was a sincere attempt by De Witt to settle the problem.[153] But it did not satisfy Cromwell who accepted it as the utmost that was to be got out of the six provinces, but then went on to wrest further concessions in the form of an Act of Seclusion from Holland, the mightiest of the provinces. With the exception of a few letters,[154] Van Beverning destroyed his correspondence with De Witt, with the result that the course of the negotiations (about which there are few English reports) can no longer be reconstructed in every detail. The secretiveness, worse, the duplicity, with which Holland treated the matter, has led to impassioned controversies, not only between Van Beverning's contemporaries but also between later historians. However, all are agreed on the main events. Thus nobody any longer believes that it was De Witt and Van Beverning, moved as they were by anti-Orange feeling, who suggested the exclusion of Orange to Cromwell in the first place. The letters of Van Beverning which De Witt quoted to prove the groundlessness of that accusation are quite conclusive on that point. Moreover, all the indications are that the demand for the exclusion was a natural consequence of long-standing English political ambitions and fears on the part of the English Republicans. True, the exclusion was also in line with the views of De Witt and his friends, but there is no doubt that they tried their utmost to keep foreign control out of the act. It is no less certain that the famous *Deduction of the States of Holland*, in which De Witt defended his policy against the attacks of the other provinces (the secret leaked out soon enough), was misleading in many important respects. Thus the claim[155] that the States of Holland had no idea that the Protector was dissatisfied with the temperament until they received news to that effect in a letter from Van Beverning and Nieuwpoort dated 10 April 1654, may be literally correct – De Witt was far too good a lawyer to commit downright lies to paper – but it was anything but frank.

We know from De Witt's own letters[156] that in late February or early March he was already having discussions with trusted and influential members of the States of Holland on what to do should Cromwell insist on more than the temperament. Quite probably the two envoys from Holland had warned De Witt that the temperament was not enough when they returned home in January.[157] Van Beverning, who left Holland again quite suddenly and secretly after a stay of some ten days, must have discussed the whole delicate subject with De Witt, and probably returned not 'with any particular instruction or orders from the States of Holland' – the *Deduction* is right to claim that – but certainly with private instructions or hints from De Witt as to what attitude he was to adopt to English demands for further guarantees by Holland against the hostility of Orange. The fact is that in the negotiations about Holland's unilateral adoption of the exclusion, De Witt not only misled the States-General, but even kept his own masters, the States of Holland, in the dark until everything had been settled. Of course, his conduct towards the States-General differed radically from his behaviour in the States of Holland. From the former he concealed his policy because he knew they would never swallow it and in the firm conviction that it was no concern of theirs; from the States of Holland, on the contrary, he not only expected full support for his policy but also for his secret negotiations which, alone, could assure his success.

In any event, he considered it essential to keep matters to

himself until, once the ratification of the peace treaty by the States-General could no longer be endangered, the States of Holland could be made to pass the Act of Seclusion, on the pressing grounds that failure to do so would undermine the peace. His hand was greatly strengthened by Van Beverning's and Nieuwpoort's letter of 10 April, claiming that Cromwell had only just presented them with the demand for the exclusion.[158] Even so, it proved impossible to persuade the States of Holland to pass the Act unanimously. After the delegates had been allowed to consult their respective States – an operation shrouded in weighty oaths of secrecy – the Act was passed on 1 May against the opposition of Leyden, Haarlem, Enkhuizen, Alkmaar and Edam. Even now De Witt did not have the document handed to the Protector at once. Cromwell had agreed to ratify the peace treaty once Holland simply *promised* to pass the Act, though with the rider that he would regard the peace as null and void if the promise were not kept. The ratifications were exchanged in late April and on 6 May peace was publicly proclaimed in England. For weeks before that, the Grand Pensionary had kept trying to stall Cromwell with assurances and protestations about the exclusion. During all that time the envoys had kept the Act in their strong-box, being careful, of course, not to let Cromwell guess that it had actually been passed, and making much play of the difficulties involved in obtaining it from the States of Holland.

Was there still a chance that the Protector might have been made to change his mind? Who can say? He had already dropped quite a number of demands in his negotiations with Holland, whose indefatigable tenacity of purpose had more than once got the better of his obstinacy. The public displays of joy, and the scenes of fraternization following the proclamation of peace in England, had no doubt nurtured De Witt's hope.[159] But then the other provinces came in to spoil his game.

Rumour had long been rife that there was something afoot between Cromwell and Holland. As early as December of the previous year, Jongestal had harboured strong suspicions against his colleagues from Holland, but he put them out of his mind, and his letters to William Frederick during the critical days of late April and early May gave no hint that anything might be amiss.[160] In January, when Van Beverning made his hurried departure from the Hague, whispers once again had it that Holland had been making private promises to England. De Witt managed to stifle the suspicions, but two days after the Act had been passed (that is, on 3 May) he was shocked to discover that Count William Frederick knew all about it.[161] The count, certainly the last man De Witt would have taken into his confidence, had learned of the matter through the treachery of De Witt's principal clerk, and there followed a flood of questions, warnings, and protests. On 8 May, Friesland lodged a sharp protest in the States-General against the policy of Holland, which had affronted not only the House of Orange but the honour and liberty of the whole country; the protest was coupled to the demand that the envoys should be recalled to account for their conduct. Most of the other provinces, including Gelderland, Zeeland, Stad en Lande, endorsed the protest, but no agreement was reached on a line of action. Next day, the two princesses, i.e. the mother and grandmother of the little prince who was the subject of the seclusion, addressed a letter to the States-General begging them to request Holland to reconsider the matter, and 'Their Noble Great Mightinesses' were persuaded to send new instructions to Van Beverning and Nieuwpoort asking them to do their utmost in persuading the Protector to content himself with the temperament.

In those days, when his whole policy was being put to the test, De Witt was far from satisfied with the attitude of the States of Holland. What hurt him most was that the deputies of his own town, Dort, showed so little eagerness to support him. Writing to his father he complained indignantly[162] that Dort, 'which was never backward on occasions like this, has sent persons whom the vain sound of a child's name and the dead letter of a humble petition by two widows have had the power so to intimidate that they have ignominiously deserted their post'.

And, indeed, there was no excuse for their faint-heartedness. True, there was a storm of indignation against the States, in Holland and elsewhere. The public talked about the matter 'in canal-boats and in coaches',[163] and in their indignation even magnified the wrong done to Orange: it was widely rumoured that Cromwell had been promised that the whole family would be exiled. One might have thought that in the prevailing public mood, the Orange party would have staged a bold *coup*. Yet, when Brederode was sent to Haarlem, an old Orange stronghold, by the States of Holland, he was able to write reassuringly:[164] 'The matter [the Seclusion] is not taken nearly as bitterly as is sometimes thought in the Hague. The peace is as welcome, nay as necessary, here as it is anywhere else.' The peace! This was indeed an argument that brooked few objections. What the States of Holland had done might not be to the taste of many, but they had at last procured the peace. 'The peace,' wrote Chanut, the French ambassador, just before the seclusion was announced, 'will add greatly to the strength of the dominant party.'[165] He was right. The States party was in a very strong position, and could stand a good deal of attack. And the opposition party was no more able to act vigorously and unanimously than it had been the year before.

The protests and denunciations of the various provinces were as vociferous as any but, in the absence of a clear lead, that was as far as the opposition went. The Orange party should have struck at once, and it did consider rushing the elevation of William III to the Captain-Generalship (with William Frederick as his Lieutenant)[166] through the States-General, thus disavowing the Act of Seclusion in public. But before embarking on that course, the party needed absolute faith in its own policy, shrinking neither from a resumption of the war nor from violent civic commotion, not to say civil war. It would have been a dangerous game. The majority, when put to the test did not dare to play it.

In addition, the attitude of the princesses acted as a damper on the more enterprising spirits in the party, led by William Frederick. We saw with how much scorn De Witt dismissed the two ladies' 'humble request'. The immediate impact of the insult to their House had caused the two princesses to settle their differences to the extent of sending a joint letter to the States-General,[167] but De Witt knew perfectly well that they were irremediably jealous of each other, and that they would rather compete for his favour than join forces against him. The French ambassador had on more than one occasion to observe[168] that the two ladies showed great submissiveness towards the States of Holland. One instance of their mutual suspicion, which paralysed the capacity of the entire party, is the French ambassador's report that some members suspected the old princess of inciting her daughter-in-law to lodge protests and complaints, merely to acerbate feelings in the States of Holland towards her. Once the States saw fit to expel Mary from the country, then she, Amalia, would remain the sole guardian of her grandson and of all his claims.

Was William Frederick himself able to give the lead when the princesses could not? One moment he thought of withdrawing as candidate for the post of Deputy Captain-General,[169] at the next he talked of having himself elected Stadholder of Overijsel and of Gelderland and of bringing the affairs of the Union to a crisis in that way. All through May and June, at any rate, he was full of plans for decisive action. Knowing that Holland was implacably opposed to him,[170] he could tell himself that he had nothing to lose in a crisis. He was quite prepared to face civil war, provided only he could be sure of French support. That was the reason why he had championed France throughout the negotiations with England, and why he now kept troubling the French ambassador with requests for advice and for assurances that he could count on French help, and particularly on much-needed French arms, in case of an uprising.[171]

How feeble the prestige of the State must still have been for Orange leaders to speak so glibly and so often of civil war and foreign intervention! Even the Hollanders, who now held sway over the entire Republic, but who had to maintain their position by underhand means, were not as confident as one might have expected. In his diary, Doubleth, a member of the *Chambre mipartie*, which was still meeting at Mechlin to settle controversial points connected with the treaty of Münster, reports a conversation with Riccen, Pensionary of Purmerend, and later a member of the High Council of Justice, and a loyal supporter of De Witt. When Doubleth expressed his great anxiety about the Act of Seclusion, which struck him as a crafty English scheme to promote disunity to the point of forcing the supporters of the Act to seek Cromwell's protection, Riccen's reply was: 'I quite believe you, and I agree that things will come to such a pass.'[172] Small wonder that many foreigners had doubts about the viability of the Republic.

In the end all William Frederick's plans came to nothing for lack of French support. The moment Chanut realized that France was being invited to meddle in a possible civil war, he began to behave with the utmost caution, even refusing to become involved in attempts to improve relations between the two princesses. On the contrary, he sent secret assurances to De Witt that France would do everything in her power to help preserve order and the union of the provinces.[173] He realized only too well that Holland had the upper hand: '*Ceux qui gouvernent en Hollande sont fermes, adroits et attentifs à leur conduite, d'où il est à juger qu'ils se pourront soustenir.*[174] On 15 May, when the crisis was at its height, the French government renewed its instructions to abstain from anything that might tend to provoke a split between the provinces, while yet maintaining the friendliest attitude towards the House of Orange. A split, according to France, would merely serve the interests of the English, who were bound to intervene, and might then be able to sign with Holland and Zeeland an act of union that had proved to be unattainable from the seven provinces.[175]

So, in spite of all the threats and talk, there was no tangible resistance to Holland's separate transaction with the Protector. Not until June were the States-General able, in the face of obstruction by Holland, to pass a resolution which, in the event, demanded no more than that the envoys in England should be ordered to communicate the instructions they had received from the States of Holland and to give an account of all that they had done with respect to it. In other words, they were not even given orders to refrain from delivering the document to Cromwell. De Witt was still delaying this decisive step; now, however, he judged that the time for taking it had come. He accordingly wrote a letter to the envoys telling them of the resolution, but complaining that it was, alas, too late to do anything about it. The envoys took the hint and delivered the Act of Seclusion to Cromwell on 10 June 1654.

It goes without saying that the Protector had paid no heed to the envoys' renewed pleas, which they put forward in accordance with their instructions of 10 and 12 May. He knew as well as the next man that the Act had now been passed and that it was in the hands of Van Beverning and Nieuwpoort. The clamour it had caused in the Dutch Republic was the last thing to soften his heart, for it only proved once again how real was the threat of Orangist plots, and it was precisely to prevent these that the Act had been conceived. Moreover, it was not Cromwell's business to promote harmony between Holland and the other provinces; indeed, it was in his own best interest that the Holland States party should fall out with the Orangists, and that is no doubt why he had been pressing for the exclusion of the young prince from the very start. As we saw, the French even thought that the Act offered him the opportunity to drive a wedge between the provinces and thus to resurrect his favourite plan for union with Holland alone. And in fact, during the peace negotiations, England had made several attempts to lure Holland away from the other provinces.[176] In any case there was less hope now than ever before that Cromwell would compromise on this particular point. De Witt could claim with apparent justice that it was the action of the Orange provinces that had made the delivery of the Act to Cromwell inevitable.

He made this claim quite emphatically in his *Deduction*[177] which appeared in August 1654. The opposition by the other provinces to the delivery of the Act had been confined to words. On the occasion of his official call on the princesses to inform them of the delivery, De Witt had issued the warning that disturbances of the kind that had occurred last year, would not be tolerated this time.[178] On 30 June (shortly after the delivery of the Act), the States of Zeeland had laid before the States-General a 'Deduction' of their own, in which the impropriety and illegality of Holland's conduct were set out with many arguments. Groningen and Friesland, too, had been very outspoken in their disapproval, and it was in answer to all these protests that the *Deduction of Holland* had been written. In it, De Witt – for he was its author – presented a forceful and detailed defence of Holland's policy, but not of his personal share in it. From the high-spirited, almost provocative, tone of this masterly piece of prose, we can glean how sound he felt his position to be. The *Deduction* was a rallying cry to the States party, which gladdened the hearts of the Holland regents, encouraged their feelings of superiority over the troublesome but impotent six provinces, and confirmed them in their stubborn opposition to the House of Orange in the name of republicanism.[179] The *Deduction* argued, *inter alia*, that no injustice had been done to the princely child who, in a free Republic, could not expect to step into the shoes of his forefathers. The Orange claim that only the Stadholders could safeguard national unity was not only challenged but refuted with the thesis, developed with much historical erudition, that from the days of medieval counts onward, it had been the nobles who had invariably initiated all the nation's feuds and quarrels. In equal detail, and by clever use of constitutional precedent (particularist actions by the other provinces who were now appealing to the Union of Utrecht), it was demonstrated that Holland had violated neither the spirit of the Union nor the rights of the other provinces.

The *Deduction* was a most remarkable political document. Not only did it refute all the attacks upon Holland, but it did so in unusually forthright terms. Take, for example, the passage in which De Witt rejected the argument that gratitude towards the earlier Princes of Orange should move the States to recognize the political claims of their descendants. Those obligations, he said, had been more than amply fulfilled in the lifetime of the ancestors themselves. And he appended an elaborate list, drawn up by three gentlemen appointed by the States to examine the financial registers from 1586 onwards, of the vast sums received by the Stadholders Maurice, Frederick Henry and William II: nineteen million guilders all told. Now this sort of argument may have impressed De Witt's contemporaries, but provides no constitutional justification of the Act in accordance with the terms of the Union of Utrecht. But then, Groningen and Zeeland were no more concerned with the constitutional issue than Holland – to them, too, the main question was whether or not De Witt's conduct accorded with the best political interests of the country.

That the Act of Seclusion, passed under the pressure of a foreign ruler, was an unhappy episode in Dutch history, nobody can deny. De Witt did his best to avoid it. True, he was not prepared to pay the price of continuing the war, but who can blame him for that when even his severest critics were not prepared to run that risk either![180] But it is difficult to avoid the impression that had De Witt had strong personal objections to the exclusion of the House of Orange as such, he would have resisted English meddling more drastically than he did. Had Holland used their delaying tactics against the Act as vigorously as, for example, they pressed for the inclusion of Denmark in the peace – who knows but that Cromwell might not have relented. According to Bordeaux-Neufville,[181] the French ambassador in London, early in January when the decisive exchanges were probably taking place, Van Beverning admitted to him quite openly 'that they wished to take advantage of every opportunity to humiliate the House of Orange, even by accepting this proposal' (i.e. Cromwell's agreement to make do with an exclusion by Holland alone). Thus while the men of Holland clearly preferred to keep foreign countries out of the matter, they would not have been politicians had they failed to appreciate that the exclusion of Orange, underwritten by the English Republic, fitted in wonderfully well with their own policy.

No doubt, it was most unfortunate that foreign policy and party strife should have been joined together in this way. But the moment the House of Orange became allied to the Stuart cause, allowing its own views on foreign policy to be dominated by the needs of that alliance, the States party was forced to take the path that culminated in the humiliation of the House of Orange. It was Orange who started it all by becoming involved in the English domestic quarrel. The first English war had been largely caused by the personal connection between Stuart and Orange. Hence the Act of Seclusion may be regarded as a direct consequence of the marriage between William II and Mary Stuart.

Gloomy years; From the Act of Seclusion to the Restoration (1654-60)

In the years between the passing of the Act of Seclusion and the restoration of Charles II to the English throne, the ties between Orange and Stuart had little influence on the foreign policy of England or the Netherlands. Both dynasties had been laid low[182] and though many of their supporters believed in a future recovery, they were bereft of all influence. The Orange party in the Dutch Republic was almost as sadly disorganized as was the royalist party in England, with the result that the two noble families became wholly dependent on foreign aid – or so, at least, they believed. As it turned out in the end, however, their restoration was the work of their own peoples.

The Orange party in the Republic – in so far at least as it did not pursue the safe course of bowing to De Witt's control – continued to place all its hopes in France. Thus as late as 1657, Sommelsdijk wrote to Cardinal Mazarin, that it was best to preach patience until the scion of 'the right branch' had grown to maturity.[183] Mazarin himself, who that self-same year drafted an instruction for the new ambassador to the States-General (M. de Thou), warned the ambassador expressly not to let himself be tempted by the Frisian Stadholder ('*homme de grand coeur et à hautes prétentions*') into a degree of intimacy that might offend the States.[184] More than ever, France felt she had to keep on the right side of the Republicans in Holland, for all the suspicion and antipathy with which French diplomats, monarchists to a man, continued to regard them. Worse still, Charles II had been driven into the arms of Spain, the enemy of France.

In the summer of 1654[185] Charles had had to leave France, for Mazarin had begun to draw close to Cromwell – needless to say not out of any great love for the Protector. Nor was the exile accorded a particularly warm reception in the southern Netherlands, where the Spanish government was no less frightened than her French enemy of incurring Cromwell's displeasure. As a result, Charles was forced to continue to Spa, in the territory of the Bishop of Liège, and the seasonal meeting-place of high-born society from all over Europe. Here he was joined by the Princess Royal who had long been anxious to see her brother, and there was a great deal of merry entertainment. The Stuarts were past-masters in the art of drowning their adversities in revels, but not everybody was edified by the spectacle of Charles squandering the money he had just received from the Emperor and a number of princes, not to mention the Princess Royal. Huygens, who had more than one confidential talk with the king in Spa, and who was greatly pleased, no less with his wise words on the necessity of establishing harmony between the princess and her mother-in-law, than with his skill at dancing and his ear for music, flattered himself with the hope that Charles was seriously resolved to return to Scotland[186] – where the rebellion had not yet been put down – but nothing came of this. Instead, Charles went on a pleasure trip to Cologne and Aix-la-Chapelle, where the princess gave her enemies grounds for gossip by kissing Charlemagne's skull, and her brother grounds for complaint by measuring his sword against that of the mighty Emperor of the West. In the spring of 1655, Charles ventured to go to Middelburg with bold plans for an invasion which, however, foundered in confusion. Later in the year, his sister rejoined him in Cologne, whence they journeyed on to enjoy the pleasures of the Frankfort Fair to the full.[187]

But then the political horizon suddenly cleared. In the autumn of 1655, Spain found herself at war with Cromwell, who had at long last made up his mind to join France, thus freeing his hands for an attack on the Spanish colonies. Charles immediately seized the chance of making common cause with the new enemy of his own foe. The Spaniards, however, were as loath to compromise themselves with him as the Hollanders had been a few years before. It took months before negotiations got going in earnest, but at last, in April 1656, a formal alliance between Charles II and the King of Spain was concluded and the exile was given leave to settle in

Bruges. This arrangement did prove advantageous to Spain, not so much at sea (where the earlier promise by Royalists that the sailors would defect from the Protector could not be made good) as on land (where a number of Irish regiments in the French service changed sides on their king's appeal).

The Stuarts were deeply divided on the line taken by Charles II. His mother, a French princess, was still staying in France, and the Duke of York was serving in the French army. It was with real reluctance that he heeded his brother's command to join him at Bruges, where luxuries were few and intrigues and feuds abounded. Mary, for her part, insisted on paying a visit to the French court at the very time when Charles was trying to come to an understanding with Spain, and prolonged her stay throughout most of 1656. Perhaps she was anxious to prevent a final break with France, for she knew that while the Spanish connection might prove advantageous to Stuart, it was unlikely to prove beneficial to Orange.

Charles himself realized this perfectly well and did not shrink from drawing his own conclusions. In December 1656, while the Princess Royal was breaking her return journey from France with a stay in Bruges, he begged the Spanish government to instruct its ambassador in the Hague to lay a proposal before the States calling for concerted action by the Netherlands, Spain and Stuart against the Commonwealth, France and Sweden. The States were to be assured that the scheme would not lead to fresh importunities on the part of the House of Orange; on the contrary, if they came to the aid of the king, they could rely on his full support in domestic matters.[188] But such proposals were unlikely to make any impression on the Hague. The Republic, freed at long last from the Orange involvement with Stuart, had been able, by a combination of great tact and great pressure, to pursue its policy of preserving a balance of power in the Baltic: in contrast to what had happened in 1644–5, this now meant keeping Sweden's growing might in check. This could only be accomplished by not getting involved in a new war with the English, who tended to side with Sweden, and with whom trade and contraband questions were causing difficulties enough. The support promised by Spain and Charles II – one almost as hard-pressed as the other – was not such that De Witt could have contemplated reversing the policy of caution and patience towards England, thus jeopardizing what freedom of action in the Baltic he now had.[189] The plans of Charles II were therefore once again condemned to failure, even though, this time, they were clearly directed against the interests of the House of Orange.

When Mary left for France – against her brother's express wish – he had not yet made his proposal, and it cannot be known with any certainty whether she ever learned of it. In any case, many of her friends and advisers refused to believe that the French court could have debased itself to the point of making common cause with the Protector, and continued to persuade her that help for her son could only be expected from France. And indeed, in the family quarrel started by Charles's Spanish policy, she sided fully with her mother and York,[190] and it is quite probable that one of the reasons for her journey to France (which badly depleted her finances[191]) was to make a public demonstration of her pro-French feelings.

Perhaps it is wrong to look for political motives behind every one of her actions. Mary Stuart was never remarkable for her political sagacity or discretion. Her conduct was governed by passion and impulse. She was the slave of her temperament, which was chiefly compounded of a frivolous love of pleasure and of pride. Thus her visit to France may well have had reasons other than concern for her son's future. To begin with she was anxious to see her mother again – after thirteen years; moreover, she was bored to distraction by her Dutch surroundings (Breda, Teilingen, the Hague), and badly needed another change of scenery. It is said that she also had the wild idea that the King of France (seven years her junior) might ask for her hand in marriage. While she was disappointed in that regard, the rest of her stay was pleasant enough. '*Jamais je nay resu tant de sivilité de ma vie*,' she wrote to Heenvliet.[192] She was not accustomed to such treatment in Holland and her naïve satisfaction is a measure of her political sense.

What she lacked above all was sufficient tact to make herself agreeable to the Hollanders; indeed, she had no wish even to try. She was convinced that her son's future depended on French help or the restoration of the English monarchy and it never so much as entered her head to look to Holland. Thus she never bothered to think that all the dancing, hunting and extravagance attendant upon the trips to Spa, along the Rhine, or to the French court, were bound to have a most depressing effect on supporters of the House of Orange, now that it had fallen from power. Had not the

Calvinistic people looked askance at Frederick Henry's worldly style of life even in his heyday? And the Princess Royal saw fit to stage great performances and masquerades even in the Hague. We can just imagine her chuckling with her aunt of Bohemia, whom all misfortunes had been unable to rid of a love of pleasure, at that foolish minister of religion who had likened their innocent amusements to the sins of Sodom and Gomorrah.[193] Yet less severe critics than the Calvinists also shook their heads. One of these was Sir Edward Nicholas, who in 1654 asked himself in irritation how it was possible that the Princess Royal, in the circumstances of her House, should have found pleasure in staging at court an English comedy with the unfortunate title, *A King and no King*.[194] But the princess was far too proud to demean herself by currying favour with the commonalty; indeed she even deemed it beneath her dignity to accommodate influential Orange supporters. 'It breaks my heart,' Hyde wrote,[195] 'to see how negligent she is of old friends.' Mazarin mentioned this fact in his instruction to De Thou (in 1657) as a matter of common knowledge. 'From natural inclination and through her having been educated among English people she does not readily deign to show favour or kindness to Dutch regents. She regards this as not being worthy of her rank and believes, moreover, that the friends of the House of Orange do no more than their duty in remaining faithful to her.'[196] Two young travellers from Holland who paid their respects to the princess at Bruges in December 1656, noted in their journal:[197] 'She received us in her customary manner, that is to say, coldly and without saying a word. In the present age this cannot please, however great the prince may be.'

In the circumstances, it was not at all surprising that some Orangists should have refused to 'do their duty', as the princess called it. More and more of them looked to the States and, indeed, in so doing they merely followed the example of the princess herself and her mother-in-law, who as we know, driven by distrust of William Frederick, repeatedly sought for a *rapprochement* with the States of Holland. Even William Frederick, who was responsible for the attack on Amsterdam and who had called for French help against the Act of Seclusion, was seriously tempted to fall in with the suggestion by Holland, late in 1655, that he accept the post of Field Marshal. It never came to that, but William Frederick nevertheless continued to cling to De Witt. Renswoude, too, once the most zealous among the zealous, was, in 1656, seeking his greatest happiness in the kind favour of *'mijn heer de Raad-pensionaris van Holland'*.[198] The report of this man's defection gave Aitzema occasion for a veritable effusion of misanthropy and cynicism. *'L'intérest gouverne le monde. – Pauper ubique jacet . . . La Hollande a beaucoup de compagnies à donner. Le jeune Prince d'Orange est pauvre, la Princesse d'Orange n'est ménagère.'*[199]

Boreel, too, gave vent to his extreme irritation. He had been incensed when his son was refused a position at the Princess Royal's court. When the princess again passed him over in appointing a new bailiff of Steenbergen, Boreel's reaction was such that she felt impelled to write to Heenvliet from Paris:

L'ambassadeur Boreel est fort impertinant ' . . Ill se mit dans un tell furie que ie ne vie jamais le pareil, en me disant que il voyoit bien quil m'estoit for peu considérable, aussi bien que les services quil avoit randu ay Roy mon Père, quil avoit faite sans y estre obligé. – Tout ce que ie luy répondois estoit . . . de ne ce point mettre en une telle rage que ie n'aimois point trop cela. Sur quoy il me dit n'avoir jamais resu obligation de moy, et come cela san ala.[200]

The Princess Royal, who thought so much of her rank, could not get used to such 'impertinent' behaviour. It merely reinforced her preference for the English, so much so that, chalking up grievances through the years, she came to hate her son's country, his people and their language, from the bottom of her heart.[201] On 18 March 1655, the States of Holland wrote to the princess, who was then staying at the castle of Teilingen, that they had been informed the king and her brother had joined her there in secret. They reminded her of the clauses in the treaty of Westminster barring 'the king' from their territory, and also of their own resolutions of July and August 1653. They accordingly asked for an explanation and for the princess's future co-operation in ensuring that the king did not again set foot on Dutch soil. In fact, the king was not at Teilingen, and the princess was profoundly hurt. As she told Hyde[202] she had the letter – 'a very uncivil letter' – translated into English 'that I may the better remember it when maybe they will not desire I should. I will send you a copy, for it deserves to be kept, I shall do the same to Dusseldorf' – i.e. to the king, who was staying there. Nor were the States the only ones to treat her with less than due respect. On 8 December 1658, she complained to Heenvliet[203] that the Council of His Highness, *'ou proprement M. Zulecome'* (that is, Huygens) had written her a letter, *'sy impertinant que ie ne man puisse assez estonner'*. She would let *'la Reine me Mère'* know *'avec quel sorte de geans que jay affaire en ce pays'*.

Her dislike of Hollanders persuaded her to give her son as English an education as possible. In 1654, when a governess had to be appointed, the Princess Royal at once put forward Mrs Howard, daughter of Lady Stanhope.[204] In 1658, it was Lady Balcarres who was proposed to fill the vacancy when it occurred. The old princess, on the other hand, knew full well how unlikely an English education would be to make William III agreeable to the Dutch. In 1656, she tried to take advantage of Mary's absence in Paris by asking the States of Holland to appoint Dutch tutors for the prince;[205] to her great annoyance, however, the States refused to co-operate with her.[206] Still, she succeeded in having a Dutch minister of religion (Trigland, son of the Contra-Remonstrant historian) appointed as teacher to the five-year-old boy. This time the Princess Royal herself had to admit that the appointment would make a good impression.[207] And in 1658, when the magistrates of Leyden called on her in Breda with the request that, when the time came, she send her son to Leyden University, she wrote to Heenvliet, full of the great advantages that would accrue to the prince from this step.[208] Not that he would be allowed to break free from English influences even in Leyden. Thus, in 1659, when the boy was thought to need a governor, her choice fell upon Nassau-Zuylestein[209], a natural son of Frederick Henry – no doubt because he was married to an Englishwoman and was dominated by her.

At all times she was a Stuart first and an Orange second. Charles was her king and she professed herself to be his subject. She could not imagine a nobler course than helping him to recover their father's throne,[210] the more so as she considered his restoration a prerequisite to that of her own son's. Once (in 1655) she even wrote to Charles that she was jealous of his kindness to the child; she was ready to obey all her brother's commands, 'except that of loving him [the little prince] (though he is my ownly child) above all things in this world as long as you are in it'.[211]

Her deep affection was, however, subject to fluctuations; at any rate it did not prevent serious dissensions. Thus Mary's stay at

Bruges on her way back from France, in December 1656, was largely spoiled by quarrels with Charles. Political differences – France or Spain – may have had something to do with them but this aspect was quickly lost sight of in the midst of intense personal arguments. What embittered the princess above all was that Charles should have seen fit to object to the presence at her court of young Jermyn, an association of which, he claimed, the world talked scandal.[212] Later there were harsh words on the subject of Lady Balcarres whom, as we saw, Mary desired as governess for her son and who, like the Jermyns, belonged to the party of the Queen-mother.

Mary was heartily sickened by all the wrangling. Once, in a letter to Heenvliet, she let drop the remark that 'for her money' she was at least entitled to 'good words'. Still, she never wavered in her zeal for her brother's great cause. Her chance to prove it came early in 1658, when it looked very much as if money might help Charles to success in the invasion of England he was planning with Spanish support.[213] Ships hired in Holland had first to be transported to Flanders. It seemed a precarious enterprise, but the princess was full of great expectations. She wrote to Heenvliet: *'Je voye que cest asteur le temps pour rendre le Roy servise. C'est pourquoy ie vous prie de me mander jusques à quelle somme d'argant vous croyés ie suis capable d'avanser.'* No half measures this time! She spoke of pawning her jewels, and even pressed Heenvliet to cede his deed of *survivance* to the Stewardship of Verelst, with which she had presented him not so long before. It proved extremely difficult to obtain his consent, but when, at long last, he bowed before her anger, she thanks him very handsomely. *'Si ce neut esté un tamps asteur où dépand absolument la ruine ou le restablissment do nostre maison, an quoy ie désire d'assister de mon pettit pouvoir, ie n'aurois jamais demandé ce quan tout autre tamps eut esté si injust.'*[215] The deed, Heenvliet informs us, was handed to the Duke of York, who put it up for sale, and was offered 13,000 guilders within the week.

But on the way from Holland to Flanders the ships were intercepted by the English and that meant the end of the entire plan. The war was, in any case, going badly for Spain, which had begun to yearn for peace: Charles's position in the Spanish Netherlands was becoming untenable. Soon after the fall of Dunkirk, in June 1658, he departed and paid a visit to his sister at Hoogstraten, where they continued their bickering over Lord and Lady Balcarres. Meanwhile another great plan was abroad, and Mary was again expected to supply the money. This time it was a large-scale conspiracy in northern England, and it was quite possibly with a view to enlisting the support of William Frederick that Charles combined his stay at Hoogstraten with a tour through the Republic. Apparently he was just about to cross the Zuider Zee to Friesland when Downing, Cromwell's ambassador to the Hague, who had only just objected to Mary's amusements at the annual fair,[216] had his attention drawn to Charles's presence and requested the States-General to expel him; which they did. The entire conspiracy had to be dropped when it became clear that Cromwell had known about it all along,[217] and the only result of Mary's zeal was an acute shortage of personal funds.

Her steward, Oudart, kept pursuing her with demands for money. In September there was no ready cash to keep the kitchen going. And if that were not enough, she now had to suffer from Charles's ingratitude as well.

For in that selfsame month came news to revive everyone's flagging hopes – Cromwell was reported dead. The report reached Charles on his way back from Leeuwarden to Hoogstraten. And the first person to benefit was Mary's enemy, the old princess, who had spent the summer on her near-by estate at Turnhout, encouraging Charles to play tennis with her daughters. Before the good news had grown stale, the king, now as good as back on the throne, was practically betrothed to Henrietta.[218] Soon afterwards, when the old princess returned to the Hague, she could not disguise her triumph from the proud daughter-in-law. '*Elle ne matretenoit,*' Mary wrote to Heenvliet,[219] '*que des plaintes que le Roy mon frère luy fit de moy. Je suis bien malheureus qui [qu'il] s'adresse a des personne qui [qu'il] sçait fort bien n'aura jamais la charité de me défandre seulement avec la vérité.*' So great was Mary's resentment that, some time later, when Charles apparently reverted to the question of her relations with young Jermyn, she wrote an indignant letter to Lady Stanhope, completely renouncing her brother and king. Charles,

'had ruined her fame; that if he were in his kingdom he could not make her satisfaction; that hereafter she would never have anything to do with him, what change soever should be in his fortune; that she was no more his subject, nor would be; that she was a free woman, and might marry, or have kindness for whom she pleased, without demanding anybody's leave; that she would not deny she was pleased with Harry Jermyn's love, and that she had a kindness for him.'[220]

She was, in any case, no longer haunted by the awful prospect of having to yield precedence to a younger sister-in-law who might one day become Queen of England. For though the usurper was dead, the English nation made no move to recall its king. Cromwell's protectorate seemed to be weathering the storm. And in November 1658 Amalia of Solms withdrew her consent to her daughter's marriage to Charles – a decision which she was soon to repent.

Meanwhile, the Stuarts felt that none of the reverses they had suffered in all the years of their exile had been as painful to bear as their neglect by England after Cromwell's death. And even when the Protectorate was abolished and the Commonwealth re-established, and *coup d'état* followed upon *coup d'état* in England, the Stuarts proved quite impotent to turn the situation to their immediate advantage.

To crown it all, the House of Orange received a severe blow as well, this time entirely due to Mary's lack of judgement. The claims of the various guardians to a say in the principality of Orange had never been settled. In practice, the Governor, Count of Dohna, was the undisputed master, and he sided quite openly with the old princess and the Elector of Brandenburg. Anxious to obtain exclusive control, and heeding the advice of her mother, Mary had approached France on the subject as early as 1654.[221] In 1658 she sent a formal appeal for help, and in that way revived her quarrel with the old princess. France lent the required assistance with more zeal than disinterestedness, and in 1660 took possession of the whole principality, then an enclave in French territory. It was a climax everyone except the Princess Royal had foreseen.

Gloomy indeed, were the years before fortune once again smiled upon the House of Stuart. True there were high hopes that the peace of the Pyrenees (negotiations between France and Spain began in the summer of 1659) would create a more favourable climate. Would not France, once it had obtained greater freedom of action, come to Charles's aid? Was it not a fact that the dissolution of the Protectorate had severely strained relations between France and the Commonwealth? Alas, all such hopes were built on sand. Dutch statesmen, for once, did not rate the chances of the Stuarts very highly even at this late stage. Towards the end of June 1659, De Witt still refused a humble request by the Princess Royal to be allowed the pleasure of her brothers York and Gloucester's company for a few days only, at Honselaarsdijk.[222] Charles, too, was forced to spend the year in exile in the Spanish Netherlands. De Witt even contemplated an alliance with the re-born Commonwealth, but developments in England were such that he deemed it wiser to adopt a policy of caution.[223]

And then quite suddenly, General Monk was able to put a stop to the confusion in England. By February 1660, he was practically in control of London and could fight it out with the Long Parliament, which was dissolved. Only then, in April, could Charles enter into direct and public negotiations with his people, who, as a correspondent of De Witt's put it,[224] were falling from one extreme to the next as the parties vied with each other in offering the Stuarts the most absolute power.

As for the States of Holland, they were not slow in swimming with the tide. To begin with, no objection was raised to the king's plan to take up residence in Breda: he thought it best to leave the territory of his Spanish benefactors, lest they demand the return of Dunkirk and Jamaica, Cromwell's spoils. And in May, when the English Convention had officially proclaimed the Restoration, the States-General of Holland immediately sent deputations to Breda to congratulate the new ruler and to invite him to pass through the Hague on his way to England. The invitation was graciously accepted. On 24 May the king set out on his journey, entering the Hague in triumphant procession. Then, on 2 June, after a week of festivities, solemn celebrations and compliments, he set sail from Scheveningen to take possession of his restored kingdom.[225]

The Restoration (Summer 1660); Mary avails herself of her brother's protection

The Restoration in England did not produce an immediate change in the relations between the two countries. The dominant party in the Dutch Republic stuck to its principle of peace with England, even though the new ruler of England had such close ties with the pretender to the Stadholdership. The king, for his part, had become steeled by adversity. He was left with few illusions about his fellow-men and he took a practical view of matters of state. He can hardly have cherished very warm feelings for the States who had done Cromwell's bidding, but then no one else had treated him very much better either – neither the French government, nor the Spanish (which had admittedly assisted – and used – him until his recovery of power seemed imminent, but had then decided to hold his person in ransom against the return of Dunkirk and Jamaica). Sweden and Brandenburg had both howled with the wolves. Even among the English, who had thronged to Breda to pay him homage, how many had not danced to Cromwell's tune while the usurper had been paying the piper! Had Charles not been a master in the art of forgetting the past, he would surely have been unable to rule his country. As it was, he had no qualms about appointing the selfsame Downing as royal ambassador to the Hague, who only three years earlier (1658) had been instrumental in his own expulsion from Holland. True, Downing had betrayed his former masters before the change was officially confirmed, but he did so only when everyone with any sense could have told that the restoration was inevitable.[226]

Hence there was no reason why the king should not have swallowed his innermost feelings against De Witt. To begin with he had need of Dutch support, knowing as he did that despite the current upsurge of royalist sentiment at home his position was by no means secure. Society was in a turmoil, the treasury sorely depleted. France and Spain alike cast longing glances at Cromwell's conquests and quite particularly at Dunkirk. Clearly, therefore, a friend on the Continent would prove extremely useful. Many historians have mocked at the speed with which the States of Holland veered from persecution to respectful recognition, calling it further evidence of their low, bourgeois cunning. Yet the same charges could be laid at Charles's door, who forgot all past insults by the Hague when he felt it advantageous to do so. De Witt and he met as two sober men of the world. To the Hollanders, a king recalled by his people was quite a different figure from a mock king, trailing from exile to exile, and Charles was intelligent enough to understand why it should be thus.

The past, therefore, was not allowed to impair good relations between England and the Republic; indeed, feelings were even more cordial than they had been in the last years of Cromwell's reign. Thus the Northern question, which had so sharply divided England and the Netherlands since about 1656, ceased to be a bone of contention when Charles decided to join the Netherlands in siding with Denmark. Nevertheless, the deeper, economic causes of the rivalry between the two countries, which had made themselves felt under the revolutionary régime as well as under the first two Stuart kings, had not been eradicated. This became obvious the moment Charles was more firmly entrenched.

As for the Orange party in the Netherlands, the change in England had a profound influence from the very start. That party, which unlike the men in power, was not so much interested in the welfare of the Netherlands as in dynastic questions, and which was not burdened with direct political responsibility, felt free to veer from being vehemently anti-English to vehemently pro-English overnight. Having formerly sought its salvation in war, it was now all for peace and friendship. Charles's ascension helped its prestige and expectations to rise enormously – the Orange party was no longer a mere cipher in Dutch politics, and that was precisely why its connection with the English royal house could once again produce such serious tensions in Dutch-English relations.

The governments themselves had not the least wish for these complications. Both Charles II and De Witt were swayed by purely national considerations. But the existence in the Republic of a dynastic party, which felt itself to depend on England, proved a weapon in the hands of England every time the two states came into conflict for whatever reason, fostering English aggression and Dutch distrust of Charles's true motives.[227]

De Witt had a sharp eye for the national danger inherent in the English connection with the House of Orange and devised his policy accordingly. He had grown up during the last years of Frederick Henry and under William II, when the Stadholders' desire to restore their royal relatives to power had posed the constant threat of war, and when Holland's determination to preserve the peace in the national interest had brought upon her the *coup d'état* of 1650. Subsequently, when he began to take an active part in politics, he had learned at first hand how the suspicions of the republican government of England continued to interfere with Anglo-Dutch relations. With Charles's restoration the situation had become far more explosive. It was no longer a case of a strong Stadholder trying to support or to restore a weak king; now a strong king – or one who would presently be strong – might well try to help his little nephew to the Stadholder's office, thus gaining complete ascendancy over him. And as we shall see, this was no mere phantom of De Witt's republican imagination.

He saw two possibilities of stemming the threat. One was, by clever management, to loosen the tie between Orange and Stuart; the other was to debar Orange from any position of power in the Republic. Only when, after a few initial successes, the first method seemed to have failed, did he concentrate on the second. In other words, his policy was not simply one of keeping the House of Orange down, come what may.

And yet, it was inevitable that the behaviour of the Orange party during the last twenty years should have favoured the growth of bitter anti-Orange feeling allied to doctrinaire republicanism. De Witt certainly had his fair share of this. The events of 1650, when a Prince of Orange supported by France had, in the interests of his English family,[228] launched his attack on the heart of Holland, the thoroughly foreign orientation of the court under the Princess Royal,[229] the party's policy of taking its cue from the Stuarts now that they were powerful once again – all this supplied fuel for the ideas of De la Court, the theorist of the new political creed, with which De Witt agreed so very largely. For De la Court the 'monarchical' party in the Republic was essentially an unnational party. Thus, while the Regents enjoyed the support of 'many good patriots and sincere lovers of Liberty, and quite particularly of many prudent inhabitants engaged in commerce as of old', the Stadholders would always have to rely on the soldiery and foreigners, people far more slavishly inclined than the men of Holland.[230] De la Court's detestation of a 'one-headed government', which was tantamount to 'death without resurrection', may at times make the modern reader smile, but only because he has no conception of the dangers that faced De la Court's generation in an age of triumphant despotism.[231]

During his stay in the Hague, the king had openly commended his nephew to the favour of the States. At the Grand Pensionary's request, Charles handed a transcript of his address to the assembly. He begged the States to show his sister and his nephew, '*deux personnes qui me sont extrèmement chères*', clear proof of their favour, '*aux occasions que la Princesse ma soeur vous en priera, ou pour elle-même ou pour le Prince son fils, vous asseurant que tous les effets de votre bienveillance envers eux seront reconnus de moy comme si je les aurois receu en ma propre personne*'.[232] It was an emotional appeal, and for the rest extremely vague and devoid of all implicit threats – the king did not make his friendship dependent upon the States' favours. And *favours* was the word he used, free favours. The recommendation, like the visit itself, amounted to a recognition of the absolute sovereignty of the States.

The king had no intention of supporting a popular movement for the elevation of his nephew. Many Orangists would have liked to see him go from Breda to Zeeland with precisely that end in view.[233] In Zeeland, as we know, the regents were always much more amenable to pressure from the commonalty, and a royal visit would certainly have provoked just such pressure. But Mary was somewhat afraid of popular enthusiasm in provinces where her mother-in-law's influence or that of Count William Frederick surpassed hers. Immediately before the Restoration, she had once again had bitter quarrels with the Princess Dowager and the Elector of Brandenburg about the French occupation of the principality of Orange. She was less inclined than ever to take advice from her co-guardians. What she dreaded above all was that the other provinces might succeed in having William Frederick appointed Lieutenant, once her son was 'designated' for the office of Captain-General. De Witt was quick to exploit this division in the Orange party. He conceded that something must be done to settle the prince's position but, alluding to the danger posed by William Frederick, he was able to persuade the king and the Princess Royal that it was far better not to aim at an immediate appointment.[234] Things would be much easier in the future, when there should be no objection to appointing the young prince to the military office, albeit without the Stadholdership – for the 'Men of True Liberty' were fully determined to prevent the dangerous combination of the two. Nor could the king have been sorry to postpone the whole ticklish problem, the more so as it did not concern him directly.[235] In any case, when he left for England, he had made no definite settlement with De Witt.

Hardly had he gone, however, when the princess changed her mind and, until the day when she herself crossed to England, she worked for the prince's appointment with an urgency that kept the Dutch political world in a state of great agitation. Only at the last minute (she was loath to leave Holland empty-handed, and the politicians were loath to see her go like that) did she agree to another arrangement.

On 27 June, the Quarter of Nijmegen urged the States of Gelderland to propose to the States-General that the Prince of Orange be appointed Captain-General of the Union. The Princess Royal took advantage of this occasion and instructed her greffier, Buysero, to approach De Witt about the implementation of the king's recommendation. Nijmegen had not proposed William Frederick for the Lieutenancy, but only for the rank of Field Marshal which, moreover, he would share with Maurice of Nassau. Was it this fact that had encouraged the princess to challenge De Witt? Or was it perhaps the warmth with which she and her son were welcomed not only in the traditionally Orange town of Haarlem, but in Amsterdam itself?[236] Whatever the true reason, not only did she exert pressure on De Witt through Buysero and personally, but she also attempted to enlist the support of the regents of Amsterdam, of all people.

When one reads the arguments she dictated to Buysero,[237] one is not in the least surprised that they carried so little weight with De Witt. 'That otherwise the king would be discontented' – seems to be the crux of the entire plea. De Witt countered by disputing the claim that the king was particularly anxious about the prince's nomination, and went on to remind Buysero of the conversations during the king's stay in the Hague. Next he said quite bluntly that the appointment was undesirable in itself. Far better that Holland saw to the prince's education and made a financial contribution towards it. Anything beyond that would be most unpopular with members of the States of Holland. Why therefore 'extort' the appointment and in doing so 'arouse bitter resentment', why provoke new 'difficulties and dissensions' as in Prince William's time, if the essential object might be obtained 'easily, and with love and sweetness'. For did not it amount to an appointment once 'His Highness was adopted as a Child of State', once the States took the trouble 'to see that he was educated in the customs and manners of these countries'? But the princess thought otherwise and continued her own campaign with the utmost vigour.

To begin with, she was able to get her brother to write her

a letter which she immediately and gleefully communicated to De Witt. In it the king, too, came out clearly in favour of an appointment (though without expressly mentioning a lieutenancy). Next, she put pressure on Amsterdam. The man to whom she addressed herself – first through Buysero, then by a personal visit to Amsterdam on 22 July – was Cornelis de Graeff of Zuidpols-broek, ex-burgomaster, uncle of De Witt's wife, a man whose influence in Amsterdam was considerable and who passed for one of the few who could get almost anything done with the Grand Pensionary. De Graeff was a man of moderate views, a man of 'ex-pediments', and hence a typical politician. De Witt had already followed his advice to slip a few words suggesting the prospect of a subsequent elevation to high office into the draft resolution dealing with the prince's education. Under pressure from Her Royal Highness, who would not content herself with this, De Graeff seemed prepared to concede a great deal more, until, discovering that the burgomasters would not follow him and spoke of the un-willingness of other 'members' of Holland, he backed down. Shortly before, De Witt had exhorted his uncle to use 'his wise and prudent counsel in persuading Her Royal Highness to acceptance of his (De Witt's) suggestion,[238] and now that Amsterdam appeared to be of his opinion, there could be no question of his relenting. Hence Mary was forced to turn to the other provinces for support. Friesland and Groningen – William Frederick was rendering her good for evil! – at once declared themselves for the appointment. Zeeland had already voted for the prince's nomination as both Captain-General *and* Stadholder. Gelderland joined in soon after-wards. It looked very much as if there would be a bitter struggle which might shake the Union to its very roots. That the princess shrank from taking the final plunge was due to one single cause: De Witt had meanwhile managed to deprive her of her main support.

Mary reaches a compromise with Holland (end of September 1660); the Education Commission; Mary's death (3 January 1661)

De Witt had clearly foreseen that the new English government would not display the force and constancy that had been so characteristic of the Protectorate.[239] The ambassador of the

States-General to England at the time was the lord of Beverweert who, being a good patriot and at the same time a good friend of the Princess Royal, had seemed the very man for this post. De Witt used him to influence Charles II,[240] and with good effect. The king, still in great difficulties, was most anxious to remain on good terms with Holland, the more so as he must have realized that, before long, he would have to apply for a loan to the States of Holland. Hence he allowed himself to be persuaded that the education clause would best serve the prince's interests, and advised his sister most emphatically – through one of her courtiers returning from a stay in England – not to issue a direct challenge to De Witt. Mary was deeply disappointed.[241] She was placing high hopes, especially in Zeeland which, on 7 August, had passed a resolution[242] that had earned the province the warm thanks not only of the Princess Royal and the Dowager Princess, but also of the King of England and the Duke of York: to ask the States-General to nominate the prince for the Captain-Generalship. At the same time, Zeeland herself nominated the prince for the dignity of First Noble as from his eighteenth birthday. Finally, Zeeland resolved to invite the States of Holland to join her in nominating the young prince for the Stadholderate. Now it was traditional for the Stadholder of each of the two provinces (so close were the links between them) to be appointed by joint resolution. A Zeeland deputation of high standing, led by the Grand Pensionary Veth, came to the Hague in September to present this plan to the States of Holland. But most of the Hollanders would not hear of it – only Leyden and Enkhuizen, and a majority of the Nobility, led by the lord of Wimmenum, voted in favour of the appointment.[243]

Meanwhile it had turned September, and Mary was about to leave for England – a departure she was loath to postpone for, as she wrote to her brother, 'the greatest punishment of this world is to live all my life here'.[244] She had not succeeded in making the king change his mind, although she had not failed to tell him that her adversaries were his as well and that they were spreading all sorts of evil rumours about his position in the restored kingdom.[245] Yet in the circumstances, she had to leave it at that. She even requested the Holland Orangist opposition to lie low.[246] De Witt's plan had prevailed: the prince was to be educated by Holland, which alone was able to provide the necessary funds. When the appropriate resolution was passed towards the end of September, it incorporated De Graeff's compromise, containing the vague promise,

that he, as a worthy servant and auspicious instrument of this state, may be instructed for the service of these countries in the true Christian Reformed religion, in all princely virtues and in the knowledge of the humours, laws and customs of these countries, the better to discharge the high offices and employments formerly held by his forefathers on commission of the aforementioned States of Holland and West-Friesland.

At the same time the States declared that the Act of Seclusion must be deemed null and void from the time the King of England had been restored to the throne.

De Witt had told the princess that while the States were happy to see to the education of her son, insistence on the prince's elevation would call forth strife that was bound to damage his interests. However, this explanation was not the whole story; had it been, De Witt and the majority of the States of Holland would surely not have taken so implacable a stand. It strikes me as unlikely that the party of True Liberty was merely temporizing until, in a more favourable climate of public opinion, they could contemptuously cast aside 'the auspicious instrument'. I believe that De Witt meant what he said when he promised that the prince's elevation was an inevitable consequence of his education. But the difference between a formal promise now and the prince's preparation without such a promise was an important one. Had the States allowed themselves to be forced into adopting the first course, the prince would at once have become completely independent of them. As it was, he still had to look to them for his elevation and would therefore be all the more susceptible to their influence.

And it was not merely their oligarchic republicanism which the States of Holland were defending against the autocratic rule of Orange. Much more than that was at stake. The cause of the oligarchy was still inseparable from that of the nation. A Prince of Orange, once elevated, would be independent of the States, and hence all the more dependent on the King of England, to whom he would have owed his elevation. And that was a danger against which De Witt had to be on his guard. De Thou, the French ambassador, tells us that De Witt never forgot Leicester,[247] the English governor, who with the help of the populace and English troops had tried to reduce the oligarchy to impotence and at the same time enforce a commercial policy best suited to England's interests. What if the Prince of Orange, nephew to the King of England and the possible Stadholder *cum* Captain-General by that king's grace, were to follow in Leicester's path? De Witt's fears on that score were shared by the entire States party,[248] and the behaviour of the Princess Royal did little to dispel their anxiety.

Had not her connection with the king been the main platform on which she had put forward all her son's claims? In her dealings with the proud Netherlanders she never gave a single thought to Dutch national feelings, not least because she was much too insensitive to appreciate their very existence. In her world, the king was so far exalted above the bourgeois States that their resistance to his wishes seemed quite inexplicable. 'I did not think it would have been possible,' she wrote to her brother, 'to see you in England and find so many violent enemies against my son.'[249] As far as she was concerned, the king was *her* king, and she did not bother to conceal that fact from De Witt. In July, when she had a talk with him and he tried to dissuade her from continuing her campaign, she kept telling him – as De Witt himself reported to his uncle De Graeff:[250] '*Que c'estoit le commandement du Roy, qu'elle n'oseroit s'en dispenser en la moinde circonstance.*' The guardian of a Prince of Orange, to whom the command of the King of England was law – is it any wonder that De Witt thought fit to take countermeasures? The princess even went so far as to promise him and his party the king's full support if only he acted as she wished, adding (on another occasion) that 'otherwise she might be compelled to deliberate with the king about this matter again and in a different sense; in which case the support might be turned entirely to the other side, which had always shown inclination and affection to the affairs of His Highness as well as of His Majesty'.[251] Such threats could not make much impression upon De Witt, who knew better than anyone else that the king had no intention of being swayed by his sister's ambitions, at least not while he stood in need of support by the Holland States party. And by the time Charles could stand on his own feet, the party was sufficiently strong to pursue its national policy even in the face of the combined opposition of England and the Orange party. So all that Mary achieved with her arrogant and menacing attitude was to irritate and estrange

Holland. Thus, reporting her second visit to Amsterdam, De Graeff wrote that 'Their Honours [the Burgomasters] did not much like her passionate zeal and suspected that there must be men who had misled Her Highness into believing that the more resolute a line she took with this state, the better would be the effect'.[252]

This was clearly not the way to deal with the regents of Holland, and yet the Princess Royal persisted in following it. Thus when she discovered that all her efforts and threats had been crowned with the adoption of De Witt's educational plan, she gave vent to her keen disappointment,[253] adding that she 'gladly accepted the resolution as an apparent introduction to a further and complete resolution, to which Her Royal Highness looks forward in the confident expectation that it will amply fulfil her hopes, thus greatly encouraging her in bearing the interests of "this" state and noble province in mind during her sojourn in England'. According to De Witt,[254] this little speech astonished and shocked all the members of the assembly, many of whom read the last sentence as 'a threat that if this more complete resolution were not adopted H.R.H. would not plead the cause of this state before the king her brother'.

Importunities and threats notwithstanding, Mary departed for England without obtaining any further concessions. When the States of Holland absolutely refused to be intimidated she realized it was time to climb down a little. This is the less surprising when one remembers that the resolution contained the bait of a considerable annual subsidy 'for the implementation of the aforesaid education in accordance with the dignity of so illustrious a personage as well as for the alleviation of his finances'. And the finances of the House of Orange were in sore need of alleviation, the more so as Charles II was in no position to repay his family debt. What was strange, however, was the way in which Mary decided to consent to the educational plan while her foot was almost on the gangway. From Helvoetsluis she wrote a letter to the States, begging them to proceed with the prince's education forthwith, if possible under the supervision of the same 'members' who had, a few days earlier, communicated the resolution to her. These 'members' were: the Nobility, Dort, Amsterdam and Alkmaar. Of the three towns, two were staunch pro-Statists; the Nobility included some who might pass for Orangists, but the two whom the princess mentioned by name, Beverweert and Noordwijk, were completely on De Witt's side. Why then did she not mention Leyden and Enkhuizen instead, or Wimmenum, for that matter?

The old princess, however, did put forward those names. During the past few months, ever since Charles's restoration had suddenly raised her daughter-in-law's standing in the party, she had kept well in the background but had not concealed her disapproval of the way in which the prince's elevation was being pressed for – by 'importuning the government' as she put it.[255] Now, however, she came back from Germany expressly to meet the Princess Royal, and was bitterly annoyed to find that she had come on a fool's errand. When she arrived in Delfshaven she discovered that the Princess Royal had already put out to sea. She now protested vigorously against the nomination of candidates to the education commission, when neither she nor the Elector had been consulted. However, the young princess's choice was too much to the liking of the majority in the States of Holland for them to heed this protest. Did Mary realize the implications of entrusting her son's future so completely to the States party? Or did she merely cling to her notorious principle, that those of Orange could easily dispense with education since faithful service come quite naturally to them? Did she intend winning over the States by complete surrender? William Frederick's friends believed that the fault lay with her advisers, Buysero and Oudart who, just like Heenvliet before them, had personal motives for keeping on the right side of the powerful States of Holland.[256]

Meanwhile the little prince, the defenceless object of so many fierce struggles, was virtually surrendered to Holland. True, the Education Commission appointed by the States in accordance with Mary's most acceptable recommendations, refused to begin its work without first trying to obtain the agreement of the other guardians. Both Weyman, the Elector's ambassador, and the old princess put forward objections or at least withheld their explicit consent.[257] Amalia even forced herself to send her daughter-in-law a letter in which, controlling her personal irritation, she implored Mary to soothe the temper of the Orangist by at least co-opting a regent from Leyden – the traditional Orange town in which the prince was now residing – to the commission. Mary replied, quite coolly, that she had no objections.[258] Though the States party refused to budge, Zeeland, acting in concert with Amalia, tried to enlist the other provinces against Holland's educational monopoly.[259] Only when Holland at long last – it was now the end of November – threatened to proceed upon the mother's authority alone, did Amalia reluctantly give way.

The combination of Holland and the Stuarts was such that she had little option in the matter. Even when the Princess Royal had still been pressing for the elevation of her son, De Witt had been able to ignore both her own and the objections of the other provinces.[260] Her defection had embittered the Orangists in Holland and abroad, and at the same time had greatly discouraged them. True, Zeeland, spurred on by the Princess-Dowager, made fresh representations in late September but in early October the Zeeland Deputies, unable to make any progress with their resolution of 7 August,[261] left the Hague in a thoroughly disgruntled mood.[262] Veth, their Grand Pensionary, had hoped to please the Stuarts with a long and learned oration in which he reminded the States of Holland of the benefits of having a Stadholder and a Captain-General.[263] Karel Roorda, a Frisan pro-States regent whose anti-Leicester forefather and namesake had been reviled by Veth, now wrote gleefully in an open letter[264] that all Veth's bowing and scraping had been in vain since neither he nor his province were apparently deemed fit for the 'honourable guardianship and supervision of the present Prince of Orange'. Wimmenum, whether at the suggestion of Mary or not, thought it advisable to offer his personal – and complete – submission to De Witt,[265] who had good reason to be satisfied, the more so as he could rely on the full support of the Princess Royal, 'avec sa prudence accoutumée',[266] as he himself put it (no doubt with his tongue in his cheek).

But could this idyllic state of affairs really last? As soon as relations with Charles II became slightly strained, the docility of the Princess Royal was likely to melt away. Nor had she so totally surrendered her son that she was unable to interfere with his education. Indeed, even before the attitude of the king had changed appreciably, she clashed with the Commission on their very first decision (8 December 1660).[267] Perhaps it made Holland's intention to turn the prince into a good Hollander more obvious than she liked to see. The decision was in two parts. First, the boy was to be moved from Leyden to the Hague, where he would be under the eyes of the States. Second, his governor Nassau-Zuylestein, was to be discharged, albeit most honourably. Zuylestein was completely under the sway by English ideas, and that was precisely why the

Princess Royal had chosen him,[268] and why she now raised such strong objections. As for the Commission, it thought it best 'to let things slide for a while'.[269]

Before they could re-examine the matter, however, the situation had completely changed. On 3 January 1660, Mary died of small-pox in London. She had felt no happier back in her own country, where her brother was restored to greatness, than she had been during the time of his humiliation and exile. Upon her arrival in England she had learned of the death of her youngest brother, Gloucester – another victim of the smallpox. Then her brother York, embittered her life by obstinately refusing to give up his unsuitable marriage to Anne Hyde, formerly one of Mary's ladies-in-waiting.[270] Mary was just thirty years of age when she died. On the last day of her life she had signed a will[271] in which she commended her son to the king and the queen, her mother. 'I entreat His Majesty most especially to be a protector and tutor to him and to his interests, by his royal favour and influence.' De Witt expressed his astonishment that she 'not only failed to appoint her only son as her sole heir, but had not bequeathed a single penny to him'. He added, somewhat testily, that she 'did not make the least mention of the States, not even of those of Holland, to whom, as supreme guardians, she had seen fit to entrust the child in her lifetime'.

REFERENCES

1. P. L. Muller, *B.V.G.*, II, VII, p. 140.
2. See Fruin, *V.G.*, IV, pp. 149 ff.
3. *Archives*, II, V, p. 6.
4. In 1654, the French Ambassador at The Hague wrote that the Loevestein party fear no one except her, 'et ce n'est pas sans raison'; *Archives*, II, V, p. 149.
5. *The Moderate Intelligencer*, quoted by G. Green, *op. cit.*, VI, p. 139.
6. In September 1647, i.e. after the death of her husband, Princess Amalia again expressed her indignation at the lack of respect shown to her by the Princess Royal; *Archives*, II, IV, p. 246.
7. 'The funeral of the Prince of Orange is to be Tuesday next, and the

King hath sent a letter to the Lord Percy, to represent his person in that sad solemnity; which is here by all knowing men thought very strange, it never being known that a Sovereign King did ever attend the corpse of any king that was not his father. But for H.M. to attend on the body of a petty Prince not of Royal Blood, is held a great diminution of Regality'; Carte, *Ormonde Papers*, I, p. 413.

8. The Princess of Hohenzollern was in possession of the marquisate of Bergen-op-Zoom.

9. *Kronijk H. G.*, XXV (1869), p. 557.

10. Carte, *Ormonde Papers*, II, p. 38.

11. *Kronijk H. G.* (1854), p. 500.

12. 'Evil people are intent on persuading her to drive out my wife and myself, and I am determined to prevent this'; Journael, p. 557 (*Kronijk H. G.*, 1869).

13. *Rawlinson Letters*, Bodleian Library, Oxford. Charles sent the required confirmation without delay. One of Heenvliet's chief supporters was Beverweert. On 21 January 1651, Charles sent the following message to Heenvliet from Scotland: 'I have (as you advised) written to Mons. Beverward, as kindly as I can, to thanke and encourage him in the way he is in, for my sister's service'; (*ibid.*).

14. Journael, p. 563. Heenvliet recorded this view as the Princess's own, but there is little doubt that he himself inspired it in the first instance.

15. Thus Charles II seemingly believed that William II's dignities would fall to his little son by hereditary right, and on 21 January 1651, he asked Heenvliet to inform him not only whom the child resembled, but also 'what care the States take for their younge Generall'; *Rawlinson Letters*.

16. Journael, *ibid.*

17. Cf. Dr. Worp's comments in Vol. V of his *Briefwisseling van Huygens*, Jorissen's introduction to the *Memoires de Constantin Huygens*, and also Jorissen's rather far-fetched *Amalia van Solms en Maria Stuart* in *Historische Bladen*.
We shall see that Amalia's reliance on Holland acted as a kind of counterpoise to the English tendencies within the party.

18. Sir Edward Nicholas, one of the leading English royalists, then resident in the Hague, explained that the old Princess's actions were mainly based on her hatred of Heenvliet: 'Chiefly, as I am told, out of a very great dislike to Monsr. Henfleet'; *Nicholas Papers*, I, p. 220. In 1654, Amalia herself gave a similar explanation to the French ambassador: *Archives*, II, V, p. 151; *Clarendon State Papers*, II, p. 234.

19. The Council of Amsterdam passed a resolution to that effect as early as December 1650: Wagenaar, *Amsterdam*, II, p. 572. See also C. G. Smit, *Bontemantel's notulen . . . 1670*, p. XII.

20. *B.M.H.G.*, 1914, pp. 117, 121.

21. See De Witt's *Deductie van de Staten van Holland* (1654); Knuttel, p. 7547.

22. For instance the affair mentioned on p. 52.

23. Aitzema, VII, p. 479.

24. *Brieven van De Witt* (W.H.G.), I, p. 3.

25. *B.M.H.G.*, 1924, p. 83.

26. Thurloe, secretary to the English embassy, wrote in 1661: 'The great interest of the United Provinces is trade . . . They make neither war nor peace, contract noe allyance, enter into noe leagues or associations, but as they can thereby promote this end'; *English Historical Review*, April 1906, 324 (from a paper on Anglo-Dutch relations, published by Professor Firth).

27. Aitzema, VII, p. 482.

28. Gardiner, *Commonwealth and Protectorate*, I, p. 323.

29. In October 1649, Strickland told Walter Frost of a conversation with a prominent Dutchman on the lines of '*faciamus eos in gentem unam*'. Strickland warned Frost (before the death of William II) to expect serious opposition. *Thurloe State Papers*, I, p. 130. Cf. Gempachi Mitsukuri, *Englisch-Niederländische Unionsbestrebungen im Zeitalter Cromwells* (1891), p. 38.

30. Cf. p. 62.

31. Cf. Aitzema, VII, p. 482. For corroboration by English royalist witnesses, see especially Carte's *Ormonde Papers*.

32. On 19 April, Sir E. Nicholas reported that they had fourteen wounded laid up: Carte, *Ormonde Papers*, I, p. 447.

33. Edward was a recent convert to Catholicism.

34. *Nicholas Papers*, I, p. 249.

35. *Brieven aan De Witt*, I, p. 17.

36. Sir Edward Nicholas makes many references to this argument: see Carte, *Ormonde Papers*. The Republican, Ludlow, too, wrote in his Memoirs, I, p. 345: 'The Dutch [were] unwilling to conclude with us whilst the king had an Army in the Field . . .'

37. *Brieven aan De Witt, ibid.*

38. Thus Dr Elias (*Het voorspel van den eersten Engelschen oorlog*, p. 127) is wrong to argue that 'the merciless exploitation of the difficulties with which, as they believed, the Commonwealth was beset' was 'the cause of the (English) war party gaining the day'. While I owe a great deal to Elias's exposition, his exclusive stress on the economic aspect makes it unacceptable in its entirety.

39. *Brieven van De Witt*, I, p. 20.

40. We lack more detailed reports about their activities: G. N. Clark, in 'The Navigation Act of 1651' (*History*, January, 1923, p. 285) has this to say: 'Unhappily the year 1651 is one of the worst-reported in our Parliamentary annuals, and we have no record of any debate or discussion on the Act (of Navigation)'. There is no reason to doubt Ludlow's testimony (Memoirs, I, p. 345) that St John, who was deeply offended by his treatment in the Hague, worked for the adoption of the Act. According to Clark, enthusiasm for the act was confined to a group in the City with special colonial interests.

41. Elias, *Voorspel*, I, p. 24. Elias cites a resolution by the Edam Council in support of the claim that when mobilization was ordered in the spring of 1652, it was directed against Sweden as well. On 22 November 1651, Sir Edward Nicholas wrote to Ormond from the Hague: 'These States are now hastening their Ambassadors for England, having great apprehensions that Mons Spring (the Queen of Swedes' agent here), who is preparing to go Ambassador into England, may there do or negotiate something in their prejudice, for it is conceived that the Queen sends to those in England about a treaty to join them against Denmark and Holland, concerning the taking the Sound out of the power of that king and these States, who having made a bargain for the profits thereof have lately raised the payments there'; Hist. Mss. Comm., *Ormond Mss.*, I, p. 230.

42. *Archives*, II, V, p. 63.

43. *Ibid.*, 73.

44. *Clarendon Papers*, III, p. 86; 9 August 1652.

45. *Archives*, II, V, p. 71.

46. Van Sypesteyn, *Geschiedkundige Bijdragen*, I, p. 204.

47. *Ibid.*, p. 191.

48. He was Justus de Huybert, a man who, on 12 June 1651, had wanted to go even further than De Witt, but who now became totally alienated from him: *Brieven aan De Witt*, I, pp. 55 ff.

49. At Middelburg, for instance, the town government shared its power with a college of twelve electors, who did not belong to the regent class.

50. Not that this support was invariably forthcoming. The Middelburg champions of William Frederick (Pieter de Huybert and Johan Mauregnault) did not really trust the old princess, who was in possession of the marquisate of Veere. In their vying for the favour of the Frisian Stadholder or of the princess, the various Zeeland groups made anything but an edifying spectacle. Cf. the letters of De Mauregnault and De Huybert appended to Van Sypesteyn, *op. cit.*

51. *Brieven aan De Witt*, I, p. 57.
52. *Brieven aan De Witt* (Scheurleer edition), V, pp. 11 ff.
53. *Ibid.*, V, p. 20.
54. Aitzema, VIII, p. 764.
55. *Archives*, II, V, p. 78.
56. See Gardiner's comments in *Commonwealth and Protectorate*, II, p. 219.
57. Who told the entire story to Van Beuningen; see *Brieven*, I, p. 72.
58. Aitzema mentions *Stad en Lande* (Groningen); Van der Capellen (*Gedenkschriften*, II, p. 394) refers to Friesland and Zeeland.
59. Van der Capellen, *op. cit.*
60. Aitzema, VII, p. 850.
61. Aitzema, VII, pp. 848, 850. De Huybert, too, used this argument in his letters to De Witt, *Brieven aan De Witt*, I, p. 52. See also such pamphlets as *Amsterdamsch Schutterspraatje* (September or October 1651), Knuttel, No. 7253.
62. The fact remains that even convinced supporters of the States party were sometimes carried away by violent anti-English feelings. See, for instance, *Ernstig gesprek*, Knuttel, 7256, which, while defending the Loevestein group against Orange slanders, nevertheless contains a violent attack on the treacherous policy that Strickland allegedly pursued throughout his long stay in the Netherlands.
63. Aitzema, VII, p. 871.
64. Aitzema, VII, p. 900.
65. Two such pamphlets (Knuttel, 7446, 7433) contained the following terms of abuse in quick succession: 'tails, rats, robbers, rascals, devils, pickpockets, floppybags, magpies'. An even more striking example of abuse is found in Knuttel 7251 (a poem!).
66. *Vervolg van het Rotterdamsch Zeepraatje*, p. 26; Kn. 7433.
67. Aitzema, VII, p. 879.
68. *Archives*, II, V, p. 101.
69. Aitzema, VII, p. 887.
70. Nicholas Papers, II, p. 24; to Hyde, 16 October 1653.
71. Aitzema, VII, p. 847.
72. Aitzema, VII, p. 874.
73. Eva Scott, *The King in Exile*, p. 377.
74. *Thurloe State Papers*, I, p. 331.
75. On 29 August 1652, Sir Edward wrote to Hyde: 'The factious party amongst the States . . . do not, will not, believe such a conjunction with the King of England will have any such influence in England as to break their naval forces'; *Nicholas Papers*, I, p. 307.
76. Hist. Mss. Comm., *Ormond Mss.*, I, p. 273.
77. See above, p. 76.

78. *Nicholas Papers*, I, p. 278.
79. *Clarendon Papers*, III, p. 98.
80. In September 1653, however, the king asked Sir Edward to assure the count 'that I have great kindnesse for him': Charles II to Sir Edward Nicholas, 28 September 1653; cf. *Evelyn's Diary*.
81. For the period under review, the Nicholas Papers contain no more than a chaotic (eighteenth century) summary of Sir Edward's letters; the originals are lost.
82. The Princess Royal's dislike of William Frederick has also been ascribed to the influence of Beverweert. Cf. Eva Scott.
83. Eva Scott, *op. cit.*, p. 363.
84. For instance, in September 1652, *Clarendon Papers*, III, p. 103; and again in December 1653, Eva Scott, *op. cit.*, p. 384.
85. Eva Scott, *op. cit.*, p. 369.
86. *Nicholas Papers*, I, p. 308.
87. 'He has as much of prejudice to those who sway there (in Holland) as you have': Hyde to Nicholas, 27 February 1653, *Clarendon Papers*, III, p. 145.
88. Eva Scott, *op. cit.*, p. 385.
89. According to Elias, *Vroedschap van Amsterdam*, I, p. 541, and Worp, *Briefwisseling van Huygens*, VI, p. 35, Johan Boreel was appointed intendant to the Princess Royal in 1652.
90. *Clarendon Papers*, III, p. 137.
91. *Ibid.*, p. 105.
92. Despite Boreel's insistence on discretion, the contacts could not remain hidden: Hyde to Browne, 31 July 1652: 'His Majestie is very much troubled that the ambassador should receive any praeiudice for his friendship to him . . . The king would have you assure the ambr. that he will be as carefull hereafter as he desyres.' From *Evelyn's Diary*.
93. Hyde's report of a letter from Aerssen to Charles II, December 1652.
94. Cf. Chéruel, *Histoire de France sous Mazarin*, I, pp. 64 and 178.
95. Eva Scott, *op. cit.*, p. 377.
96. Fears were even expressed by so staunch an Orangist as Van der Capellen: *Gedenkschriften*, II, p. 414.
97. *Nicholas Papers*, II, p. 1.
98. *Clarendon Papers*, III, p. 105.
99. *Archives*, II, V, p. 106.
100. *Clarendon Papers*, III, p. 145.
101. *Ibid.*, p. 177.
102. *Ibid.*, p. 141. The letter is wrongly dated 6 February 1653; it was sent on 6 March.
103. Eva Scott, *op. cit.*, p. 380.

104. Receipt of this letter was confirmed on 18 March.
105. See *Clarendon Papers*, III, p. 159.
106. *Brieven*, I, p. 95.
107. Thurloe State Papers, I, p. 314.
108. Wagenaar, *Vad. Hist.*, XII, p. 239.
109. *Brieven aan Witt*, I, p. 61.
110. *Hollandschen Ruyker*, Amsterdam 1653 (Kn. 7439), p. 8.
111. When the States of Holland were not in session, their powers were vested in the town authorities.
112. According to a contemporary witness (*Thurloe State Papers*, I, p. 324), only about half the population of Amsterdam supported the prince, so that the Amsterdam magistracy still enjoyed far greater popular support than did the authorities of most other towns in Holland.
113. See Wicquefort, *Histoire des Provinces Unies*, II, p. 216.
114. Wagenaar, *op. cit.*, XII, p. 292.
115. Aitzema, in *Thurloe*, I, p. 300.
116. Aitzema, VII, p. 909.
117. Aitzema, in *Thurloe*, I, pp. 315, 359.
118. *Brieven* (Scheurleer), V, p. 191.
119. Disparaging remarks about them can be found in *Clarendon State Papers*, III. Several letters by Massey and others (February to May 1653) are contained in Hist. Mss. Comm., *Ormond Mss.*, I.
120. 27 March 1653; Hist. Mss. Comm., *Ormond Mss.*, I, p. 275.
121. *Ibid.*
122. *Nicholas Papers*, II, p. 4.
123. On 24 April 1653, Massey wrote: 'I have spoken with Dr Sturmer, minister in the Hague (who is the king's faithful friend and servant) and with Junius of Amsterdam and other ministers well affected unto H.M. and the House of Orange, and understood their sense therein, and humbly beg of your Excellency you would employ your power and interest in H.M.'s favour to persuade him to shew himself more affected to religion and more to countenance the Reformed Churches.'
124. *Clarendon State Papers*, III, p. 55.
125. Princess Royal to Nicholas, 21 July 1653, from *Evelyn's Diary*.
126. *Clarendon State Papers*, III, p. 184; *Thurloe State Papers*, I, pp. 371, 381.
127. *Brieven van De Witt*, I, p. 55. When it suited her, however, the princess was not above giving the people an opportunity for anti-States manifestations, for instance, in August, when she exhibited her little son to the excited public after his inauguration as Baron of Breda. Wicquefort, II, p. 216.
128. On 14 August 1653; *Nicholas Papers*, II, p. 18.

129. De Witt to Van Beverning, 24 July 1653; *Brieven van De Witt*, I, 101.
130. *Briefwisseling van Huygens*, V. p. 179.
131. *Brieven aan De Witt*, I, p. 99. According to a French observer, the Orangist Zeeland regents were afraid of their own policy: Colenbrander, *Zeeoorlogen*, I, p. 73.
132. On 18 July 1653; *Brieven aan De Witt*, I, p. 82.
133. The first formal proposal to that effect was made on 31 July 1653: *Verbael gehouden door H. van Beverningk* (1725), p. 53.
134. *Thurloe*, I, p. 382 (8 August 1653, NS).
135. Preserved in English translation only.
136. *Brieven aan De Witt* (Scheurleer), V, p. 206.
137. According to Blok (*Geschiedenis*, III, 51), De Witt 'exerted himself to make the States give serious attention to the English demands'; this was not, in fact, the case.
138. *Clarendon State Papers*, III, pp. 208, 213, 220.
139. *Briefwisseling van Huygens*, V, p. 186.
140. Eva Scott, *op. cit.*, p. 477.
141. All this according to a draft treaty communicated to the envoys (unofficially) at the beginning of October: *Verbael....*, pp. 150 ff.
142. On this question the Orangists saw eye to eye with the Loevestein faction; political and theological considerations alike made them reluctant to accept the ruling party in England as brothers in the faith. Bowman, *The Protestant interest in Cromwell's foreign relations* (Heidelberg, 1900), p. 4, quotes an interesting passage from the *Nouvelles ordinaires de Londres*, 1/21-8/28 May 1653 (?): 'Les lettres de Paris du 23 disent que l'Ambassadeur de Hollande y résident avait dit en bon lieu qu'il étoit expédient, que la guerre entre les deux Républiques durât, peur d'une autre de Religion plus cruelle.'
143. See Geddes, *op. cit.*, 373, note 2. Geddes quotes from 'Ms. De Witt' and mentions a letter of 10 December to Brederode; – not in *Brieven aan De Witt*, W.H.G.
144. Aitzema, VII, 988.
145. On 10 December. Chanut was first received by the States-General in November: *Brieven van De Witt* (Scheurleer), V. 264.
146. *Brieven aan De Witt*, I, 84.
147. *Verbael...*, 200.
148. *Brieven van De Witt*, I, 116 (2 January 1654).
149. Aitzema, VIII, 66.
150. Chanut, after a conversation with De Witt, put it as follows: 'Leur raisonnement est cecy: la paix est très-nécessaire à cet Estat; certaine, s'ils traitent seuls; douteuse, s'ils y meslent nos intérests.' (*Archives*, II, V, 129).

151. See his correspondence with Chanut, *Archives*, II, V.

152. Geddes, *op. cit.*, 392 ff.

153. Japikse, *Johan de Witt*, 74. – In *Nicholas Papers*, II, 59, we can read that Beverning, who abstained from wine in England, made good the omission when he returned to Holland and, in his cups, confided to a friend that when the negotiations became stuck on Article 12, 'he and some powerful men with Cromwell fixed upon that expedient (the temperament)'. Cromwell informed Van Beverning that he himself would never have thought of the exclusion, if Van Beverning had not raised the point and had assured him that the States-General would agree to it. – This story is so improbable that it deserves no credit, the more so as it came from sources hostile to Beverning (Nicholas was quoting Sommelsdijk, who was certainly not among Beverning's confidants).

154. These enabled De Witt to prove that the original suggestion of the exclusion had come from Cromwell and not from himself. See *Brieven*, W.H.G.

155. *Deductie* (Knuttel, 7547), 3.

156. *Brieven aan De Witt*, I, 127.

157. At any rate, by January, Cromwell had agreed to accept the ratification of the exclusion by Holland alone (Bordeaux-Neufville, see Geddes, *op. cit.*, p. 389).

158. De Witt kept a confidential letter, in which Van Beverning expressed the hope that Cromwell might still change his mind, from even his closest associates (Geddes, *op. cit.*, p. 407).

159. Aitzema, VIII, p. 101.

160. *Ibid.*, p. 99.

161. *Brieven aan De Witt*, I, p. 153.

162. *Ibid.*, p. 161.

163. *Brieven aan De Witt* (Scheurleer), V, p. 342.

164. *Brieven aan De Witt*, I, p. 128.

165. *Archives*, II, V, p. 138.

166. *Ibid.*, p. 144.

167. *Ibid.*, p. 142. – 'Better late than never', as Hyde put it. (*Clarendon Papers*, III, p. 241).

168. *Archives*, II, V, pp. 138, 141, 145.

169. *Ibid.*, p. 144.

170. *Ibid.*, p. 146. ('*Sans* l'aversion des Hollandois' should no doubt be read as: *sous* or *dans*.)

171. *Archives*, II, V, p. 148.

172. Doubleth replied that he would sooner die than see this happen. Fruin, Uit het dagboek van een Oud-Hollander, *V.G.*, IV, 227.

173. *Archives*, II, V, p. 145.

174. *Ibid.*, 149. He continued: 'S'il n'arrive que les peuples deleurs

propres villes, persuadez d'ailleurs, s'élèvent contre eux et les destituent.'

175. *Archives*, II, V, 146. The following reference to William Frederick occurs in a letter by Chanut dated 21 May (*op. cit.* 149): 'Son intérest est différent du nostre; car il se figure aisément que l'assemblée de ces provinces estant une fois dissous (?), il en tomberoit pièces en son partage, et pour cela il n'appréhende point dutout ce démembrement qui nous fait horreur.'

176. Bordeaux-Neufville in Geddes, *op. cit.*, 385. Also in *Zeeoorlogen*, I, 78.

177. *Deductie van de Staten van Holland*, pp. 9 and 10.

178. A. W. Kroon, *Jan de Witt contra Oranje*, p. 92.

179. After reading it deep into the night, Gerard Schaep had this to say about De Witt's little book: 'The Lord God be praised that there is still so much vigour and upright Holland blood in the hearts of faithful and brave regents. Because by all this soft talk and toleration we have almost from free-born men become slaves, not only of our envious and ungrateful allies' (the other provinces) 'but even of alien and foreign women and children'; *Brieven aan De Witt*, I, p. 131.

180. In the States of Holland, only Edam declared 'that their honourable principals were of the opinion that the proposed Act was inconsistent with the liberty of the Province of Holland and felt that, in the circumstances, it was better to continue the war': *Brieven aan De Witt* (Scheurleer), V, p. 341.

181. Geddes, *op. cit.*, p. 389.

182. See the gloomy tone sounded by De Wilhelm as early as August 1654: *Briewisseling van Huygens*, V, 219.

183. *Archives*, II, V, p. 178.

184. *Ibid.*, p. 172.

185. See Eva Scott, *The King's Travels (1654–1660)*.

186. *Briefwisseling*, V, p, 114.

187. 'Young Princes think of nothing but pleasure'; Nicholas commented bitterly: Eva Scott, *op. cit.*, p. 108.

188. Macray, *Calendar of the Clarendon State Papers*, III (1876), p. 217. Four Memorials to Don Juan, of which the last two were presented by the Earl of Bristol on 22 December 1656. The second one read: 'Since France, Sweden and Cromwell are themselves united against Spain, and are endeavouring to draw the United Provinces into league with them, and the present rulers there, although sensible of their danger if Cromwell prevails, are so apprehensive of the restoration of the House of Orange to power that they consider nothing else, the king desires that the Spanish Ambr. at the Hague may not only press reasons on behalf of his own master, but

may likewise negotiate with leading men in the name of the King of Gr. Br., and represent the benefit that would accrue to their country and themselves from the joint protection of the two kings, and undertake that they shall receive no prejudice from the P. of O., but all possible advantage from a prince so obliged as it is in their power to oblige the King of Gr. Britain.'

189. The suggestion in the last footnote that the States were solely concerned with keeping the House of Orange at bay strikes me as being dictated by party bias. I stick to my view, expressed on p. 125, that, in the period under review, the Orange-Stuart connection had little influence on the foreign policy of either England or the Republic.

190. Clarke, *Life of James II*, I, p. 282.

191. Rawlinson Letters, Oxford.

192. *Ibid.*

193. Elisabeth of Bohemia to Charles II; *Thurloe State Papers*, I, p. 672.

194. *Nicholas Papers*, II, p. 66. The play was by Beaumont and Fletcher (1611).

195. *Clarendon Papers*, III, p. 174; 27 June 1653.

196. *Archives*, II, V, p. 169.

197. *Journal d'un voyage a Paris en 1657-1658*, publié par A. P. Faugère, 1862. The travellers were Orangists.

198. De Wilhelm to Huygens, *Briefwisseling*, V. p. 255.

199. Aitzema in *Thurloe State Papers*, V, p. 700; 22 December 1656. Renswoude, in his capacity of President (for the week) of the States-General, had obliged his new masters by appointing Van Beverning Treasurer of the Union, a position Holland had promised him as a reward for his services in England, but which the Orange provinces had managed to block.

200. 10 March 1656, Rawlinson Letters, Oxford.

201. The Princess Royal, who had lived in the Netherlands from her eleventh year onwards, conversed with the Dutch regents in French until the end. See, for instance, *Brieven van De Witt* II, pp. 241, 249. As we shall see below she even had difficulty in reading Dutch.

202. *Clarendon Papers*, III, pp. 267.

203. Rawlinson letters, Oxford.

204. *Thurloe State Papers*, II, p. 284.

205. *Ibid.*, V, p. 259, Aitzema, VIII, p. 643.

206. On 3 March 1656, she complained to Heenvliet about the Dowager Princess's attitude to Pauw (one of the proposed tutors). Her letter went on to say: 'Pour le Prince Guillaume (William Frederick), ie croye quills santandent fort bien, car ills ne sont que plein de fourberies'; Rawlinson Letters, Oxford.

207. 'Pour cela que vous me mandes touchant Mr Triglandius, ie l'approuvre, car ie croy comme vous dit (dites) qun ministre flamand plaira plus au peuple qun français'; to Heenvliet, from Paris, 18 Febr. 1656; Rawlinson Letters, Oxford.

208. *Ibid.*

209. The French ambassador described Zuylestein (born 1608, natural son of Fred. Henry) as pro-French, and alleged that Amalia was opposed to his appointment: *Archives*, II, V, p. 187. He also claimed that Zuylestein was dominated by his English wife: *ibid.*, p. 197. Her name was Mary Killigrew and she belonged to the Princess Royal's court. In Jan. 1662, Wicquefort wrote that the prince's governor 'l'élève tout a l'anglaise et selon la volonté du Roy d'Angleterre': *ibid.*, 216.

210. According to Jorissen, Fabius, *et al.*, she made half the income of the Orange family over to her brother; as far as I can judge this claim has no foundation and is simply taken from Green, *Lives of the Princesses*, etc., Vi, p. 211. The Orange fortune was already heavily encumbered by the extravagant expenditure of Frederick Henry and William II, and there was little left to make over. His sister made Charles a monthly allowance of 1,000 guilders, of which the younger brother, Gloucester, was to get half. From time to time, as we shall see, the princess did, however, make great efforts to raise larger sums for specific purposes.

211. *Thurloe*, I, p. 644: 'Besydes, you are so partially kind to him that I feare at last (? fear lest) my desiring your kindness to him wil turne to jealousie hee may take some from me; for I must assure you that I shall obay all your commands, except that of loving him (though he is my ownly child) above all things in this world, as long as you are in it.' (1655?). Fabius, *Leven van Willem III*, 40 takes quite a different view of the meaning of this passage.

212. Undated letters in *Thurloe*, I, p. 622 ff.

213. Clarke, *Life of James II*, I, p. 330.

214. On 31 Jan. 1658; Rawlinson Letters, Oxford.

215. 9 March 1658; *ibid.*

216. Lane to Nicholas, *Cal. St. P., Dom.*, 1657–8, pp. 349 ff.

217. *Thurloe State Papers*, VII, *passim.*

218. Eva Scott, *op. cit.*, p. 369. Her account is mainly based on unpublished letters in Clarendon Mss, Oxford. Macray's *Calendar* does not extend beyond 1657.

219. On 11 Oct. 1658; Rawlinson Letters, Oxford.

220. Eva Scott, *op. cit.*, p. 374.

221. Johanna Sernee, *Het geschil over het prinsdom Oranje, 1650–'60*, pp. 65 ff.

222. Princess Royal to Heenvliet on 29 June 1659: 'Je vous prie de dire

à M. le Pensionnaire leur arrivée icy comme à une personne que
m'a toujours témoignée tant de bonne volonté; que ie luy prie
quil me veuille faire sçavoir par vous si il croyt que l'arrivée de mes
frères icy pouroit en aucune fason desplaire a Mess. les Etats de
Holland, quand ie luy peut assurer que se ne sera que pour fort
peu de jours et que leur intention n'est pas seulement d'approcher
La Haye plus près quils sont à présent . . .' – And on 1 July: I see
from your letter that my brothers cannot stay here. 'Ils sont
résolue de partir dans deux jours, que i'espère empechera qu'on ne
prene des resolution contre eux.' Rawlinson Letters, Oxford.

223. October 1649: *Brieven aan De Witt*, II, p. 115.

224. Dolman; Brieven aan De Witt, I, p. 306.

225. Japikse, *Verwikkelingen tusschen de Republiek en Engeland van
1660–1665*.

226. See Japikse, *op. cit.*, p. 117.

227. In 1662, Turenne advised D'Estrades to kindle Dutch suspicions
against England by warning De Witt that an Orange restoration
was being planned by the English with a view to increasing their
influence in the Republic. *Recueil des Instructions, Hollande*, I, p.
247.

228. De Witt himself inserted this phrase in De la Court's *Het interest
van Holland*: see facsimile in Japikse, *Johan de Witt*, p. 200.

229. A fact that did not escape the regents of Holland; cf. footnote 179.

230. *Aenwyzing der gronden en maximen*, 1669, 334, 322, 420. See also
the following remark by Downing on 1 July 1661, quoted in Japikse,
op. cit., App. IXa: 'They have made a rule that they will prefer no
forreiner' (in the army) 'a thing never before done in this Country,
nor would now bee, but that they are lookt upon as more inclining
to the interest of the P. of O.'

231. Cf. *De Stadthouderlijke Regeeringe in Hollandt en West – Vrieslandt*
(anon. – the author was Uytenhage de Mist), p. 106.

232. Aitzema, IX, p. 863.

233. Japikse, *Verwikkelingen*, p. 10, note 1.

234. De Witt to Beverweert, *Brieven* (Scheurleer), IV, p. 9.

235. The Princess Royal believed the King had merely failed to exert
himself on the Prince's behalf, because his own position was not
yet strong enough. Journal of Buysero, Van Sypesteyn, *Geschiedkundige Bijdragen*, I, p. 224.

236. On 17 June, at the time of the Princess's visit to Amsterdam, the
French ambassador wrote: 'N'y ayant plus de doubte que le Prince
d'Orange rentre dans les charges de ses pères': *Archives*, II, V, p.
197.

237. Van Sypesteyn, *op. cit.*

238. *Brieven aan De Witt*, II, p. 242.

239. He pointed this out to the French ambassador; *Archives*, II, V, p. 205.
240. *Brieven aan De Witt* (Scheurleer), IV, p. 12.
241. She wrote on 20 August: 'I hear you are changed in your opinion concerning my son, which if it be true, and that you continue in it, I fear it will be our total ruin, in this conjuncture of time that our friends are so well disposed'; Green, VI, p. 307.
242. Aitzema, IX, p. 940.
243. Knoop, *Johan de Witt contra Oranje*, 108 (based on Amsterdam Council minutes).
244. Green, VI, p. 310.
245. *Ibid.*, p. 309.
246. Japikse, *op. cit.*, p. 28, note 5.
247. *Archives*, II, V, p. 200. Letter of 12 August 1660.
248. On 23 July 1660, De Witt informed Beverweert that he had warned the princess: 'qu'il n'est nullement à propos de presser et de forcer les inclinations de nos membres, si l'on veut éviter l'ombrage et la jalousie, principalement dans le temps que le Roy de la Grande Bretagne est restably dans son throne au plus haut degré; ce que j'appuyois par l'expérience de la jalousie qu'a donné le mariage de son Altesse Royale, au grand préjudice du feu Prince Henry de glorieuse mémoire'; *Brieven* (Scheurleer), IV, p. 8.
249. Green, VI, p. 309.
250. *Brieven*, II, 244. She spoke French with De Witt.
251. That, she informed Buysero, is what she intended to tell De Graeff; Van Sypesteyn, *op. cit.*, I, p. 237.
252. *Brieven aan De Witt*, II, 2.
253. Aitzema, IX, 966.
254. Letter to Van Beverweert; *Brieven* (Scheurleer), IV, p. 29 (in French). What made the bad impression even worse was the widespread belief that Sommeldijk had drawn up this document.
255. *Brieven aan De Witt*, II, p. 303.
256. Van Sypesteyn, *Geschiedkundige Bijdragen*, I, p. 137.
257. *Brieven van De Witt*, II, p. 250.
258. Japikse, *op. cit.*, App. VI. That reply had even been drawn up in consultation with De Witt: *ibid.*, 129.
259. *Brieven aan De Witt*, II, p. 252.
260. *Archives*, II, V, p. 203.
261. See p. 142.
262. *Archives*, II, V, p. 206. They expressed their displeasure in a letter to the Princess Royal; Aitzema, IX, p. 988.
263. 10 September; Aitzema, IX, pp. 943-63.
264. Printed (1664) in Aitzema, IX, p. 983.
265. De Witt writing to De Graeff that Wimmenum had promised to

apply 'all his ingenuity' to the conversion of other opposing members, added ironically: 'With which, as you are aware, the Lord God has abundantly blessed him'; *Brieven*, II, 243. Wimmenum had sufficient wit to realize which was the stronger party.

266. *Brieven*, II, p. 250.

267. Japikse, *op. cit.*, p. 132.

268. Cf. note 209.

269. Japikse, *op. cit.*, p. 133.

270. De Witt, who sympathized with the Princess Royal, could not understand how the King could have approved of that marriage; *Brieven*, II, p. 283.

271. Green, VI, p. 326.

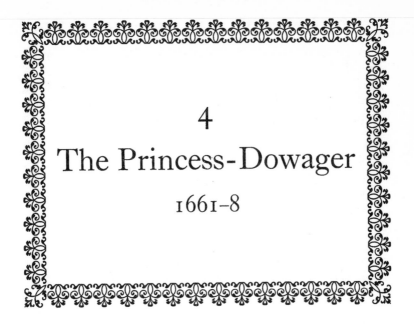

4
The Princess-Dowager
1661–8

Charles II tries to gain control of the Orange party

In fact, the death of the Princess Royal plunged the whole question of the prince's education into doubt once again. De Witt questioned her right to make over her guardian's share to her brother, the king.[1] As he saw it, once the education offer by the States of Holland had been accepted, they had become the boy's guardians-in-chief, and this they remained, even after the death of the Princess Royal. The king, the Dowager and the Elector were at best 'subsidiary' guardians.[2] It was a somewhat tenuous thesis and De Witt felt it should be presented to the king 'with the utmost moderation and with great discretion'.[3] Should the king refuse to agree, however, the States ought 'to wash their hands of the whole business and let the high-born pretenders fight it out among themselves'.[4] If the child's foreign relatives could not be persuaded 'to defer and entrust absolutely and unreservedly the personal education of His Highness and all that went with it to Their Noble Great Mightinesses',[5] so that the prince might grow up to become a loyal Hollander, then it was better to have nothing to do with the whole matter. But then, of course, the prince would also be debarred from any position in which his foreign ties and inclinations might prove harmful.

Since the 'subsidiary' guardians were unlikely to allow themselves to be reduced to mere puppets, De Witt decided to hoodwink Charles II, the more so as Oudart and Buysero – the first-named had been appointed executor to Mary – were prepared to support him in any course he might choose. The king would be asked to do little more than give formal consent to his sister's decision, a step that was in line with his in-born indolence and his known indifference to the affairs of his little nephew. And then there was the additional bait of the prince's annuity – in its absence, demands, on the prince's behalf, for repayment of moneys advanced to Charles II and to his father, would obviously become more pressing.[6]

De Witt did his utmost to consolidate his position by reaching agreement with Zeeland. Thus he told his colleague Veth[7] that, if Zeeland and the other provinces would waive all their claims to the guardianship, His Majesty could be more readily persuaded to leave everything to Holland.

And indeed, had all the provinces made common cause, the king would never have jeopardized his nephew's future by forfeiting the goodwill of Holland. Knowing this, De Witt tried to clinch the argument with Zeeland – the most likely candidate – with promises that Holland would not employ the political power of Orange (Veere and Flushing!) against her, and of other favours.

Nor was it necessary to send Charles himself away empty-handed. Could he not be fobbed off with the regency of the principality of Orange which – or rather the claim to which, for the principality was under French occupation – he had been so anxious to secure?[8] And could this promise not be used to drive a wedge between the king and the Elector? That the Elector and the old princess would oppose Holland's claim to the young prince was only to be expected. True, they had started out by being exceedingly amicable, thus succeeding in taking De Witt in for some time. However, it was not with friendly intentions towards him that, in the middle of March, they sent Maurice of Nassau (representing Amalia) and Weyman (representing the Elector) to England for discussions with Charles II.

Until then Beverweert's negotiations with Charles had been fairly satisfactory. On 21 January, the king had confirmed the agreement between his sister and Holland in an affable letter to the Education Commission.[9] The Commission replied with profuse thanks, but purposely omitted any phrase amounting to a recognition of the king in the capacity of guardian.[10] Meanwhile Beverweert continued exploring the ground, and his reports were not at all pessimistic. But before De Witt's plan was definitely made known in England, Holland began to act as if it had already been passed by all concerned. This became clear during an incident involving the famous iron chest.[11]

On 1 February 1661, the Education Commission persuaded the Court of Justice of Holland to seize the chest, until then preserved in the offices of His Highness's Council, on the grounds that the removal would safeguard the contents until the prince reached his majority. It was undeniably a high-handed step, and both the Elector and the Princess-Dowager protested against it. In England, fears were voiced that the Commission might open the chest simply to rake up the events of 1650, thus implicating and ruining a number of leading Orangists. However, when the assurance that the intention was rather the prevention of any tampering with the chest, was received by the king's principal minister and Chancellor, Sir Edward Hyde, now raised to the rank of Earl of Clarendon, he professed himself to be 'well-pleased'.[12] Unfortunately this mood was not to last. In March, the envoys of the Elector and Dowager arrived in England. Doubtless it was they who opened the king's eyes to Holland's true intentions. This they were able to do more readily in that the States of Holland, meeting on 9 March, ordered the chest transferred from the Court of Justice to their own record-office.

Only then did Charles realize what was going on – that Their Noble Great Mightinesses regarded themselves as Chief Guardians and hence did not deem it necessary to await the result of their negotiations with himself. His protests were loud and fierce. Clarendon told the States envoys that he had never seen the king so angry.[13] No longer could De Witt take advantage of his understanding with Oudart and Buysero – the king's wrath was concentrated on Oudart, who had got him to sign the letter of 21 January, and William Frederick and his supporters congratulated themselves that the false servants were being unmasked at last.[14] The entire past conduct of the States and of De Witt came under attack. Nothing at all had been done for the prince, nothing had come of the promises made to the king in the Hague. The Chancellor addressed the ambassadors in enraged, haughty and threatening tones.

In fact, there was more behind English irritation than displeasure at the guardianship settlement. In the months that had passed since his stay in Breda and the Hague, the relationship between Charles II and the States had undergone a great change. While the king's position was still uncertain, he had not dared to antagonize the States of Holland which, in their turn, hoped he might be willing to temper the rigid commercial policies initiated by the Republican régime. For the leading party in the Netherlands this had always been the crux of their attitude to England, and in order to obtain commercial concessions they were even willing to include in the terms of an alliance, vaguely mentioned in the Hague, the promise of support against possible internal enemies of the king. To that purpose, Beverweert had been sent to England with all speed, in the van of the party of negotiators. His colleagues, however, were very slow in following and it was not until November 1660 that Van Hoorn from Amsterdam, Van Goch from Zeeland, and Ripperda from Groningen, joined him in London. All were instructed to make the signing of a political alliance contingent upon a commercial treaty in which, as in the specious plan of some years ago, free competition would be fully guaranteed.

But even before their instructions had been finally confirmed, it had become clear that there would be very little free trade in practice. In September 1660 the Navigation Act had been renewed. However loosely it had been implemented, Dutch merchants had hated the Act with all their hearts and the renewal proved that the new ruler was not immune to the spirit of jealousy which animated the English merchants. The king might be anxious to keep on good terms with the Dutch but he was unable to make economic concessions. He might be trying to revoke the policy of the usurper but felt that people were comparing his own and finding them wanting far too often. The City in particular remembered how its special interests had been protected under the Commonwealth, and Charles felt that his honour would suffer if he now stood up less staunchly as a champion of England's trade and navigation. True, a moderate like Clarendon kept reminding him that he must step gingerly while his finances were still in so parlous a state but this counsel was brushed aside by those favouring a tough policy with Holland. They soon afterwards found a leader in the Duke of York; and men like Thurloe and Downing, who had acquired their political methods and economic views under Cromwell, proved his willing tools.

In these circumstances, the relationship between Charles II and the States was bound to be clouded. The king's plan for raising a sizeable loan in Holland met little encouragement from the Dutch, once they discovered that the Navigation Act had been resuscitated from the ashes. Before the year of 1660 was out, the talks in London had become far less friendly as England kept pressing home old grievances and claims. International relations, too, took a turn that acted as a damper on Anglo-Dutch friendship. Portugal turned to Charles II for help against Spain, which threatened to subdue her smaller neighbour now that the peace treaty of the Pyrenees had forced France to leave Portugal to her own fate. The Dutch-Portugese war was not yet over, so that Portugal's discomfiture would normally have been welcomed by the States, and quite particularly by the Dutch East India Company; but the fact was that Charles's marriage to Catherine of Braganza was throwing such Portuguese possessions as Bombay and Tangiers into England's lap and this was rather disquieting news for Amsterdam, who knew the English would use them for staging attacks on Dutch ships. For a time, it looked as if England would have to pay for these acquisitions with a war against Spain, but Louis XIV, just freed from Mazarin's tutelage, hinted to Charles II that he would be glad to see him come to the aid of Portugal. France's duel with Spain, in other words, was not yet over. And Spain did not dare to do anything about it.

At the same time Louis – and perhaps the two moves were connected – suggested to Charles that they should co-operate in challenging the presumption of the Dutch Republic. Simultaneously with their mission to London, the States had also sent an embassy to Paris. The change of government in England and the peace between France and Spain had created a new state of affairs in Europe in which the States were caught between the Kings of France and England, a position they did not relish in the least. To try for friendship with both, but if necessary to play off one against the other, was the obvious Dutch policy. And now Louis XIV was proposing to England that they prevent this game by keeping each other fully informed of the negotiations with the Dutch! This proposal never worked in practice, but it must have left the English government with the impression that they could take what steps they pleased in their dealings with the States.[15]

English anger at Holland's resolution of 9 March 1661, then, is not fully explained by the sudden realization that De Witt had attempted to obtain exclusive control over the young prince. But the discovery that the friendship of the States was not as sincere as had been hoped, inevitably made Charles II change his attitude to the guardianship problem, now that his somewhat sweeping attention had suddenly been focused on it anew. No longer did he feel it right to leave the child's future in De Witt's hands; far better to keep the young Orange under his own thumb, thus gaining a precious weapon if ever it came to an open break. These considerations determined the line he took with the envoys of the Elector and the Dowager. While the States of Holland, replying on 1 April 1661, to the English protests against their high-handed procedure, made it clear that they would wash their hands of the prince's education unless they were recognized as guardians-in-chief, the relatives concluded a new guardianship treaty over the head of the States.

It must be admitted that this treaty was a moderate document. The guardianship of Holland would not be brushed aside lightly – the House of Orange stood to gain too much from it, both politically and also economically. It was also understood that English influence must not appear too brazenly. Charles consented that the Princess-Dowager should exercise the guardianship on behalf of all the relatives. Not that he was prepared to trust her to the same extent as the Elector did – ever since the events of 1658, he had felt rather cool towards her.[16] But he realized that an attempt to gain direct political control of the House of Orange would make an exceedingly bad impression. Instead, the States of Holland were to be requested to appoint a new Education Commission which would include representatives from the Orange towns,[17] and be open to checks by the Princess-Dowager and deputies from the other provinces. In that way De Witt's party would no longer have a dominant say in the prince's education. The relatives further agreed to retain Zuylestein as the young prince's governor.[18]

The only question was now whether the States of Holland would agree to the new scheme. No one was, of course, in any doubt that De Witt would be against it. And, in fact, his attitude was quite unequivocal. In the absence of guarantees that the prince would be turned into a good Hollander, the States could not possibly promise him the eventual command of the army, and had best wash their hands of him altogether. De Witt had expressed this opinion more than once. The States themselves, undoubtedly under his guidance, had taken the same view in their resolution of 1 April. And yet when at last, in September, the new plan was proposed to the States by the prince's high-born relatives, it took them a long time to turn it down.

In the interim, the Orange party had become greatly emboldened under English encouragement, thus justifying all the States' worst fears with regard to them. In June 1661, Downing – Sir George Downing since the Restoration – re-appeared in the Hague as the king's ambassador. His instructions were, ostensibly to act as mediator in the peace negotiations between the Dutch Republic and Portugal. In point of fact, he did his utmost to obstruct the peace which he knew would bring the States considerable commercial advantages. More generally, he was to keep a watchful eye – this was Clarendon's clear intention – on De Witt and Van Beverning, in other words on the Holland States party, 'who play the devil at present'.[19] According to a separate instruction[20] he was to do his utmost to urge Holland to continue interesting herself in the prince's education, but on the conditions agreed upon by the relatives. In addition, he was to consult with the Princess Dowager and the Elector's ambassador as to what further demands might be pressed on the prince's behalf – to that purpose he was instructed, with the help of the princess and the ambassador, to foster the interests of the 'true friends' of the House of Orange, in other words to encourage and strengthen the Orange party.

Downing was a man of indomitable energy. It was this quality which, together with his knowledge of commerce, made him an esteemed servant of his government, albeit disliked for his rude, impudent, self-assured manners, and his shameless lack of principle, which had given offence even during the Restoration period.[21] Perhaps this last charge was unfair, for though it was true that he had served and betrayed Cromwell and the Commonwealth and now served the king with so much zeal that in 1662, for instance, he was instrumental in the abduction at Delft and transportation to

England of three regicides who ended up on the gallows – with the States looking on in dismay but inactively[22] – Downing was always consistent in his determination to champion the cause of England's commercial imperialists. Holland was their enemy, and hence Dutch trade must be cut down. Equal privileges, liberty – all that was so much nonsense from which only the Hollanders could derive benefit. Their connections, their experience, their formidable capital, made this quite inevitable. But England was superior in the political field, and Downing knew how to make full use of that. He loathed the Hollanders. Words of disapproval, of envy, of contempt, flowed from his pen whenever he wrote about them to his principals. From his instructions, he culled what pinpricks he could find, with ingenious zeal powered by his hatred of everything Dutch. He was known in the Hague as a quarreller, and all his diplomatic missions, under the 'usurper' (to use the word he himself used later on) as well as under the king, strained relations to breaking-point.

This was the man who immediately upon his arrival in the Hague reached a close understanding with the Orange party. Subsequent relationships of a similar kind between various French ambassadors and the States party have been seized upon by modern historians as being of greater importance. To some extent this is due to the passion with which William III, in 1684, denounced the secret relations between the Amsterdam burgomasters and d'Avaux, and to the publication of d'Avaux's damning *Négociations* in the eighteenth century. However, these relations were not nearly as criminal as the incensed Stadholder suggested, though they were bad enough in all truth. The name of d'Avaux became a synonym for foreign meddlers in Dutch policy, and *ces coquins d'Amsterdam* a term of general abuse. But long before d'Avaux, Downing had already found the way to the town councils and to the chambers of the opposition leaders, and the Orangists allowed themselves to be duped long before the Amsterdamers did and by one of the bitterest enemies the Dutch nation ever had.[23] 'To be duped' is putting it mildly. There were some who let themselves be bribed, among them Bottsma and Van Haren, two gentlemen from Friesland. Downing's connections with Bronckhorst, deputy for Gelderland, are also open to suspicion. And if no more deputies figured on the English pay-list, then, as the ambassador himself sadly remarked, it was due to no other cause than the English government's penury.[24] The small provinces, accustomed to *douceurs* by Frederick Henry and William, proved an easy prey to other paymasters. Nevertheless it would be wrong to take foreign bribery for the decisive factor of Orange success.[25]

Anglo-Orange co-operation was directed first of all towards promoting the interests of the Prince of Orange. Not that the English gave their help without ulterior motives even at that stage. As Downing expressed it: 'The king can have no firme friendship in this Countrey without the Prince of Orange and his restitution.'[26] Which can be freely, and yet faithfully rendered by: 'The present government in the Hague protests the national interests so force-fully, that it would be to our advantage to have it replaced by a more tractable one.' How right Downing was emerged soon afterwards, when the Orange party co-operated with Downing not only in calling for the elevation of the prince, but also in weakening De Witt's plain refusal to make further concessions, once the negotiations on the economic differences had broken down.

At first, as we saw, Downing concentrated all his efforts on the prince's elevation. To that end he enlisted the ardent support of Sommelsdijk, who contended that a satisfactory settlement of the education problem was not enough – unless the king made the signing of any treaty with the States of Holland ('a peace' as Down-ing put it) dependent on the prince's elevation, Charles's prestige with the Orange party would suffer, and the ruling party would be able to keep the prince under its thumb for good. Realizing that if this demand were presented prematurely, De Witt would wreck the negotiations on some pretext or other, Sommelsdijk proposed that negotiations be continued until the treaty was ready for signature, at which point the States would be faced with an ultimatum: the king would only sign if the States designate the prince for the offices of his ancestors. The people would never allow to have their trading interests vitiated by a refusal to yield on that one point.[27]

These were the tactics the Princess Royal had been advocating for a long time. The Dutch Orangists never appreciated – to the detriment of their position as it emerged soon afterwards – the humiliating aspect of this policy. They kept recalling the Act of Seclusion. If Cromwell had been able to impose his will, was it not a blemish on the king's honour if he could not now do likewise? And if the States had committed their injustice under compulsion, could not a little mild pressure be applied to force them to make amends?

Now that the two governments were getting on so badly, the Orange party was clearly in a good position to bargain with England. Downing was whole-heartedly in favour of supporting it with might and main. But in London, Clarendon, disabused of his great hopes in France, had begun to adopt a more moderate policy. He believed that 'a peace' with Holland should not now be endangered: a relaxation of the prevailing tensions was too badly needed for that. Moreover, Clarendon, unlike Sommelsdijk and the other Orangists, realized full well how Downing's policy would hurt the national susceptibilities of the Dutch people: 'I pray upon what grounds, in reason or policy, can the Kinge, in the renewinge a league with the States-Generall, demande that they should choose a Generall of his recommendačon? and what harangues would De Witt make upon that subiect, that the King of England will not make a peace with them excepte he may give them a Generall, Admirall, and Stateholder, who must alwayes remember to whom he owes the benefitt?'[28] Clarendon went on to remind Downing of the ambassador's own reports, according to which De Witt was even then inciting public opinion against the king by an appeal to national sentiment. And he concluded that efforts to promote measures on behalf of the Prince of Orange would only become feasible once the treaty had been signed and all suspicion on the part of the Dutch people were removed.

And in fact there is much evidence that public opinion was disturbed and that, more even than in the previous year, when relations with England were still good, the pro-Orange zeal of the English was damaging the prestige of the House and of the party. De Witt had warned Downing in so many words that 'foreign interposition' could only have an untoward effect.[29] When Buat, the prince's gentleman-in-waiting, called on Van Beverning after a visit to England, to tell him of the king's dissatisfaction, Van Beverning retorted that the king might be master in England but that he had no business to dictate to the States of Holland. Wicquefort, who communicated this incident to the French Secretary of State,[30] emphasized again and again that, now that the underlying commercial motives of England were becoming clear, even the people, as distinct from the more consistently republican regent class, were disinclined to allow England to foist a Stadholder on their country.[31]

Withdrawal of the education offer (30 September 1661)

Thus while the English government did not press for the prince's elevation, Downing, as we saw, kept meddling with the education problem. He had instructions to consult the Princess-Dowager and the Elector's ambassador on all questions touching upon the affairs of the House of Orange, but failed to get an active response from the ambassador – the Elector, less even than Clarendon – was not prepared to antagonize the Holland party. When Weyman's attempts to obtain concessions from De Witt proved abortive, he and Downing sought direct contact with the 'members' of Holland, visiting most towns in person and presenting his case to them.[32] In this they proved highly successful.

Even with the relatives' new demands, the education plan was obviously far less offensive to the Hollanders than the elevation, the more so as many of them were anxious not to fall out with England and Brandenburg over this question. The arguments of moderate and well-meaning men are exemplified by two letters to De Witt – one from his uncle De Graeff and one from Van Thilt, burgomaster of Haarlem.[33] Both show concern lest relations with England deteriorate. De Graeff thought that an estrangement was likely once Holland washed her hands of the prince's education. Van Thilt, a man who was thought to be of the Orange party in the Holland States, was nevertheless aware of what he called 'the covetous and unreasonable nature' of the English. For all that, he was anxious to keep on friendly terms with them, 'by all possible means, reasonable or questionable – even if it meant spending a notable sum of money'. De Graeff hoped that an agreement would prove possible by which 'His Highness may prove to be the link through which the alienation between us and the king may be prevented as much as is feasible'.

De Witt met these pious wishes with unruffled courtesy, but with cool deliberation. Clarendon's ill-tempered sallies to the Dutch envoys in March 1661,[34] had hurt both his personal honour and that of the state and he was disinclined to reply with further concessions. 'The States,' he wrote to De Graeff, 'are so offended by the rude treatment it has pleased the Lord Chancellor to mete out to meesieurs Van Beverning and Van Hoorn,' that anyone pressing them for an annuity to the prince was bound to make himself 'suspect and disagreeable'. He did, however, have lengthy discussions with his fellow deputies in the Education Commission on the claim that the prince might be instrumental in preventing the further alienation between Holland and England.[35] His conclusion was that the prince could only play that part provided that Holland was recognized as sole 'master' of his education. If, 'on the contrary', no regular intercourse and no regular supervision were possible; if the prince were 'inbued with foreign maxims and English pride'; then he was bound to 'provide constant cause for misunderstandings between the two nations'. It was therefore necessary in the prince's own interest as well as that of the country, to make a further attempt to obtain complete control of his education. If this proved impossible then 'it would be safer to leave the aforesaid education entirely in the hands of the guardians' (i.e. the relatives); the alternative was that the States, as educators in name only but without power to effect the prince's education in any way, would be responsible for a poor education and, moreover, be forced to agree to raise the prince to a position which, 'His Highness having been badly educated and in affection estranged from this state, might for this same state turn out to be most harmful, or even ruinous'.

The education Commission was in full agreement with De Witt, and so was the *ad hoc* committee appointed by the States to examine the matter. And yet, according to Downing, who was possibly anxious to give an exaggerated view of his own influence, the initial resistance of nine towns had to be overcome[36] before a resolution on the lines of De Witt's proposal could be passed. The opposition was led by Haarlem, and Enkhuizen framed the most violent protests. These went unheeded, and when the resolution was finally passed on 30 September 1661, it explained that the States, although firmly convinced of their right to act as guardians-in-chief, thought it inadvisable to enter into a discussion with the 'high-born personages', the prince's relatives, on that point, and therefore renounced their right and annulled all previous resolutions on the subject of the prince's education.

Holland had thus divested herself of all responsibility for the young prince. The 'highborn personages' had pitched their claims too high, with the result that they now went away empty-handed.

Their demand 'that Holland should come to the prince's aid and support him in his debts and maintenance and yet be given no special authority over his education' – that, according to Aitzema was 'wanting your hair smooth and curly at the same time'.[37] The old princess and her advisers had misjudged the situation – they had hoped 'by England's great authority to have their own way completely, but it had the contrary effect'.[38]

While these arguments had been proceeding, the prince's education itself had hardly even begun. The members of the Commission had paid the prince no more than fleeting visits in Leyden, and these could have had little influence on the development of his mind and personality. Now he came wholly under the thumb of his grandmother, and his future was more uncertain than ever. The States of Holland had made it clear that they regarded him as a private person and that, since he was now so obviously tied to his uncle the King of England, they were determined to block his progress to his forefathers' high office.

The French alliance (March 1662); the Orange party looks to England

The education episode had done much to undermine the prestige the English government enjoyed in the Republic; public opinion at large was incensed, and even Amalia and her most devoted servants spoke bitterly of the high pretensions of the English nation and of the covetousness of the clique who had passed from the service of the Princess Royal into that of the king.[39] Yet the Orange party seemed more than ever dependent upon English support. Of their other possible allies, Brandenburg was far too cautious to become too deeply involved. Worse still, the old link between Orange and France, which had survived Mazarin's approaches to Cromwell, now came to a sudden end. Factors on both sides contributed to this débâcle.

William Frederick, the heir to William II's pro-French tradition, had been losing influence ever since 1655. He had been forced to submit to De Witt and now lived in hopes of one day being appointed a Field-Marshal. Amalia of Solms had never been as pro-French as the Princess Royal, who had been influenced by her mother. Ever since Amalia, some fifteen years earlier, had been won over to the peace of Münster by Spanish promises of estates in the southern Netherlands, the French had ceased to trust her, and the possession of those estates and her unsatisfied claims kept her dependent on Spain. In addition, she greatly resented the French occupation of the principality of Orange. Huygens, who had been sent to Paris in 1661 to plead on behalf of the young prince, was highly indignant about the reception he was given. 'Revelling in their prosperity,' he reported, 'they are self-satisfied and proud beyond measure, so that in the matter of our authority in Orange I have had to swallow a lot of talk and arrogant conclusions that I should never have allowed to go unanswered in the Hague.'[40] The Dowager herself was so hurt by the tone adopted by Paris that she gave Huygens express orders not to besmirch the honour of the House by any 'soumissions et souplesses'.[41] But no matter what the envoy did, his mission was doomed to failure. It was a first sample of the new spirit reigning in the France of Louis XIV.

True, when he chose to do so, the great king could be accommodating enough. But French policy no longer saw any advantages in an alliance with the House of Orange. Hence Clarendon's hopes that Louis would help to influence the States in favour of the Prince of Orange were sorely disappointed. The French, like the States themselves, were afraid that, if the Orange party ever came to political power in the Republic, it would inevitably look to England rather than to France, not only on account of family relations[42] but also because of the French occupation of the Orange principality. Nobody knew better than Louis XIV that the principality would never willingly be restored. General political considerations, too, persuaded French statesmen to prefer friendship with the Netherlands to friendship with England, and whoever wanted friendship with the Dutch Republic could not do without De Witt. Yet the French proposal to England in March 1661 jointly to put the Holland States party in its place, shows that the French were still vacillating. It also shows how dangerous the situation was for the Republic, and how greatly it was in the Dutch interest to draw France away from England. Had Clarendon been assured of French support, he would surely not have gone to such great lengths to restrain his war party. But Louis was thinking of other matters. These, too, would have dangerous consequences for the Republic, but for the time being the French king was anxious to keep the peace.

What he wished above all was to conclude the work interrupted in 1659 by the peace of the Pyrenees, and which he had taken one step further by his marriage: the disintegration of the Spanish empire and the occupation of the Spanish Netherlands. He was well aware of the disquiet these plans were causing in the northern Netherlands, and that, in the long run, they were bound to meet with English resistance as well. For the moment, however, De Witt posed a greater threat than Charles II. The Spaniards were making great overtures to the Hague in the hope of obtaining an alliance for the protection of the Southern Netherlands.[43] Their feelings for Charles II, on the other hand, were damped by his Portuguese marriage. Charles's financial embarrassment, moreover, was such that he had been forced to sell Cromwell's most glorious conquest, Dunkirk, to France. In the circumstances, Louis XIV felt free to make considerable concessions to De Witt. And if by siding with the Grand Pensionary he could at the same time rid the Republic of all English influence, so much the better!

What delayed the negotiations in Paris most of all was the emergence of a new current in the French policy towards the Dutch Republic. The traditional view that friendship with the Republic was a counterpoise to Spain was gradually crumbling before Colbert's belief that Dutch trading predominance posed by far the greatest threat to France. In this Colbert was at one with Downing. To Colbert, the most important thing was to develop France into a great commercial and colonial power and, as far as he was concerned, this meant breaking the Dutch monopoly. With his tariff on foreign merchandise and his *Compagnie du Nord*, he started the series of aggressive tactics that the Dutch negotiators were desperately anxious to see revoked. In this they had only little success (the tariff was slightly reduced). In the end, the two countries found common ground all the same because, for France, political considerations (the isolation of Spain) still predominated over economic ambitions and because, for the Republic, English commercial imperialism still seemed the more dangerous of the two threats. Hence it came about that, in March 1662, Louis, in spite of English pressure, conceded the demand of the States that the Franco-Dutch treaty would not only guarantee the territorial integrity of both contracting parties, but also the Dutch right to fish off the British coast. The alliance built on these foundations appeared to ensure the safety of the ruling party in the Republic as well as of the Republic itself.

The political *rapprochement* did not, however, put an end to economic antagonism, and this became more acute as Colbert succeeded in getting a firmer, though never a dominant, grip on French policy. As for Louis xiv himself, his main interest in the treaty of 1662 was to fasten the Republic down against the day when the Spanish inheritance was due to be shared out. In view of the poor state of health of Philip iv and that of his sickly little son, this might happen at any moment. In that case, what was to become of the southern Netherlands? Even a man like Sommelsdijk, whose main complaint had been France's contemptuous treatment of the House of Orange, now began to realize that the country as well as the House was in danger.[44] De Witt, leader of the party which had warned against this threat even in the days of Frederick Henry and William ii, was certainly not blind to it now. But European relations being what they were, it seemed impossible to avert the threat by direct action. No steps against France were to be expected from Charles ii. The offers from Spain may sound tempting today, but De Witt knew well enough that Spain had little power or energy when it came to fulfilling her promises. Hence he looked to his alliance with France as a means of persuading Louis, in an amicable way, to drop his claims to at least part of the southern Netherlands. If the king proved intractable, it was time enough to bring other pressures to bear on him.

Meanwhile the troubled relations with England were a further incentive for keeping on good terms with France. In retrospect, in the full knowledge that the political menace from France would soon afterwards overshadow everything else, one is tempted to condemn those Dutch politicians who pooh-poohed the French threat and concentrated on the economic threat from England. Louis xiv was the last man to let himself be turned from his purpose 'in an amicable way'. He was prepared to encourage De Witt's hope that France would support the small Republic in her struggle with England, only to take advantage of the weakness of De Witt's position *vis-à-vis* Charles when the time came. De Witt proved to be the loser in the end.

But this was due to the cards fate dealt out to him, rather than to lack of political sagacity or skill. De Witt found himself between the Scylla of France's dynamic territorial expansion and the Charybdis of England's commercial rivalry. At critical moments, the political threat of France (with a strong admixture of economic pressure under the influence of Colbert) would invariably over-shadow the economic threat of England. Not that commercial quarrels with England did not impinge upon vital interests of the Dutch state, which tried with might and main to protect its econ-omic predominance, or even to expand it wherever possible (for instance in India). And in the early sixties, circumstances conspired to encourage them in the attempt, doomed though it was to failure.

Louis XIV was outwardly complaisant and concealed his true intentions. England, on the other hand, demanded a price for her friendship that no country with any claims to dignity and strength could afford to pay. The negotiations which opened in London at the end of 1660, made it perfectly clear how badly disposed the English were to Dutch commercial interests.

We saw that all hopes of entering into a possible alliance evapor-ated during the first few months of these negotiations. The English lodged so many objections and claims that the discussions began to look more like peace negotiations, and did, in fact, continue with a changed objective: a treaty for the settlement of controversial issues. De Witt had no wish to make difficulties for England. On the contrary, he was the spokesman of the party that had tradition-ally advocated good relations with England, no matter who was in the saddle there. He was most anxious to have the various conflicts resolved and was prepared to make any concessions for the sake of peace. But he could not consent to anything resembling a com-plete abdication. There might be those in the Republic who recom-mended the elevation of the prince as a cheap way of winning England's favour. De Witt knew better than the fainthearted that the elevation as such was not what the king was really after: he merely desired it because he thought his nephew might prove a useful instrument in vitiating the hated commercial policy of Holland. But the attitude of the Orange party towards the negotia-tions could not but confirm the Grand Pensionary and his friends in their conviction that such were, indeed, Charles's plans.

Hence De Witt welcomed the French alliance of March 1662 as a release from the necessity to bend over backwards in his dealings with England. He had no fears of a head-on clash. He was right in trusting that Clarendon, however exigent and intractable his agents might be, would, for the time being at least, shrink from war, and that some show of inflexibility would not come amiss in the negotiations.

Yet here he was constantly hampered by members of the States of Holland or the Generality who kept hinting to the English that they were prepared to make further concessions and would never allow the situation to get out of hand. De Witt's predicament was that of every Dutch leader, be he Stadholder or Grand Pensionary, for such was the Dutch constitution. In January 1662 Amsterdam, behind De Witt's back, gave assurances to the English government that she was prepared to concede one of the disputed points – the demand that even claims not previously raised should be submitted to arbitration.[45] Though Amsterdam soon afterwards recanted, she never owned up to her lapse in the States of Holland.[46]

Much more serious was the obstruction of the Orange party. In August 1662, Downing wrote impatiently that all the trouble was being caused by the adversaries of the Prince of Orange; his supporters were quite ready to meet most of the king's wishes, although they would not be sorry if it came to war, since war would certainly lead to the 'inclusion' of the prince.[47] This view is corroborated by many other sources. Sommelsdijk, for instance, who kept up his confidential contacts with the English ambassador,[48] looked at matters in much the same light. He informed Huygens with unmistakable satisfaction that the negotiations with France were likely to founder on the question of the fishing rights, with the result that the States would have to climb down, *'lequel asseurément donne beau jour pour faire valoir à mesme temps les intérests de Monsr le Prince.'*[49] In the States-General, Friesland and Groningen opposed the stand of the Dutch negotiators,[50] and in this they enjoyed the support of Gelderland and Overijsel. In short, the hand of Downing made itself felt everywhere. Van Haren, a man who took English bribes, was exerting pressure on Friesland, and promised to use his influence on Van Renswoude of Utrecht. In Gelderland, Downing worked through Bronckhorst; in Overijsel he had yet another accomplice.[51]

In time, the negotiations began to hinge on the fate of the *Bona Esperanza* and the *Bon Adventure*, two ships that had been seized by Holland thirteen years earlier. While Holland contended that the matter had been solved by the treaty, England argued that, since the fate of the ships had been the subject of a law-suit, the law ought to take its course despite the treaty. De Witt warned that, if the English had their way, a precedent would be set for a host of 'similar frivolous claims', but his suggestion that the

English should be brought to heel by the threat of a recall of the ambassadors[52] was opposed by the pro-Orange provinces. By dint of great effort, De Witt nevertheless succeeded, in August, in getting the States-General to agree that his tactics should be tried after all. His majority was slender in the extreme – Holland and Zeeland were his only consistent supporters. The deputies of Overijsel and Utrecht abstained; the Groningen deputy voted with Holland, although his instruction did not really permit him to do so. Feelings ran high. De Witt produced private letters from Van Hoorn, one of the ambassadors in England, who had warned him that giving way would only open the door for new chicanery on the part of the English government.[53] But, as Downing reported,[54] the inland provinces exclaimed: 'Whate dothe this businesse concern us, we will not fall out with the king for two ships.' And Jongestall of Freeze, who, in 1654 was one of the ambassadors in England (the other was Beverning) 'tould some of the principall of them of Holland this weeke that they looke what they do, for that if a breache should happen they must not onely not expect any assistance from them but the contrary'. This kind of language served both to undermine the determination of the Dutch government and to encourage English intransigence.

It should be noticed that while the inland provinces now felt that they were not sufficiently interested in ships to go to war, they had thought the question of ships sufficient grounds for hostilities in the days of William II. Clearly, they were motivated by party feelings in both cases.

To make things worse, the unanimity of Holland, too, became shaken. Once the decisive resolution had been passed by the States-General, Haarlem and Enkhuizen insisted that an extraordinary meeting of the States of Holland should be called in order to reconsider the whole question; they were afraid that war might ensue once the negotiations were broken off. Van Thilt, one of the Haarlem burgomasters, wrote to De Witt that 'misunderstandings' with England ought to be avoided, the more so as they would once again bring into the open 'the weaknesses residing in our Republic'. And, in fact, the States of Holland were reluctant to take things to extreme lengths. The ambassadors in England were authorized to make one further concession – which completely undermined De Witt's position. The question of the two ships remained unsolved and although a new treaty was now concluded (September 1662, ratified January 1663), the fate of the *Bona Esperanza* and the *Bon Adventure* was one of the chief issues that led to the outbreak of war two years later.[55] And, when all is said and done, it was Downing's intrigues with the Orange party that had made it impossible to reach a final settlement.

Under Downing's vigorous and unscrupulous guidance, the Orange party had won a great tactical success, and this despite the fact that, as we saw, the party's connection with England had greatly weakened its influence in the Netherlands at large.

It will be remembered that Clarendon had refused to agree to Sommelsdijk's suggestion that the signing of the treaty be made dependent on the elevation of the prince. Instead, Clarendon favoured the idea of launching a surprise attack on De Witt once the treaty had been ratified. De Witt, he believed, could then be beaten with the old stick of the Act of Seclusion, or rather with the proof that it was he who had first suggested the exclusion of Orange to Cromwell. When such proof could not be adduced,[56] Downing for one, was not dismayed for, as he wrote, all that mattered was that 'as much dirt as can must bee thrown on De Witt'.[57]

At Cleves, in the autumn of 1661, after Holland's decision to wash her hands of the prince's education, the Elector, the Dowager, and Downing as representative of Charles II, reached agreement to petition the States for the elevation of the prince as soon as the Anglo-Dutch negotiations had been concluded. The petition was to be accompanied by a sharp reminder about the Act of Seclusion and a vague allusion to the manner in which it had been brought about. Downing thought this was putting the cart before the horse. The mere fact that the treaty had been signed greatly strengthened De Witt's position – just as in 1654, when Cromwell had obtained the seclusion, or at least a binding promise of it. Now there was the further complication that the Elector had lost interest in the whole affair, that France had concluded an alliance with the States, and that the popular commotion, which had caused so much concern to De Witt in 1660, had subsided. Moreover, Zeeland had drawn closer to Holland, and the old princess was uncertain whether she should side with Charles II or with Holland.

In these circumstances, the English were reluctant to insist on Dutch acceptance of the Cleves demands. The Dowager's hesitations[58] were well known to them and suspicions of her intentions intensified their unwillingness to plunge into wild adventures on behalf of the young Prince of Orange. English reluctance contributed to the final disintegration of the Orange party, and decided the old princess to place all her hopes in Holland. England gave her no support even on the question of the principality, and all requests for repayment of the family's accumulated financial claims – the dowry of the Princess Royal, the advances to the Stuarts by Frederick Henry, William II and his widow – fell on deaf ears.

The Princess-Dowager turns to Holland (17 March 1663)

In the Republic's political battles, Zeeland had always played a part of crucial importance. This was chiefly because the province had only a very small number of 'members' – six towns, of which two were permanently subject to Orange influence, as was the seventh member, the First Noble – and that majorities could therefore be easily upset.[59] Veth, the Grand Pensionary, did his best in 1660 to gain the support of what he thought was then the leading party, and his calculations went astray. Moreover, economic questions, which invariably tended to make Zeeland side with Holland against England, had come to the fore once again, with the result that the two provinces, and their Grand Pensionaries, had joined forces. Holland used the old dispute about the respective powers of the two provinces over their common courts of justice and other outstanding questions, to get Zeeland's support on the question of the Prince of Orange.

As early as February 1662, Downing had reported 'a plot' by Holland to get Zeeland to agree to a new Act of Seclusion. Great promises have been made to the Zeelanders, he wrote, but 'God be thanked, I got to know betimes of this combination . . . and the States of Zeeland have broken up without having taken any decision'.[60] Downing, as Sommelsdijk explained, was a good deal more zealous in this matter than the Princess-Dowager, who needed a great deal of urging before she wrote to Zeeland (she showed a draft of her letter to Downing).[61] An agreement had meanwhile been drawn up between De Witt and Veth, but Veere and Flushing were still opposing its adoption. Thibaut of Middelburg, on the other hand, who had always been regarded as an Orangist, now supported the agreement with Holland,[62] and the Dowager, too, did not oppose it too vigorously. In September 1662 at about the time that the negotiations between the States-General and England were nearing their conclusion and talks between Zeeland and Holland were being resumed, Downing hinted that the Princess Dowager had obviously decided to postpone her visit to the Hague until such time as the town Pensionaries had settled their differences.[63] Apparently she was afraid to take sides openly, but the English had begun to feel that she was slipping out of their grasp.

In that atmosphere even the deputies of Veere and Flushing gave in. True, on returning home from the Hague, they were disowned by their councils, and the two towns blocked the ratification of the agreement in the States of Zeeland. While it is impossible to retrace all the tortuous paths of the old princess's policy, there seems little doubt but that she supported the council's action. Thibaut, the burgomaster of Middelburg, at any rate, wrote to De Witt scornfully about the timidity of vassal towns that allowed themselves to be swayed by 'a woman's passion'.[64] It took months before the States of Zeeland at last decided to ignore the protests of Veere and Flushing and to ratify the agreement. Even then, Holland had first to drop the import duty on salt, to which the Zeeland salt refiners objected, before the documents were finally sealed and delivered in December, two months after Veth's death.[65] The Grand Pensionary's successor, Pieter de Huybert, a zealous Orangist, was probably chosen in an endeavour to assert Zeeland's independence of her powerful sister province.

The agreement itself, however, marked a great success for Holland. It laid down[66] that, in the matter of the appointment of a Stadholder or a Captain-General, the two provinces would act in consort and after mutual consultation, and that the question of the appointment or designation was in any case not to be raised before the prince had attained the age of eighteen years. It was, moreover, expressly laid down that any decision by the States-General on the Captain-Generalship would have to be unanimous. This gave Holland a respite until November 1668, provided, of course, that Zeeland stuck to its bargain. But even if she did not, Holland was in a much stronger position now. For even while the Princess-Dowager was still tacitly encouraging resistance by Veere and Flushing, she had ceased giving support to the Orange party. Early in 1662, Sommelsdijk had already objected to her 'hesitation'.

In July, she began openly to side with the States party, when she presented the States of Holland with a long memorandum in which she asked them to implement their resolution of September 1660 regarding the prince's education.[67] Her request was bound to fall on deaf ears since, arguing that she, the grandmother, should not be totally excluded from the guardianship, she did not offer Holland the absolute control over the prince's education that De Witt had always considered so indispensable. Still, the memorandum paved the way for a compromise, which was not, however, defined in any detail. Even so, the very emphasis with which the States were assured that it had never been the intention of the 'high-born personages' to exclude them proved that the princess was beginning to change her mind. De Witt had no doubt but that once embarked on this path, she would continue along it. The reply to the memorandum was delayed, and De Witt, in a conversation with Downing, let fall the remark that the Dowager was sure to see sense in the end.[68]

And indeed, after the conclusion of the Anglo-Dutch treaty, when the English government appeared both unable and unwilling to champion the prince's cause before the States, the Princess-Dowager came round completely. Early in 1663, she sent Milet to England to inform Charles that the only way of ensuring that the prince would ever enjoy the dignities of his ancestors, was to accept De Witt's conditions. The king laid the matter before his council and, on its advice, replied with an unconditional *fiat*. It was a sad admission of English impotence. In September 1661, the States of Holland had, according to Downing, as good as declared: 'Take your child, and doe what yee will with him.' Now the uncle proclaimed that he was able to look after the child no better than the grandmother.[69] The position of their 'Noble Great Nightinesses' must indeed have seemed unassailable in those days!

And so on 17 March 1663, when the Princess Dowager addressed a formal request to the States of Holland to take charge of the prince's education, she added:[70] 'We shall conform to everything Your Great Mightinesses will think serviceable and fitting for the above-mentioned prince.' She only permitted herself the remark that she was willing to be consulted, and the king, in a letter supporting her request, put the matter a little more strongly. Oddly enough, it was at this very time that the Princess-Dowager incited Veere and Flushing to obstruct the pact between Holland and Zeeland, thus antagonizing the States of Holland. At any rate, when their answer came on 27 April, it amounted to a polite refusal.

'*La considération du passé, la constitution de notre corps et plusieurs réflexions importances*' – these were some of the rather strange explanations with which they justified their decision.

Apart from these documents, which were intended for publication, we know very little about the deliberations in the States or about the talks they must have had with the guardians. D'Estrades tells us[71] that, before the Princess-Dowager made her public request, she sent a certain Friquet to sound out De Witt. Friquet met with an exceedingly cool reception. D'Estrades himself tried to convince De Witt that it would be wiser not to reject the offer outright, but to make conditions that would place the prince completely in the power of the States. Did De Witt dismiss this plan as impracticable? His papers include the draft of a letter to Clarendon[72] in which he assured the chancellor that he had not failed to draw the attention of the States his masters, to '*l'affection dont S.M.* . . . *continue d'honorer ceux qui sont encore de la main de la feue Princess Royale, son soeur, auprès de la personne de M. le Prince d'Orange, son fils*'. The irony was barely concealed. That the king gave renewed evidence of his affection for these gentlemen could only mean that he intended to prevent their removal from the prince's entourage once the States had agreed to resume the guardianship. And if there was anything to strengthen the States' objection to the guardianship, it was the setting of precisely such limitations to their powers.

However, all this is merely surmise on my part. For despite the declarations of 1660 and 1661, the States refusal may well have been based mainly, and perhaps even exclusively, on rigid republican sentiments. After all, things *had* changed during the last few years. The position of the States had grown much stronger, that of the Orange party much weaker.

True, being familiar with the final outcome, we can detect other factors at work as well. There was, for instance, the growing opposition to the policy of the States by the ministers of religion. In spite of all the pains the Great Assembly took to assure them of their orthodoxy, relations with the clergy had never been very cordial. We saw how the ministers, despite their strong disapproval of the manner in which life at court was being conducted, grieved for William II and did not forget William III. As the young prince grew to manhood, their devotion to the illustrious House quite naturally became an increasingly important element in political life. The Restoration in England further enhanced this trend. It became customary in clerical circles to glorify Charles II as the leader of Reformed Christendom, much as Elizabeth, James I and even Charles I had been revered before him.[73] The expulsion in 1662, from the Church of England of 1,200 Presbyterian ministers, a clear breach of the promises made at Breda, did a greal deal to dampen Dutch ardour for the English crown, but the growing conflict between the Reformed Church and secular authority helped to keep its flame alive. At Utrecht, after a bitter quarrel over the disposal of ecclesiastical possessions, in which Voetius played a prominent part, two ministers were expelled from the town and province. One of them, Teellinck, was offered a living in Zeeland. The States of Holland, on the other hand, sided quite openly with the Utrecht magistracy, thus increasing the bitterness of the orthodox faction and strengthening their determination to resist all meddling and supervision by 'political commissars'. Just before the rejection by the States of the Dowager's latest request, the ministers had been given an instruction that increased the tension even further: they were told, in public prayers, to mention their Noble Great Mightinesses (the States of Holland), before Their High Mightinesses (the House of Orange), and the Prince of Orange not at all. This emphasis of provincial sovereignty and the implied principle of secular authority over the church, together with the slight to the House of Orange, caused a storm of indignation in the States of the other provinces, and among the commonalty as well.[74]

The States of Holland preserved their equanimity in the face of all these protests. They were obviously convinced that it was no longer necessary to take the slightest interest in the fate of the young prince, and were hopeful that their policy of exclusion could be prolonged indefinitely. This was both presumptuous and short-sighted, but then such is the general behaviour of political parties riding high. And the States party was now so firmly entrenched that it could steer an uncompromising course at home without putting its foreign policy at risk. The Orange party, on the other hand, could do nothing but wait and keep quiet. The Dowager did not show any resentment at Holland's refusal to accept her proposal; indeed, ignoring the criticism of most of the adherents of the illustrious House,[75] she persisted in seeking the friendship of Holland. Buysero, who invited De Witt to his country house near the Hague so that the Grand Pensionary might meet the princess over dinner, helped her greatly in this pursuit.[76] In dealing with the affairs of Zeeland, she soon afterwards came to heed the advice of Thibaut, De Witt's friend, who in 1664 'suddenly' gained her respect,[77] – much to the annoyance of Pieter de Huybert. Charles II, too, swallowed the States' refusal to resume charge of the prince's education, and did not allow it to strain his relations with Holland.

Brief rapprochement with England; Colonial conflicts; War (January 1665)

Later in 1663, it even began to look as if the Republic and England were drawing still closer together. Shortly after Louis XIV had sent Godefroy Comte D'Estrades, a high-ranking diplomat who had just negotiated the sale of Dunkirk at the English court – to the Hague, De Witt opened discussions to discover what precisely France intended to do about the southern Netherlands, and if possible to reach an agreement that would help to safeguard the Republic. He soon drew from D'Estrades the admission that Louis regarded as invalid the abdication of her rights to the succession which his Spanish consort had been 'compelled' to make at their marriage in 1659. The question then arose what price the Republic would demand for agreeing to Louis's interpretation. De Witt began by suggesting a partition of the southern Netherlands. It appeared all too soon, however, that he could not get his own people to accept that solution: Amsterdam was opposed to any plan that would bring Antwerp into the States-General, thus preventing the continued closure of the Scheldt. Hers was a purely selfish argument, but one that nevertheless preserved the Netherlands from disaster. For the new frontier acceptable to De Witt was based on purely strategic considerations: it ran right across Dutch-speaking territory, from Ostend to Naastricht and would have left Ypres and Courtrai, Audenarde and Alost, Brussels and Louvain to France, thus abandoning them to the same irrevocable gallicization that was the fate of Dunkirk. Next, the talks turned to the establishment of a South Netherlands Republic, allied to the Dutch, and under the protection of France. This, too, was not a very promising plan, as we may gather from the fact that D'Estrades recommended it to his government with the rider that the independence of such a republic was unlikely to endure for long.[78]

While trying to discover what bait they must offer to gain the Republic's support for Louis's plan to gain mastery over the remainder of the Spanish monarchy, the French hit upon that remarkable 'law of devolution' which would enable them, albeit with the help of far-fetched arguments, in the name of the queen, to press claims not to the entire heritage, but at least to Brabant and Namur. And to this territory, their argument ran, the Queen would be entitled upon the death of her father, Philip IV, and not upon that of Carlos, her unhappy little half-brother. Moreover, in 1663, arguing that a bird in the hand is worth two in the bush, Louis decided to abandon any idea of buying Dutch acquiescence, if not co-operation, with the very part of the monarchy to which he was entitled by the 'law of devolution'. D'Estrades did not, however, break off the negotiations there and then. France was anxious not to antagonize the Republic until the last moment, and although no settlement was effected, Louis managed to emerge from the discussions without destroying the impression that he was a moderate man.

Yet in the summer of 1663, when D'Estrades had expounded the invalidity of Maria Theresa's solemn renunciation of her rights, and De Witt had begun to consult the many-headed government of Holland about the various compromise solutions, Dutch public opinion suddenly became aware of Louis's true ambitions, and was most seriously disturbed by this discovery. Downing, returning to the Hague after nearly a year's leave, noticed it all with great pleasure. For him, who invariably placed economic above political considerations, the only thing that mattered was that the turn of events was bound to make De Witt more receptive to English demands.[79] His government, however, took a more serious view. Thus Clarendon, at least, pleaded with De Witt to join a common front against French plans for Europe.[80] But was he really in earnest? He, who now evinced such uneasiness about the future of the southern Netherlands, had only a year ago helped to give the French an outstanding staging post for an attack on that very country, by ceding Dunkirk. And, in fact, Downing acted with the utmost reserve when the Spanish ambassador to the Hague tried to convince him, no less than the States of Holland and the States-General, of the need for joint action in opposing the French threat.[81] De Witt, too, could get no more out of Downing than an assurance that England would not like to see the French in possession of the southern Netherlands. Even early in 1664, when French troop movements were causing great uneasiness and it looked as if an attack on the southern Netherlands might be mounted at any moment, Downing still remained a passive spectator, while Holland made desperate attempts to reach agreement with Spain. All that De Witt could do with Clarendon's letter was show it to D'Estrades, in the hope that the Frenchman might be persuaded (De Witt himself was not) that the States had other irons in the fire, should France refuse to reach an arrangement.[82]

Meanwhile, the Grand Pensionary and the English ambassador engaged in an unprecedented exchange of compliments: in the autumn of 1663 heated debates in the English Parliament once again gave the impression that a civil war was imminent, and De Witt called on Downing to offer assistance in that eventuality. Charles II's reign, so he said, seemed more advantageous to the Republic than any other régime England might choose.[83] His offer of help could be declined, for the danger had only been apparent, but Downing for his part assured his visitor that the English government did not intend to interfere in the quarrel between Holland and Zeeland, which was then assuming disquieting proportions. In point of fact, Downing no longer enjoyed special relations with the Princess-Dowager, who had formerly done his bidding in Zeeland.[84]

And in all, therefore, Holland's treatment of the young prince did not impair her relations with the English court. But the *rapprochement* did not last for long. Fear of a French onslaught on the southern Netherlands was not so grave at the court of the Stuarts that De Witt could have risked raising his policy upon it. Downing had not changed. Back in England, he at once reverted to his old method of voicing economic grievances, and pursued it so vigorously that he succeeded in making it the dominant issue. As a result, De Witt was forced to swallow his distrust of Louis XIV and to focus his attention on the renewed threat from England.

All this had nothing to do with the Prince of Orange – in contrast to the first English war, the causes of the second were purely economic. It was with full justice that Downing, the zealous protagonist of the economic policy, was described as the author of that conflict.[85]

He worked at it with indefatigable energy. To begin with he

re-opened the affair of the two ships, which dated back to 1649, and which, because of opposition by the Orange party, had not been settled conclusively in 1662.[86] Then he brought up a number of new problems, with equal passion. He was helped by the fact that the Dutch East India Company which, in a last tremendous spurt, had just succeeded in driving the Portuguese from their possessions in India, dealt rather high-handedly with English merchantmen who challenged the company's monopoly. At the same time, the interests of the Dutch West India Company on the Guinea coast had begun to clash with those of the Royal African Company, in which the Duke of York and many other high-placed and influential personages had an active interest. All these conflicts were symptomatic of English reluctance to acquiesce in the dominant commercial and colonial position of the little Republic. Downing made as much of these difficulties as he could, inciting his government to stand firm, and exerting himself to the utmost to 'expose' the arguments and subterfuges of the Dutch Companies and the States. To Downing, England was predestined to command the seas, to leadership in commerce, and to ownership of settlements and colonies in the East and West. The fact that English sailors and merchants had to put up with Dutch arrogance and commercial predominance, struck him as a monstrous reversal of the natural state of things. Many Englishmen thought so too, and Downing could count on a great deal of public support for his policy. And to quicken the king's resolve, he never tired of assuring him that the Republic would always shrink from a war, that threats would always make her climb down, that she was too divided to resist concerted pressure.[87]

His observations of internal dissensions, of the unwillingness of the inland provinces to protect the interests of Holland and Zeeland, and of the pro-English leanings of the Orange party, persuaded him to persist in these illusions, the more so as he discovered that Dutch statesmen were prepared to suffer his rude remarks and for all their dilly-dallying, to meet most of his complaints. However bitterly aggrieved De Witt and his friends might feel, they never forgot that their country, as the dominant commercial power, had much more to lose than an England striving for dominance; that both through its situation and its very much larger fleet of merchantmen, the Republic was infinitely more vulnerable; that, moreover, she had to explore every avenue to preserve the peace before she could count on the support of the inland provinces in a war in which the interests of the latter were not directly involved. But Dutch patience had a limit, and this Downing failed to understand.

The Republic began to realize that the situation was becoming critical when, on 22 April 1664 (OS), the English House of Commons, in an outburst of passion and anger, passed a resolution censuring Holland's intolerable presumption, and promised the king its utmost exertions in case he took measures for securing his subjects' rights. That demonstration was meant to strengthen Downing's hand; instead it caused the States to alert their men-of-war. Meanwhile, Charles II, relying on questionable historical arguments, had made a present of the New Netherland, then in the possession of the West India Company, to his brother the Duke of York (in private of course); to secure it, he sent a secret expedition which succeeded in taking possession of the colony. Even before the news of the conquest reached the Republic in October, the situation had deteriorated considerably. In July, a report had come in that an English squadron under Holmes, acting for the Royal African Company, had attacked possessions of the Dutch West India Company on the coast of Guinea. True, the English government had given an assurance that Holmes had not acted under their instructions, but it did not, for all that, speak of restitution. As for the next conquest, the seizure of Cabo Corso, Charles II assumed full responsibility for it [88] later in the year. On August 11, the States-General sent a signal to De Ruyter, who was cruising in the Mediterranean, to recapture the Guinea posts.

The way in which this decision was taken shows better than perhaps anything else how considerably party divisions weakened the Republic in its conflict with England. Though the friends of England were unable to block the order to De Ruyter, there was good reason to fear that they would betray it to the English ambassador, when the success of De Ruyter's expedition depended entirely on secrecy. Hence De Witt (in co-operation with the secretary of the Amsterdam Admiralty, David de Wildt) had to resort to a ruse: he had the decision passed by a special committee of the States-General which was dominated by him. It was later rushed through the full assembly as if it were a mere formality. Whom was De Witt so anxious to deceive? Apparently[89] he took quite special trouble to mislead Renswoude, whose conversion to the States party he did not yet fully trust, and a Frisian deputy. As for people outside the assembly, De Witt believed[90] and even the Zeeland deputy De Huybert agreed with him,[91] that the secret must be kept closely from everybody connected with the House of Orange – Veere and Flushing for example. So successful was De Witt, in fact, that even when rumour about the decision was rife, Downing felt sure that nothing could have been decided by the States-General of which he had no knowledge. It was not until December, when reports of De Ruyter's victory came in from Guinea, that the world at large learned the truth, and at the same time took note that the Republic did not take provocation lying down.

But by then it had become difficult for the English government to retract. The ambitious Arlington, Clarendon's younger rival, foresaw rich profit out of the prizes to be gained, and a special royal commission was set up to distribute them.[92] The French ambassador was still trying to act as mediator, and in their talks with him, the States demanded that all the possessions seized unlawfully from the West India Company must be returned. Arlington, for his part, argued that there was no point in negotiating before defeat had made the States see reason, and that no peace could satisfy England by which she did not, as guarantee of Holland's compliance, obtain certain towns in pawn, in the way Elizabeth had held Brielle.[93] In January 1665, a surprise attack was launched on the Dutch Smyrna fleet sailing back home – this again in the hope that a forcible action would induce Holland to bend her knees. The treacherous attack was resisted courageously, and the States replied with an order to the Dutch navy to use violence against the English in European waters as well. Letters of marque were issued. In March, England declared war. Oddly enough, the ambassadors of both countries remained at their posts: Downing in the Hague, Van Goch in London.

France's defection; Disaster at Lowestoft (13 July 1665); Orange activities

That the second English war turned into a triumph for the Republic, was due above all to De Witt's great energy and resolution. His leadership during the three years now under review represents the peak of his career and places him among the few great statesmen in Dutch history. The enormity of his task can only be appreciated if, in addition to his strategic difficulties – which were, indeed, formidable – we also bear in mind how very considerably the Constitution impeded the action by any Dutch leader, and quite especially of a Grand Pensionary, and, worse, how much indifference, pusillanimity, obstruction, and even treachery, he and his supporters had to face.

The public at large was pro-Orange, though not necessarily pro-English. Profound irritation with England was widespread, and the official interpretation of the origins of the conflict was widely accepted. No one challenged the many pamphlets denouncing Holmes and the attack upon the New Netherland. The war had clearly been forced upon the Netherlands and the new taxes levied by the States of Holland were paid without demur. And yet, many Dutchmen found it difficult, if not hateful, to recognize the States and the Grand Pensionary of Holland as the true representatives of the country's interest and honour, so much so that, at the slightest set-back, they were ready to listen to the insinuations of the Organists, who were systematically pro-English, and according to whom the King of England was not a bitter enemy, but a benign Protestant ruler. Each reversal was, moreover, the signal for reminding the inland provinces that what the war was all about was simply the protection of the sectional interests of Holland. And before the triumph of 1667 was achieved, there were a good many set-backs and reversals.

Besides preparing the Dutch navy for battle, De Witt's primary concern was to keep France to the promises she had made in the treaty of 1662. There was a clear *casus foederis*, and in order to obtain the armed support stipulated in the fifth article, De Witt sent Van Beuningen, one of his ablest and most trusted colleagues, to Paris in December 1664. Boreel was obviously not equal to the situation, and what was worse he was whispered – for it must not be send out aloud[94] – to be pro-English in his heart of hearts. It will be remembered that his son had a post in the young prince's household, and as it turned out later, the young man had taken out English naturalization papers.[95]

Louis was most reluctant to accede to De Witt's appeal for help. His main concern was still his wife's claim to the Spanish Netherlands, and nothing was more likely to upset that claim than a war with England, which was bound to drive Charles into the arms of

Spain. Yet Louis did not like to see the Republic defeated either, for that would seriously upset the existing balance of power. From the Hague, D'Estrades sent the warning that the friends of England, who had always been sceptical about the promises of France, were already boasting that they had been right all along and that the States régime was about to topple. This did make some impression, and the French ambassador was instructed to hold out 'hope'. Once or twice, France even let it be known that she might be willing to do something more concrete in exchange for a Dutch undertaking to assist in the conquest of the Spanish Netherlands. De Witt rejected that idea out of hand, stating quite bluntly that, as long as he had any say in the matter, he would never consent to such bargains. 'The point at issue is whether or not His Majesty is willing to implement the treaty of 1662, not whether Holland should sign a new treaty that would probably be honoured no more than the old.'[96]

After tarrying for months, the French finally sent a special mission to England for the purpose of mediating between the two warring countries. This was simply another delaying tactic, yet Louis and his ministers, with a degree of hypocrisy that the Dutch must have found particularly galling in their distress, and with the high-flown unction so typical of his reign, gave out that no great king had ever behaved more generously towards a troublesome ally, and that the little Republic was being singularly ungrateful. The mission, which became known by the foolish name of *la célèbre ambassade*, included the Duke of Verneuil and Courtin, a man of wide diplomatic experience. It made no haste, and indeed was not meant to do so.

Deprived of the aid on which she had been counting, the Republic had to look to her own resources. Louis did not rate her chances very high, and his advice was not to stake the Republic's welfare on the uncertain outcome of a war. But De Witt and the States could not afford to play a waiting game. Trade required that the sea should be kept open. General dissatisfaction, the machinations of the enemy within, the continual displays of hostility by Downing, who regularly entertained members of the Orange court and was on intimate terms with the Spanish ambassador – everything made it imperative that De Witt pull off a coup.

In April, De Witt himself, as delegate to the States-General, went to Texel in order to speed up the preparation of the Dutch fleet. He went there not only because he knew that the weight of his position would help to settle conflicts within the Admiralty, but also in order to familiarize himself personally with maritime matters.

While he was unable to remedy a great many of the organizational defects he had observed, he did not forget them. His visit, moreover, earned him the respect of the sailors, who came to revere him more than they did the supreme commander, Wassenaer of Obdam, who had been retained in his post simply because his noble birth set him above the jealousies of professional sailors. 'Setting the Younker above the tars', had been the phrase in the days of Frederick Henry, and even then the system had not worked satisfactorily.[97] The second generation of Tromps and Kortenaers, and in Zeeland of Evertsens, did not look upon themselves as lowly 'tars'. De Ruyter, the greatest of them all, had started from the bottom, and he was even now sailing the oceans, no one knew precisely where. For weeks De Witt stayed on at Texel, addressing and encouraging the crews as he went from ship to ship.

On 23 and 24 March, the Dutch fleet, including a squadron from Zeeland under Jan Evertsen, finally put to sea. It numbered more than a hundred heavily armed vessels – the strongest naval force the Republic ever had sent out. The States awaited news of their first encounter with bated breaths. When the first dispatches gave a hint that the admiral was irresolute, the State resolved to appoint special commissaries with full authority to act with him or even to overrule him. De Witt himself volunteered for this dangerous post. Then, on 13 June, the sound of cannon was heard in the Hague. The first sea battle had begun, and it ended in a heavy defeat for the Dutch.

Wassenaer lost control of his fleet the moment he engaged the English off Lowestoft. He incurred heavy losses, and when his flagship blew up, confusion became general and a number of captains fled from the scene of battle. Jan Evertsen reached the Maas with ten badly battered ships. That nearly eighty vessels were safely brought back to Texel was largely the achievement of Cornelis Tromp, who had taken it upon himself to hoist the admiral's flag and successfully covered the retreat.

The fact that the States régime was able to survive so great a shock was clear proof that it was more firmly entrenched than many observers believed; De Witt's inspired leadership kept it from bowing to England and daily infused it with courage. His was a difficult task for, as D'Estrades[98] wrote immediately after the defeat, consternation was rife among the deputies to the States of Holland; many were anxious to conclude a peace on whatever terms England might be pleased to grant, and to elevate the Prince of Orange to his ancestral offices.[99] The story went round that the crew of several ships had refused to fight unless the prince's flag were raised.[100] It was unfortunate for the States that the man to return home with the most glorious record should have been Tromp, widely known as an Orangist and never bothering to hide that fact. Leyden was the scene of a minor riot reminiscent of the black days of 1653: drummers recruiting for the navy in the name of the States, were first abused and then attacked by a number of women, who seized their drums and tore them to shreds. 'The devil take the States, drum for the Prince!' Similar scenes occurred all over the country'[101]

More alarming still was the fact that in their grumblings, the people so often expressed the belief that the war was merely the result of the exclusion of the Prince of Orange;[102] to their way of thinking, the King of England was embattled against De Witt and his party, but not against the Dutch people.

They completely misunderstood the situation, the more so as the English government had given them no grounds for this belief. There had, in fact, been many attempts to obtain an open declaration from England that she had gone to war on behalf of the Orange cause. Thus in January 1665, one of England's agents or spies in Holland – namely Van Ruyven, De Witt's disloyal clerk, now in Leeuwarden – had written a lengthy letter on behalf of 'a number of gentlemen, friends of the King of Great Britain and of the Prince of Orange':[103] all of them took it for granted and with great satisfaction to boot, that France would back out from her obligations and that De Witt's ensuing fall would clear the way for the elevations of the prince. That, they asserted, was also in England's interest, for only an Orange régime was capable of living on honourable terms with England. No English government could or should negotiate with the present rulers. The ostentatious preparation of the Dutch navy was entirely De Witt's work, and the sailors themselves were such zealots for Orange that the States were bound to have difficulties with their recruiting campaign. Let the King of England therefore openly declare that he is taking up arms on behalf of the prince. Then the best part (*la plus saine partie*) of those entering the service will take the side of the prince under the king's protection. And let handbills be distributed throughout the Republic with the emphatic declaration that it was De Witt and his coterie who alone had obstructed the prince's appointment.

That advice was not followed. The English Chancellor, Lord Clarendon, in particular, took the view he had expressed before:[104] that declarations in favour of Orange would merely be grist to De Witt's mill, uniting national sentiment behind him and behind the slogan of no concessions to foreign interference. That objection was not wholly unfounded. In the waiting period before war was finally declared, the deputies of Holland had been able to sting their fellow regents to more vigorous action against England by the mere mention of possible English intermeddling.[105] In a pamphlet of about that time, a Hollander and an Englishman were shown playing cards. The Hollander said: 'What is our game about? Is it the Orange apple? If so, we must change it, for I will not allow strangers to play for such stakes in my garden.'[106] Similar sentiments were expressed after the declaration of war as well, and they pointed to a very real feeling among the Dutch people. Nevertheless, at moments of crisis, the belief that Charles II, like the Dutch commonalty, was anxious to achieve the elevation of the prince, thus fusing the cause of Orange with that of England in the popular mind, posed a serious threat to the States party, or rather to the whole country, locked as it was in struggle with England. In the disturbances following the defeat at Lowestoft, this became so obvious that the English government quickly abandoned Clarendon's policy of neutrality in the matter.

Meanwhile the House of Orange itself was living in high hopes. The States of Holland were informed that Zuylestein, the prince's governor, had proposed a toast to 'the King of Holland and his lieutenant'.[107] The Princess-Dowager, at any rate, was more discreet. She gave strict orders that the prince's pro-English attendants – Zuylestein and his wife and the Heenvliet-Wottons – were not to continue calling on Downing – without effect as far as the last two were concerned.[108] The old princess fully appreciated the need of sparing national sensibilities. She reproached De Witt for his distrust of the adherents of her illustrious House, as evinced in the secrecy with which he had issued his orders for De Ruyter.[109]

She made a point of keeping all doors open. Thus while she continued to maintain close contact with the Holland States party
through Buysero, she also heeded the many excited voices now
clamouring for the prince's elevation, be it as a means of persuading the King of England to halt the war, or of fighting him more
effectively. Had not Tromp himself told the young prince that the
battle would have had quite a different issue had it been fought in
his name? In July, the princess kept putting off a trip to Buren
in the expectation that 'something would be done for her grandson,
if only by appointing him Admiral-General, which would give
great satisfaction to our sailors'.[110] Courtin, impressed by the
patriotic fervour the war had aroused in England (which, at times,
assumed somewhat unpleasant forms for the mediators), predicted
that De Witt was certain to take another licking, thus helping the
Orange party to power, or else make a sudden peace without informing France: 'Waging war is clearly no job for merchants.'[111]

The States stand firm; De Witt sails with De Ruyter (August–November 1665)

'As haughty as ever,' D'Estrades wrote of De Witt, and even
Downing, who from the safety of his house in the Voorhout, fitted
out like a fortress against possible mob attacks, watching and
chuckling at the general consternation, had to admit that De Witt
put a brave face on it at the Binnenhof.[112] Only two days after the
disaster, De Witt left for Texel carrying a fresh authorization from
the States-General. The watchword was: sit tight, have the fleet
repaired as soon as possible, and then put to sea again. De Witt was
not the only one to take that attitude – else his task would have
been insuperable. The nation at large had been aroused against all
vacillation and the narrow pursuit of self-interest. 'The first round
counts for nothing,' so ran one of the typical popular pamphlets,
'watch out for the next.'[113] Profound shame was voiced in other
pamphlets, all of which mentioned the defeat in sober tones but
described the future with confidence.[114] 'The hearts of cowards lie
revealed by this small loss,' exclaimed one of the pamphleteers.
A number of young men from regent families applied to the States
for leave to serve at sea: one of them was Ouwerkerk,[115] Beverweert's son. Renswoude, the old turncoat, however, still asked
Downing for favours and promised to use his influence in the

States-General on His Majesty's behalf (and, as Downing himself commented,[116] was working zealously for peace on 'acceptable' terms). But for the time being, all such efforts had to be made in secret; in the assembly itself not a single voice was raised for compromise, nor was any time wasted on regrets or squabbles. Van Beuningen in France, who had to face the brunt of Louis's displeasure when the king first learned that the States had ignored his advice to avoid war at all costs, was able to report, only a few weeks later, that matters had been redressed by 'admirable and vigorous conduct'.[117]

At Texel, the Grand Pensionary and his fellow delegates had to struggle manfully against overwhelming odds. Reports of their determination caused the shares of the East India Company to rise again. 'Cost what it will,' Downing warned his government on 19 June already, 'they will have their fleet out.'[118] And as a matter of fact, on 24 June, a squadron set sail to give protection to Dutch merchantmen returning from the East Indies.

De Witt's most urgent task was to restore the morale of his sailors. All discipline had gone, and no change was possible before those captains who had shirked their duty were brought to book. One problem called for the direct intervention of the deputies: the commanding officers, and especially Tromp, though inveighing against the cowards, refused to summon a court-martial. Tromp, moreover, travelled to the Hague without leave, in order to plead that this hateful business ought not to fall upon his officers but upon the Boards of Admiralty; an untenable thesis, as De Witt pointed out. De Witt was grimly impatient of the widespread reluctance by a nation long unaccustomed to such measures, to see strong justice done. In his view, at any rate, the salvation of the navy depended upon it. In the end, Tromp let himself be persuaded and a court-martial was held, but even then the deputies had to play a much more active part than De Witt deemed proper. Three captains were sentenced to death, a good many more to exile, to having their swords broken by the hangmen, and so on. At the same time, there were rewards for those who had acquitted themselves well. Their number was not large, and in some cases the reward could only take the form of a solemn funeral.

As a result of the measures, there was now a marked shortage of senior officers. Everyone looked forward with longing to the return of De Ruyter, who had with him a number of experienced captains and who seemed himself to be the man cut out for the supreme command. While he was still away, Tromp had to be accepted as second best. But after all the States had had to endure from him, they endorsed his appointment only after some hesitation, and simultaneously passed another resolution which showed clearly their reluctance to entrust the fleet to a hothead, and an Orange one at that – they appointed their own delegates to supervise his conduct of the campaign. This was customary in the army, but had never been done in the navy (although it had been considered when Obdam was suspected of wavering).

In the event, it was De Witt himself who took charge of the conduct of the new naval expedition, on which depended the fate of the country and the régime. His fellow delegate, Huygens from Gelderland, was then more than eighty years of age. Tromp, to whom De Witt was the very personification of the meddlesome States,[119] was anything but pleased. De Witt's other enemies railed at his lust for power, and his nearest relatives were dismayed to learn that he intended to stake the family fortune on the venture. Louis XIV, too, made no secret of his annoyance. De Witt himself was calmly conscious that he had no alternative. There was no one in the navy who could be safely charged to take full responsibility for the campaign, and he was the only outsider whose advice senior officers might be expected to heed, the only man, moreover – as the deputies to the States declared – with sufficient self-confidence to contradict the officers and if necessary to compel them to act against their opinions.[120] Was this bragging? De Witt proved the justice of his claims on 14–16 August, when he took the Dutch fleet through the Spaniards' Inlet, without accidents, an unheard-of achievement. All the pilots had asserted that this would be impossible, and the officers had been sceptical. De Witt, who had supervised the taking of soundings, now had the satisfaction that the outcome had confirmed in practice what he, after a preliminary examination, had declared must be feasible in theory.

Meanwhile there were renewed hopes that, at this critical juncture, Louis XIV might at last decide to take more positive steps. The king did indeed temper his constant carpings with assurances of deep concern, but all that he did in practice was to instruct his emissaries in England to address fresh admonitions to Charles II. If these proved ineffective, then – so D'Estrades was allowed to assure the States, but not in writing – Louis would give the States cause for satisfaction. And, in point of fact, he did oblige them in July, when he adopted a vigorous attitude to a new threat, this time from the east. The Bishop of Münster, Bernhard von Galen, had for a long time been at daggers drawn with the States-General. The bishop entered a claim to the lordship of Borculo, and in order to check their impetuous neighbour, the States had made contact with the disaffected citizens of Münster – to the bishop's further annoyance and to no benefit to themselves. But when the bishop seized the opportunity of the war and tried to obtain English subsidies for an attack on the Republic, Louis let it be known both in Münster as well as in London, that he would come to the defence of the Netherlands. The States' army was miserably feeble, especially now that it had been used to come to the aid of the navy. Hence Louis's promise of support was exceedingly welcome.

At the same time De Witt, who used to travel from Texel to the Hague to look after the country's foreign affairs, had time after time to listen to D'Estrades' warnings against the reckless policy of putting the Dutch fleet at risk once again. Though he remained quite firm on that point, De Witt was forced to make minor colonial concessions which would enable the French mediators to make a new offer to England.

The fleet had not yet set sail when, on 6 August, De Ruyter, with his small squadron loaded with rich English booty, put in at Delfzijl, to the utter delight of the entire Dutch nation. After the defeat of Lowestoft, his adventurous and so miraculously successful expedition was doubly welcome. A second piece of good news reached Holland at about the same time: an English attack on the Dutch merchant fleet, including the ships from the Indies, which now that the English were in command of the sea, had sought shelter in the neutral port of Bergen, had been repulsed with considerable losses to the enemy. The Danish government,[121] which had reached a secret arrangement with England that in return for allowing an attack in Danish waters, they would receive half the booty, now began to wonder whether co-operation with the States might not after all be more profitable.

Meanwhile the States of Holland had lost no time in elevating De Ruyter to a rank above Tromp's, whereupon the States-General invested him with the supreme command. It was a great relief to the ruling party to place at the head of the navy a man who accepted their policy without question, and who was, moreover, as prudent and cool of judgement as Tromp was reckless and incalculable. The change was, however, no mere act of political bias. De Ruyter was more than twenty years older than Tromp, highly esteemed and beloved of the sailors, while the people were even more profoundly impressed by his romantic world voyage than they had been by Tromp's heroic cover of the retreat from Lowestoft. For all that Tromp, who, with De Witt, had helped to make the fleet ready for sea and to carry out its complete re-organization, was bitterly disappointed, and understandably so. But the step he took to express his dismay was quite inexcusable. He began by declaring that he could not possibly serve under De Ruyter and insisted on resigning. It was only after serious warnings from the delegates that he would be taken before a court-martial and charged with refusing to obey orders in time of war, that he grudgingly bowed to the inevitable. On 10 August, De Ruyter appeared before the fleet, which was already stationed outside the harbour, and was wildly cheered by the assembled officers and men. That same day, the fleet set sail. The object was to wrest back command of the sea, to avenge Lowestoft, and to cover the voyage home of the merchantmen from Bergen. This last task was per-formed without difficulty, but there was no encounter with the English fleet. The two antagonists missed each other time after time. Early in September, moreover, a heavy storm scattered the Dutch fleet and, at the end of the month, when it was back again in home waters, and De Witt and De Ruyter were making great efforts to get it ready for a new attack, it was once more hit by a heavy gale. In spite of this and of the lateness of the season, the fleet did cross to the English coast, but illness and death so ravaged the crew that, at the beginning of November, the Dutch were forced to return home with empty hands. It was a disappointed De Witt who resumed his post of Grand Pensionary in the Hague, without bothering to take a day's rest between his two arduous jobs.

Downing's intrigues; Anti-French feeling in spite of Münster; A proposal by Overijsel (20 October 1665); D'Estrades' activities

His friends had missed De Witt painfully, especially during the last phase of his absence.

At first, the hopeful mood set up by De Ruyter's homecoming

had continued, fed as it was by the bracing reports from Bergen. In July, the English were not a little disappointed, and at the same time irritated, to see that the threat from Münster had the untoward effect of bringing Louis XIV closer to his ally. As a counter move, the English government gave Downing secret instructions to enter into separate peace negotiations with various Dutch politicians. Downing had long been urging that policy, on the grounds that nothing good would come of French mediation, and that a separate peace could be had for the asking. At the same time he did not forget to stress that any peace must be contingent on the condition that the States shed their deeply anti-English – and anti-Orangist! – leaders.[122] On 31 July, Arlington wrote to him that the king and Clarendon were convinced that 'all wise and good Dutchmen' would realize how much to their advantage was an agreement that would rid them of the menace of French self-seeking. Dutch attention should be plainly directed at the dangers of the French plans for the southern Netherlands, where the interests of the Republic coincided with those of England. Unfortunately, the conditions Arlington suggested as a reasonable basis of negotiation were unlikely to prove acceptable to the States, who as Arlington insisted would have to make the first move, since that was what honour demanded.[123]

Especially interesting was Arlington's suggestion that such a move would be received the more favourably in England, 'if ushered in by some friendly action towards the Prince of Orange'.

Arlington, unlike Clarendon, had always looked upon the Orange party as a stick with which to beat the arch-enemy De Witt, and now that so many Orangists were offering their services, and France had begun to meddle more directly, he thought it was time to strike.

However, when Downing received his new instructions, De Ruyter's appearance off Delfzijl had helped to raise the mood of the Dutch people to such an extent that he did not dare mention Arlington's severe peace conditions to anybody. In fact, only a little while earlier, no less a personage than Van Beverning had suggested a meeting, 'to see if we cannot find an accommodation'; and on 18 August, Downing complained that he had heard no more from him, 'nor anything pointing towards peace, since De Ruyter's homecoming'.[124]

Downing's position was becoming increasingly embarrassing

for other reasons as well. In England, Cunaeus, secretary to the Dutch embassy, had been arrested. The ambassador's protests only elicited the reply that the secretary had paid illegal visits to prisoners. In fact, the English regarded Cunaeus as De Witt's tool and wanted him removed from the presence of ambassador Van Goch,[125] who was less ardent and, moreover, a man of no ability. The States now retaliated by ordering a number of arrests in the Netherlands, though retaliation is not, in fact, the correct term since many of Downing's agents had, in fact, violated the tenets of international law in more than one way.

War in that age interfered much less dramatically with the life of nations that it does today. Thus if an English prisoner of war found his lot hard to bear, he could offer his services to the Dutch fleet and was readily accepted.[126] Numerous Englishmen were still living in the Republic, quietly pursuing their business in Amsterdam or Rotterdam, and restricting their political activities to occasional talks with Dutch businessmen. Not that they did not run into trouble from time to time. Thus Sir William Davidson, who had remained at his consular post in Amsterdam, reported indignantly that the populace suspected him of having bribed Jan Evertsen, and that a furious mob had attacked his innocent book-keeper in the streets, calling him a spy.[127] As a matter of fact – the English archives show it clearly enough – Holland was riddled with spies, though it was not only Englishmen who were involved. Moreover, the English residents were divided into parties, which worked against and betrayed each other. The English or Scots supporters of the Commonwealth, who had gone into exile in 1660, the 'fanaticks' as the Royalists used to call them, hated Charles II with a more passionate hatred than did the Dutch; they looked down upon Downing as a turncoat, and never forgot that, in 1662, he had been instrumental in the capture of the three unfortunate 'regicides' who had believed themselves safe in the Republic. This faction was anxious to serve the States in every possible way, though, as De Witt realized, they were not the best men to be recruited for counter-espionage. For that job, he employed Colonel Bampfield, an adventurer who, during the English disturbances, had served both sides in turn and had lately succeeded in worming his way into Downing's confidence. It was he who supplied De Witt with damning evidence against a number of the ambassador's agents.

The first victim was Oudart who, as we saw, was a member of the prince's council and who, once the guardianship project was shelved, went over wholeheartedly to the English side. Downing protested against his arrest, on the ground that Oudart was a naturalized English subject, who had been in Downing's employ ever since 1664. The States, for their part, argued that Oudart was still in the service of the Prince of Orange, and hence subject to the Dutch law, according to which he had compounded serious felonies.[128] Downing himself believed that the States were anxious to extort from Oudart the name of the printer whom he (Downing) had employed (imprudently enough) to publish his notes to the States in Dutch translation. Though Oudart did not know the man's name,[129] he had helped the ambassador by many acts that amounted to espionage, and by pressing various deputies to accept the English peace terms.[130] An English officer, who had just left the States service and was now staying at Downing's house, whence he worked furiously against De Witt and for peace, was the next man to be arrested. The States came even closer to the ambassador's person when they apprehended Gringham, his secretary. Protesting away, Downing began to feel some anxiety for his own safety,[131] and towards the end of August he quietly left the Hague. The States could congratulate themselves on having rid themselves of a hotbed of espionage and intrigue. Davidson absconded soon afterwards, and a few months later, Oudart and Gringham were exchanged for Cunaeus.

The States régime, meanwhile, suffered greatly from De Witt's absence with the fleet. D'Estrades kept grumbling that no important decision could be taken. Vivien, the pensionary of Dordrecht, who was filling De Witt's place, lacked the courage to endorse any new plan. But the worst was that fault-finding and discouragement were rife in the assembly. The indecisive outcome of De Witt's naval campaign cast a shadow over Dutch optimism; the relief at Louis's stand against the Bishop of Münster gave way to impatience, particularly when, at the end of August, it appeared that Louis's ambassadors in England had offered the enemy even larger concessions than those to which De Witt had reluctantly consented before his departure from the Hague. Hostile voices were saying that the French alliance seemed to serve no other purpose than to prepare the way for a humiliating peace.

In the face of French pressure, De Witt's own supporters, who

had built high hopes upon French friendship, maintained bitterly
that the Republic was able and determined to defend her honour
and interests against England, come what may. That is what Van
Beuningen and Van Ghent, of Gelderland, a prominent figure in
the States-General, told Lionne in Paris, and what Van Beverning
said to D'Estrades in the Hague. Louis, for his part, felt the Dutch
were not nearly grateful enough for his declaration that France
would break with England if his offers were rejected. Had he not
taken yet another step towards fulfilment of the promises of 1662?
In fact, he had only issued the declaration out of concern for De
Witt's position. Without the Grand Pensionary's support, the
French-Dutch alliance could not survive for long; his fall would
make England the master of Dutch policy. Now that was something
Louis wanted to prevent; but remembering Spain, he was equally
anxious to avoid a *war* with England.

All in all, Louis greatly underestimated the Republic's power
of resistance, and did not understand what importance the Dutch
attached to the protection of their colonial interests. So great was
public irritation at his attitude, that many Dutchmen began to
heed the advice of Downing and his Orange sympathizers: that it
might be better to treat with England directly. In September,
Dutch opinion was again riveted on French plans for the southern
Netherlands – Philip IV of Spain had died and there was reason to
fear that Louis would try to press his wife's claims. Downing was
no longer there to make capital out of the situation, but Van Goch
was still in London, where, as Van Beuningen put it, he had
'lamentable audiences with a king, who was his country's open
enemy.'[132] Early in October, Charles used one such meeting to
intimate that he would be glad to receive a direct Dutch peace
offer; French mediation was to no purpose.[133] At that point the
Bishop of Münster had begun to act upon his threats. His army
had crossed the frontier, occupying not only Borculo, which the
bishop was claiming as his own, but also tracts of Gelderland,
Twente, and even of Salland. Meanwhile the feeble States army –
recruiting had only begun after July, when Prince Maurice had
been given the command – kept on the safe side of the river Ijsel.
Charles II told Van Goch bluntly that peace with him would mean
peace with the bishop. But while this dictum was still on everyone's
lips, Louis XIV let it be known that he had sent out a relief corps.
This announcement undoubtedly stiffened resistance to England,

but at the same time the prospect of being saddled with French troops and being beholden to Louis also strengthened the voice of those who clamoured for a compromise with England.

Distrust of France had always been rife in De Witt's party, and for very good reasons at that, as the future was soon to show. It also revealed that De Witt had not bargained away his freedom of action, as many had accused him of doing. His policy was supremely realistic. In order to stand up to England, he needed the French alliance, but as soon as England ceased to pose a threat to the country's interests and the greater menace came from France, he was ready to change his tack. His difficulties were considerably increased by the fact that Dutch public opinion was not as free to choose between the two powerful neighbours as he was – for many Dutchmen, friendship with England and hatred of France were matters of principle or of party, with the result that their opposition to De Witt's policies was no less blind than their interpretation of his motives.

All diplomatic intercourse with the hyper-sensitive court of France, for ever anxious about its honour and swollen with conceit, was a great trial. But that was not what the Dutch people held against Louis, at least not before he finally turned tyrant. To them he was the champion of Catholicism, while England was seen as a fellow Protestant power. It was no accident, therefore, that so many ministers of religion should have loudly voiced their objections to the French alliance, much as Dathenus had preached against Anjou eighty years, or Smout against Richelieu thirty years, before. Preachers could follow in their path the more fervently now that the marriage of 1641 had joined the House of Orange to England, and that France had annexed the principality of Orange.

The conflict with Münster had greatly stirred up anti-papist feeling. A vehement riot shook Arnhem in August, when a plot was discovered to deliver the town into the bishop's hands. There was also much irritation at the behaviour of the Spanish Netherlands. Not only was the bishop supplied with officers and soldiers, but troops from Spanish Brabant kept raiding the States territory, ostensibly in order to preserve the peace, and with the Spanish governors making profuse declarations of neutrality. In the southern provinces, meanwhile, Flemish writers issued a stream of pamphlets gleefully prophesying the collapse of the Republic, to which the North replied with vehement denunciations of all priests and monks.[134] Even so, it would be wrong to reduce the conflict to one of religion only: it was a Protestant ruler who financed the bishop's campaign, and a Catholic ruler who was threatening the Catholic southern Netherlands. Moreover, Gamarra, the Spanish ambassador, worked hand in glove with Downing, until the day the Englishman departed from the Hague, and even afterwards found a ready ear among those of the Orange party.

But all this did not prevent the ministers of religion from advocating peace with England and preaching distrust of Catholic France. Their pleas were often wrapped in references to the elevation of young William of Orange. Take the Reverend Sceperus of Gouda, who had this to say in September 1665:[134] 'Let us avoid all further bitterness, so that English and Dutch blood, united as they are in that great and worthy personage gracing Holland's Court, may no longer be locked in bitter antagonism.' His long-winded sermon, so crammed with quotations from Rome and the Old Testament that it became almost unreadable, was by no means unpatriotic; on the contrary, Sceperus argued most forcibly that a war between Holland and England was a bar between brethren, and that 'the Reformed world' would be the loser no matter which of the two sides won in the end. His sermon was deemed sufficient provocation for his suspension by the Gouda magistrates;[136] his flock, however, stood by him and collected money for the continued payment of his salary.[137]

A much more serious breach was the sermon of the Reverend Lantman, delivered two months later at the Hague itself. The very text he chose was a challenge to the States: 'I will go and return to my first husband, for then was it better with me than now.'[138] He went on to attack the French alliance, mentioning the St Bartholomew's massacre of 1572, the French Fury at Antwerp in 1583, and the subjection of La Rochelle, the Huguenot stronghold. There was nothing unusual in all this: the St Bartholomew's massacre had often been quoted by pamphleteers as an argument against the French alliance,[139] but in the case of Lantman, the States of Holland could do no less than suspend one who had insulted an ally and publicly challenged his country's foreign policy from a pulpit in the heart of the capital. Even so, it took only a month for him to be restored to office – after apologies and protestations that his intentions had been quite innocent. His colleague Simonides, who declared from the pulpit that common gratitude demanded that the young Prince of Orange be restored to the offices of his ancestors, was let off with a mere reprimand.

These and similar incidents may help to explain why, in the last week of October, while De Witt was cruising off the coast of England with the Dutch fleet, his policy should quite suddenly have come under strong fire. It all started with Van Goch's report of his audience with Charles II. An enormous commotion was caused by a surprise resolution of the Overijsel deputies in the States-General.[140] It not only called for compliance with 'His English Majesty's wish that an embassy be sent to England, but stipulated that the person best fitted to lead the mission was someone for whom Charles was known to cherish 'a singular affection' – to wit the Prince of Orange. Moreover, to strengthen the prince's authority the States would have to appoint him Captain- and Admiral-General, and seeing 'the tenderness of his years' provide him with a Lieutenant. At first, it looked as if Zeeland and Friesland would associate themselves with the Overijsel motion and that several towns in Holland, too, were sympathetic to it. Buysero, the greffier of the prince's council, immediately sprang into frantic action informing every member of the States in turn of the keen desire of other members to see the prince installed in high office.[141] He even told Fannius, a cousin of the Grand Pensionary and one of De Witt's close confidants, that complete discord could only be avoided if the prince were made a member of the Council of State thus paving the way for peace with England.[142] Van Goch, on whose report of 4 October, all the plans had been based, now wrote that he was sending his son – ostensibly to talk about an exchange of prisoners but, as most people supposed, also to go further into the matter of a separate peace. France, for one, was highly suspicious of these moves.

Excitement rose higher still when Van Beverning informed the assembly of Holland that he had decided to resign from the Treasurer-Generalship. His speech was tantamount to a declaration of his lack of confidence in the Grand Pensionary. Compared with this, the defection of Overijsel, a 'three-penny province' as it came to be called, was a minor disaster. For while Overijsel had the excuse that the Münster invasion had brought her dire trouble[143] and peace with England was her only hope of salvation, Van Beverning's disaffection shook the unity of the most powerful province of all, one on which all De Witt's authority was based.

On learning the news, D'Estrades hastened to Van Beverning in a desperate effort to get him to change his mind. He spoke of the confidence Louis reposed in him, and of the grave repercussions his resignation would have on De Witt's position. But Van Beverning said quite plainly that matters had come to a sorry pass and that he wanted no further responsibility for them. The state had been left in the lurch for far too long. It was now being assailed by two parties, both under the thumb of the King of England: the commonalty and magistrates were rightly alarmed at England's unprecedented display of power: a fleet of a hundred ships and an army of 30,000 men (he meant the Münster army) were drawn up against Holland, and England had further resources with which to beat the States unless they came to terms and kept the peace for evermore.[144]

This language must have pleased the Orange party, among whom faint-heartedness was exceedingly rife in those days. Take a pamphlet,[145] which, judging by its reasoned arguments, must have been the work of a man of some education. The pamphlet asserted that no war could be more harmful and intolerable to the Republic than the one with England. The Republic could never hope to win seeing that the Dutch fleet had been 'scraped together from different nations',[146] moreover, 'the English nation is more audacious and bellicose than ours'; England, finally, had the geographic advantage and did not have to look for help to treacherous France! Conclusion: what the Republic needs is peace and the only way to obtain it was to discover 'acceptable ways by which to persuade the King of England to sweeten the bitter opinion for which we have given him cause . . . on more than one occasion . . . All too often have we brushed aside recommendations by that king, which, as sensible politicians, we ought to have accepted without demur, if only to show our goodwill to the king, as on similar occasions we have not failed to do with regard to France. That the King of England has reason to feel aggrieved no one can deny in these circumstances, and on no point more than in the treatment of the Prince of Orange.' The writer went on to claim (quite wrongly) that promises made to Charles II in 1660 had not been honoured; he spoke of ingratitude towards the House of Orange; and he concluded with the assertion that it was through the prince that the King of England might be turned from an enemy into a friend, thus greatly enhancing the Republic's prestige in Europe. This line of thought, which betrayed so little faith in the national cause, was typical of the feelings of many Protestants and of the Orange party in particular.

De Witt's friends were now clamouring for his immediate return. Several deputies in the States of Holland took the Overijsel motion seriously enough to consult their town governments about it. Amsterdam, in particular, showed a marked lack of 'boldness'.[147] D'Estrades sent reports to France of so alarming a tone that Louis was exceedingly glad he had authorized the ambassador to promise a declaration of war against England; it now seemed the only way to prevent Holland's submission. Yet D'Estrades felt the situation could be exploited in quite other ways. Confusion was now such that he asked himself whether France could not use the army corps she was sending out against Münster to obtain a foothold in the Republic. He was thinking quite particularly of Gulik or Maastricht.[148] Once in possession of these, it would be possible to dominate the Republic, without having to bother about those un-accountable States assemblies or the town magistracies. And if Gulik or Maastricht were unobtainable, a coup might well be brought off in the very heart of the Republic.

There were Friesland and Groningen, for instance. The Stadholder, William Frederick, had died on 31 October 1664, and his widow, the daughter of Frederick Henry and Amalia, was acting as deputy-stadholder for her little son. She was on bad terms with her mother and had made no secret of that fact in her talks with D'Estrades. After she had offered her services to France quite openly – she objected strongly to the English atmosphere in which her young nephew was being educated in the Hague – her confidants Van Haren and Bottsma filled in the details. (The reader will remember these men for their close relations with Downing). They now talked of an occupation of Münster, after which Louis might deal with Friesland and Groningen as he pleased; the princess could count on the support of the governors of Koevorden and Steenwijk and on many more. Indeed, the claims and promises they made were so reckless that one would be inclined to discount D'Estrades' report, were it not that it was all so very much in the tradition of the late William Frederick. An old claim by William Louis (William Frederick's father) now served as a pretext for a request that France offer financial assistance to the princess.

Bribing had become second nature to D'Estrades in the crisis and, if we are to believe him, he was a past master at it. The noblemen of Gelderland and Overijsel, ruined by the invasion, were said to be eager for 'gratifications'; the town magistrates of Holland were all of them said to be open to corruption – with the exception of the two De Witts, Van Beuningen and Van Beverning. But then D'Estrades was a braggart, a man who falsified his own letters for the sake of future generations, and many of his claims were patently false.[149] He betrayed himself not only with obvious exaggerations, but also by telling demonstrable lies. That he did hand out money here and there is probably true enough: at any rate he received considerable sums for that purpose. But the claim that it was French money alone that stopped the Dutch from succumbing to English temptations ('the Spanish, the English and the Orange parties' are all fighting with the same weapon), that it was only by bribes that he, D'Estrades, managed to avert the danger of an elevation of the young prince and of the signing of a peace which would have meant a rupture with France – all that does not fit the picture of the situation as we know it. D'Estrades' principals, whom he no doubt tried to dazzle with the importance of the role he was playing, were all too pleased to read his gibes about the unpredictable and inconstant behaviour of 'a popular government', but not even Louis was completely taken in, or so his replies to the ambassador suggest. For us, at any rate, the violent fluctuations of Dutch public opinion were dictated by changes in political circumstances and not by mere greed. It is not only quite unnecessary, but betrays a lack of understanding of public reactions in war time generally and of Dutch history in particular, to argue that instead of real *men* with a variety of national, political, religious sentiments scrambling among themselves, the Dutch were mere puppets jumping this way or that as Spaniards, Englishmen, the Princess Dowager, or the French ambassador tugged at the purse-strings.

De Witt continues in office; Louis recalls his ambassadors from England (November 1665)

In the midst of this crisis, De Witt, as we saw, at long last returned home. Within a few days and with his customary composure, he gave his own view of the situation in letters to his brother Cornelis and to Van Beuningen. The disasters at sea (he meant the storms) and advances by Münster's troops had caused 'the minds of many prominent and well-meaning regents, not only in the other provinces but even in Holland', to become 'considerably upset and depressed'. And 'those who were out to suppress the country's freedom' (i.e. the Orange party) 'were making full use of the occasion. But God be thanked, I cannot at present observe but that all good patriots have taken heart again and that matters are going well.'[150] The Overijsel proposal, De Witt continued, had only made such a great impression on the people because they assumed that it was supported by others, an idea that had been spread abroad by Buysero and the like. But now everyone had come to realize how ludicrous and how humilating the plan really was. In Zeeland, De Witt's emissary, Colonel Bampfield, had little difficulty in persuading Burgomaster Thibaut of this fact. Unfortunately, the Zeeland Grand Pensionary, Pieter de Huybert, who had succeeded Veth in 1664, was a man whose political views differed radically from De Witt's. He and his cousin Justus, who had become secretary to the States of Zeeland at practically the same time, were staunch Orangists, and objected to a close alliance with France on religious grounds.[151] But Huybert's influence was not very great at the time and, moreover, eclipsed by marriage links between the powerful Thibaut and Veth-Vryjbergen families, with both of whom De Witt was on friendly terms.[152] It appeared that, even in Overijsel, not everyone was pleased with the motion of the provincial deputies – Van Pallant and Van Langen – the more so as they had acted without due instructions and now had to apologize to their own States.[153]

In short, there had been a panic, not unnatural in the critical circumstances, and then a more balanced reaction and a return to a sense of national dignity. The entire episode, moreover, had been influenced not so much by foreign bribes, as by the absence of De Witt. 'If only that taskmaster had stayed away for another month, our plan would probably have succeeded.' So spoke Van Pallant, adding bitterly that Zeeland had left him in the lurch.[154]

The fact that De Witt could keep control of the situation was in no small measure due to the assistance he obtained from France, not in the form of *livres* and *ecus*, but of political support. The French ambassador had no need to disclose Louis's intention to declare war on England – the danger did not become acute enough for that. But the French government not only dispatched auxiliary troops, but had come to appreciate that the patience of the States must be strained no further. It was a blow to Louis XIV's pride that, despite all his negotiations, he was now facing a rupture with England and, moreover, facing it at a moment when the death of his father-in-law, Philip IV, had brought the Spanish prize within his reach. The southern Netherlands, which had been sympathetic to England and Münster, now greeted the approaching rupture between England and France with relief as a safeguard of their own territorial integrity. Even so, Louis realized that a collapse of the States régime, which would lead to the creation of an Orange state under the thumb of England, had to be prevented at all costs. In the circumstances, however, he felt entitled to demand guarantees that the Republic would stand by him once he had broken with England.

Hence De Witt's first task was to obtain a declaration from the States of Holland that they would not enter into separate negotiations with England. The Grand Pensionary and the French ambassador exercised joint pressure on the town governments, and by 14 November, D'Estrades was able to dispatch a courier with the message that the States had voted unanimously in the sense demanded by France.

Things now proceeded apace, the more so as the English government, once again yielding to a wave of war fever, rejected a third peace proposal by the French negotiators out of hand. Louis decided to recall his envoys from England, and demanded that the States follow suit by recalling Van Goch. But this was easier said than done. For though the towns had made a promise in an endeavour to obtain French help, and though they were relieved that the peace plan and the untoward concessions to England contained in it had been shelved for good, doubters and Orangists alike were anxious to avoid a final break with England. So strong was their opposition that De Witt considered leaving Van Goch at his post, even though Van Beuningen implored him not to give a handle to French suspicion. The matter was settled when Van Goch's son, returning from England declared – a pleasant surprise for De Witt[155] – that the English court had no real desire for peace. This decided the States to take the final step. In their letter of 11 December 1665, notifying Charles II of their ambassador's recall, they once again assured the king of their desire for peace. At the same time, they made it clear that they demanded a return to the *status quo* or the acceptance of a state of *uti possidetis*.

Brandenburg; Denmark; Peace with Münster (April 1666)

It now looked as if the war would continue through the winter, and with France fighting on the side of the Republic. De Witt and D'Estrades were busily negotiating about common naval action, and particularly about the difficult problem of the naval command. Nobody foresaw that their plans would never have to be implemented. In October 1665, the Duke of Beaufort was ordered to transfer his fleet from the Mediterranean to the West. When, after long delays, he arrived at Dieppe towards the end of September 1666, the campaigning season was nearly over and, in any case, he had missed De Ruyter. Meanwhile, Pradel's small army corps had done well against Münster, although the French soldiery made themselves thoroughly unpopular by their rude treatment of the population. Moreover, relations between Pradel and Prince Maurice, the supreme commander, were far from good and his clashes with the Field Deputies of the States-General were fiercer still. In any case, before the year 1665 was out, the Bishop of Münster was compelled to evacuate the territory of the States and was facing an invasion of his own.

The diplomats of the belligerent countries were hard at work all over Europe to find assistance for their own side and to frustrate help to their adversary. England, as Louis XIV had rightly foreseen, looked primarily to Spain – since a French attack on the Spanish Netherlands seemed merely a question of time, England hoped to gain Spanish support with a promise of keeping the French at bay. But there were many obstacles. To begin with, there was England's alliance with Spain's enemy Portugal: English diplomacy had failed to patch up a quarrel that had dragged on ever since 1640. Colonial interests played their part as well. The upshot of it all was that the Spanish government, which even in peacetime had felt its empire slipping from its grasp, felt unable to sever relations with the France they hated but also feared. All that Louis had to do – and even this he felt to be a heavy price for his alliance with the Republic – was to postpone his attack on the southern Netherlands.

The English had no better luck in gaining the support or at least the neutrality of the Scandinavian countries. Here, French support stood the Republic in good stead, even though France pressed the States to make further concessions to Sweden and Denmark. In the end, England was completely isolated. In February 1666, Denmark entered into an alliance with the Republic, which cost the States a great deal of money, and England even more disappointment. At the same time, Münster was cut off from all help except financial support from England, and this proved inadequate – the bishop had based all his plans on the support of other German principalities, and quite especially of Brandenburg.

In December, the Elector of Brandenburg travelled to Cleves, where his own interests were at stake. Here he was besieged by ambassadors from the States-General, from France, and from England. The States ambassador, Van Beverning, arrived at the end of January 1666. His position in the town of Gouda was so strong, that De Witt had gone to great trouble in regaining his support and in urging him to serve on the mission to Cleves, even sending a solemn deputation from the States of Holland.

In France, Van Beverning's ostentatious resignation as Treasurer-General in October was, quite naturally, remembered against him, and his tendency to avoid the French ambassador at Cleves greatly intensified suspicions, the more so as he was reported to have had a conversation with the English envoy.

All the same, the negotiations with the Elector proved successful. The Elector had grievances of his own against the States and, like everyone else, tried to make use of their present embarrassment to have these grievances remedied. In particular, he wanted the States to withdraw their garrison from the town of Orsoy. Nevertheless, on 16 February 1666, when he signed the treaty, it made no mention of Orsoy, but contained his promise to urge the bishop to conclude peace and, in case the bishop proved refractory, to assist the States with troops (to be paid for by the Republic). This new threat left the bishop no choice but to give way. In spite of an eleventh-hour promise of further subsidies by Sir William Temple, the English resident at Brussels, Münster made peace in April 1666.

Arlington plays off the Orange party; Instructions to Vane (November 1665)

France had had no cause for alarm about Van Beverning's alleged conversation with Vane, the English envoy at Cleves – it never took place. But they had good reason to distrust Van Beverning, all the same. The English were known to be most anxious to make contact with all enemies of France and of De Witt, in an effort to undermine the dangerous alliance, and to have built high hopes on Van Beverning. Arlington was in a far better position now than he had been in July 1665 to interfere in the Dutch party struggle: in October, he had been appointed Secretary of State. His hand could be clearly seen in the instruction which Sir Walter Vane took with him to Cleves, and which contained the following passages:[156]

You shall let [the Elector] know that wee looke upon the rise of this warre betwixt us and the United Provinces to bee, not from the Estates, but only from de Witte and his faction and adherents out of an animosity to our Nephew the Prince of Orange and his family, and therefore that wee doe not thinke that wee or the Elector [another uncle of the prince] can have any firme friendshippe with that country, so long as they have such power, and the more for that they are wholy guided by French counsels . . . Itt is evident that this warre has allready wrought so farre as to make the people weary of their gouvernement in a great measure to cast their eyes upon the Prince of Orange, witnesse the frequent affronts put upon the Drummers that were employed for the levying of men, if they did not make use of the name of the Prince, witness also their ordinary discourses in their boats, the preaching and praying of their ministers, their cryings out of late against the new forme of prayer [see above], and the late resolution of the province of Over-Isel for the sending of him in Ambassade to Us, and making him General and Admiral. When the warre shall have pinched them a little longer, itt is not to be doubted but other provinces will followe their example and that this Establishment is the only means for us both to have any settled quiet with them and for the keeping up the protestant interest here. [Coming as it did from a Stuart who was soon afterwards to entertain plans for restoring Catholicism in England, this is an amusing touch. The instruction was, of course, adapted to suit the taste of the Elector.] Therefore you shall desire that by his influence amongst the people of those provinces especially in Guelderland and Frise, hee does sturre up the friends of the family of Orange to apprease and laye hold of this opportunity for the shaking of the Act of Seclusion and the late Treaty between Holland and Zeeland[157] and the Lovesteins party, assuring them that wee shall stand by them, and that when the Prince shall be restablished, we will hearken to very moderate terms of accomodation, and that itt would not only bee very dishonourable to us to make peace without *his* inclusion, whose exclusion was a maine part and inducement to the treaty with Cromwell, but that then de Witte and his party would so roote themselfe in the gouvernment as that there would remaine very little hopes of the Prince's ever obtaining anything afterwards. You shall also endeavour that the Elector possesse the Princesse Dowager of Orange hearewith . . . You shall also hearewith deliver to the Princesse Dowager our letters, assuring her of our harty kindness to her and her family, and that wee do not designe the ruin of the United Provinces, but only just and reasonable securitys for the injurys wee suffered by them, and that wee looke on this warre as the only product of de Witte's malice to her and her sonne [read: grandson] . . . You are to endeavour to worke upon the Electress of Brandenburg upon the same accoumpts, and also upon the Princesse of Nassau [the Governess of Friesland] if shee bee there [both daughters of Amalia].

This document gives us an important glimpse into the attitudes and intentions of the English government. In the event, Vane's mission remained completely unsuccessful. The Elector, as we saw, did not let himself be swayed from signing a treaty against Münster. And as for the Prince of Orange, the Elector – like Clarendon before him – had issued a stern warning that if England now championed his claims, it would look as if she were trying to force the Republic's hand. The Electress, too, had foreseen this objection, but she had nevertheless begged Vane to persist; so great was her enthusiasm for the Orange cause that she did her utmost to undermine the alliance against Münster.[158] And though the evidence is not conclusive, it would appear that not only his wife, but her mother as well, seems to have pressed the Elector to pay heed to Vane.[159] In the face of all this pressure, Van Beverning volunteered the assurance[160] that Holland would be able to protect the Prince's interests without outside assistance (we shall learn below what precisely he had in mind). Whether the Elector needed that assurance we cannot tell; in any case he refused to be swayed by his womenfolk. He even forwarded an anonymous letter from a Dutchman,[161] urging him not to ally himself with the States until these had restored the prince to his father's offices, to the States, that they might trace the writer. As for Vane, his hopes that Van Beverning would get in touch with him remained unfulfilled.

Buat and Sylvius negotiate with Van Beverning (Autumn 1665–January 1666)

Vane's expectations that Van Beverning would take the first step were not only based on the latter's resignation or on vague utterances of doubt or dissatisfaction – Van Beverning was highly temperamental and, moreover, loved a glass of wine – but on other factors, as well.

In November 1665, the States-General had sent Van Beverning to Maastricht to be present at the reception of the French auxiliary corps. His fellow deputy was Henry de Fleury de Coulan, Seigneur de Buat, St Sire et La Forest de Gay, a French nobleman who had grown up in Holland, where his father had served in the States army. He himself had been a page at the Orange court, and still held a post there; he had married the daughter of Musch, the late Greffier of the States-General and another well-known champion of the illustrious House. Buat had visited England as a member of the retinue of the Princess Royal, the widow of William II. After her death, the Princess-Dowager saw to his promotion in the States army and also got him an annuity from Charles II (to be set off against the Stuart debt to Orange); the promised annuity was paid irregularly, as was usual in England at the time. It was to discuss this matter that Buat had travelled to England once again and, being a brave and cordial fellow, he had become a popular figure at court. Though Buat was anything but a diplomat or statesman, Arlington remembered him when, after Downing's departure from the Hague, he wished to continue the agitation for peace without France. Buat was away in Paris when, in September 1665, Sir Gabriel Sylvius sent him a letter containing a detailed offer of peace.

Sylvius, like Oudart, Zuylestein, Wootton-Heenvliet, Boreel jr., and one might say Buat himself, had been one of that group of servants of the House of Orange to whom the dynastic interests of Orange and Stuart were the crux of all political alignments. By origin he was neither Dutch nor English: he hailed from Orange. Coming to England in the service of the young Princess Royal, he had stayed on there after her death and had found a place in the English public service. He was on intimate terms with Arlington, the rising star in the English political firmament, and it was certainly on the instigation of Arlington that he had written to Buat. A little later, Sylvius was sent abroad: in early January we find him at Antwerp, corresponding with Buat in the Hague, and making appointments for a personal meeting. Great plans were clearly afoot.

When Buat received Sylvius's first letter in Paris, he took it to Van Beuningen. Needless to say, the latter was not impressed with a peace offer that had no other purpose than to divide the Republic from France, and that must have made reference to the elevation of the Prince of Orange.[162] Van Beverning, on the other hand, as Buat discovered on their joint expedition, was more open to persuasion, and this despite the fact that he had shrugged off Buat's pro-English speeches in the past.[163] While chatting about the state of the world with his companion, the Holland States deputy now let his tongue run away with himself.

'He said,'[164] (as Sylvius later told Arlington) 'that he did not agree with the Grand Pensionary De Witt, whose policy was too ambitious and did not serve the state's interests. A decent peace was what all patriots ought to strive for and he, Van Beverning, would always be ready for one.' Buat, seizing the chance to gain this powerful man for the prince's cause, fell in with his argument and assured him that there was every possibility of securing a decent peace, provided only they went the right way about it: 'If only the Republic made a gesture towards the Prince of Orange, the king would surely listen to any peace offers they might have to make. And he advised Van Beverning to work towards that objective. To which Van Beverning replied that he was quite willing to do so [it will be remembered[165] that, in August, he had had thoughts of approaching Downing] but that he knew that the king had heard malicious stories about him. If only he could be sure he would be well received, he would gladly be of help. Buat then offered to write to me [Sylvius], suggesting that I should show his letter to the king, and told Van Beverning that he had no doubt but that he [Van Beverning] would have reason to be satisfied with the reply.'

Buat now set to work with a will. Not only did he write to Sylvius (as we saw) to obtain a reassuring message for Van Beverning, and an invitation for both of them to visit England, he also informed the Princess-Dowager of what was happening, so that she might do what she could to land this unexpected catch for 'our party'.[166] The Dowager invited Van Beverning to call and showed him Buat's letter, whereupon he told her that he was still of the same mind. Towards the middle of December, Sylvius had a secret meeting with Buat somewhere near Rotterdam, during which he learned so many particulars about the political situation and the great chances it offered, that, as he put it himself, he might have written a book instead of the fairly circumstantial report that has come down to us. On that occasion, Sylvius was introduced to several of the leading Orangists. At Christmas time, he paid another visit to the Republic and even ventured to go to the Hague.

Meanwhile, the Republic was in a great political turmoil. We shall see that Sylvius's original reports were much too hopeful, but we know from other sources that the state of public agitation on which he was counting existed in fact. The Overijsel proposal might have been rejected, but the problem of the prince's elevation had not thereby been disposed of for good. The Orange party was convinced that the moment for it had now come. Among the public at large, a desire for reconciliation with England was coupled to a more patriotic sense of outrage at the deplorable weakness the army was displaying against the Bishop of Münster's forces. According to Aitzema, people were murmuring that

we allow ourselves to be bitten by a mouse; we are assailed by one whom formerly we should have counted for naught and were able to compel and keep in his place by merely pulling an angry face. And all this because the army lacks a general, an illustrious head. How well and creditably would not the work of war have been performed under the Princes of Orange![167]

Old Maurice of Nassau was incapable of restoring discipline, and his officers were looking to Orange.[168]

Naturally the youth of the prince proved a great handicap. Another difficulty was to make the popular clamour of the people for Orange be heard in the federal assembly, where the party was weak. Sylvius expressed great annoyance that the representatives of the prince's interest remained so inactive and seemed resigned 'to sleep in the expectation that the power of England will compel Holland' to come to the aid of the young man. He had warned them that 'if they wanted support from the king, His Majesty hoped that they for their part would make an effort to build up a party; and to that end they are now working with all their friends.'[169]

In any case, the public mood was such that the Orange party could have made things exceedingly uncomfortable for De Witt. Sylvius expected a revolt. A change, he thought, had become inevitable. The people were grumbling openly against the States, and the impending 'restoration' of the prince was on everyone's lips.[170] In Holland, taxes had been raised to pay for the war. Now that, as a result of the Münster invasion, the inland provinces were unable to make even the small contribution they had 'consented', Holland had to bear a very heavy burden and this at a time when her trade was so badly disrupted. The well-to-do citizens, the wealthy merchants, might stick it out for a few years, but the poor, the labourers in the ports, the fisher folk, had begun to suffer grave deprivations. The situation was even worse in Zeeland, where there was a preponderance of the poorer classes.

Sylvius believed that De Witt enjoyed little support from even the ruling circles. The reason why three provinces besides Holland still stuck to him was simple. Utrecht – according to Sylvius – was swayed by Renswoude, alleged to be a blind follower of Holland's policies (which he was not, in fact); in Gelderland, the poverty-stricken nobility was utterly dependent on Generality jobs, and these were now doled out by Holland. This left Zeeland whose regents had the reputation of being pro-Orange, but had nevertheless seen fit to conclude a treaty with Holland (in 1663) by which any decision about the prince's future was postponed until he reached the age of eighteen. There, no improvement was to be expected as long as the Dowager was unwise enough to antagonize the powerful Thibauts and Vrijbergens, now allied in marriage. Sylvius accordingly set his greatest hopes in dissension in Holland herself. He knew that, since the death of De Graeff, the uncle of De Witt's wife, the States party could no longer count on Amsterdam. Opposition was rife in several other important centres as well. The little towns of North Holland were all of them pro-Orange. If a man with the renown and ability of Van Beverning had only dared to give the opposition a lead, he might well have drawn the whole of Holland away from De Witt.

That, at any rate, is how Sylvius saw the situation after his first visit in December. But, as he himself was quick to remark, there was just one major snag: Van Beverning seemed already '*un peu refroidi'*.[171] And when one looks at the situation from the Dutch point of view, one realizes that De Witt did, in fact, hold strong cards. Sylvius and Buat never tired of ranting and raving at his cunning and impudence in trying to make his fellow-countrymen believe that the King of England did not really want peace. That lie, they claimed, was the foundation of his power. But *was* it really a lie? Was it not the only correct conclusion to be drawn from the *célèbre ambassade*? The peace Charles sought was one in which Dutch interests would take second place to English – and it was such a peace that Sylvius now tried to obtain with the help of the Orange party. A man like Buat heeded him eagerly, simply because he failed to realize that what he was advocating was not honourable peace but abject surrender. He accepted at their face value the most hollow assurances of love and peace as readily as he did the most far-fetched accusations against the States party. Nor was he the only one to do so – in the prevailing atmosphere of party passion, animosity towards De Witt, worship of Orange, hatred of France, it was not surprising that many regents should have been equally credulous. But while most Dutchmen, including their regents, might let themselves be deluded by phantom promises of a peace that required no greater effort than a gesture to the Prince of Orange – when it came to the crunch they were wise enough to look at the substance rather than the shadow of Charles's offer. And when they did, they saw that De Witt was not being swayed by mere obstinacy.

Sylvius himself realized that in order to mobilize Orange opinion against De Witt and his policy, more was needed than the general assurances of goodwill he was able to offer. Buat was met with flat disbelief when he told the burgomaster of several towns how kindly Charles was disposed towards the Netherlands. A letter Sylvius had specially written for him, and with which he was asked to win over the burgomaster of Amsterdam, contained nothing but generalities either. All his friends were agreed that vague promises were not enough. Only if they knew what precisely was in Charles's mind, could they launch a successful campaign.[172]

So, at the turn of the year, Sylvius crossed to England (which had sent him many warm professions of interest and encouragement) to report and to receive more precise instructions. Some time earlier, he had suggested that the king should use the letter recalling Van Goch as the occasion for a reply in which he should once again stress his peaceful intentions. If it was thought proper to have him, Sylvius, deliver that letter, he would, with the help of Buat, ensure that it was printed and widely distributed, so that every man in the street should come to know it.[173] But the English preferred to use Van Goch himself as their tool. Before he departed, he was made to learn his lesson by heart and on 11 January, he recited it before the States-General, not so badly either. But then, as Sylvius complained a week later, after a talk with Van Goch,[174] De Witt had gained a stranglehold over the former ambassador (according to Sylvius by playing on his love of money – the more probable explanation, however, was that, back in the Hague, the ambassador was at long last able to shake off the spell the English court had cast over him) 'so that he is no longer the same man and seems to be struck dumb'.[175]

The royal reply communicated by Van Goch made no mention of the proposal contained in the letter recalling the ambassador,[176] it was nothing but propaganda. The king had never wanted the war; he had been compelled to wage it by the high-handed treatment of his subjects and the orders to De Ruyter to start hostilities off the Guinea Coast. In his conversations with the French mediators the king had not rejected any, even the most presumptuous suggestions, and he had recalled his ambassador in the Hague only when the arrest of his secretary 'by the States of Holland, who are in reality the authors of this war', proved that the ambassador's person was exposed to danger. Nevertheless, he still deplored a war which might have such dangerous consequences for Protestantism, 'for the Protestant religion which is infinitely dearer to Us than any interest of state; and we wish that you may cherish the same peace-loving sentiments so that we can unite in indissoluble bonds, well knowing that you will therefrom gather more fruit than from alliances which will make you pay for their assistance with harsh conditions prejudicial to the interests of your state'.[177]

What Charles was thus trying to do was to address Dutch malcontents over the heads of their States. Overijsel and Gelderland, groaning under the Münster invasion, were given to understand that it was merely Holland's commercial interest and Holland's pride that had caused the war. The ministers of religion were given a text for a sermon on the war between brethren. The innate suspicions of France were played upon: the French conditions to which Charles alluded were clearly the demand for a slice of the southern Netherlands. The whole thing then, was blunt and clumsy propaganda, but yet not entirely devoid of cunning, and, as Sylvius had foreseen, the king's letter was 'kept very secret', so as 'not to rouse the commonalty to sedition', as a respectable Hague lawyer explained in a letter to his brother then abroad, adding:[178] 'Some copies are being handed round; if I can get hold of one I shall send it to you.' He also informed his brother that several lampoons against the regents had appeared. He had heard one being read, but did not himself wish to burden himself with such stuff; it might be dangerous.

A few days later, when Sylvius returned from England, Buat assured him that the king's letter had had 'a wondrous effect in all towns, and especially in the larger ones of Holland, where the longing for peace is acute'.[179] His friend, Burgomaster Kievit of Rotterdam, a brother-in-law of Cornelis Tromp, had been so much impressed by the document that he had stopped his town from authorizing its deputies to support certain decisions on foreign affairs in the States. These decisions all tended to tighten the links with France, and Buat's friends were successful in getting Amsterdam, Haarlem and Leyden, to vote against them as well. What D'Estrades was particularly worried about was the refusal by the various towns Sylvius had approached to contribute the sums they had already 'consented to', and though quite unaware of Sylvius's activities, he was, in fact, counteracting them by treating the deputies to a series of dinners.[180] On the whole, he was not dissatisfied with the course of events, the more so as France's approaching rupture with England inevitably strengthened De Witt's position.

On 18 January, Sylvius arrived in the Hague. It was characteristic of the time that the war seemed no reason for deferring the announcement of the betrothal of Freule van Beverweert, the sister of Nassau-Odijk and Nassau-Ouwerkerk, to, of all people, Lord Arlington, the English Secretary of State. That alliance could not but strengthen the distrust with which De Witt and many others regarded the policies of the Orange court. But civic leaders in the Hague went out to compliment the young lady and, soon afterwards, when she left for England via Antwerp, she was given a send-off as if the country she had adopted were a close ally.

This time, Sylvius had arrived with more concrete proposals, with which he hoped to persuade Van Beverning to come out into the open at last. But the bait his principals had devised was too poor to be swallowed by so seasoned a diplomat. Van Beverning saw only too clearly but was merely trying to create further dissension. Even an abler man than Sylvius would have found it hard to disguise this fact, and Sylvius's report of his conversations with Van Beverning makes it all too clear that he was not born to practise diplomacy.

His very reception by Van Beverning made it clear how little importance the latter had come to attach to England's peace offers (if their intrigues deserve to be called by that name). He explained in the kindest possible way that in spite of his promises to Buat, he had found it impossible to decline the mission to Cleves, once the States of Holland had come in a body to invite him, and that he had merely postponed his departure for Cleves not to miss the privilege of meeting his visitor from England.[181] In fact, he had by then decided to fit in with De Witt's plans and to do what he could to further them – D'Estrades rightly concluded from his acceptance of the Cleves mission that the Orange party was powerless after all.[182]

Sylvius credulously swallowed the apologies. When Van Beverning left him for an hour to 'think over' the points of his message, he never realized that his interlocutor had gone to consult De Witt.[183] (Van Beverning had previously told Buat that he had informed De Witt that Sylvius would be conveying an offer from England.) And when Sylvius tried, after their meeting, to compose a report for his English principals of Van Beverning's comments on complicated colonial and commercial questions, the task proved too much for him. His report was never finished. As he put it himself, his memory failed him, and his suggestion that Van Beverning made concessions on one important point barely deserves credence.[184]

Expectations of the conspirators; De Witt's Turenne plan (February 1666); Sylvius's peace proposals rejected

To write his defective report, Sylvius went back to England. On 2 February – a week after Louis XIV had declared war – new conditions were drafted which allegedly met most of Van Beverning's objections. However, the new document remained extremely vague on the question of the war indemnity, on the precise method by which the commercial interests of the two countries were to be co-ordinated, and about the claims of His Majesty's allies. Only on one point was the document quite specific:

> If His Majesty can be certain that the States will conclude an alliance with him and against France – which is truly the only way for them to secure their safety and to guard themselves against too close a vicinity of France – and if, moreover, His Majesty can be convinced that the peace will be followed by the restoration of the Prince of Orange, then His Majesty is prepared to leave the manner and the conduct of that affair to their judgement entirely; and in that case you may tell them that, according to your belief, they would be able to obtain some reduction of the sum suggested by His Majesty (the indemnity, put at 200,000 pounds sterling) or at least a longer term for the payment.[185]

It will be seen that the English government intended, not only to break up the hated Dutch-French alliance but to drag the Republic into an anti-French bloc. Arlington, for one, believed firmly in the practicability of such a scheme.[186] As for the proposals concerning the Prince of Orange, these were inspired by the advice of 'some men well inclined for the interests of His Majesty.'[187] 'If the king demands a large sum of money' (so he was told), 'they will rather pay up than lose the peace; but if the peace has to be bought dearly, there will be less inclination to do anything for the Prince of Orange and more excuse for doing nothing. His enemies will benefit.'

The last view shows that Sylvius met with objections from even his English contacts or, at least, that these contacts were aware that the prince's elevation did not depend on his devoted adherents alone.[188] Worth nothing also is the following reflection, by which Sylvius's Orangist friends tried to further their cause. 'The influence which the king can exercise in the future through the prince and his party will be worth to His Majesty a good deal more than some millions in his hands.'

On 14 February, Sylvius arrived at Rotterdam after a journey fraught with dangers: the whole of Western Brabant (he was once again travelling via Antwerp) was in an uproar following a raid by a gang of soldiers from Münster. When Sylvius finally arrived, Buat, who had been waiting for him impatiently, immediately summoned a council of war with the Rotterdam regents Kievit and Van der Horst.

The supporters of the Prince of Orange were just then in full cry. Five provinces in the States-General were pressing for his appointment to the Captain-Generalship. Gelderland and Utrecht, of which Sylvius had only just said that they did De Witt's every bidding, had suddenly changed sides. Zeeland alone, observing the 1663 agreement, still supported Holland, where several towns had begun to waver. In quiet times, the clamour for the prince would hardly have posed a threat to the established order; but, in the circumstances, De Witt had cause to be worried about the English intrigue, of which Van Beverning had kept him informed. At any rate, Sylvius's table companions in Rotterdam assured him that De Witt and D'Estrades were desperately uneasy, now that Charles II's demand for peace could no longer be ignored.

In fact, De Witt made a rather strained attempt to regain the initiative. For some time past, he had been aware that it was time to do something about the high-handed manner in which the prince's future had been shelved in 1663. Now that the English were using the elevation of Orange as a pawn against him, it had become imperative to take the wind out of their sails. Even before Sylvius's visit in January, De Witt had given the Princess-Dowager assurances to that effect. However, the princess doubted his word, and wondered whether more could not be gained from reliance on England. All the same, she reported De Witt's assurances to the elector and so did Van Beverning,[189] who was greatly encouraged by De Witt's change of mind.

The moment had now come to translate intentions into practice, and early in February, De Witt surprised the States of Holland with a concrete scheme for the prince's future. William was to be made a cavalry general (in which rank Frederick Henry had served for years), and, as there was an urgent need for a capable army leader, De Witt further intended to offer the supreme command in the impending campaign to the Duke of Turenne. This choice, he hoped, would prove acceptable to the Orange court. Turenne's mother was a daughter of William the Silent; he himself was one of the most renowned commanders of the period; his conversion to Catholicism was not yet accomplished. De Witt's adversaries, however, looked upon Turenne as a mere tool of the French court, and hence decried the whole idea as a plot to bring the young Orange under French domination. In his conversations with D'Estrades De Witt did indeed lay emphasis on the fact that the appointment would help to tear the prince from England and to join him to France. He even suggested that Louis should personally call for the appointment of the prince, so that the latter would feel dependent upon the king's favour. At the time, he brought up the subject of the inconclusive 1663 negotiations about the fate of the Spanish Netherlands: how advantageous would it not be for the king if he could count on the assistance of the Republic when moving against that country! . . . One cannot suppress the uneasy feeling that De Witt, in resisting the English party, was leaning over backwards to appease the French. True, he meant to give Turenne no more than a temporary position; moreover, he believed that the offer of help in the Spanish Netherlands was the only way to stop France from attacking points of greater strategic importance. This calculation, at any rate, was mistaken, just as was Louis's belief that he could conquer without De Witt's help and was therefore in a position to reject it.

It was not at all surprising that the entire pro-English and pro-Orange party should have risen up in arms against the Turenne scheme. What may look astonishing, however, is that the Princess-Dowager should have agreed to it. The reason was, no doubt, that she was clever to see through the English professions of peace, and that she felt impressed by the strength of De Witt's position. Like Van Beverning, she had come to see the error of her ways. After all, France *had* at long last declared war; a treaty with Denmark *had* been signed and a treaty with the Elector was ready for signature. Now, the knowledge that the Elector was going to range himself on the side of the States must have weighed very heavily with Amalia. She was sufficiently sharp-witted to warn Buat against the dangers to which he was exposing himself – Louis was likely to retaliate by sequestering all his estates in France. The warning greatly frightened Madame Buat, and this despite Sylvius's many assurances that her husband's mission would earn him great renown at home and abroad.[190]

It goes without saying that the Dowager's attitude was bitterly resented by Sylvius's friends, who claims that she had let the pensionaries of France talk her round. They were particularly incensed to find that De Witt was now able to ask the Dowager's approval as a stick to beat the opposition.[191] However, in that they were quite wrong. Rotterdam and Haarlem took an adamant stand in the States of Holland, and now that Sylvius had brought over the new English peace conditions, De Witt's position was considerably weakened. The conspirators decided that Buat himself should inform De Witt of the new conditions (Van Beverning was away at Cleves), and that a number of towns should be told beforehand so that they might keep a strict eye on De Witt when he was eventually forced to lay the matter before the States of Holland. 'In case he plays false,' Sylvius wrote to Arlington, 'they will pull him up unsparingly.'[192] Kievit and Van der Horst took charge of Delft, Leyden and Haarlem; they still had hopes that Gouda, too, might join them despite Van Beverning's defection. In the Hague, Buat and Sylvius set to work on a number of deputies from the Northern Quarter, and Sylvius was able to persuade Burgomaster Blauw of Purmerend that England and the King of England had been badly misrepresented. Diederik Pauw, a relative of Buat and also of Valckenier, the up-and-coming man of Amsterdam, went to work upon the latter. The Dowager, too, was approached and the emissaries did actually succeed in making her back down a little.

De Witt received Buat on 15 February, and was handed the English document, or rather its first three points only;[193] the fourth, dealing with joint action against France and with the future of the Prince of Orange was kept for the 'friends' alone. Buat, moreover, showed the Grand Pensionary a personal letter from Arlington, in which the latter attested to the sincerity of the peace proposals and expressed (in accordance with the original plan) a desire to see Van Beverning as envoy to England, where Buat himself would also be welcome.[194]

From Sylvius's hastily written report[195] we gather that De Witt raised immediate objection to a number of vague and ambiguous points. Yet Sylvius also dilates at length on the amiability of his reception and on the hopes De Witt had apparently held out to him. De Witt's own account of the meeting to Van Beuningen has quite a different ring.[198] Though the fourth article was kept from him, he was quick to discern that 'it was the intention to separate this state from France'; and, in fact, he pointed out to Buat that if the king were serious, he ought to offer conditions to the two allied countries simultaneously. Not only did he send a full report to Van Beuningen, but he related the entire interview to D'Estrades. Arlington's letter to Buat naturally revived D'Estrades's distrust of Van Beverning, and Van Beverning felt compelled, during a brief visit to the Hague, to call on D'Estrades and to clear himself as best he could.[197]

Meanwhile the matter came before the States of Holland, and De Witt sent for Buat to tell him the result (probably on 21 February). De Witt's account – intended for Sylvius – amounted to the following:

The three points 'were too general, too obscure, and also, in so far as they could be understood: unreasonable'. His Majesty should reassure the States in two respects:

Firstly, that the whole affair was not intended to impart to the commonalty the impression that whereas the King of Great Britain was desirous of peace, the Dutch government was rejecting it, or at least, the conclusion of peace was being obstructed by some of its regents and ministers. Secondly, that the proposals were not mere inventions meant to cause dissension between the allies. That, in order to avoid that impression, he, Buat, being charged with such weighty matters, should not hold discourses with so many people, or after wine, protest that the King of England was truly desirous of peace and that their High Mightinesses could have peace any time they pleased – as I have been informed he has done on various occasions.

Moreover, offers should in future be addressed to France as well, and in any case he, De Witt, would always immediately communicate them to France. The States had nothing to add to their declaration of 11 December[198] as long as the king did not express himself more clearly. Nothing was changed, except that France was now in open war with England.[199]

After the confused and excited tenor of Sylvius's and Buat's reports, the clearness of this language does one good. The dashing cavalry captain, who could talk so confidently at table, must have felt small indeed when faced with the strength of De Witt's outspoken reply. And, indeed, one is tempted to dismiss all Buat's self-important doing, all his bragging and plotting, as so much froth that had nothing to do with the realities of the situation. 'For two days,' Sylvius wrote on 19 February, 'they (the States of Holland) have debated the question *chaudement*, yesterday until eleven at night, which is most unusual.' But he did not know any particulars: secrecy had been preserved wonderfully well. 'As far as I can judge,' Sylvius continued, 'the king must benefit even if the worst comes to the worst. Suppose the affair does not take the turn we are hoping for, we shall still have the pleasure of seeing them fight among themselves.'[200] A fine gloss on their sincere attempt to restore the peace!

Nevertheless, the plotters could boast that their friends had been instrumental in getting the Turenne plan shelved:[201] De Witt was thwarted at the critical moment by Louis XIV's refusal to grant Turenne leave to accept the appointment. More than that, the king received the idea of appointing the Prince of Orange to any post with marked displeasure. Meanwhile, D'Estrades painted a gloomy picture of the situation.[202] Apologizing for De Witt to Louis, he explained that a powerful cabal in the States of Holland had set up such a clamour for the elevation of the prince, that De Witt was willy-nilly forced to make small concessions to it. 'He is in a depressed mood and quite cast down.' In a letter to Lionne, D'Estrades went further still, when, in the spirit of Courtin,[203] he wrote: 'All that I can tell you is that a Dordrecht lawyer does not dispose of the strength of mind one will find in a man of birth.' And naturally it was he, D'Estrades, who helped the little burgher to recover his courage. The man whose stubborn attitude after the defeat of Lowestoft and during the commotion over the Overijsel proposition had compelled the Frenchman's admiration, was now said to be steeped in gloom. 'Several friends from the towns have deserted him. He admits that he needs help with his overwhelming task to lead so many divergent minds.' D'Estrades' sneer at De Witt and his class was, in fact, merely a reflection of his own pessimism. A mood of despondency is the last thing one can deduce from De Witt's own letters, always exemplified by iron self-command. The Frenchman was right, however, in thinking that De Witt felt the interference of Buat and his friends a severe strain on the resolute and successful pursuit of his policies,[204] though no more than that.

His difficulty was not so much the rejection of a peace based on the totally inadequate conditions brought over by Sylvius, as the mounting agitation in favour of the Prince of Orange, which, if the English party remained in control of it, would inevitably undermine the alliance with France and also the resolve to stand up to English pressure.

Failure of conspiracy and continued intrigues (March–August 1666)

As a result of De Witt's firmness, the English government lost interest in Sylvius's efforts. 'Our Messenger is returned out of

Holland,' Arlington himself wrote to a friend, 'and with an answer
he thought entirely to our satisfaction; but examining it none of
us here make that iudgement of it. I am afraide De Witt is so
powerful and soe engaged with France thatt wee shall gett nothing
of them but what wee gett by fighting.'[205] And so he himself
dictated the next letter Sylvius wrote to Buat. In it, De Witt was
said to have made his reply under pressure from the French party,
with the result that the king now felt he could do no more for the
peace.[206] In a second letter, marked 'confidential', the old tune was
nevertheless struck up again. The real cause of the king's disappointment, the letter alleged, was Holland's failure to hold out
any hope for the Prince of Orange. Nothing would make the king
moderate his demands so much as 'the assurance that the Prince
of Orange's interest should be granted'; and more of that nature.

But even Buat realized that nothing was to be gained by that
approach. His reactions were those of a desperate man. On Zuylestein's advice, he threw Arlington's first letter into the fire.[207]
And, indeed, how could he, who had always assured the regents
of the king's desire for peace, now suddenly confess that the king
had lost patience? And so he kept on begging his English correspondents to persuade the king that by concluding peace he would
even now be able to frustrate all the French plans at the same
time restore the prince to office. He told Arlington[208] of 'a large
party which he had formed for the peace and consequently for my
little master'. His state of mind is reflected even more clearly in
the draft of this letter (his spelling of French was so unintelligible
that he often got his wife to edit his letters) – the original phrase
had been 'For *His Majesty* and my little master'.[209] For peace, he
believed, would so consolidate Charles's position in Holland, that
he would 'come to be the greatest king in the world'. And, as he
informed Sylvius a few days later,[210]

if I had produced the [Arlington] letters, the party of His Majesty
would have surely made common cause with those ready to abandon
themselves to France . . . Your party is the largest, but it has been led
to believe that the King's assurances of his inclination towards peace
are no more than a feint, and that His Majesty wants only to create
dissension amongst them. You will see that the King must disabuse
them. In God's name, make the best of this advice.

But all his appeals fell on deaf ears, for the English government had meanwhile embarked on an even riskier scheme. The plan originated with the English resident at Brussels, Sir William Temple, who had been studying the French threat to England from close quarters and who had instructions[211] to warn the Spanish governor that the Holland States party might well go beyond the Dutch-French alliance of 1662, and make promises to France that would prove detrimental to the Spanish Netherlands. He was in touch with Wevelinchoven, a member of the prince's council,[212] who had come to Brussels in connection with a lawsuit involving one of the Orange estates in the South; Wevelinchoven carried a letter from the Dowager in which she begged the king's resident to support the interests of the king's nephew.

Wevelinchoven did not belong to the Dowager's immediate circle. Like Oudart, he was a supporter of the Princess Royal and as such he had always looked for salvation to England. Temple found him so agreeable that he decided to make him privy to a plot he hoped to get approved by the English government. The king was to be asked to declare that he would not listen to peace proposals before the Prince of Orange had been restored, though once that was done he would be very moderate in his demands. 'Wevelinchoven assures me,' Temple wrote to Arlington, 'if that were done the tenth men in Holland would not contribute to the warre, that the Prces friends are much discouraged to see his Maty takes no notice of his interest, that as the Prince without the Kings favour & assistance has no hopes in his fortunes so his Maty without the Prces greatness can never be secure of Holland.'[213] So far, the plot was no more than a variation upon the theme of Buat and Sylvius. But Temple also had a new tune to play, for he went on to say:

That ye young Prince who I am assured is forward in his under-standing as well as stature should be possest by this commissioner how necessary it is to deliver himself from his grand-mother's tutelage and those persons company and service whom De Witt's faction has placed about him and to govern himselfe (beeing now upon his sixteenth year) by His Matyes advice and under his protection that when the Prince has received this infusion hee should pretend some short gourne [journey] of pleasure in his yacht with such few persons as are his owne and being out at sea should make for Zealand and land either at Terveur or Flushing which are both his owne (as wee receive most encouragement by the persons I shall there take care to sound) that beeing there hee shall declare his escape to have been made upon the apprehentions of danger to his person at the hague and upon a desire of giving a sudden and happy ends to the miseries of his countrey by mediating a Peace with England if the States Grall thought fit. If this can be compast the rest may be favord by his Matyes fleet from sea and by levies which ye Bp of Munster is continually making here as well as many others whom his Matyes name would soon send out of those countreys if wee desired it. I can not imagine but this must give an immediat shake to Holland engage the Duke of Brandenburgh as well as all other friends of the Orange family and preserve his Matyes honour in condescending to a more reasonable peace in other points if it bee necessary if his Matyes thoughts should lye this way I think Master Sylvius and master Nypho [the English consul in Antwerp] may bee useful to mee in it and should bee glad order may be sent them to consult with mee and take their measures from mee . . .

Though Temple's letter suggested that he himself had devised the scheme and that he still had to broach the subject with Wevelinchoven, it seems highly improbable that he should have asked his government to entertain the idea before he had first obtained assurances that the indispensable mediator was prepared to act. Moreover, the plan betrays intimate knowledge of relations in Orange court circles: we shall see in a moment how close the Dowager would draw to De Witt's party and how the antagonism between young William and his grandmother would become accentuated as a result. Temple also had a keen appreciation of the political importance of Zeeland, not to mention of its strategic importance as a potential staging post for English men-of-war and Spanish troops.

However, in the spring of 1666, Temple's plan still impressed his government as being far too adventurous. The king, as Arlington at once replied, was of the opinion that nothing would give greater pleasure to his enemies than an attempt on his part to stir up William III against his grandmother[214] and that was that – for the time being.

For a time it even looked as if, what with the failure of Sylvius, the English government was about to accept the only practicable condition for peace: the inclusion of France. In April, a provisional conference was held in the palace of Charles II's mother (who, after his restoration, had stayed on in her native country). Those present were Lionne, Van Beuningen and Hollis, the

English ambassador at the French court, whom gout still prevented from returning home. But the English broke off the negotiations before they had started in earnest. Instead they again turned to allies in whom they themselves had lost faith: the ill-organized and leaderless Orange party. The Buat intrigue was far from dead.

From time to time, Buat was sent letters for transmission to De Witt, who replied in due course. The English government kept urging the dispatch of an envoy to London. De Witt charged Buat to 'cut off' all hope of such a mission, and to leave 'not the least expectation for its success'.[215] Buat, however, felt certain that, with the help of his friends, he would still overcome De Witt's 'obstruction'. His reports were, at times, flagrant violations of truth,[216] and so the meaningless exchange was continued, though the English government had realized by then that recourse to arms had become inevitable if they were to achieve their aims – they would, as Arlington put it, have to see what they could 'get by fighting' rather than through the Orange party.[217]

William made a 'Child of the State' (April 1666)

But before things came to that, De Witt saw to it that the cause of Orange was publicly divorced from that of England. The failure of Sylvius's negotiations greatly facilitated his task, as Buat's bitter complaints make abundantly plain. In any case, De Witt judged that the time had come to topple the platform from which irresponsible peace intrigues could be launched time and again.

We have seen that France was opposed to De Witt's plan.[218] On 26 February, when, following Louis's refusal to 'lend' Turenne, the States decided to 'continue' Maurice of Nassau[219] and took no resolution concerning William of Orange, the king congratulated them, and himself, on that step. But De Witt felt that matters could not be left at that. In his heart he may have agreed with Louis's view that it was foolish to expect support from the prince. 'I won't dream of lending myself to so pitiable a part,' Louis had written of the prince's appointment, 'he would be the first to laugh about it with the English.'[220]

And in that the King of France was not mistaken. William, now fifteen years of age, had for some time had his own ideas about public affairs (Temple was well-informed). He was not likely to feel grateful to anybody for the privilege of his elevation:

he felt himself called to high office by his birth, by a higher power, as his tutor Trigland would have expressed it. When the young prince was told in January that the States of Holland regarded circumstances as 'too critical and too dangerous' for someone of his age to be appointed, he retorted: 'I shall render the state at least as much service as the Grand Pensionary did last summer.' Aitzema, who reported this reply in one of his secret newsletters to the English government[221] added: '*Ce jeune Prince devient de plus en plus fort généreux, gentil, sage et aymable.*' The old cynic was writing with his tongue in his cheek, for the prince's *bon mot* was anything but generous or amiable – his retort was, in any case, no good augury for the success of De Witt's attempts. In the Turenne plan, too, the lad had raised his voice. Reared as he had been on grievances about his principality, he had been unable to follow the tactical turn-about of his grandmother, whose bitter resentment of Louis xiv's arbitrary action still rang in his ears. A few years earlier, meeting D'Estrades in the Voorhout in the Hague, he had refused to make way for his coach. Now, against the express wish of his grandmother, he consulted 'his friends' – probably Van Zuylestein, his governor, perhaps the younger Odijk, now Arlington's brother-in-law, and no doubt Buat as well – about the Turenne plan and encouraged them to incite 'his party' against it. The prince was clearly a young man with a will of his own, but De Witt simply had to persist in his new course, and once one accepts the general direction of his policy, one cannot but admire the execution of it. On 4 March he wrote to Van Beuningen:[222]

As for the person of his Lordship the Prince of Orange, it seems incontrovertible to me that the general inclination of the Members (of the States of Holland) at present tends to this, that he will, first and above all, visibly and in fact, have to be detached from all correspondence, inclination and affection with and towards the present enemies of the state, and therefore also from the education and daily conversation of English and pro-English women and men and that, as long as this has not been effected, during the present war all promotion of the afore-mentioned Prince of Orange would cause suspicion to the allies and be contrary to the security and service of the country.

In order to make sure he had not misrepresented the general view of the members, De Witt had this declaration read out aloud and verbatim in the States of Holland assembly, and he could now affirm that he was speaking in their name.

Is it not surprising that not one voice was raised against that declaration? What had become of all Buat's friends? Probably they were discouraged by Sylvius's failure, and hence did not dare to protest when the other deputies – under the tactful leadership of their 'servant' – vented their annoyance at the machinations of the previous month. The reader will have observed that the declaration, as formulated by De Witt, was in complete agreement with the general policy for which he had managed to obtain the States' approval in September 1661.[223] And there was more than outward consistency: in both cases, his appeal was directed to national self-respect, a sentiment deep-rooted in the States of Holland. It was just then being challenged from a new quarter: the Elector of Brandenburg, having signed his treaty, had ventured to address to the States-General a very cautious recommendation of his nephew, and the deputies were incensed at such foreign interference. 'Tomorrow,' they exclaimed, 'the King of France might well recommend the Dauphin! . . .'[224] In his reports to England, Aitzema pointed out that the Grand Pensionary could not have acted as he did, had not the majority of the States of Holland expressed the wish to remain 'without a head'.[225]

And yet De Witt did intend to follow his negative declaration to Van Beuningen by a positive step concerning the Prince of Orange. The mood of the commonalty was such that it was impossible to continue the policy of complete exclusion. Much had changed since 1663, and notably the attitude of the ministers of religion, who were busily stirring up public unrest.[226] The Orange court itself had sprung into feverish action. Young Odijk gave sumptuous dinners to supporters. The prince visited Rotterdam, the chief centre of the English conspiracy, and it was Buat's friend, Van der Horst who had the honour of receiving him at his house, to the enthusiastic cheers of the crowd.[227] Amsterdam gave the prince an equally enthusiastic reception. 'The strong pressure for the restoration of the Prince of Orange,' as De Witt himself put it,[228] has 'already found a loud echo in the very body of Holland.'

What made it particularly imperative that something should be done about the prince was that the Zeeland regents could no longer hold out against their people. We can readily believe Aitzema[229] that they themselves had 'as little taste for the nectar of personal power as had those of Holland, even though they had not suffered what Holland had at the hands of the prince in 1618 and 1650.' It was fear of the clergy and of the commonalty incited by them, that caused the Zeeland deputies in the States-General to press for measures against the Papists, who, as they were quick to point out as well, were behind the support of Münster by the Spanish Netherlands.[230]

The States of Zeeland planned to have the prince appointed general of cavalry and a member of the Council of State. De Witt himself had but recently raised the question of the first of these appointments in the States of Holland, but only in connection with his abortive Turenne plan. He now managed to get the States to reject it, just before the Zeelanders could bring the matter up. About a month after the decision to 'continue' Maurice of Nassau, on 25 March, the States of Holland decided to propose other candidates for the various subordinate commands: only Edam and Enkhuizen were still for appointing the prince to the cavalry generalship.[231]

On 26 March, the Grand Pensionary of Zeeland announced the arrival of a deputation from his States, and in the afternoon one from the States of Holland met in conference with them. De Huybert, who was no doubt whole-heartedly in favour of the Zeeland policy, if only for the pleasure of thwarting De Witt, acted as spokesman for his province, and requested that a fuller conference might be held in order to attain the indispensable unity between the two provinces. The little drama that ensued is described in a letter by Coninck, a regent of Hoorn, to his uncle, a burgomaster of that town. 'His lordship Jan' – as the Orangist writer called De Witt[232] – tried vainly to represent the matter as settled by the resolution of the previous day and, moreover, as falling within the agreement concluded by the two provinces in 1663. The rejoinder by his Zeeland colleague that he, De Witt, himself had wanted the prince to serve under Turenne, and why not then under Maurice, was difficult to counter. His own Hollanders were divided among themselves, and De Witt found it impossible to persist in his refusal to refer the matter to their States. The plenary States assembly turned out to be as divided as the Holland delegation and, to the annoyance of 'his lordship Jan', a further discussion was decided upon which, alas, confirmed the decision of 25 March. Coninck, and this deserves notice, had remained hopeful all through the proceedings. Kievit had assured him that the Princess-Dowager had told him personally that she had never arrived at any understanding with De Witt; that he had reason to believe that Haarlem and Leyden would lay a new proposal before the assembly, that Rotterdam and Hoorn would support it, and then 'we shall have peace with England, as I know for certain'. And Kievit and Coninck thereupon went to dine with the prince.

But all these expectations came to nothing, for the Dowager *had* reached an agreement with De Witt after all. On 2 April, she addressed a humble memorandum[233] to the States of Holland, much as she had done in 1663.[234] In it she professed the desire to let her grandson benefit by 'that instruction and stimulation that would teach him to understand and recognize the good and salutary rights, privileges and maxims of the state', the better to become qualified for 'such charges and employments as Your Noble Great Mightinesses might think proper to confer upon him'. She ended by expressing the hope that she and the prince, her grandson, 'might have the honour and happiness' of seeing the States provide for the requisite lessons under their direction.

Her memorandum was a remarkable document and represented a striking victory for De Witt, who could not have hoped for more had he dictated it himself.[235] The young prince was being handed over to Holland on De Witt's conditions – a return to the education agreement of 1660 which Holland had torn up because the 'high-born personages' had been unwilling to agree to its conditions. The memorandum was immediately referred to a special committee, and by 13 April, Their 'Noble Great Mightinesses' were able to pass a resolution by which the arrangement was given detailed form. By 15 April, all the necessary appointments had been made: the education commission of 1660 was revived, two places, vacated by death, were now filled with equivalent 'members' (that is how Valckenier came to replace the late De Graeff). At the same time, the Grand Pensionary reported that he had read the resolution to Her Highness and that she 'had thanked Your Noble Great Mightinesses most politely for the favour, honour and affection rendered by it to (her grandson) and the entire house'.

These protestations of gratitude notwithstanding, the new arrangement was in fact a great humiliation for Orange. Not only was the prince to be subjected to the Holland education commission but 'the appointments and qualities of all those who are at present engaged and in charge at His Highness's court were abolished automatically', and 'for weighty considerations of state' not one of them would be reinstated. The young prince was, indeed, and most abruptly 'detached . . . from the education and daily conversation of English and pro-English men and women'. Zuylestein and Boreel were indemnified in other ways; Bromley had to return to England;[236] Buat, too, lost his position at court.[237] Zuylestein's place as governor was taken by Baron Van Ghent of Gelderland. The other posts were reserved for men of proven reliability. Thus when one, Cabeljauw, a younker and captain of horse, was recommended, De Witt's cousin Fannius warned that the younker was still a cornet in Buat's company and a great friend of his: very likely therefore the recommendation had been obtained by Buat, 'so that through his good friend he might retain his influence at court,' and Cabeljauw was rejected.[238]

A victory for De Witt, we have said. But how much better it would have suited him to decline the Dowager's request, as had been done in 1663, and wash his hands of the prince once again! Holland might be recovering her influence over the young man, but in fact he was once again recognized as 'a worthy servant and instrument of great hope for this state'.[239] Child of the State, that was what the prince was now called – albeit unofficially. As in the past, the phrase held out a promise for the future; only this time the future that was six years nearer. No wonder that the 'Men of True Liberty' among the regents showed some hesitation when the Grand Pensionary surprised them with his new arrangement.[240] Reynst, the sheriff of Amsterdam, declared that he and Valckenier regarded the choice between acceptance and rejection as a choice between two evils, but that, in view of the weakness and half-heartedness of the majority in the corporation, and in view also of the danger that the February clique might use the affair to discredit the regents with the commonalty and the ministers of religion, they had decided to bow before the inevitable. Even then it took some urging before Valckenier could be persuaded to accept a seat on the education commission.[241]

The Orange party, too, showed annoyance at the unexpected agreement between the Dowager and the Grand Pensionary. The Zeelanders, in particular, were highly incensed. They, who had exerted themselves so fervently for the prince, now found themselves abandoned by the Dowager much as they had been in

1660 (when the Dowager had tried to play them off against her daughter-in-law);[242] once again they were treated as if the prince were the concern of Holland alone. In Holland, too, the most zealous supporters of the House were inclined to inveigh against the Dowager, who seemed to care for nothing but the support of their powerful adversary. They were more bitter, said an informant of the English government,[243] than ever the pro-States men. And for good reason since, as we saw[244] Amalia had kept hoodwinking them with soothing assurances up to the last moment.

William himself, when pressed by his grandmother shortly before she sent her memorandum, had expressed his utter aversion to the entire scheme, so much so that she had had to take matters into her own hands. To betray his party, whatever its faults, and to seek the friendship of its enemies – all that went quite naturally against the grain of the proud boy. And when the plan became a reality, what pain did the separation from his friends not cause him! To Boreel, the ambassador in Paris, he wrote that Boreel's son had been moved from the court against his wish, nay in spite of his opposition, and that he meant to restore him as soon as cir-cumstance allowed.[245] By all accounts, the prince was particularly attached to Zuylestein, so much so, in fact, that he brought himself to call on the French ambassador and to implore him, with tears in his eyes, to use his good offices with De Witt on Zuylestein's behalf; he promised that if Zuylestein were allowed to stay with him he would send the latter's English wife to one of his estates for the duration of the war, and he would guarantee that Zuylestein himself would not in any way act against the wishes of Holland. As for himself, he was prepared to confide himself to De Witt and to regard him as a father. He also assured the ambassador explicitly that he meant to follow the example of his forefathers and to side with his French Majesty. It was wronging him to contend that his blood relationship made him subservient to the King of England: as Child of the State he would recognize no interests other than those of the States and their allies.[246]

Can Louis XIV have overcome his distrust when he read these protestations?[247] It was, at any rate, impossible for D'Estrades to plead for a man like Zuylestein – all he could do was promise to talk with De Witt about the ex-governor's pension. However pain-ful, William had to accept Van Ghent as his new governor. When D'Estrades soon afterwards offered Van Ghent a pension on behalf of Louis, he had to report that it was declined, albeit with professions of loyalty.

The commonalty, meanwhile, took scant notice of the changes of personnel at court, but whole-heartedly cheered the only thing that mattered to them: the bright promises for the prince's future. That such expectations should have been aroused was something the States of Holland had been unable to avoid by their manœuvres. Aitzema, the experienced observer, free from bias, with no other sentiments than those of amused interest, compared the prince straight out with 'the rising sun'; the States were wrong to expect anything from a mere change of his servants, for whoever served him would automatically come under his spell.[248] A deputy in the States-General, Aitzema went on to report, had mocked at the title of 'Child of the State'; Holland would soon be a child of the prince.[249] For the benefit of his English paymasters he also described a contemporary print on which De Witt and the members of the education commission were depicted as trying to thrust a large prince back into a small cradle.[250]

It was only too natural that the question of the prince's position should not have been removed from the political arena by Holland's successful stroke. On the contrary, the other provinces began to press for his appointment to Union office with greater insistence than ever. Zeeland, profoundly mortified by the turn events had taken – De Huybert, their Grand Pensionary, treated the matter as a personal insult[251] – was busily engaged in negotiations with the other provinces. Holland had suggested that the two should hold a special conference, so that they might agree on a common line of action, but this was no more than an attempt to pacify the Zeelanders and it came too late. All the provinces except Holland were now anxious to bring the prince into the Council of State; Gelderland still pressed for the Captain-Generalship, but now that the war with Münster was drawing to a close, the others were prepared to drop that matter – at least for the time being. Holland maintained that the prince could not possibly be taken into the Council of State now that the State was at war with his uncle, and her veto was enough to stop proceedings in a matter that called for a unanimous decision in the States-General. Moreover, in spite of all the opposition to his policy, the general view was that De Witt's party had strengthened its position enormously. The prince himself had bowed to the inevitable. D'Estrades reported that he was behaving with exemplary tact, so much so, in fact, that the government ventured to make use of his services when they felt the need to hearten the sailors in Texel. In May, the prince accordingly visited the fleet, distributed a few barrels of beer, was loudly cheered, and gave a great boost to the recruiting drive.[252]

Four Days' (June) and Two Days' (3-4 August) Battle; Quarrel between De Ruyter and Tromp

At last, in the early days of June, the fleet was ready to sail out again. As in the previous year, Louis XIV preached caution, but in vain: the Dutch decided not to wait for support from the French fleet. Strenuous work had been done – some thirty ships put to sea, all of them better armed than even the greatest ship of the previous year. De Ruyter, on board of the new De Zeven Provinciën, was in supreme command and, as De Witt could testify, on most harmonious terms with Tromp, who served under him. Tromp had repeatedly visited Den Helder, seeing to the equipment of the fleet in his capacity of Commissioner of the States-General, but did not himself join De Ruyter's first expedition which, after only a few days at sea, had its first encounter with Monk. A false rumour that the French Admiral, De Beaufort, was coming up from the Mediterranean, had caused the English to divert a squadron, so that the Dutch contingent was superior in number. The battle was still proceeding two days later when the diverted squadron, hurriedly recalled, appeared on the scene to redress the balance. But by then it was too late, and on the fourth day the English made a fighting retreat to base, leaving the Dutch in control of the sea. The English had suffered exceedingly heavy losses. Six ships had been captured, seventeen destroyed, 5,000 men killed, not less than 3,000, among them Admiral Ayscue, taken prisoner. De Ruyter's fleet, too, was so badly battered that it had to put in at the Wielingen.

De Witt hastened to greet the victors, and supervised the work of re-equipping the fleet with furious energy. To his mind the Boards of Admiralty were far too slow. Now that the victory was still fresh in everyone's mind, he was able to speed up the recruiting drive, for shortage of men was still the fleet's great difficulty. On 4 July, De Ruyter put to sea once again (Zeeland once more placed old Jan Evertsen at the head of her fleet, much to De Witt's annoyance), with secret instructions to force the Thames estuary. De Witt was most anxious to inflict another heavy blow on the enemy, thus forcing him to talk peace, before he had time to refit his own limping fleet. But De Witt foresaw that the sailors – he had got to know them well last year at the Spaniards' Inlet! – would make the most of the difficulties of the unfamiliar waterway, however simple he might, with an abundance of maps and particulars, represent the enterprise to be. And as a matter of fact it was not attempted; all the States fleet succeeded in doing was to block the Thames for a while.

De Witt concealed his disappointment from De Ruyter. But the resulting loss of initiative led to a heavy set-back. The English fleet, too, had sailed out, and in the encounter that began on 3 August in the southern part of the North Sea, Monk quickly gained the upper hand. The Frisian and the Zeeland squadrons were thrown into great confusion by the deaths of Tjerk Hiddes de Vries and Jan Evertsen. There were moments when De Ruyter thought all was lost, but in the end, with masterly seamanship and unfaltering courage, he managed to bring most of his heavily damaged ships back to the Wielingen. However, the English were now in even more complete command of the sea than the Dutch had been two months earlier. Moreover, while they kept cruising defiantly off Zeeland, the Dutch faced not only the problem of refitting their fleet once again, but also a vehement quarrel between De Ruyter and Tromp.

In the battle, Tromp's squadron had given chase to the English rear with such passion that it completely forgot the distress of the supreme commander and the main body of the fleet. De Ruyter felt that he had been left in the lurch and, though generally a quiet man, he fell upon Tromp, who arrived in the Wielingen one day later, with the most violent reproaches. Nor did he spare Tromp's officers who, as De Witt rightly remarked, had had no alternative but to follow their admiral. And all this abuse was vented in the full hearing of the men.

De Witt did what he could to calm down the excited tempers. He was even prepared to forgive Tromp's absence from the first court martial, on the grounds that De Ruyter had warned him off his ship. De Ruyter was prevailed upon to apologize for his outburst of passion, and the two men drank each other's health. But on 13 August, Tromp, believing the De Ruyter's report blamed him for the entire defeat and egged on by political mischief-makers, wrote a letter to the States-General that could not possibly be glossed over. He accused De Ruyter of jealousy, 'because to me, with a small force, God Almighty granted the advantage whereas to him, with a larger force, He sent discomfiture';[253] and arrogantly demanded satisfaction or dismissal.

The States took his behaviour very badly. For all his superior fighting qualities, the man clearly lacked the power of self-command, as he had shown time and again in battle and now on shore as well. All the difficulties he had caused during the previous year were recalled, and it was decided to dismiss him. Summoned to the Hague, he was full of remorse, promised satisfaction to De Ruyter and obedience in the future. De Witt fully expected that the States would accept his apologies, but, 'taking into consideration the changeable and ill humour of the afore-mentioned Tromp, and it being alleged that once having fallen into a passion he is incapable of restraining himself, so that no reliance can be placed in such promises', the members refused to budge.

It goes without saying that Tromp's political sentiments weighed heavily with the States as well. In spite of this, De Witt did his best to spare him for the navy. But Tromp had attracted a 'cabal' round him and, in his letter to Their High Mightinesses, he had spoken of the 'confusion' in the fleet that would inevitably occur if justice were not done to him. This had sounded very much like a threat. D'Estrades watched the affair with uneasy feelings: he feared that the States might lose control over their ships.[254] The shock of the defeat was in any case bringing back the dangers of the earlier crisis. Bitter talk was heard on all sides about the French navy, which took so long to accomplish the voyage from the Mediterranean. With public temper in such turmoil, a man like Tromp could easily cause a catastrophe. An Orange supporter, filled with distrust of the Grand Pensionary (who deserved better of him), Tromp, 'with his great heart and less great intelligence' (as Wicquefort said of him),[255] proved a willing tool in the hands of such plotters and zealots as his brother-in-law Kievit (who was then a Commissioned Councillor, a post of some importance, since the Commissioned Councillors represented the States of Holland when these were not in session). A few days after the return of the fleet, an account of the battle was being passed from hand to hand: it was entitled *Report*, and Sommelsdijk junior, who had been on board of Tromp's ship, was said to be its author. The pamphlet amounted to a most irresponsible vilification of De Ruyter and was a paean of praise to Tromp. The States were startled, particularly when it emerged that Kievit, not Sommelsdijk, was the author.[256] The quarrel between Tromp and De Ruyter threatened to become one between Orange and the States of Holland, between pro-English and pro-French policies, between peace and war.

The English were quick to take advantage of the dissension, and on 20 August, fell upon the roadstead of the Vlie, inflicting severe damage on the Dutch merchant fleet and on the island of Terschelling. An attack had been expected, and the Grand Pensionary had intended that the navy, which was not damaged nearly as badly as it had been the year before, should put to sea before the English could strike. However, with the prevailing mood, it had seemed safer to keep the fleet in harbour, and precious time was lost while the men got out of hand and many of them deserted.[257] And now, of course, the air resounded with the loud laments and bitter complaints of the stricken merchants and shipowners.

Buat discovered (18 August) and sentenced (October 1666)

It was fortunate for the States that, at that very time, the chief link between the opposition and England was snapped. On 14 August, the States summoned Kievit to explain his authorship of the scurrilous pamphlet. On the 20th, the day the English invaded the Vlie, the States confirmed the dismissal of Tromp. And in that same week, on the 18th, Buat was arrested on charges of corresponding with the enemy, and locked up in the Gevangenpoort (the state prison in the Hague).

The unhappy man had gone on plotting all this while. Of his letters since the great disappointment of February, but a few have been preserved. We have seen how he could distort the truth, presenting mere wishes as facts. In a letter of 8 June, he looked forward anxiously to the impending naval encounter; he spoke of scoundrels in England who kept sending reports to bolster up the courage of the Dutch – conveniently forgetting that he was doing just that, albeit in the opposite direction. And on 11 June (the Four Days' Battle had just begun): 'If we are beaten, I assure you that certain persons will have to face an astounding charge.'[258]

He was deceived in his hopes, but continued his intrigues all the same. Indeed, after their set-back, the English were inclined to take his activities a little more seriously again. In July, Sylvius came to Antwerp once more and was told by Buat that 'the friends' were planning great things. He handed Sylvius the draft (composed with the help of Kievit[259]) of a letter which the English government was to send to the States-General by way of introducing a new peace campaign. Because the Dutch fleet was in temporary control of the sea, it took Sylvius a considerable time to get back to England. Then, the English fleet put to sea again, and all English ports were kept closed. As a result, he was unable to contact Buat until after the second sea battle, when England was again riding high. He said so explicitly in his letter, adding that the project discussed at Antwerp would have to be abandoned. 'The peace-loving party of our friends could not but have been strengthened by the defeat; let the well-affected towns now draw more firmly together and take a forceful decision, then support from England will not be wanting.'[260] Two of the usual, non-committal letters to De Witt by Arlington and Sylvius were enclosed.

Buat called on the Grand Pensionary to deliver these letters, and with quite staggering negligence left the one marked *pour vous mesme* in his hands as well. That letter was treasonable, and when Buat came to claim it back, De Witt told him that he had put the document in the hands of the Commissioned Councillors. These ordered Buat's arrest and had his house searched. The zealous but clumsy conspirator failed to make good use of the many hours left to him, while the bureaucracy came slowly into action. Perhaps he counted on Kievit, a member of the Commissioned Councillors,[261] to whom he explained the unfortunate accident that same afternoon.[262] The letters left in his house were not many, but one of them was so compromising that the destruction of the rest proved of small avail. It was the draft – in his wife's handwriting – of the letter of 19 March to Arlington, in which he complained of the coolness of the last replies he had received from England, and made much of the party he was getting together 'for the peace' (or 'for His Majesty') 'and for my little master', and of his wish to strengthen the position of that little master and to make the King of England 'the greatest king in the world'.[263]

Buat was questioned by members of the Commissioned Councillors of Holland, assisted by the Grand Pensionary. Kievit was not among them. He was already in trouble over his pamphlet and his relations with Buat were now a matter of common knowledge.[264] The first aim of the interrogation was to discover which of the regents were involved in the plot, and who precisely 'the friends' were. Buat did not reply directly, but his remarks indicated that several men from Haarlem (Burgomaster Van Thilt and Pensionary Fagel), and from North-Holland, together with Van Amerongen of Utrecht were involved. His papers also included a recent letter (2 August) from Renswoude, who stated that the States of Utrecht were much inclined towards peace and asked for a copy of the latest letter Buat had received from England.

For some days, little progress was made, until at last, on 24 August, Buat suddenly became more communicative. He now confessed that, after receiving the letters from England mentioned in his draft letter of 19 March, he had been summoned to Zuylestein's house (through an halberdier in the service of the Prince of Orange), where he had met Kievit and Van der Horst. It was they who had advised him to burn the letter in question, and all his references to 'good friends' and 'a party' had been based on their assurances.[265] The States of Holland, acting upon the report of the Commissioned Councillors that self-same day, decided to instruct the Holland Court of Justice to 'proceed with all possible vigour' against Buat, Kievit and Van der Horst, and against all others who might be found guilty with them.

Buat was examined by the Court on 26 August and again on 13 September. The Court also summoned Kievit and Van der Horst to appear before them a fortnight later, but took no measures to prevent their escape. Only after they had 'retired' to the Spanish Netherlands (a term used by a former burgomaster of Rotterdam to explain the failure of Van der Horst to present himself), were orders for their arrest issued.

There is little doubt but that the Court was not over-anxious to get to the bottom of this painful affair. The men mentioned by Buat in response to the more pressing questions of the Grand Pensionary and the Commissioned Councillors were not even called. Van Thilt was afraid to leave Haarlem for a whole year. Bol and Fagel, who were as deeply implicated, did, and nothing happened to them. Years later, William III claimed that De Witt, who had every intention of prosecuting Fagel as well, was so dumbfounded when the latter suddenly turned up in the assembly of the States of Holland, after a prolonged 'illness', that he let the matter rest. That story was, however, part of the legend (the bloodthirsty Grand Pensionary, the undaunted Fagel, who succeeded him in 1672) which the victorious party later wove round the actual events.[266] In reality, most of the accomplices were simply left to stew in their own juice, while Fagel, as we shall see, loudly protested his support of the then rulers of Holland. When Buat was asked for the names of Kievit's and Van der Horst's contacts, he replied that 'he had no knowledge thereof.' And the Court left it at that. Odijk was only heard when he asked for a chance to clear himself. And there is no evidence that the States, after those first examinations by the Commissioned Councillors, were more curious than the Court itself.

Yet they followed the trial attentively, and the judges' evident reluctance to bring even Buat to justice forced them to spring into action. First, they summoned the Court before them and treated it to a homily by the Grand Pensionary. De Witt pointed out that all correspondence with the enemy was prohibited; he quoted the most offensive passages in Buat's letter and expatiated on 'the mischief of lax justice'. In October, by which time the States' impatience had been strained to breaking point, a deputation of pensionaries proceeded to the Court in order to repeat De Witt's observation. The deputation was led by Vivien; De Witt himself had gone to visit the fleet a few days earlier. The States' interference in the due process of justice may strike the modern reader as quite unjustifiable, but it was a fact that the Court had proved reluctant to discharge its duty and had given clear examples of 'laxity'. And when all is said and done, the States did no more than insist that the Court ruled 'in accordance with the existing laws and proclamations' – anything short of that would merely spur the English on to fresh intrigues and would be rightly resented by Louis XIV, to whom Buat's activities had but one object: the exclusion of France from the peace negotiations.[267]

But no pressure was exerted on the Court to hunt down Buat's accomplices. Apparently even the most ardent States supporters were loath to be responsible for the commotion that a full-scale investigation, with the inevitable implication of a host of regents, would undoubtedly have stirred up – they felt that the rigorous prosecution of the main culprits would prove a sufficient deterrent. That two of these, namely Kievit and Van der Horst, had decamped, must have been a relief to many of the conspirators: these two knew more than Buat, that happy-go-lucky libertine, whose own wife testified with admirable tact, that he was 'a military person, not understanding the subtilities of politics'.[268] This was, in fact, a valid plea for mercy but as everyone else was dropped from the case, it became increasingly difficult to let him off lightly. The affair had caused a great upsurge of popular revulsion against all those who were making common cause with the enemy. Several towns sent in resolutions demanding sharp retribution. Pamphleteers condemned the prisoner in advance.[269] And so Buat became the scapegoat.

Perhaps scapegoat is putting it too strongly, for Buat had, in fact, committed a capital crime. No doubt he was naïve beyond measure, but no one could gainsay the fact that he had deceived the government he was supposed to serve, had intrigued against it, had served, not its interests but those of the enemy. And when the Court at long last passed sentence on him on 6 October, it took all these matters into account. Buat was found guilty of 'engaging in a dual correspondence with the enemy, in part openly and with the knowledge of the High Government, in part without its knowledge and against its express orders; of making a distinction between the said High Government and his so-called good and well-intentioned friends and traducing and calumniating the Government throughout by pretending that it did not desire peace, when in fact it was striving for peace on just grounds in accordance with the treaties and general resolutions of state, though not as the plotters would have liked for the benefit of the enemy and to the discredit of this state and its allies'. And this was no more than the plain truth, though not the entire truth, for the Court refrained from mentioning that Buat had been motivated throughout by the wish to see justice done to his 'little master'.

According to Aitzema, the Court did originally include a reference to Buat's desire to make Charles II 'the greatest king on earth' with the help of his 'little master', but that reference had been struck out 'as being odious to that eminent House'.[270] The Court included several Orangists, and it is worth noting how plainly their party bias made itself felt in their attitude to the accused. One of them, Van der Graeff, apparently a timorous man, used the excuse of a press attack on his person to withdraw from the case.[271] The number of members was thereby reduced to eight, including a Zeelander (The Court of Holland was, in fact, the Court of Holland and Zeeland) who, in accordance with the attitude adopted by his province, voted against the death sentence. (Zeeland was seriously offended when she learned that Holland, too, had engaged in secret negotiations, thus behaving no better than Buat.) Of the seven Hollanders, three were known to be staunch States supporters (one of them was De Witt's cousin, Fannius); all of them voted for death. Two, Sixty and Van der Goes, pleaded for a milder sentence (Sixty because he was not convinced that Buat had worked for a peace without France – which was, however, a patent fact). The remaining two, Van Nierop and Van de Honert, began by taking the milder view but came round when they heard their colleagues' arguments.

All this was perfectly understandable. No one could argue that making common cause with the English was a harmless matter, but Orangists, however patriotic, could not forget that Buat had been acting on the prince's behalf all along and that his execution was bound to be regarded as a triumph for the States party. It was typical of the situation, that the Elector of Brandenburg should have felt compelled to address a plea for clemency to the States of Holland – which was politely turned down.

As for the Princess-Dowager and the prince, they happened to be staying with the Elector at Cleves when the case began. It was clearly no accident that, in September, they went for 'a little trip' to Maastricht; this with the approval of William's new guardians (the prince was invariably accompanied by Baron Van Ghent). Only when the trial was over, did they return to the Hague. On 24 August, De Witt had informed the prince of some of the most extraordinary passages in Buat's letter to Arlington of 19 March – without comment, since the letter spoke for itself.[272] The prince immediately assured him that Buat had acted entirely 'without his participation and communication' and that he 'openly and to the highest degree disapproved of (Buat's) doings'. De Witt expressed his gratification and said he would communicate the prince's assurance to his fellow guardians and 'wherever else it might be useful'.[273]

Even so, the Buat affair was played off by pro-States pamphleteers against all Orangists in general and the House of Orange in particular, and there is no doubt that the cause of the House suffered greatly. There was an upsurge of doctrinaire Loevestein Republicanism, and a loud beating of the national drum. A particularly, but not atypically, coarse expression of popular sentiment was a pamphlet entitled *The Sincere Dutch Sailor*.[274] According to its publishers, the author, H. van V., had already rendered his fatherland similar service during the disgraceful and treacherous attack on Amsterdam (1650). H. van V. preached 'obedience to your High and Lawful Government' and was in cordial agreement with a Professor of Deventer University, according to whom the most dangerous enemies of the State were not the English, but those citizens who in the name of Orange incite the mob against their regents and are anxious to bury the state with the help of Orange. Tromp (a self-seeker, a coward and a traitor! . . .) thought that being his father's son entitled him to the supreme command hence his friendship with the Orangists, who argued the same way. 'All these men are corrupt.'

No doubt scurrilous pamphlets like these were frowned upon by many, and not by Orangists alone. Other pamphleteers tried to redress the balance, pleading that 'attacks on the former princes, and especially on the last Stadholder's behaviour in Amsterdam' might at long last be forgotten.[275] Yet their voices fell largely on deaf ears. 'It is unfortunate,' Aitzema wrote early in September, 'that Buat has been able to tie the cause of his little master to that of England and of the peace.'[276] A few weeks later, Temple, who earlier in the year had been devising such bold plans, concluded that 'the prince's party is seriously weakened by the exposure of Buat'.[277] People everywhere recoiled from a party that had so blatantly engaged in intrigues with the enemy. 'Nobody with a single drop of good Holland blood in his veins, wishes to see a king, already so formidable at sea, being turned into the greatest king in the world.' So Aitzema wrote in the twelfth quarto volume of his great chronicle (1668),[278] and although one may smile at this sudden outburst of patriotic fervour in an old cynic – and this while the enemy was paying him for his news letters – it is all the more evidence of the strength of the current on which he thought it safe to drift along. And there is little doubt that the prince, at whose court Buat had served only six months ago, and where Zuylestein had held a dominant position, the prince, who had dined with Van der Horst in Rotterdam and who had received Tromp and Kievit at his own table,[278] would have been gravely compromised had not his grandmother been wise enough beforehand to place him under De Witt's personal guardianship.

Their feelings of relief must nevertheless have been mixed with bitterness. William III, who had shed tears over the separation from Zuylestein and Boreel, was never able to put Buat and Kievit from his heart either. Buat, above all, had been loyal to the bitter end. On 11 October, the day of his execution, he had stepped out in a black cloak, followed by servants clad in black, and accompanied by two ministers of religion, to stride proudly through the ranks of the soldiers linking the streets of the Hague. Though his arms were tied, he was able to doff his hat to the judges pronouncing sentence in the court room, to all his acquaintances who had come to witness his end; and to his little master's empty room of state in the Binnenhof. On the scaffold the Reverend Vollenhovius offered 'a learned, solemn and lengthy prayer'; of which many spectators thought 'that he made it too long and wearied the patient'.[280] Buat himself was saying a prayer when the blow fell. The public at large remained unmoved by his death; it was not until later that he was raised into a martyr for the Orange cause.

Buat, we have said, had been guilty of a capital crime against the national state. Now 'the state' meant something quite other to our seventeenth century ancestors than it does to us today. To begin with, we are far more willing to concede that the state has legitimate claims on us. In the seventeenth century, on the other hand, these claims were still challenged by party, religious, dynastic and personal loyalties, as we have had ample opportunity to discover in the course of this account. In a way this is, in fact, our leading theme. When, in my arguments, I have judged issues in the light of national sentiment or interest, it was not because I think that they represent the highest criteria at all times and in all circumstances. But the Dutch state had been established and endorsed – not only by laws and proclamations, but also by political thought at its best. Those who, for whatever reason, tried to play fast and loose with national claims, moved against the mainstream of history. They were behind the times or, in the full sense of the term, reactionaries. De Witt's considered view that Buat must be punished was not the result of personal resentment or party passion, but sprang from a deep wish to see justice done, and hence to preserve the state.

And the fact that he was aware of the difference constitutes part of his historic greatness.

It is not surprising that he saw God's hand in the miraculous disclosure of hidden dangers.[281] The States régime was enormously strengthened by the fall of Buat and Kievit. Not only had the plotters been laid low, but, more important still, the primacy of the state over mere party interests had been asserted with unmistakable force, and this proved of unestimable importance when dealing with the new menace posed by Tromp. As early as 30 August, a Haarlem newsletter reported[282] that, after the first 'consternation' of the fleet, Tromp's dismissal was almost completely forgotten – 'respect for the state had increased'. In other words, Tromp's 'cabal' had been eliminated as well.

One observation must still be made. However sincere De Witt's conviction of representing the state might have been, his position of servant of Holland and yet master of the conduct of the Union's foreign policy, contained an element of contradiction. Thus the Zeeland regents, among others, were inclined to regard the entire Buat affair more as a party quarrel than as a victory of the law.[283] De Huybert, in a memorandum to the States of Zeeland, complained bitterly that the official part of Buat's negotiations had been conducted by one province, over the heads of all the others. The Grand Pensionary of that province had presumed to 'cut off' all English hopes that a negotiator might be sent, without consulting the other provinces. Buat had been blamed for carrying on a 'dual correspondence'; but in the negotiations with Cromwell about the Act of Seclusion, the ambassadors of Holland had likewise carried on a dual correspondence, 'one with, the other without, the knowledge of Their High Mightinesses, worse, directly against their intentions and resolutions.'[284]

De Witt was a statesman, a builder of national consciousness. His ability and whole-hearted devotion were immune to the envious polemics and rancour of his Zeeland colleague. And yet De Huybert pointed to a defect in the constitutional basis of his edifice, a defect that De Witt could not help but that he could not remedy either, a defect that was overshadowed and yet caused by the realities of the political struggle, and that, at moments of crisis threatened to assume disastrous proportions.

England prepares to negotiate (October 1666)

Buat's conspiracy was the culmination of English attempts to use the Orange party for their own purposes. That line of approach had not been cut off completely, but for the time being at least it was blocked by the discredit into which the Orange party had fallen, and by sudden popular revulsion of anything that smacked of foreign interference. England even found it difficult to obtain the usual political reports from Holland; which, as Arlington wrote, had never been a problem 'till they were grown suspicious through Mr Buat'. One correspondent was said to have been 'frightened into a deep silence'.[285] Arlington was doubtless referring to Aitzema, whose messages ceased arriving after 21 September. Van Ruyven who, as we saw, was another writer of informative letters, had by then fled to Brussels. The papers left behind by Davidson, the Scottish consul in Amsterdam, contained compromising particulars about him. They also incriminated MacDowell, the former Scottish resident, who was sent to prison and even to the rack, but survived the ordeal.

Early in September, Sylvius returned to England from Antwerp, all his hopes crushed. Kievit, on the other hand, arrived in London full of optimism. He had been assured by Arlington through Sylvius (who regretted that he could think of no way to assist Mr Buat in his misfortunes) that His Majesty would, in time, reward him for his services.[286] Kievit was now asked to write a letter to the States of Holland[287] in which he tried to excuse his own conduct, asserting that he had acted in accord with the six provinces and most towns in Holland, and stressing that the king and the Duke of York (with whom he had, in fact, discussed the matter), were anxious as ever to conclude a peace and that an envoy should accordingly be sent to England. He also kept in touch with a correspondent in Holland,[288] and in October he, too, felt impelled to advise Arlington not to mention the Prince of Orange when promoting a peace mission (in which he still believed).

The English government did not wait for his advice. It had begun a correspondence with the States-General, ostensibly about the return of the body of Admiral Berkeley, who had been killed during the Four Days' Battle, yet studded with professions of England's desire for peace. In October, Charles II gave the explicit assurance that it was not his intention 'that your state should be subjected to any change, that in your own territory your authority should be diminished or your freedom impaired by dependence upon any prince' (compared with the instruction of November 1665 to Sir Walter Vane (see p. 218 f.), this was a considerable climb down!); moreover, that he did not pretend to any authority over the seas; apart from what his forebears had always possessed. But Charles still wanted negotiations which, he suggested, had best be preceded by the dispatch of the mission to England that had been under discussion for a whole year. On 25 November, the States replied with the warning that they would never let themselves be persuaded to enter into *separate* negotiations, and proposed *general* negotiations at a neutral place. As for the various English claims – indemnification, a deal regarding trade with India, and the restoration of Pularoon, one of the Spice Islands – the States felt unable to improve on their offer on 11 December 1665: a choice between *status quo ante* and *uti possidetis*. Sweden had offered to act as mediator long ago, and now persuaded Charles to drop his demand that a States official should come to London for separate negotiations. But Charles was still anxious to make the best of a bad bargain, and now proposed to send his own envoys to the Hague, where the States' allies were represented. His design was only too transparent – in the Hague, as Arlington explained to a friend, the peace-loving people of Holland would be the judges, whereas elsewhere the King of France would have the final say.[289]

An English merchant at Rotterdam, who, that winter, still found it possible to send reports across the sea, described the warweariness he observed all round about him. A war with England – so he argued, not without justification – was felt to be a very heavy visitation:

> England lyeth in the way of the trade of this country to the westward and these people dayly loose there shipps taken by the English, there trade decayes and taxes increase . . . War is chargeable work and this year all inhabitants here must pay the hundreth penny or 1 p.c. of there estates, besides all other taxes, which are infinite and is deadly burdensom, and like to be more, whilst the war continews, and this without any trade – considerable – saddens mens mindes beyond expression . . . The longer this war continews, the more his majestie will have his will of this country.[290]

But war often hinges on the question which of the two weary contenders has the greater power of resistance. And in spite of the heavy losses suffered by Dutch merchants – certainly much heavier than those inflicted upon the English – in spite of all the many mutterings, squabbles and divisions, there was no doubt that the Republic had a greater will to persevere.

To begin with, England had suffered great depredations from the plague of 1665 and from the great fire that had laid London low in September of that year. Moreover, Charles II, too, had his hands full with the opposition. Parliament had little faith in his attitude to Protestantism, however unctuously he may have referred to it in his propaganda. There were also many other objections that caused Parliamentary resistance to his war policy, and Charles had good reason to fear a lack of financial support. A revolt in Scotland had just been put down, but Catholic Ireland was in a state of unrest as well. English ministers were beginning to admit to each other that the war had come to be an unbearable burden. No hopeful news had come from Spain, and though intrigues with Orange still seemed to offer the best chance for making the peace, the pressure had grown too great and disunity in the cabinet too marked, for England to insist on talks in the Hague.

Naturally, Holland had been quick to see through the latest English scheme. D'Estrades received instructions to oppose the offer, but De Witt needed no prompting in the matter. Nevertheless, he realized that public opinion would be incensed at a summary rejection of what must have looked a very generous English offer. And, indeed, many voices in the States-General were raised against Holland's uncompromising attitude – De Witt's province had meanwhile resolved not to admit enemy envoys to its territory for the duration of the war. In the draft reply which Holland subsequently submitted to the States-General, the refusal was somewhat tempered by interpreting 'neutral place' as including the Generality Lands. The decision by the States-General to send a letter to that effect without consulting the provinces, and without a unanimous vote, elicited protests not only from Friesland and Zeeland, but also from two urban councils in Holland, namely Alkmaar and Enkhuizen. Zeeland let it be understood that she was willing to convene the peace congress in Middelburg – an idea quite unacceptable to Holland, which felt strongly about the unreliability of that province, its divisions and its special relations with England. The two protesting provinces even threatened that they would withhold their 'consent' to the continuous prosecution of the war, which served merely to bolster up Holland's obstinacy and about which they had not even been consulted. All in all, as De Witt complained in a letter to Van Beuningen, the King of Great Britain had clearly attained his objective with the envoy scheme, namely 'division and altercation both between the provinces among themselves and between the state and its allies.'[291] Matters began to look even grimmer for Holland and De Witt's policy, when Gelderland and Overijsel, too, declared for a meeting in the Hague. But such was England's weakness that she suddenly came round: before the end of March, she declared her readiness to agree to a neutral meeting place and suggested Breda.[292] Kievit's correspondent was indignant. The only reason why 'the friends' had acted with so much vigour was that they had relied on the assurance that His Majesty would stick to his guns.[293] Just before the peace congress opened, therefore, the Orange party was taught once again how little reliance could be placed on England.

As for De Witt, he had scored yet another diplomatic victory, which not only strengthened his position at home but his hand against England as well. One of the Swedish mediators had meanwhile brought him assurances of the king's personal esteem. At the same time, England agreed to accept the proposals of 11 December 1665 as a basis for negotiations.[294] But the most striking proof of the impotence to which the English government had fallen sway was the decision, as early as February,[295] to lay up the fleet of war, or at least the battle-ships. For some time, England had been unable to pay her sailors regularly, and the only way to keep the ships manned was with the help of press-gangs. In no sphere was the contrast with the Republic more striking. For while England, in her exhaustion, took the coming of peace for granted, the wharves at Ij and Maas were preparing furiously to get the ships ready for battle by the summer. Throughout that spring the English government kept receiving warnings from its informants in Holland that, despite all the peace talk and the strain the heavy war taxation was imposing on the resentful merchants, a new maritime expedition was being prepared with all speed.[296]

England at Breda (May–June 1667)

Even before the negotiations at Breda had begun, Europe witnessed yet another crisis: D'Estrades informed the States that, on the basis of the alleged rights of his queen, Louis had asked Spain for the immediate cession of parts of the southern Netherlands. A strong French contingent, commanded by Turenne, had already launched an attack. The reason why Louis felt free to act now when, ever since the autumn of 1665 he had felt his hands tied by the war with England, was simply that England's weakness had suddenly been brought home to him.

Yet English weakness was not, in fact, the full explanation. England had embarked on two contradictory policies simultaneously. This duplicity, which strikes us today as being the result of confusion rather than of treachery, had been a characteristic of English policy ever since the Restoration. Its cause was the profound division between Charles II and his people. Charles had always wanted an alliance with France, and as early as 1662, he had hinted to D'Estrades that he needed French help to subdue his rebellious subjects. He never rid himself of the fear that Parliament might treat him as it had his father, and indeed, a Catholic in his heart, he was completely closed to the passions and prejudices of his people. Thus, though Louis XIV had preferred an alliance with the Republic, and had even allowed himself to be dragged into the war with England, Charles continued to look to France. The unanimity with which England waged war on the Republic did no more than bridge the gulf between ruler and people for a short time. Of Charles's ministers, Arlington may be said to have represented the national mood, for while the people were undoubtedly behind his demand for colonial and trading advantages, they would also have liked to see Holland – albeit a subdued Holland – on their side against France, especially against French ambitions in the Southern Netherlands – hence their policy towards Brandenburg, and their plottings with Buat and Kievit. That being the case, it is easy to understand why their intrigues and appeals should have found a ready echo among war-weary Netherlands Protestants in general and the Orange party in particular. De Witt, for his part, was right in concluding that all the English really wanted was political and economic dominance, and that Charles was not to be trusted.

In the event, Charles II was forced to give Arlington a free hand, even allowing him to plead in the king's name for the cause of Protestantism, because the war with France left him no alternative. But the wider aims of that policy were never his. Early in 1667, Arlington was still examining the possibilities of a separate peace. This time he did not consult the Prince of Orange, but sought direct contact with De Witt. The intermediary was no less a personage than the great Hapsburg diplomat, Baron de Lisola, a man born in Franche-Comté, then a Spanish possession, and now in the service of the Emperor, with a deep-felt mission to warn and arouse Europe against the plans of Louis XIV.[297] Clarendon, less actively anti-French than Arlington, made difficulties before he agreed to the colonial concessions that Lisola considered needful to gain De Witt's support. Even so the intermediary was asked to demand an indemnification and a substitute for Pularoon. Yet De Witt could not possibly entertain the idea of meeting bankrupt England by a policy of saving bankrupt Spain, at the expense of his French ally, the less so as, after two years of strenuous effort, peace on his own terms now seemed to be within his grasp; if need be, he wrote to Van Beuningen, he would go to England to fetch such terms in person.

But even while Lisola was pleading for an anti-French alliance, Charles was using St Albans (whom we have met under the name of Jermyn as Mary's lover) to sound Paris on the very opposite of that policy. He was authorized to persuade France to conclude a separate peace and what he had to offer in exchange was far greater than Louis's faith in the Dutch alliance: on 18 April 1667, letters were exchanged between the two kings (behind the backs of the English ministers) by which Charles promised not to enter into any alliance against France for one year in exchange for a French promise to return the island of St Christopher in the West Indies; Louis now considered that his war with England was over. Van Beuningen noticed with growing impatience that the true substance of St Albans' negotiations was being kept from him,[298] but there were indications enough to enable him and De Witt to guess at the truth. The sudden French attack upon the southern Netherlands – and this without any consultation of the Dutch ally (another clear breach of a promise) – coupled to an equally sudden French withdrawal from the common naval campaign despite recent preparations – the French fleet was now assembled in North-Atlantic harbours – all that showed unmistakably which way the wind had begun to blow.

A French move towards the southern frontier of the Republic was felt as a nightmare by all parties in the Republic. De Witt, who even at the height of his predicament with England, had resolutely refused to let himself be drawn into commitments on behalf of 'the queen's rights', did not hesitate for a single moment. He immediately instructed Van Beuningen[299] to inform France that her action could not but 'tend to detract from the friendship between France and this state' and that it would make Their High Mightinesses increasingly averse to 'the neighbourship and contiguity of France'.

In these circumstances, he, too, began to look for peace with England, and Van Beuningen agreed with him.[300] But De Witt had not prepared the fleet for nothing. If the English thought that, at the last moment, and in fear of France, he would allow himself to be robbed of the fruits of his country's exertions, they would be sorely disappointed.

For one thing, he was not prepared to change the basis of the negotiations. The peace would have to confirm the state of *uti possidetis* and restore the treaty of 1662. Now, these conditions were by no means unfavourable to England. They amounted to the surrender by the States of New Netherland, and the exchange of a few factories on the West coast of Africa. However, just before, on 28 February 1667, a Zeeland fleet contingent (this was a strictly provincial enterprise) had conquered Surinam, and in the eyes of the Dutch, that was not a bad exchange for New Netherland. The English negotiators (Downing was not among them; he now held a post in the Treasury and it was with bitter regret that the notorious trouble-maker saw himself excluded from the negotiations) kept mentioning an indemnification, and especially a substitute for Pularoon, to which the Dutch felt entitled by the *uti possidetis* principle. The States, accordingly, declined both substitute and indemnification and, moreover, demanded that the confusing provisions of the 1662 treaty, which had been formulated as a result of collusion between Downing and the Orangists,[301] should now be eliminated. In addition, they wanted the Navigation Act to be mitigated: goods from Germany and the Spanish Netherlands carried along the rivers Rhine and Scheldt in Dutch bottoms were to be admitted into England. France did not support the additional demands, since the alliance merely obliged her to maintain the States in their actual possessions. And so the *Bona Esperanza* and the *Bon Adventure*, those two ships conjured up in 1662 out of cold judicial documents, made their ghostly re-appearance at Breda, with De Witt firmly determined this time to exorcize them for good.

The chief Dutch negotiator was Van Beverning, who was again co-operating smoothly with De Witt.[302] But in the circumstances, with England so feeble and the Republic so menacingly strong, the English could not even count on help from De Huybert, the second negotiator. A reporter of the English government who was staying at Breda, observed regretfully: 'It seemeth, because they are ready before us and have now no enemy to encounter, they are apt to think it will ever be so and they doe so much flatter themselves that his Ma[ty] wanteth both men and money, that they think it now a very fit time to impose what conditions they please upon him, insomuch that it hath been publickly discoursed in most places – even amongst ye rest by the Ambassador Hubert, who otherwise is a pretty well inclined man and a greate lover of the house of Orange.'[303]

A lover of the House of Orange! Even at Breda, the English still looked for help from that quarter. True, the instruction to the two envoys, Hollis and Coventry, not to disembark in Zeeland, showed a certain respect for the position of Holland which, what with the antagonism between the two Grand Pensionaries, might take offence; but the Zeelanders and De Huybert were nevertheless to be treated with great politeness.[304]

And there was still hope for co-operation from Holland itself. Kievit's friend kept sending the most favourable reports,[305] and – *mirabile dictu* – the English continued to take them seriously. D'Estrades, on the other hand, reported that the Prince of Orange used every possible occasion to assure the regents that he 'knew no other interests than those of the state'[306] – suspicions against him were evidently strong after the Buat affair. And yet Clarendon saw fit to write blithely to the English envoys that they were to reject 'with contempt' the 'insolent demands' of the States and 'to see that the reasonableness of the king's offers and the unreasonableness of *their* demands might be made clear to those who are desirous of peace!' And if Amsterdam was, indeed, as zealous for peace as Mr Kievit's friends kept assuring him, it might still be possible to frustrate De Witt's ambitious plans.[307]

The attack on Chatham (June) and peace (July 1667)

At the very moment when Clarendon was writing his letter, 18,500 Dutch sailors had already put to sea under De Ruyter. To begin with the fleet consisted of ships from Holland alone; the Zeeland and Frisian squadrons were not yet ready. In Zeeland, an anxious watch was being kept on the French advance in Flanders; Friesland was hampered by lack of money. De Witt made certain that the attack on 'London's river', which his officers had been too cautious to launch after the Four Days' Battle, would go off smoothly this time. He could not leave with the fleet himself (the French menace in the southern Netherlands made his presence at home indispensable) but he persuaded the States-General to send his brother Cornelis along with De Ruyter as their deputy, and with express instruction 'to deliberate and to proceed with vigour and rather to take a risk than return without some notable accomplishment'. The ships carried assault troops and two English skippers to act as pilots, one a true 'fanatick', the other a fugitive from English justice – he had evaded paying the king's tolls.[308] And Cornelis de Witt made good use of his explicit instructions. At the council of war, all officers without exception judged the plan to be impossible of execution; a few of them mocked it openly. De Ruyter himself wavered. In the end, however, they did not refuse their orders, and as a result struck a blow at English pride that shook the entire kingdom to its foundations. The fort at Sheerness was taken; the wharves and magazines at Chatham destroyed, and most of the English fleet at anchor there burned, sunk, or captured; there is no need to tell the well-known story in detail. The panic in London, a run on the bank, a flight to the provinces, and the helpless government at their wits' end – all this shows how much the blow had struck home. Johan de Witt was convinced that even more might have been done, but after days of holding out against the reluctance of the officers, and the objections of De Ruyter himself, he finally gave way and abandoned the idea of an attack on Woolwich.

The Grand Pensionary had good reason for satisfaction, if only because the English were at last brought to reason at Breda.

D'Estrades had done what he could to prevent the attack which, he felt was bound to prolong the war. This, he now alleged was precisely what De Witt wanted – his very position rested on that, and, moreover, he was using the fleet to line his own purse.[309] On 1 July, one of the Englishmen at Breda, shocked by the humiliation, wrote a letter in which he expressed his own bitterness at the weakness of his government, and the fear of 'sensible men here' that peace has now moved even further off, since the king will not take so sensational a blow.[310] But Clarendon wrote to his envoys that, 'although peace can be bought at too high a price, it would suit us highly in the circumstances and we are not in a position to decline. Peace is needed to calm people's minds, and would free the king from a burden which he is finding hard to bear.'[311] Shortly before,[312] he had insisted on restitution for the two ships; now he gave way on that as on all other points. On 31 July, a peace treaty was signed in full accord with the proposals that De Witt had dictated to Van Beverning in May. The raid on Chatham, had, all of it, been De Witt's doing. He had designed it, he had prepared it, he had executed the plan through his brother and against the obstruction of the officers. More remarkable still was the shrewdness of his political calculation. Immediately before the attack he had written his brother a letter in which he had called him 'the best plenipotentiary in that matter [the peace]'.[313]

One problem remained. The English envoys had been told that the peace treaty must include the restoration of Kievit and other Orangists to office; also of Wootton and the other English officers who had been dismissed in 1665. But Kievit's apology to the States of Holland had been rejected 'with scorn';[314] in December, the Court of Holland, trying him *in absentia* had convicted him of high treason and condemned him to exile. In that respect, his sentence was more severe than that sending Van der Horst into exile, or even than Buat's death sentence; for in neither case had the term 'high treason' been used, and 'high treason' involved the confiscation of personal property.[315] Kievit's restoration, therefore, was no small matter. No doubt, the English government thought it could put him to better use in the Republic than in England; yet their insistence on that point is yet another proof of their complete misunderstanding of conditions in the Republic. In the event, all their efforts proved in vain, and the peace treaty was signed all the same. The English envoys had realized by then that the States-General could not be of help even had they wanted to be, for the sentence had been passed by Holland and the States-General were powerless to revoke it. 'As far as I am concerned,' De Witt wrote to Van Beverning, 'England may shelter Mr Kievit *cum sociis*, and even treat him to festivities, and invest him with all honour and dignity,' but the request to restore him in Holland is so 'exorbitant' that it need not be contested with great arguments; it was enough 'to declare simply and soundly that their High Mightinesses *cannot*, and Their Noble Great Mightinesses *will not*, do it'.[316]

There the matter rested for the time being, but once the peace treaty had been ratified, Charles himself wrote to the French and Swedish envoys asking for their mediation in the matter, and, beyond that, addressed himself directly to both the States-General and the States of Holland. He gave his royal word that Kievit, before leaving Holland 'had never held any direct or indirect correspondence with us;[317]' which was all too obviously untrue. Meanwhile D'Estrades, too, put in a plea for forgiveness – a striking proof of the way the French attitude had changed as a result of Louis's new war. D'Estrades was quite suddenly 'unable' to understand why Holland should refuse to show mercy to what was, in fact, a plotter and tool of the enemy, and by so doing encourage other adversaries of the States régime. He argued that nothing more was involved than extending the customary post-war amnesty to Kievit, and added that Holland was quite unfeeling in taking revenge on English and Scottish officers who had stayed in their service and whose properties at home had been confiscated. It seems that Van Beverning went along with him as far as the officers were concerned: D'Estrades at least alleged that he called it a shame, but said that he could do nothing about it.[318] Yet the case of the English officers was quite different from that of a man found guilty of high treason. Even so, the other provinces, led by Zeeland,[319] put great pressure on Holland for his restitution, so much so that Kievit's 'friend' felt most hopeful. Towards the end of July, he also mentioned support in Holland: 'Our great friend Mr Calterman of Haarlem' was president of the States-General for that week and if Charles's letter arrived during Calterman's term in office, 'he might achieve a great deal with the help of Zeeland.'[320] Coventry, one of the English envoys, aired the problem with Kievit's friend. The latter observed how useful Kievit's restoration would prove to the position of the Prince of Orange, and the envoy assured him that he had found a good deal of sympathy among the States plenipotentiaries in Breda.[321] But Holland remained obdurate; in the States assembly not a single voice spoke up for Kievit[322] and, as De Witt pointed out with glee: the States-General had no say in the matter.[323] By way of compensation, the English government saw fit to bestow a knighthood on Kievit in September, and while it continued in its great efforts to have Sir John Kievit rehabilitated in his own country, it realized that De Witt had the upper hand for the moment – the peace conference had left England in no doubt that what promises of support she had obtained from Kievit's friends were quite worthless. 'Not one person so much as ventur'd a visite to ye Ambassadors;' was what their chaplain Dr Mews[324] wrote disconsolately in August: 'by which you may see hoe much hee [De Witt] hath yem in awe.'

The raid on Chatham and the peace of Breda gave a powerful boost to national pride. 'It is not to be expressed, how high the spirits of the Dutch are at present,' the English merchant Tucker wrote from Rotterdam. 'They expect the English shall truckle under them hereafter, and that, where and when a Dutchman is present, an Englishman must hold his peace . . . The English will hardly bear the braggings and boastings of the Dutch. . . .'[325] Clearly, the (justifiable) glorification of the great feat of arms of Cornelis de Witt in poetry and painting had its disagreeable side as well. But the Dutch had so often shown pusillanimity towards their great neighbour, that they were bound to swagger now they had scored so resounding a victory. Abroad, too, there was no longer so much of that contemptuous talk about Dutch 'lawyers' and 'merchants'.

Inevitably the victory cast its rays over the régime, whose leader had steered the ship of state so resolutely and brilliantly into port. There was even an upsurge of Republican fanaticism. Thus Naeranus, a leading Remonstrant publisher in Rotterdam, saw fit to publish a letter from England in his *Rotterdamse Donderdagse Zee-en Post-tijdingen*, whose author alleged[326] that recent events have driven many people in England to say 'That countries are better off under the States than under a king; . . . and that what reputation the English had gained against the Dutch at the time they had a Republic under a Protector, now that they are a Kingdom is lost again and much more besides to the same Dutch.' Consequently 'a change is in the air' over here (in England).

This article caused violent indignation at Breda: Lord Hollis pressed Van Beverning, who in turn pressed De Witt, to have the 'licentious and seditious' writer punished, and the paper was suspended.[327] The High and Mighty States, albeit they had not scrupled to make use of the services of 'fanaticks' during the war and had even not refrained from coupling their attack on London with a call to insurrection, could not afford to tinge their foreign policy with Republican ideals. Yet the letter was merely one instance of a general upsurge of Republicanism.

Triumph of the States party; The Perpetual Edict (5 August 1667)

In terms of party strife, all this meant simply that De Witt was better able to resist the demands of the Orange party.[328] Yet there was one circumstance which, in spite of everything, greatly encouraged De Witt's enemies.

This circumstance was Louis XIV's invasion of the southern Netherlands, which began in late May and continued all through the summer. At the end of August, Lille fell into French hands and when Alost followed in early September, the French were in a position to strike at Ghent and Bruges, and at Brussels on the other side.

The threat to the southern frontier revived the old problem of the army high command. Zeeland and Friesland once again proposed the Prince of Orange, and also repeated the demand that he be appointed to the Council of State. In one respect these proposals met with less resistance than they had in 1665: the entire fabric of 1662, on which De Witt's foreign policy had been based, had disintegrated, and there was no longer any reliance on D'Estrades.[329] The anti-French party had been proved right. There was an urgent need for friendship with England and, as in 1665, much was made of the argument that the elevation of the Prince of Orange was the way to win the King of England.[330] As against this, there was the fresh memory of the Buat affair, and De Witt's plea that this approach had not only been wrong-headed but endangered the country's independence did not go unheard.

Yet as he found, there was so much weakness even 'in our own body' [the States of Holland][331] that he felt immediate precautions were needed to forestall any possible surprises or panic. Though he fully realized that Orange could not be sent away empty-handed, and that some of the promises implicit in declaring the prince a Child of the State would have to be implemented, he also felt that the mood engendered by Chatham and the peace provided the right climate for demanding binding guarantees that central power would remain vested in the States themselves.

Ever since the cry that 'something must be done for the prince' first went up in 1660, the States of Holland had let it be known that all they were prepared to consider was a military position. To them, the greatest danger was the Stadholdership and, *a fortiori*, its combination with the Captain-Generalship. It was that unholy combination to which Frederick Henry had owed his overweaning power, a power from which the States had suffered so grievously in 1650 under William II, and which had turned the Stadholders into dictators of foreign policy.

This was the train of thought which gave rise to the three resolutions that the States of Holland passed unanimously on 5 August 1667. One of them, the Perpetual Edict, can only be understood in connection with the other two, namely the immediate appointment of Maurice of Nassau as field marshal (together with Wirtz, a man from Holstein who had served in the Swedish army and about whom De Witt had received the most satisfactory reports), and the invitation to the prince to serve in the Council of State, 'where he might acquire the knowledge needful to the political conduct of military campaigns and fit himself to what military service the States might decide to appoint him'. But all this was to be dependent upon the third resolution, the Perpetual Edict, which laid it down, in the most solemn manner, that the States of Holland would never again allow any Captain- or Admiral-General to be Stadholder of any province; that they would try to obtain similar resolutions from all the other provinces; and that an oath to that effect would have to be sworn by any future Captain- or Admiral-General; moreover, that they themselves would never again appoint a Stadholder, and that this office 'was for all time abolished in the province of Holland.'[332] The resolution also laid it down that the Nobility and the eighteen urban councils were forbidden ever again to leave their own election to an outsider. The individual regents making up the 'members' (the nobility and eighteen towns) of the States were also asked to swear an oath on this 'Perpetual Edict and Permanent Law', and it was stipulated that, in future, no one was to be admitted either to the town councils or to the Nobility who had not first taken that oath.

All the councillors of the eighteen towns and all the representatives of the Nobility in the entire province of Holland did indeed take the oath, though only six months later, after fruitless attempts to obtain the co-operation (the 'Harmony', as it was called) of the other provinces. In Holland itself, there was apparently but one dissenter: Aitzema tells us that in the small town of Breda, an old man was heard to say: 'I am old and deaf and cannot hear the oath very well; I shall rather leave. And so he did.'[333] One cannot help wondering about that degree of unanimity. What had become of all the Orangists with whom Buat and Kievit had concocted such ambitious plans? What did Burgomaster Blauw of Prumerend feel, or Coninck of Hoorn, or pensionary Fagel and burgomaster Calterman of Haarlem, when they took the oath? After the great change of 1672, Orangist pamphleteers were quick to explain that all these right-thinking men had not dared to come into the open. Whosoever showed the slightest opposition, was treated as one of the *bons amis* and a supporter of le petit maistre. 'Whosoever spoke out, was playing with his head.'[334]

In fact, it seems certain today that the Edict itself was the work of one of those 'right-thinking' men, namely Fagel who, it is true, drafted it with the help of Valckenier. No doubt, Fagel was anxious to use 'these brave proposals for the conservation of Liberty'[335] the better to clear his name from the odium of the Buat affair. Perhaps he was really shocked when the treasonable aspects of the intrigue eventually came to light. As for Valckenier and De Witt, they were pleased to help the conversion of their vacillating colleague. Naturally, there was another side to the proposal as well: it seemed to pave the way for a settlement with the prince, the more so as his appointment to the Council of State was being stipulated as well. The prince himself and his grandmother thought this to be disappointingly little, and were dismayed at the entire transaction, for like so many good Orangists, they had expected nothing less than a complete restoration.[336] But it was something – in fact, too much for many States supporters, who for that reason found the Edict as distasteful as their opponents did.

Thus De Witt had to defend the Edict to his loyal follower Lambert Reynst of Amsterdam. In the preparatory talks not only

Edam and Enkhuizen, where the Orange party was strong, had been slow to come round, but also Dort, Delft and Rotterdam, generally the strictest of republican towns (the last-named since the downfall of Kievit and Van der Horst).[337] In the Amsterdam council, De Witt's staunchest supporters were up in arms – Bontemantel voted against the proposals in the preliminary discussion and took the oath with obvious reluctance; ex-burgomaster Hooft thought it 'strange to swear today how one will cast one's vote in a few years' time, provided the fashion has not changed by then'.[338] This, at any rate, is how the Orange party must have looked upon the oath, and it was at them that Hooft was directing his cynical remark. De Witt, he felt, was deceiving himself if he thought he could settle the future in this way.

The other provinces, as we saw, held out much longer against the Edict, with the result that the Harmony was not signed until 1670 – but more of this later. Meanwhile, most people were impressed by the striking unanimity of the powerful province of Holland. The Stadholdership had been rejected by its entire regent-class, and there could be no promotion for the prince, not even his 'introduction' into the Council of State, so long as all the other provinces failed to obtain Holland's co-operation by agreeing to pay the price of the 'separation' of the high offices. The public view – if we may go by Aitzema[339] – was that Orange had suffered another setback and that Buat's intrigue had been responsible for it.

Louis's invasion of the southern Netherlands (May 1667) Triple Alliance (January 1668); Peace of Aix-la-Chapelle (May 1668)

But before we continue the life story of young William and of the 'Harmony' project, we must take a closer look at the attitude of the English government and at its relations with the States from the summer of 1667 onwards.

The widespread belief that there was a necessary connection between the Orange question and English support against the new French threat in the Spanish Netherlands had no substance in fact.[340] De Witt might be suspicious of the Prince of Orange, but that was no reason for remaining passive while the King of France perpetrated acts of aggression, and though William was kept waiting for his promotion, England nevertheless saw eye to eye with the Republic on the matter of the southern Netherlands.

Not that either England or the Republic drew the necessary conclusions straight away, and this despite the fact that their similarity of interests was brought into the open even at Breda. Van Beuningen kept writing from Paris that it was imperative now to seek the friendship of both England and the Emperor. But this was easier said than done. Lisola, zealous as ever, was actively fostering an anti-French coalition, but his imperial master regarded this as a hopeless enterprise and in the end allowed himself to be swayed by French diplomacy into signing a secret treaty, by which he was promised part of the Spanish inheritance upon the, generally expected, death of Carlos II. Brandenburg, too, considered it safer to make a deal with the powerful French king. As a result, the completely helpless Spanish monarchy had no alternative but to look to the two Maritime Powers, whose mutual strife it had but recently watched with so much satisfaction.

The isolated English government was left to face a deeply indignant nation. Fear of Parliament led to the dismissal of Clarendon, who had to flee to France. Clarendon had been the chief advocate of a separate peace with France,[341] and the English had good reason to reproach him (as they reproached the French) that his policies had not avoided the Chatham disaster. As late as June, Clarendon had written to the envoys at Breda that the French advance in Flanders posed no threat to England.[342] Public opinion in England, as in the Netherlands was, by contrast, profoundly disturbed by that advance, and now looked with hatred on the man who had sold Dunkirk, and on all Catholics and Jesuits to boot. Above all, however, there was a passionate desire to vindicate the nation's honour by a powerful campaign in aid of the Spanish Netherlands.

The entire second half of 1667 was spent in talks about co-operation with the Republic against the French threat; the Dutch were represented by the new States ambassador in London, a Zeelander (as the States ambassadors in England customarily were) and the special envoy Meerman from Leyden who, being a Hollander, could correspond more intimately with De Witt.

At first, however, the negotiations made little progress. The States – as we shall see in a moment – were still exploring other possibilities, but the principal obstacle was the fact that the

English government, secretly, and going directly against public opinion, was still trying to sound France on what concessions she would be prepared to make if she were left a free hand in the southern Netherlands. Now that had been the very line taken by St Albans.[343] Clarendon might have been sacrificed, but Charles II had not changed – his main objective was still to gain Louis as an ally against the Republic. This fact cannot be stressed enough, and explains much of what followed. Only when Louis replied that he could not consider such an alliance while the Republic stood by the treaty of 1662, did the English government swing round and make serious attempts to come to terms with the States.

The man they sent to the Hague for that purpose was Sir William Temple, who, as we saw, had previously dreamed up the plan of a Zeeland insurrection against De Witt.[344] At Brussels, however, he became convinced of the French danger, and now believed whole-heartedly in the policy which he had been sent to present in the Hague. Thus there is no doubt that he was sincere when he assured the Dutch that his government had now made its final choice and would abide by it – he was completely ignorant of Charles's recent proposals to France.

Outwardly, at any rate, everything now seemed smooth sailing. The English government, so Temple explained, had come to appreciate that they and the States had identical interests in the Spanish Netherlands. On the thorny question of the Prince of Orange, Temple had instructions to assure De Witt 'that the consideration of the prince's interests must in no ways impede or disturb the great interests the nations have in common, which must always go beyond those private interests'. In other words, the English government, which had tried to make use of the prince for their own purpose when the two nations were at war, now acknowledged the primacy of the States.

The policy which Temple had come to expound to De Witt involved the famous Triple Alliance, i.e. the grand alliance between England, the Dutch Republic and Sweden against the exorbitant claims of France, with which the name of William III has become inseparably associated. That, at least, is an obvious reading of the event of January 1668. But this was certainly not the intention of De Witt (and even less so of Charles II). And, indeed, the Treaty was to have completely unforeseen consequences.

The Republic, too, had been pursuing negotiations in two directions: with Spain and other powers that seemed interested in saving the southern Netherlands from the French, and with France, in order to reach an understanding at the expense of Spain. Only – and here was the crucial difference from the English approach – in its negotiations with France, the Republic had no intention of surrendering the whole of the Netherlands; it fully intended to fob off France with as little as possible, and have the remainder divided into independent cantons or left under Spanish rule. Nor was there ever any question of entering into an anti-English alliance with France.

I have pointed out that Van Beuningen had given much thought to the advantages of an anti-French coalition. Lisola, as we know, was preaching this all the time. And indeed the idea arose quite naturally from the circumstances. In October, Van Beuningen returned from France with grim forebodings. Colbert's tariff policy had caused much resentment in Amsterdam, where Van Beuningen was listened to as an expert in foreign policy. In early September, the hard-pressed Spanish governor of the southern Netherlands and the Spanish Ambassador to the Hague had proposed that the States should occupy Ostend, Bruges and a few fortresses in return for a pledge of auxiliary troops. That was to the liking of many in the Republic, including De Witt, but much precious time was lost (as usual) while the provinces examined the proposals, and by the time they had done so, Spain had withdrawn the offer. No help seemed to be forthcoming from the Emperor or from England either, and De Witt was thrown back upon his old plan which, in fact, he had never completely abandoned, to reach an agreement with France on the lines suggested in 1663. The danger that the States might otherwise accept the Spanish proposals impressed Louis enough to adopt a more positive attitude towards the Republic in late September. He called a halt to his advance and agreed (to the States, whose interest in the matter he thus recognized) to content himself with the part of the southern Netherlands which he claimed as his due (or rather his Queen's due). He left Spain the 'alternative' of ceding a considerable stretch of country in the south, contiguous to France, or else of leaving to France those parts already occupied by her. In addition, the Franco-Dutch negotiators discussed possible armed intervention by the States, after the truce, should Spain be unwilling to acquiesce in the proposed amputation. Van Beuningen and others at first raised serious objections,[345] but finally came round when they realized that this was the only way in which France could be made to promise that, should the war between the Republic and Spain be resumed, she would attack parts of the Spanish empire other than the southern Netherlands. This then was the general policy on which Holland agreed on 10 December. The final details were decided on 14 December, after deliberations between De Witt and Prince Wilhelm von Fürstenberg, a West German ruler who may be said to have acted as agent for France. The final agreement contained one secret stipulation that D'Estrades would have read with a good deal of indignation: the Kings of England and Sweden (and whoever else might be willing to come in) would use force not only against *Spain*, but also against *France* should she still try to evade her obligations.

A few days later Temple returned from England, where he had gone for final instructions, and by 23 January 1668, the alliance was signed (the Swedish ambassador joining in without having received clear directives). Holland had had her way, but she now found herself embroiled in a defensive alliance that went beyond her original intentions. De Witt, for one, had never been en-thralled by the idea. He had told Temple quite plainly that the vacillations of the English court did not inspire him with any confidence in a policy of close association. Were his suspicions lulled by Temple's obvious sincerity? I doubt it very much; the more likely explanation is that he found it impossible to offend England once he had gained her co-operation in a scheme that might all too easily give her a chance to make a deal with France at the Republic's expense. Temple had threatened with that very possibility on the occasion of his first visit. Much as the prospect of a seizure of the southern Netherlands by the Republic and France had forced England to come to the negotiating table, so De Witt could not risk driving England into the arms of France. Yet England and the Republic felt so little confidence in each other that they had to seek safety in a grand alliance.

Meanwhile, De Witt did his utmost to assure the French government that they had nothing to fear, that the alliance was no more and no less than the French themselves had asked. In his explanations he laid constant stress on the fact that the alliance was primarily directed against Spain. Temple did not make De Witt's task any easier by the enthusiastic way in which he presented the alliance as the beginning of a great new Anglo-Dutch friendship. And the English government spoilt the whole game when, one month later, they informed the French of the secret stipulation.[346] Partly as a consequence of his country's geographical situation, which made the fate of the southern Netherlands a matter of primary concern to the Republic, and as a result of England's unscrupulous tactics, De Witt had willy-nilly been manœuvred into a position in which the maintenance of good relations with France, on which his diplomacy had been based all along, had become impossible. He made that discovery too late, and, as it were, reluctantly. Yet the annoyance with which the Triple Alliance was received at the French court, and especially the revelation of the secret article, were quite unmistakable. For a moment, it looked as if the French would brave the entire Alliance and proceed with their war of conquest. Van Beuningen who was sent to France to present the advantages of the Triple Alliance, was struck by the menacing tone the French adopted towards him. But Louis XIV was not a man for immediate action, and caution won out in the end. In May 1668, the peace between Spain and France was concluded at Aix-la-Chapelle on the agreed terms. Spain chose to cede the towns and districts that France had already occupied, thus creating an explosive situation.

However, Louis had been hurt in his deepest pride by the presumption of mere republicans, who dared to play the arbiter between kings and who had the temerity to block his path. He was the more indignant in that he had just assisted these self-same men and, moreover, at a moment that did not suit him in the least (the Republic itself had been more impressed by the obvious reluctance and meagre quality of his help than with its reality), who now saw fit to make common cause against him with the very enemy from whom he had saved them! So far he had felt himself bound (albeit retraining a degree of royal liberty) by the treaty of 1662; now the States might argue for all they were worth that they had not offended against the treaty, that they had done no more than impose the king's own alternative upon the Spaniards – Louis felt himself released from all obligations to them.

When we spoke of England's 'unscrupulous tactics', we were referring, not to Temple, who took up his post in the Hague with the firm conviction that the Triple Alliance, the work of his hands, was the rock on which the foreign policy of his government firmly rested, but to Charles, who used Temple's obvious sincerity as a means of misleading De Witt. Subsequent events were to make it quite clear that Charles II had not abandoned his real intention, an alliance with France, and that, as far as he was concerned the Triple Alliance was merely a convenient tool for allaying the suspicions of Parliament – which rejoiced at his 'protestant' policy – and above all, for undermining (at last!) the good relations between the Republic and France, which stood so ominously in his own way.

The preliminaries of the Anglo-Dutch alliance[347] have been dealt with in such detail because it was the beginning of the difficulties in which De Witt's foreign policy became bogged down and on which it finally foundered. And as De Witt's relationship with the House of Orange, and the connection between Orange and Stuart, played an important part in these developments as well, though only incidentally.

There had been many differences of opinion in the government of the Republic as to the correct course to steer between France and Spain, before it was quite suddenly decided to reach an agreement with Temple, in which the provincial States were not even consulted. And the differences of opinion had by no means been along the usual Orange and pro-States division, even though a man like Dohna, the Swedish ambassador (a cousin of the Princess-Dowager and a brother of a governor of Orange, who had had to suffer a great deal from the French) spoke at times as if the deep-rooted pro-French sentiments of the Grand Pensionary was the only obstacle to peace with the Spaniards.[348] But even Amsterdam and Rotterdam, two staunch Republican centres, had joined with Haarlem, the home of Fagel and Van Thilt, in showing definite reluctance to a break with Spain. Zeeland, the most outspoken Orange province, had been foremost in advocating the partition of the Spanish Netherlands, which was tantamount to close co-operation with France; Utrecht, which had already accepted the Harmony, i.e. the 'separation' of the offices of Stadholder and Captain-General, and had been the only province to join Holland in abolishing the Stadholdership, was the last of all to give her consent to threatening Spain with armed force. Nor is there any evidence of attempts by Temple to gain Orange support for his policy or even to make contact with them. His instructions for the critical negotiations in January had, indeed, ordered him to offer emphatic assurances to De Witt and to promise, in almost so many words, that the English government would not meddle with the Prince of Orange.[349] And when the prince appeared at the dinner which De Witt gave in honour of the new ally, and the English ambassador treated the nephew of his king with all the respect and courtesy due to him, De Witt had no reason to fear that these civilities might cast a shadow over the warm friendship of the two new allies.

The Harmony challenged (1667-70); Zeeland's animosity towards Holland

His alliance with England and successful mediation between France and Spain, helped to consolidate De Witt's position once again. In July 1668, he was re-elected for the third time running, and with much pomp and circumstance. Motions of gratitude, a considerable present in money and an increase of his (rather meagre) salary, showed how highly appreciated he was by the States.

For all that, the Harmony between the provinces had, as we know, not yet been sealed, and the prince's future remained unsettled, much to William's own discontent. Outwardly, his relationship with his governor and his guardian remained unruffled. The young man kept seeing De Witt regularly to receive instruction about affairs of state. In January 1668, when, with his noble friends, he staged a symbolic play about the peace of Breda[350] (in French, naturally, and what poor French it was! . . .) all official bodies in the Hague came to witness the spectacle and bickered about questions of precedence. The prince, in the course of his role (as Mercury, in Roman dress and with a plumed helmet) hinted not obscurely at his hope to be allowed to serve the state in arms, as, in fact, he was entitled to under the Perpetual Edict. It was not a secret, however, that his ambitions went beyond that and that he could count on the support of governing circles outside the province. In face of the united attitude of the Holland regent class, this did not pose a very grave threat, but deserves our attention none the less. For in trying to understand the history of the Republic, we are frequently compelled to take note of purely local conditions in the seven provinces, and even in the various districts and towns. In each, the major political problems assumed quite distinct forms, under the influence of local narrative conditions, interests, and family ambitions. The unity of my narrative demands that much of this should be skipped, but ignoring these complications altogether would be tantamount to a distortion of the true picture.

At the end of 1667, after months of discussion in which Holland used all her power over the various provinces, only Utrecht, Gelderland and Overijsel had endorsed the Harmony. This gave De Witt a majority in the States-General, and Holland was now able to address the remaining provinces with the authority of the High and Mighty Assembly itself, which, indeed, sent 'deputations' of its own to the provincial States of the tardier members. For a time, it even looked as if these efforts might be crowned with success, the more so as the provinces were divided among themselves.

Friesland and Groningen raised very special objections: the proposal would put an end to all their hopes that their own Stadholder, young Henry Casimir, might one day become Captain-General – in case, for instance, his cousin at the Hague were to die and the direct Orange line were thus broken. His mother, who acted as Governess of the provinces during his minority, therefore did her utmost to frustrate Holland's plans.

We have the letters in which Fagel, sent North as a member of the deputation of the States-General, reported his experiences to De Witt. The Haarlem pensionary addressed the Friesland regents as a true supporter of the States party, warning them against the anti-Republican ambitions a powerful Prince of Orange was bound to entertain, and adding that it had been due solely to a succession of miracles that William I, Maurice and William II had not become masters of the state (the first-named and the third thanks to their untimely deaths, the second through his lack of decision): it would be tempting God to count on a fourth miracle. And he found a good deal of agreement among the Frisian regents. But Karel Roorda, still proud of his namesake who, seventy years before, had led the opposition against the then Stadholder of Friesland, and who was himself as strict a republican as any Hollander,[351] nevertheless took a gloomy view of the situation. It was not, as in Zeeland, fear of the commonalty which made the Frisian regents hesitate, it was fear of the Governess. Roorda told Fagel with some bitterness that it was the latter's province which had, years ago – in the days of Frederick Henry – helped to put power in the hands of the Frisian Stadholder; now the Stadholder's court had the support of a political party, and many of those who thought otherwise were afraid to say so openly, the more so as there was no real need for them to do so; after all, Holland would hold up the elevation of the prince even if Friesland abstained. And, in fact, both Friesland and Groningen declined to endorse the Harmony.

Much the same happened in Zeeland, though only after much excitement and squabbling. In the prince's own town of Veere, half of the town council fell out badly with the Dowager and appealed to the States of Zeeland for help. They threatened that if they did not get satisfaction they would ask the States to allow the town councils to appoint their own magistrates (the Stadholder or his guardian, i.e. the Dowager, had a say in the annual appointment of burgomasters and aldermen). The other faction occupied the town hall and hoisted the Orange flag on the tower. The States sided against the Dowager and saw sedition in the Orange flag. Amalia sent Huygens to mediate on her behalf, and the compromise he obtained after exhausting discussions conceded much more to 'the rebels' than was to his liking.[352] But De Witt's confidant Bampfield sent even more gloomy reports to *his* patron![353] The connection between the Veth and Thibault families on which De Witt had built such high hopes in 1665, had proved unable to weaken the influence of De Huybert. The situation in Zeeland had become even more complicated by the rise into prominence of Nassau-Odijk, the son of Beverweert, and hence a brother-in-law of Arlington. Before 1660, Nassau-Odijk had almost been ruined in Paris, where he had run up large debts and had fallen into general disrepute. Charles II had nevertheless seen fit to make him a large gift of money after the Restoration,[354] and in 1664 he had married the daughter of a wealthy Zeeland regent. De Huybert, himself, though he had been hurt so bitterly by the Dowager's 'treason', had remained an unswerving Orangist, and probably looked upon the Perpetual Edict, which had driven a new wedge between the Orange court and Holland, as a chance to parade Zeeland's fervour for the House.

His attitude was plainly tinged with an element that had often stood the Orange party in good stead in the small provinces: envy of Holland, and jealousy of Holland's Grand Pensionary. Those sentiments were barely concealed in Zeeland's notorious address to the States-General of January 1668. This document, which was intended as a reply to Holland's complaint that Zeeland had fallen into financial arrears, contained a bitter attack on Holland's complacency, and her quest for domination. The document went on to belittle the victory at Chatham, poured scorn on Holland for having shown little vigour in the war against Cromwell, and asserted that Zeeland had known far better than her haughty sister how to take advantage of England's exhaustion, when she had sent a naval expedition under Crijnsen to capture Surinam. Much the same note was struck in the resolution by which Zeeland, a few months later, definitely rejected the Harmony project.[355] The rejection and the assertion that Zeeland intended to adhere to the resolution of August 1660[356] went hand in hand with a long list of accusations against Holland: the Act of Seclusion of 1654 and the prayer formula of 1665, were denounced as offences against the Union; the deeds of the Princes of Orange praised highly above 'the exploit in the river of Chatham'; a host of setbacks and mistakes in the conduct of foreign policy since 1650 were recalled and laid at Holland's door. 'Behold,' a Holland pamphleteer wrote with unusual vehemence[357] (for vehemence called up vehemence) – 'behold the work and the style of the Grand Pensionary of Zeeland ... a slave sold to the House of Orange, and implicated in the conspiracy and actions of that self-same Buat, who paid with his head for his wish to make the King of England "the greatest king in the world".'[358]

Meanwhile the Orange court's displeasure at Holland had grown to such dimensions that the Dowager, at least for a time, thought it best to reverse what may be called her habitual policy: she seriously entertained the idea of using Zeeland as a lever against Holland.

REFERENCES

1. *Brieven van De Witt*, II, pp. 278, 280.
2. *Ibid.*, 283, 290.
3. *Ibid.*, 280.
4. *Ibid.*, 279.

5. *Ibid.*, 278.
6. The precise amount had still to be settled, and uncertainty about the final figure was a strong weapon in the hands of Holland; *Brieven van De Witt*, II, p. 34.
7. On 24 January 1661; *Brieven van De Witt*, II, p. 280.
8. *Ibid.*, p. 278.
9. Japikse, *Verwikkelingen*, app. VII.
10. *Ibid.*, p. 135.
11. Fruin, *V.G.*, IV, pp. 149 ff.
12. *Brieven van De Witt* (Scheurleer), IV, p. 94.
13. Japikse, *op. cit.*, opp. VII. Beverweert and Van Hoorn to the States of Holland on 25 March 1661.
14. Van Sypesteyn, *Geschiedkundige Bijdragen*, I, p. 157, note 3.
15. The documents on which Clarendon's story (*Continuation*, I, 1043) is based are found in the supplement to the *Clarendon State Papers*, III. The first proposal from France was made in March 1661. But by June, Clarendon had begun to feel uneasy about the course of the Dutch negotiations in France.
16. He had abandoned any idea of marrying her daughter, because, as he told Clarendon (*Continuation*, I, p. 492) of 'her mother having used him so ill when he proposed it'. The old princess, for her part, was bitterly disappointed at the concessions which the envoys in England were compelled to make: *Briefwisseling van Huygens*, V, p. 360.
17. Haarlem, Leyden, Enkhuizen and Rotterdam.
18. *Brieven van De Witt* (Scheurleer), IV, p. 142.
19. *Clarendon State Papers*, III, Supplement, p. XLVIII; from an undated note the King and Clarendon exchanged during a sitting of the Cabinet Council: Chanc.: 'I am of opinion that nothing is of more importance than to send away Sir G. Downing or somebody else into Holland, both in respect of your nephew and your own affairs, to watch De Witt and Bevering, who play the devil at present. It will be necessary to think of it out of hand.' – King: 'It is certainly most necessary.'
20. Japikse, *op. cit.*, app. VIII b.
21. See Clarendon's characterization of Downing, *Continuation*, 1116.
22. Downing wrote a number of jubilant letters about this unsavoury business. See Japikse (*op. cit.*, pp. 193 ff), and a letter to Sir E. Nicholas in *Nicholas Papers*, Br. M., Egerton 2538; 14 March 1662: 'Not a thing hath happened theise many yeares that hath occasioned so much discourse heere, saying that they are now noe longer a free countrey and that now no man is sure heere. I am glad they are gon. When I carried the order of their delivery to the Bailie of Delft hee said: "Mr. vous avez atraper Messrs les Estats:

had they imagined that you could have taken them they would never given you an order to doe it."' In a pamphlet entitled *Aenspraek aen de burgery van Amsterdam*, 1672, Knuttel 10562, we can read that 'the seriousness and love towards the welfare of the commonweal' of burgomaster Hooft 'appeared notably when he alone in the assembly of Holland spoke against the faithless surrender to Downing of the English Parliament men'.

23. As we saw (p. 121), William Frederick made the most objectionable proposals to Chanut even earlier, when he agreed to the partition of the country. The secret understanding which Frederick Henry and William II had with French diplomatists was hardly less reprehensible.

24. For further particulars from Downing's unpublished letters at Oxford, see Japikse, *op. cit.*, p. 183.

25. See p. 213.

26. Japikse, *op. cit.*, app. IXa.

27. Lister, *Life of Clarendon*, III, p. 143; Downing to Clarendon, 24 June 1661.

28. 16–26 August 1661; Lister, *op. cit.*, III, p. 167.

29. Japikse, *op. cit.*, app. IXa.

30. *Archives*, II, V, p. 208.

31. *Ibid.*, 21 April, 1661: 'Quand les Anglois auroyent formé un dessein de ruiner le peu d'affection que reste icy pour la maison d'Orange, il n'y sçauroyent mieux réussir qu'ils font. Toutes les villes mesmes qui ont esté jusques icy dans ses intérests, declarent contre ces gens-là, et de fait il n'y en a pas une qui ne juge que ce n'est point l'avantage de l'Etat d'avoir un général et gouverneur du pays dépendant du Roy d'Angleterre.'

32. Japikse, *op. cit.*, p. 152.

33. *Brieven aan De Witt*, II, pp. 35, 38.

34. See p. 165.

35. *Brieven aan De Witt*, II, p. 296.

36. Japikse, *Verwikkelingen*, p. 152. A comparison with Aitzema, X, pp. 85–7, suggests that Downing represented the opposition as more important than it actually was.

37. X, p. 87.

38. X, p. 85.

39. *Briefwisseling van Huygens*, V, p. 361.

40. *Ibid.*, p. 369.

41. *Ibid.*, also *Archives*, II, V, p. 213.

42. In a memorandum which Turenne sent to D'Estrades, when the latter was sent to the Hague, we can read the following: 'La parenté proche du roi d'Angleterre avec le Prince d'Orange . . . lui donne aussi beaucoup d'avantages pour avoir une grande cabale

en ce pays-là contre les intérêts du roi . . . Une des plus capitales affaires du pays est l'établissement du prince d'Orange que je ne croirois pas mauvais, hors la liaison qu'ill a avec le roi d'Angleterre. Mais ces choses-là peuvent changer selon les temps. Mais présentement je crois que M. d'Estrades doit maintenir M. de Wit et sa cabale;' *Recueil des instructions, Hollande*, I, p. 246.

43. Louis XIV mentioned this in a letter to D'Estrades: see D'Estrades's *Lettres et Négociations*, I, p. 277.

44. *Archives*, II, V, pp. 218, 220.

45. *Briefwisseling van Huygens*, V. p. 383.

46. Japikse, *op. cit.*, p. 190.

47. *Ibid.*, p. 256.

48. Downing kept showing him letters from his government; *Briefwisseling van Huygens*, V, pp. 384, etc.

49. *Ibid.*, p. 406.

50. Japikse, *Verwikkelingen*, p. 179.

51. *Ibid.*, pp. 183, 189, note 4.

52. *Ibid.*, pp. 191, 221.

53. Downing to Nicholas, particularly on 22 August 1662 (OS), Nicholas Papers, Br. Mus., Egerton 2538.

54. Downing to Nicholas, 29 August 1662 (OS); *ibid.*

55. Dr Japikse considered this concession 'almost incomprehensibly imprudent' on the part of the States; *op. cit.*, pp. 223.

56. Japikse, *op. cit.*, p. 243.

57. *Ibid.*, p. 241, note 5.

58. In January 1662, for instance, Sommelsdijk wrote that the old princess seemed inclined to dismiss Van Zuylestein, who had come to symbolize the English connection; Sommelsdijk was opposed to this move, and apparently thought that his correspondent (Huygens) shared his views: *Briefwisseling van Huygens* V. p. 385. Cf. Japikse, *op. cit.*, p. 203.

59. 'Un hausse-qui-basse continuel' as Brasset put it: *Archives*, II. V, p. 20. – The seventh member, i.e. the prince, was 'dormant' during his minority.

60. Downing to Nicholas, 3 February 1662 (OS), Nicholas Papers, Br Mus. Egerton 2538.

61. *Briefwisseling van Huygens*, V, p. 375.

62. In 1661, a French observer described Hendrik Thibaut as the most powerful man in Zeeland; *Archives*, II, V, p. 210. In March 1662, Sommelsdijk complained bitterly of Thibaut's support for Holland; *Briefwisseling van Huygens*, V, p. 409.

63. Downing to Nicholas, 2 September 1662 (OS), Nicholas Papers. 'Meanwhile,' Downing concludes, 'De Witt makes it his businesse to gratifye them in their personall and provinciall concerns.'

64. See Thibaut in *Brieven aan De Witt*, II, p. 121.
65. *Brieven aan De Witt*, II, pp. 433–53.
66. Aitzema, X, p. 519.
67. Aitzema, X, p. 378.
68. Japikse, *op. cit.*, p. 255.
69. *Ibid.*, pp. 252, 257; app. XI.
70. Aitzema, X, p. 837.
71. 22 February 1663; *Lettres et négociations*, II, p. 98.
72. *Brieven*, II, p. 431. For the letter to which this was a reply, see Japikse, *op. cit.*, p. 260.
73. See p. 49.
74. It is significant that in May 1663, De Witt should have felt it necessary to assure Veth that the States of Holland had no intention of challenging the Synod of Dort; *Brieven van De Witt*, II, p. 434.
75. See the correspondence of Sommelsdijk and Huygens. Cf. Van Ruyven in Japikse, *Verwikkelingen*, p. 260.
76. *Brieven aan De Witt*, II, p. 121.
77. Van Sypesteyn, *Geschiedkundige Bijdragen*, I, p. 162.
78. *Lettres et négociations*, II, p. 317.
79. Lister, *op. cit.*, III, p. 149.
80. Japikse, *Verwikkelingen*, p. 272, note 5; the letter is not included in *Brieven aan De Witt*.
81. Lister, *op. cit.*, III, pp. 251–2.
82. *Lettres et négociations*, II, p. 306.
83. Japikse, *op. cit.*, app. XLII.
84. *Ibid.*, p. 274.
85. Wicquefort to Lionne, *Zee-oorlogen*, I, p. 240: 'Cette guerre est son ouvrage'.
86. See p. 46.
87. See Japikse, *Verwikkelingen*, app. XLIX ff.
88. Japikse, *op. cit.*, p. 394.
89. Van Wijn's views (*Aanmerkingen bij Wagenaar*, XIII, p. 122) are ingenious but are largely based on hypotheses. From Van Ruyven, *Zeeoorlogen*, I, p. 145, which is far from clear, we nevertheless gather that De Witt rejoiced at having obtained Renswoude's signature to a document he had not read.
90. See Downing: *Zeeoorlogen*, I, p. 147.
91. See Japikse, 'Buat als diplomaat', *B.V.G.*, IV, IV, p. 66.
92. Violet Barbour, *Henry Bennet, Earl of Arlington*, p. 82.
93. *Ibid.*, pp. 83 ff.
94. *Venetian Calendar*, XXXIV, p. 63.
95. D'Estrades, *Lettres et négociations*, IV, p. 259. See above.
96. *Ibid.*, III, p. 27.
97. *The Netherlands in the 17th Century*, I.

98. D'Estrades, who obviously wanted his government to intervene, may have painted the situation in somewhat too gloomy colours. The same is true of the alarming reports Wicquefort was sending to Lionne. In early August (by which time the mood of panic had begun to recede), Louis himself wrote to his envoy that he could not believe all these prophecies of revolution and that De Witt's position seemed strong; *Lettres et négociations*, III.

99. *Ibid.*, III, p. 215.

100. *Zeeoorlogen*, I, p. 209.

101. *Ibid.*, p. 236.

102. *Ibid.*, pp. 231, 249.

103. St P. For., Holland, p. 174; 3 January 1665; signed Bucquoy. In 1652, Van Ruyven had been discovered to hold a private correspondence with William Frederick.

104. Cf. *Continuation*, p. 249.

105. Japikse, *Verwikkelingen*, p. 329.

106. Quoted by Van Vloten, in Arend, *Algemeene Geschiedenis des Vaderlands*, IV,[1] p. 715.

107. Wicquefort to Lionne; *Zeeoorlogen*, I, p. 224.

108. *Ibid.*, p. 199.

109. See p. 192.

110. Wicquefort to Lionne, 2 July 1665; *Zeeoorlogen*, I, p. 241.

111. 2–22 June 1665; *op. cit.*, p. 218. It is amusing to read in the *Venetian Calendar*, XXXIV, p. 222, that this M. Courtin, son of a merchant family, found his birth an obstacle in English court circles.

112. *Lettres et négociations*, III, p. 214; *Zeeoorlogen*, I, p. 197.

113. *Nederlander en Engelsman tzamen redenkavelende over den zeestrijt*, etc.; Knuttel, p. 9069.

114. Cf. Knuttel pp. 9068, 9070, 9071.

115. Beverweert was an Orangist, but a true Hollander at heart. See Downing, *Zeeoorlogen*, I, p. 211.

116. *Ibid.*, p. 228.

117. *Brieven van De Witt* (Scheurleer), II, p. 106.

118. *Zeeoorlogen*, I, p. 210.

119. See, for instance, Bampfield in *Brieven aan De Witt*, II, p. 129.

120. *Brieven van De Witt*, III, p. 90.

121. Norway was part of the Danish kingdom.

122. *Zeeoorlogen*, I, p. 240.

123. Arlington to Downing, 21 July (OS), Add. 22920, Br. Mus. (Downing Papers). Arlington demanded a war indemnity; a satisfactory arrangement for the East, and indemnification in Guinea.

124. Japikse in *B.V.G.*, IV, IV, 79. Colenbrander has omitted this

important passage in his edition of Downing's letters, *Zeeoorlogen*, I, p. 286.

125. See p. 197 f.

126. *B.M.H.G.*, 1917, p. 370.

127. *Sir W. Davidson in de Republiek, B.V.G.*, IV, V, p. 384.

128. Aitzema, XI², p. 796.

129. According to Downing himself: Goodison, *England and the Orangist party.*

130. Japikse, *Buat als diplomaat B.V.G.*, IV, IV, 63; *Brieven aan De Witt*, II, p. 198.

131. Aitzema (XI², p. 796). On 25 August, Downing himself wrote to Arlington (St P. F., Holland, 177): 'For God's sake seize nobody, for yn [then] my family will al be seized and wt [what] care they for Van Gogh, I assure you not two straws in comparison of an occasion for to take mee'; Goodison.

132. *Brieven van De Witt* (Scheurleer), II, p. 128.

133. Van Goch reported this conversation in a letter of 4 October 1665; see Aitzema, IX², p. 1015; cf. *Brieven van De Witt* (Scheurleer), IV, p. 480.

134. See, for instance, Knuttel, p. 9144, 9186, 9230, 9252.

135. His sermon was published in 1666, with additions, under the title: *Juda en Israel teegens Benjamin, mitsgaders Engelant teegen Hollant, voorgestelt uit Judic. 20 : 27, 28 ;* Knuttel p. 9398.

136. Aitzema, XI², p. 987.

137. *B.M.H.G.*, 1936, p. 44, note 3.

138. Hosea, 2, 6. See Aitzema XI², p. 1034.

139. See, for instance, Knuttel, p. 9559.

140. Aitzema, XI², p. 1015.

141. *Brieven van De Witt*, III, p. 150.

142. *Brieven aan De Witt*, II, p. 201.

143. Aitzema, XI², p. 1016.

144. D'Estrades, *Lettres et négociations*, III, p. 478.

145. *Observatie van eenen Amsterdammer gheschreven aen eenen goeden Patriot op het suject van desen teghenwoordighen Orlogh met Enghelandt ;* Knuttel, p. 9391.

146. This claim was exaggerated. No doubt there were a good many Germans and Scandinavians and even Englishmen among the crew since, as we saw, national dividing lines were not so sharply drawn as they are today. But the navy did present a different picture from the army. Thus Knuttel 9068, *Hollantse ontsteltenis*, etc., tells us that the sailors were far less slavish then the soldiers, because, among other reasons, they were largely composed of Netherlanders.

147. *Resolutiën Holland*, 28 October 1665; cf. *Brieven van De Witt* Scheurleer), II, p. 117; 18 November 1665.

148. To be obtained by way of negotiation, the first from the Duke of the Palatinate – Neuburg; the second from the States-General themselves. What precisely D'Estrades had in mind is unclear; *Lettres et négociations*, III, p. 486.

149. One does not have to be an uncritical admirer of the Holland regents to be shocked by the insinuation that every burgomaster of every voting was open to bribes. See my article about D'Estrades's exaggerations in *Nederlandsche Historiebladen*, 1939.

150. *Brieven van De Witt*, III, pp. 149 ff.

151. *Brieven aan De Witt*, II, p. 199 (report of Bampfield).

152. *Ibid.*, p. 202 (ditto).

153. Aitzema, XI^2, pp. 1019 seq.

154. *Brieven aan De Witt*, II, p. 204. Temple, too, wrote from Brussels: 'De Witt is returned to the Hague in high time to prevent the mastery of the Orange faction;' 10 November 1665, St P. F., Flanders, 33 (Goodison). In fact, Zeeland changed her attitude before De Witt's return. See the important resolution of 31 October: Aitzema, XI^2, p. 1032.

155. *Brieven van De Witt* (Scheurleer), II, p. 136.

156. Published (from a copy in the B.M.) by R. R. Goodison in *Further correspondence relating to the Buat affair*, *B.M.H.G.*, 1936, pp. 43 ff. The authenticity of this document cannot be doubted, although it is not found in the P.R.O.

157. The treaty of 1663.

158. Vane to Charles II, 8 January 1666, from Cleves; *B.M.H.G.*, 1936, p. 52.

159. From Buat, reported by Sylvius: *B.M.H.G.*, 1936, p. 32.

160. *Ibid.*, 58: Vane to Arlington, 2 February 1666, from Cleves.

161. *Briefwisseling tusschen de gebroeders Van der Goes*, I, p. 240; *B.M.H.G.* 1936, p. 56; Vane to Arlington. The Elector supposed that the letter came from 'the well-intentioned party', but left Vane in the dark about its contents.

162 As Buat testified at his trial.

163. See p. 172.

164. *B.M.H.G.*, 1936, p. 27. Sylvius's report to Arlington, based on oral communications by Buat.

165. See p. 204.

166. *B.M.H.G.*, 1906, p. 544.

167. Aitzema, XII, p. 239.

168. Aitzema wrote this in one of the secret news letters he was still sending to England: P.R.O., Newsletters, Holland; quoted by Goodison, *England and the Orangist party*.

169. To Williamson, 19 December 1665; *B.M.H.G.* 1936, p. 25.

170. *Ibid.*

171. *B.M.H.G.*, 1936, 35: Sylvius to Arlington, Antwerp, 22 December 1665. Vane soon afterwards received a letter from Dolman, an English officer in the States' service, which alleged that Van Beverning was anxious to meet Vane, at least if the latter could tell him anything more. The fact that Dolman was a staunch pro-states man throws a curious light on this incident; *op. cit.,* p. 53.

172. *B.M.H.G.*, 1936, p. 28: Sylvius to Arlington (Antwerp ?), 19 December 1665.

173. *B.M.H.G.*, 1906, p. 546: S. to A., the Hague, 25 December 1665.

174. *B.M.H.G.*, 1936, p. 29.

175. St. P. F., Holland, 179; Sylvius to Arlington, the Hague, 19 January 1666. This letter has escaped the attention of Del Court and Japikse as well as of Goodison. For the sake of completeness I am publishing it in *B.M.H.G.*, 1939.

176. See p. 215.

117. Aitzema, XI², p. 84. The document is dated 16 December OS (26 December (NS).

178. *Briefwisseling tusschen de gebroeders Van der Goes*, I, p. 236. The Van der Goes family was Catholic, and as such, supporters of the Emperor and the King of Spain. Cf. Aitzema, XI², p. 807: 'This letter, Holland therein being hatefully censured, was much suppressed.'

179. *B.M.H.G.*, 1906, p. 534.

180. *Lettres et négociations*, IV, p. 51.

181. *B.M.H.G.*, 1906, pp. 555 seq.

182. *Op. cit.,* IV, p. 52.

183. This is a supposition by Japikse: *B.V.G.*, IV, IV, pp. 89 seq.

184. Japikse, *loc. cit.,*.

185. *B.M.H.G.*, 1906, pp. 561 seq.

186. See his hopeful utterance to Ormond, *B.M.H.G.*, 1936, p. 12.

187. *B.M.H.G.*, 1906, pp. 558 seq.

188. This appears even more clearly from a letter by Mme Sommelsdijk to Vane early in January. This actively pro-Orange lady warned him against mentioning the prince in the peace offer to the States-General: *B.M.H.G.*, 1936, p. 54.

189. *B.M.H.G.*, 1936, p. 58. Cf. *above*.

190. Fruin, *V.G.*, IV, p. 267.

191. *B.M.H.G.*, 1906, p. 566 – the slander that De Witt had been bribed with French money was soon afterwards refuted when it appeared that France would not hear of the plan.

192. *B.M.H.G.*, 1906, p. 571.

193. This appears plainly from *Brieven van De Witt* (Scheurleer), II, p. 184.

194. *Brieven aan De Witt*, II, p. 277.

195. *B.M.H.G.*, 1906, p. 572.

196. *Brieven van De Witt* (Scheurleer), II, p. 184.

197. 'Il a fort protesté n'y avoir aucune part, et que cela venoit de Buat, qui est au Prince d'Orange, qui (Buat) l'a nommé de son chef au Mylord Arlington, qui est son (Buat's) ami, pour entrer dans cette négociation, qu'il (Van Bev.) a rejettée dès qu'il (Buat) lui (Van Bev.) en a parlé'; *Lettres et négociations*, IV, p. 146.

198. See p. 215 f.

199. *Brieven van De Witt* (Scheurleer), II, p. 181; 25 February 1666, to Van Beuningen.

200. *B.M.H.G.*, 1906, p. 575; to Arlington.

201. *B.M.H.G.*, 1936, p. 41; to Williamson, same date. This letter contains a remark similar to the one from the other letter, quoted above: 'Nostre affaire est en tel estast que quoy qu'il arrive nostre Maistre y aura de l'avantage.'

202. *Lettres et négociations*, IV, p. 145 seq; to Louis XIV and to Lionne, 25 February 1666.

203. See p. 199.

204. Aitzema, for one, did not notice any hesitation on De Witt's part. On 28 February, he wrote: 'Grande résolution et promptitude dans le party de la France et ses allies et de l'autre côté rien'; P.R.O., Newsletters, Holland, Goodison.

205. Arlington to Ormonde, 24 February (6 March NS) 1666, Carte Papers, 46; Br. Mus.; Goodison. Before that time he was highly optimistic: Browne's *Miscellanea Anglica*, 383; *ibid.*

206. *B.M.H.G.*, 1906, p. 579.

207. *Ibid.*, p. 582: Buat to Sylvius, the Hague, 19 March 1666. Buat called him 'un de mais melieurs amis'.

208. In the letter, a draft of which was discovered after Buat's arrest and which proved most damaging to him. The letter appears in Aitzema, XII, 355; and also in the notes to Wicquefort, *Histoire des Provinces-Unies*, III, 262.

209. De Witt pointed this out in his letter to the Prince of Orange: *Brieven van De Witt*, III, p. 213, note 5.

210. *B.M.H.G.*, 1906, p. 585.

211. See, for instance, *Arlington's Letters* (1701), I, p. 59: Arlington to Temple, 9 February OS. 1666.

212. His brother served on the council of Leyden.

213. Temple to Arlington, received on 21 February (OS); St. P. Flanders; Goodison.

214. *Arlington's Letters*, I, p. 58.

215. De Witt to Fannius, 4 September 1666: *Brieven*, III, p. 225.

216. For instance when he assured the English that the States had decided to propose that France enter into negotiations with

England, since otherwise the States themselves would have to do so: *B.M.H.G.*, 1906, p. 587.

217. Temple, for his part, wrote that 'we shall not reduce Holland to reason without breaking De Witt's party, which is to be done by means of attempts to elevate the Prince'; 26 March 1666, to Arlington; P.R.O., St. P. F., Flanders; Goodison.

218. See p. 233.

219. Rather: they decided to introduce a proposal to that effect in the States-General.

220. *Lettres et négociations*, IV, p. 131.

221. On 29 January 1666; Newsletters Holland; Goodison.

222. *Brieven van De Witt* (Schuerleer), II, p. 199.

223. See p. 174 ff.

224. Aitzema, XII, p. 747. It is surprising to note what indiscretions: particulars about discussions in the States, speculations about the intentions of the regents, and comments of all kinds, Aitzema could permit himself to put into print so soon after the events. Vol. XII appeared in 1668. In his secret news service to the English Council of State, Aitzema, of course, said a good deal more still.

225. 'S'il ne savoit pas les intérieures intensions du gros de la Hollande estre, pour se maintenir sur ses maximes de demeurer encore sans chef'; Newsletters, Holland, 16 March 1666; Goodison. – See also *Brieven van De Witt* (Scheurleer), II: De Witt to Van Beuningen, 18 March.

226. Aitzema in Newsletters, Holland; Goodison.

227. Aitzema, XII, p. 747.

228. *Brieven van De Witt*, III, p. 169: to L. Reynst, 3 April 1666.

229. Aitzema, XII, p. 227.

230. Ibid., p. 228.

231. *Brieven van De Witt* (Scheurleer), II, p. 220.

232. *Kronijk van het H.G.*, 1852, p. 432 ff. Cf. *Brieven van De Witt*, III, 169 ff.

233. Aitzema, XII, p. 239 ff.

234. See p. 183 f.

235. The claim of De Guiche: *Mémoires*, p. 223.

236. Charles II had sent him over with a gift of horses in 1665; *Cal. St. P. Dom.* 1664–5 and *Cal. of Treasury Books*, 1660–65.

237. In his article *Buat als diplomaat, Bijdr. Vad. Gesch.*, IV, IV, 105, Dr. Japkise wrote that there is 'no conclusive evidence' for the supposition that Buat was denied admittance to the court. In a newsletter to the English government, Aitzema stated that Buat had been ordered to his garrison at Bergen-op-Zoom: Newsletter, Holland, 16 April 1666; Goodison. Another reporter too, mentions

Buat's expulsion: *Zeeoorlogen*, I, 303. On hearing of Buat's arrest, D'Estrades said: 'M. du Buat, qui étoit auprès du P. d'O. avant qu'on eût changé sa maison' (*Letters*, etc., IV, p. 420)

238. *Brieven aan De Witt*, II, p. 281.

239. See p. 185.

240. Elias, *Vroedschap van Amsterdam*, I, CXV, alleges that De Witt made this proposal 'in consultation with' Valckenier and Reynst, but the letters from Reynst in *Brieven van De Witt*, II, p. 278 f. prove (as Fruin rightly remarked) the opposite. The towns which, on 2 April, 'took over' the plan (that is to say agreed to put it before their principals) were among De Witt's staunchest supporters: Dort, Delft, Amsterdam, Gouda, Schiedam, Brill; the most pronounced Orangist towns (Haarlem, Leyden, Enkhuizen, Hoorn) were among the ten members prepared to act immediately: *Brieven van De Witt*, III, p. 173 (from an annotation by Bontemantel).

241. *Brieven aan De Witt*, II, p. 279 seq.: L. Reynst, 6 and 19 April 1666.

242. See p. 147 ff.

243. *Zeeoorlogen*, I, p. 303. Cf. Van Ruyven to Williamson, 4 June 1666, Newsletters, Holland, 48: 'Tous les honnêtes gens en murmurent grandement;' Goodison. – Cf. also De Guiche, *Mémoires*, 222.

244. The Zeelanders, too, were said to have been taken by surprise: *Zeeoorlogen*, I, p. 203.

245. Japikse, *Prins Willem III*, p. 128.

246. *Lettres et négociations*, IV, 223: D'Estrades to the King, 15 April 1666.

247. According to Aitzema (XII, p. 228) France could not possibly trust the prince, because she knew she had 'displeased him with the demolition of Orange'.

248. Newsletters, Holland, 16 April 1666: Goodison.

249. Aitzema, XII, p. 228. This, incidentally, is one of the quotations used by Goodison in evidence of Aitzema's authorship of these Newsletters.

250. 'In a later letter;' Goodison. The print, says Aitzema, was banned immediately.

251. See Wicquefort, *Histoire des Provinces-Unies*, III, p. 409.

252. 'Sa présence a fait prendre service à plus de mille matelots,' D'Estrades, *Lettres et négociations*, IV, p. 282.

253. Aitzema, XII, p. 101. Cf. Wicquefort in *Zeeoorlogen*, I, p. 466.

254. *Lettres et négociations*, IV, pp. 413, 418.

255. *Zeeoorlogen*, I, p. 467.

256. The ins and outs of the affair appear from a memorandum in

Kievit's file. It is a rough copy of a Holland States resolution and contains a summary of Kievit's deposition. After his return from the fleet, Sommelsdijck had apparently visited the house of Maarten Harpertszoon Tromp's widow (Kievit's mother-in-law) and in the presence of company (amongst them Kievit) had recounted his experiences during the battle. It was on this story that Kievit had based his report. Next day, he showed it to his brother-in-law, Harpert Tromp, the brother of Cornelis. In the absence of Kievit, Tromp, and also a certain Molewater, made a copy; and at the behest of Cornelis's sisters (one of them Kievit's wife) sent it to Amsterdam for printing.

257. *Zeeoorlogen*, I, 468 (Wicquefort) and 469 (notice from Haarlem).
258. *B.M.H.G.*, 1906, pp. 588–591.
259. *Brieven van De Witt*, III, p. 219.
260. Aitzema, XII, p. 354, and Wicquefort, III, p. 260.
261. That, at least, is what Japikse supposes: *Brieven van De Witt*, III, p. 228, footnote 1; in view of Keivit's desperate position (about which more in the text) I am inclined to doubt it. But one cannot help wondering about Buat's failure to take to his heels.
262. This appeared during the hearings; *Crimineele Papieren Hof van Holland*, A.R.
263. See p. 234 f.
264. On 19 August, Kievit was examined by the States about the 'Sommelsdijck Report'. – D'Estrades immediately connected Buat with 'Tromp's cabal': *Lettres et négociations*, IV, p. 420. Cf.: *Zeeoorlogen*, I, p. 468.
265. Hearings at the A.R.
266. *Journalen van C. Huygens den zoon*, III, p. 64 f. (1682).
267. D'Estrades pressed unrelentingly for a severe sentence and there is little doubt but that Louis XIV would have thought very ill of any sentence other than the death penalty. D'Estrades – of course! – made it appear that it was his intervention that swayed the court.
268. The Commissioned Councillors examined her in her own house: file of Buat trial, A.R.
269. Aitzema, XIII, p. 184.
270. Aitzema, XII, p. 362.
271. See Fruin, *V.G.* IV, p. 286.
272. *Brieven van De Witt*, III, p. 214.
273. *Ibid.*, p. 220.
274. Knuttel, 9330; 9341; the author calls himself H. van V.
275. Knuttel 9339.
276. Newsletters, Holland, 3 September 1666; Goodison.

277. S.P.F., Flanders, 28 September 1666; ditto.
278. XII, p. 357.
279. The prince kept open house even after he became a 'Child of the State'. Thus Tromp called on him in June to tell his story of the Four Days' Battle: Japikse, *Prins Willem III*, I, 132.
280. Aitzema, XII, p. 360.
281. *Brieven van De Witt*, III, p. 216.
282. *Zeeoorlogen*, I, p. 483.
283. See, for instance, J. Boreel's comments in confidential letters to Van Kinschot on 22 August and 4 September: *Codex H.G.*, II, I, pp. 76 seq.
284. Aitzema, XIII, p. 186. – How offensive the States party found these comparisons may be gathered from the pamphlet *Den Zeeuwsen Buatist, of Binnenlandsen Verrader, ontdekt in een oproerig en landverdervend pasquil genaamt 'Consideratiën van de Heeren Gecomitteerden Raden van Zeeland, etc.'*; Kn. 9662.
285. *Arlington's Letters*, I, p. 101: to Temple, 12–22 October 1666.
286. Minute of a letter from Arlington to Sylvius, 24 August 1666, S.P.F., Holland; Goodison.
287. Kievit to Arlington, with the request to let him know through Sylvius whether it were thought desirable to make any alterations in the draft of his letter: S.P.F., Holland; Goodison. (October, but the correct date must have been 10 September).
288. The letters of Kievit's correspondent at the P.R.O. are translations, in Sylvius's hand. Goodison did not succeed in identifying this man.
289. 5 January (O S) 1667; to Ormond: Carte Papers, B.M.; Goodison. A similar observation by Temple, 18 February 1667: *ibid*. See also the *Diary of Samuel Pepys* under 17 February (O S).
290. Samuel Tucker, 11 February, 18 March 1667; *B.M.H.G.*, 1917, pp. 365, 370, 366.
291. *Brieven van De Witt* (Scheurleer), II, p. 454.
292. Aitzema, XIII, p. 35: 18–28 March 1667.
293. Translation in Sylvius's hand, about 15 April 1667: S.P.F., Holland; Goodison.
294. Aitzema, XIII, p. 44.
295. Keith Feiling, *British Foreign Policy, 1660–72*, p. 206.
296. See for instance *B.M.H.G.*, 1917, p. 371 ff.
297. He had just published his *Bouclier d'état et de iustice*, an impressive indictment of France.
298. A few months earlier, Louis XIV had boasted that he would keep nothing from his allies. Cf. Japikse (*Louis XIV et la guerre anglo-hollandaise, Revue Historique*, 1908, p. 56). However, the April agreement was certainly not communicated to the Republic – and

Dr. Japikse's claim that this agreement did not entail important changes, is immediately contradicted by his own remark: 'Dès sa convention particulière avec Charles II, il (L. XIV) avait abandonné toute idée d'hostilité contre l'Angleterre.' No less erroneous is Keith Feiling's assertion that France and the Republic kept each other informed about the Lisola and St. Albans missions: *British Foreign Policy, 1660–72*, p. 219.

299. 12 May: the new orientation had been evident since April. *Brieven van De Witt* (Scheurleer), II, p. 498.
300. *Brieven van De Witt* (Scheurleer), II, pp. 512, 517, 531.
301. See p. 183.
302. The best summary of the States' demands is given in De Witt's letters to Van Beverning: *Brieven*, III.
303. *B.M.H.G.*, 1917, p. 411: P. du Moulin to Arlington, 24 June 1667.
304. S.P.F., Holland: instruction to Hollis and Coventry, 18 April OS 1667; Goodison.
305. Chiefly about the other provinces. 'We' have won over Gelderland, Zeeland, Friesland and Overijsel 'to give all imaginable satisfaction to H.M.', etc.; an English translation in Sylvius's hand S.P.F., Holland, about 15 April 1667; Goodison.
306. *Lettres et négociations*, V. p. 279 seq.; 30 June 1667.
307. Clarendon to Hollis and Coventry, B.M., Add. Mss. 32094; 31 May (OS) 1667; Goodison.
308. *B.M.H.G.*, 1917, p. 384 seq.
309. *Lettres et négociations*, V, 381.
310. *B.M.H.G.*, 1917, p. 416.
311. 14 and 21 June (OS) 1667; Goodison.
312. 7 June (OS); ditto.
313. *Brieven van De Witt*, III, 302: 22 June.
314. *Cal. St. P., Dom.*, 1666/7, p. 157.
315. See Fruin, *V.G.*, IV, p. 302.
316. *Brieven van De Witt*, III, p. 332: 10 June 1667.
317. Aitzema, XIII, p. 139. – Afterwards, Arlington assured the new Dutch ambassador that he had never heard of Kievit before the latter's arrival in England; even Sylvius, who had conferred and dined with Kievit and Van der Horst repeatedly, asserted the same 'very assuredly'! – *Brieven van De Witt* (Scheurleer), IV, p. 548 seq.
318. *Lettres et négociations*, V, p. 411.
319. De Huybert in person intervened on Kievit's behalf: letter in S.P.F., Holland, 5 September 1667; Goodison.
320. In a French translation; Goodison. On 15 April, Kievit's friend wrote: 'It's commonly spoken of ye likelyhood of your returne

with honour', but, he added, if K. were mentioned by particular recommendation only, 'De Witt may yet oppose it and your friends will not have too good a foundation . . .'; in an English translation, S.P.F., Holland; Goodison.

321. Letter received on 28 July (OS?) 1667, S.P.F., Holland; a summary in Goodison.
322. *Brieven van De Witt* (Scheurleer), IV, p. 526.
323. Aitzema, XIII, p. 304.
324. *B.M.H.G.*, 1917, p. 424.
325. *B.M.H.G.*, 1917, 423.
326. *Brieven aan De Witt*, II, p. 372.
327. *Ibid.*; See also *B.M.H.G.*, 1917, p. 421.
328. Kievit's 'friend' wrote early in August: 'Nous voyons clairement que par (le) dernier suxces de Monsr de Whit l'advancement de Monsr le Pr. Dorange auquel il y avoit beaucoup de disposition se recule presentement, car lon voit que Monsr de Whit et sa caballe par ceste heureuse action seront extremêment fortifiés dans leur crédit'; S.P.F., Holland; Goodison. Cf. *B.M.H.G.*, 1917, p. 424.
329. *Lettres et négociations*, V, p. 381; 30 June, from Breda.
330. According to a letter by Kievit's friend, received on 30 August 1667, (S.P.F., Holland; Goodison) this is what Gelderland told a deputation from Holland, which had come to win the province over for the Harmony Project.
331. *Brieven van De Witt*, III, p. 363.
332. *Resolutiën van consideratie*, II, p. 801.
333. Aitzema, XIII, p. 356.
334. I have found this phrase in three pamphlets: *Den Grooten Witten Duyvel*, Knuttel 10319; *De heldere dageraad*, etc., 1672, Kn. 10311; and *Vriende-praetjen over het Eeuwig Edict*, Kn. 10333 (all three of 1672). Pamphleteers often copied one another.
335. De Witt to Reynst, 8 July 1667; *Brieven van De Witt*, III, 363.
336. Aitzema, XIII, p. 311.
337. *Brieven van De Witt*, III, p. 372 note; also C. G. Smit, *Notulen . . . 1670 . . . door H. Bontemantel*, introd. XVI. Data about the origins of the Perpetual Edict are few and far between. One senses a lack of political correspondence during this period; even the valuable De Witt archives show serious gaps. Hence we have to make do with Bontemantel's notes, written years after the events. De Witt's letter of 8 July to Reynst seems, in fact (as Fruin has noticed), to confirm that the idea did not come from the Grand Pensionary. Fagel and Valckenier cannot be considered as members of 'a middle party', especially during this period. Smit takes this view, following Japikse and Fruin; see my *De wording van het Eeuwig Edict* in *Studies en Strijdschriften*. In the text (p. 314) I have

mentioned Valckenier's veneration of De Groot's *Verantwoordinghe*. As for Fagel, his letters to De Witt from Friesland in the spring of 1668 (see p. 280) are full of the spirit of Freedom and show his dislike of tyranny under a Stadholder. It is true that Fagel had taken a different line in the past and that he would afterwards change his tune once again. But the Frisian letters entitle me to assert that he was deeply shaken by the Buat intrigue. The theory that Fagel supported the Perpetual Edict in the interest of the Prince and the Dowager presupposes that he was playing an intricate game of dissimulation – in any case, the Orange court would have nothing to do with it.

338. Smit, *Notulen . . . Bontemantel*, p. XVII.

339. *Saken van Staat en Oorlogh*, XIII, p. 353.

340. This view was even held by many leading citizens of Amsterdam, as witness a memorandum in Oudart's hand, presumably based on an original document he received from Holland, and marked 'Copia for My Lord Arlington'; S.F.P., Holland; Goodison: 'Nonne mirabile in auribus vestris Patres Principis adoptivos (sc. the Holland States) promotioni, quam omnes urgent Provinciae, obstrepent? . . . Deputati Amsterodamenses rogati an quid sinistri sentirent de Rege Galliarum, responderunt se plus damni expectare ac metuere a Regis Galliae successibus quam a promotione Principia Auriaci.'

341. See p. 176.

342. It would only confound the Dutch and make them sue for peace the more quickly, England not having to yield a thing: 7 June (OS); B.M., Add. Mss., 32094; Goodison.

343. See p. 262.

344. See p. 235.

345. Amsterdam and Rotterdam because of their trade interests in Spain; Utrecht because of the injustice towards the King of Spain, whose lawful rights were universally admitted.

346. Keith Feiling, *British Foreign Policy, 1660–72*, p. 257.

347. It was, moreover, one of the most intricate and confused episodes in diplomatic history. I know of no really satisfactory account. Keith Feiling's *British Foreign Policy, 1660–72* (1930) is often to the point, as is his whole, often brilliant but more often irritatingly obscure work, the main historical virtue of which is the underlying attempt to view diplomatic events against their overall political background. Feiling, however, does not really know or understand De Witt and exaggerates his pro-French attitude. Thus when he writes: 'A majority of Dutch provinces would hear of nothing for Spain beyond the alternatives, while the English resolutely made a defensive alliance the condition of any negotiation' (p. 254), he is

not, in fact, stating two irreconcilable attitudes. Two pages before, moreover, he mentioned 'a defensive alliance' as one of the points of 'De Witt's platform'! – When he cites an utterance of Dohna about De Witt's pro-French sentiments, he omits to add that his authority, Wicquefort, himself remarks upon its partiality (Feiling, p. 242, note 1; Wicquefort, *Histoire des Provinces Unies*, III, p. 382). – Somewhat surprisingly, Feiling writes as if he were the first 'to dispel a legend', to wit that the Triple Alliance as an anti-French move was De Witt's work. Dr. Japikse (whose *Johan de Witt* is repeatedly quoted) had done so fifteen years before. – Dr. Japikse's exposition is convincing in many respects, but he also, in my opinion, lays too much stress on De Witt's determination to use threats against Spain alone. On one point he even makes a mistake (p. 259). He observes that in the resolution of 14 January 1668, Holland went a step further than in the resolution of 10 December. 'It was resolved . . . to promise positively that a Dutch army would march into Belgium, if Spain refused peace on the conditions offered by France.' But he fails to mention that it was also resolved (and resolved before Temple's decisive visit) to make war on France in consultation with the allies in case France contracted out. Feiling does mention this fact, but calls it 'hardly more than a pious aspiration, reflecting rather the acute differences of opinion between the Dutch provinces', – an assertion that, in my opinion, can hardly be substantiated.

348. See note, p. 347.

349. He had instructions to 'endeavour to quiett all jealousy and apprehension he (De Witt) may have of Our wishing to lessen his credit in that government and of Our concerning Ourselfe for Our nephew ye Pce of Orange to the prejudie there of': Instruction of 1 January (O S); printed in Courtenay, *Life of Temple*.

350. *Ballet de la Paix, dansé par le Prince d'Orange*. The play was published by Van Wouw, Imprimeur ordinaire de Son Altesse Monseigneur le Prince d'Orange. Facsimile of the title-page in Japikse, *Prins Willem III*, I, p. 145. – I cannot agree with Dr. Japikse's interpretation that certain passages were allusions to the Prince's further ambitions.

351. See p. 147.

352. *Briefwisseling van Huygens*, VI, p. 226.

353. *Brieven aan De Witt*, II, p. 404. See above.

354. *Nieuw Nederlandsch Biographisch Woordenboek*, I; art. by P. J. Blok.

355. In March, the Commissioned Councillors of Zeeland proposed a project which served no better purpose than 'to divert and amuse the common people'; Aitzema (XIV, p. 253).

356. See p. 142.
357. *Praatje in 't ronde*, etc., Knuttel 9763, p. 20. Dated Dordrecht, 1669.
358. The reader will recognize the unhappy passage from Buat's letter to Arlington: see p. 249.

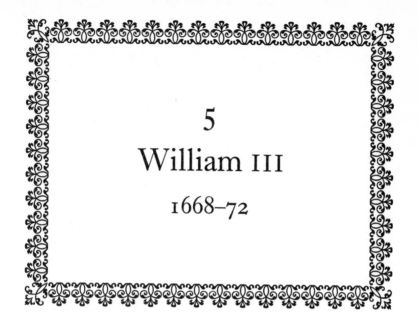

5
William III
1668–72

William's journey to Zeeland (September 1668)

This change of attitude was reflected in a sensational event that, at one and the same time, marked William's entry into politics. In September 1668, he suddenly travelled to Middelburg to ask the States for his admission as First Noble. His expedition had been prepared in secret by Huygens and the De Huyberts[1] acting on the Dowager's instructions. With a number of friends – Odijk was one of the party – the prince went first to Breda, ostensibly on a hunting trip; his governor Van Ghent had been left behind in Gelderland, and the guardians in the Hague suspected nothing untoward. Then William quite suddenly made for Bergen-op-Zoom, where a Zeeland States yacht picked him up.

When he reached Middelburg, the prince had his presence announced to the States by his intendant, and was immediately assured of their keen pleasure. If the truth be told, quite a few members had been privy to 'the plot' from the start, while others harboured quite different feelings and would have resisted far more vociferously had they not been taken 'by surprise'.[2] Not that they would have withheld the First Nobleship – after all, there was the resolution of August 1660 which, as everyone knew, would have to be implemented sooner or later, but there was always the chance of restricting the prince's powers by means of a 'settlement'. Now no one so much as dared to raise the subject. At the reception, on the first day of the prince's arrival, the commonalty displayed clear signs of the liveliest enthusiasm. The local militia lined the route, all windows facing the street through which he passed in his ornate coach drawn by six horses, and even the roofs, were crowded with spectators, and so was the Abbey Square, where he took up quarters; carriages drove to and fro, and the populace expressed its joy by firing interminable salutes. In these circumstances, the prince's installation next day, i.e. on 15 September, as First Noble went off without a single protest. 'It was much too dangerous to oppose the wish of the people,' wrote a hostile pamphleteer, 'especially when it is remembered how tumultuous, seditious and wicked the Zeelanders are.'[3]

The States of Zeeland were, of course, fully entitled to admit the prince as one of the seven 'members' of their assembly. No doubt they were a little startled when he immediately – a warning from his grandmother and from Huygens arrived too late – appointed Odijk as his representative. Not even the De Huyberts were pleased. Zierikzee summoned up its courage to protest in the presence of His Highness himself – a protest on formal grounds. But by then the step could no longer be revoked.

What must have worried the States of Holland most (apart from the wilfulness of their ward) was the explosion of popular feeling. In his 'congratulatory address', Dominee de Mey ascribed the country's prosperity to the prince's forebears, and prophesied an even more glorious future for the prince himself, welcomed his 'protection', and compared him to Emperors, kings and other great leaders. That was going much too far and, as Aitzema remarked, ran counter to 'the maxims and consequences of Holland's Perpetual Edict'.[4] The Holland pamphleteer who dissected De Mey's oration, expressed his disgust at 'all that exaggerated flattery and servility', and at 'these blasphemous comparisons with saintly actions'. But that, as he wrote scathingly, was only to be expected in Zeeland, where the preachers were still allowed to pray for the Prince of Orange, and did so with much more fervour than they displayed for their true masters (the States of the province):

> As soon as they come to mention the House of Orange and Nassau, they cast their eyes upwards and inflect their voices as if their lives depended only upon the welfare of that young sapling and on the rest of the House of Orange, but when they, as I said, pray for their lawful Authority, they just mumble as if they were praying for a woman lying-in, or for a sailor setting out on a dangerous voyage; which they do so much by rote that they have nearly done before they give it so much as a thought.[5]

Aitzema asked himself whether His Highness, 'by so over-riding his guardians, had not done more harm than advantage to his cause'.[6] Nor was he the only one to wonder. Amalia herself noticed the repercussions with great uneasiness – Holland had clearly taken offence at the triumphal declarations of the prince's supporters. She immediately reverted to her old view that the States of Holland could not be ignored, and William was given a hint, through Huygens, who shared Amalia's views, to break off his stay in Zeeland.

Yet it still looked like a challenge to Holland when the Dowager immediately afterwards, and with the approval of England and Brandenburg, resigned her share in the guardianship, in favour of the prince himself: in other words, when, on his eighteenth birthday, she declared William a major and handed him the administration of his estates and the leadership of the House of Orange. The first alone was no small task, and the Prince's Council had been quite unable to discharge it satisfactorily. There were troublesome debtors, lawsuits without number (about Geertruidenberg with Holland, about Lingen with a German neighbour, etc.) and a host of outstanding claims. In particular, Charles II had not repaid his heavy debt, which encouraged the Spanish government not to keep too closely to its obligations under the treaty of 1648. In March 1669, the idea was mooted that the prince should go to England himself to plead his cause. It took a year and a half before the final decision was taken: the journey threw up grave political issues. Moreover, the prince's foremost task was not so much the collection of debts as establishing his precise standing with Zeeland and Holland.

William discovers the inadequacy of Zeeland's support; His ambitions

The self-willed announcement of the prince's majority (the Dowager had simply communicated it to the States of Holland) greatly angered De Witt: to be declared a major before reaching the age of twenty-three, the prince, like every other citizen of Holland, needed the express permission of the States (*veniam aetatis*). De Witt would have liked to retaliate with the dissolution of the education commission, and pressed for a re-examination of the prince's position and future, but he received little encouragement from Valckenier in Amsterdam,[7] and so the education commission continued. De Witt himself continued giving his lessons, for Holland refused to recognize William as a major. Yet from now on Holland's guardianship meant even less than it had before. Meanwhile, De Witt had obtained the consent of Amsterdam (Reynst complained[8] that it was not an easy job) for a measure that was meant as a safeguard against further untoward consequences of the new connection between Orange and Zeeland. By the resolution of August 1660, Zeeland had promised the prince not only the First-Nobleship but also the Stadholderate. Should he acquire that as well, Zeeland might well demand that, in accordance with precedent, the prince be given a seat on the Council of State. Holland, firmly determined that all the provinces must accept the Harmony first, blocked this possibility by passing a resolution that debarred separate provinces from introducing their Stadholders into the Council of State *ex officio*.

But this was a challenge the prince no longer cared to take up; in fact, he did not so much as ask for the Stadholdership of Zeeland. In that office, as he knew full well, Holland's Perpetual Edict would have barred him from the Captain-Generalship. But seeing that he was not prepared to enter into open conflict with the States of Holland, he might as well have refrained from making his sensational journey to Zeeland in the first place. True, he was First Noble now and as such was one of Zeeland's delegates to the States-General, but when it came to his real objectives, Zeeland proved of little help to him, and the only result of his flamboyant gesture was that he had learned to appreciate the full importance of Holland.

The attitude of the English government must also have contributed to that realization – England clearly had but the one wish – not to get involved in the affair.

Temple had arrived in August 1668 as Ambassador, supplied with the instruction that he was to give precedence to the king's nephew. That was a point that had never been cleared up since William's public encounter with D'Estrades five years ago, and it was no small matter that, by the new instruction, England now officially recognized him as a member of her royal family.[10] At the same time, however, Temple was instructed to take care not 'to give any unnecessary jealousy to the States; which caution you must especially observe towards that which is called the Prince of Orange's party, by whom you may be privately informed of many things relating to their government, which you will not easily learn from others, but taking heed not to be put by them upon any thing that may disturb our good correspondence with the States . . .' In other words, he was to advise the prince to depend upon the 'goodwill of the States rather than on any particular faction', but the advice was to be tendered 'with such a temper and discretion as not to lose the friendship and dependence any considerable person hath upon his family.' A veritable tight-rope act this, for both the prince and his English adviser. All that Temple was told to do directly for the prince (apart from the question of precedence) was to ask De Witt for help in restoring his shattered finances – a request that cost Charles not a penny. As for repaying his own family debt to Orange, Charles continued to turn a deaf ear to all pleas.

The Zeeland affair had made it crystal clear to any who still doubted it that the English government had no intention of sacrificing its present interests to the needs of the Prince of Orange. Thus Arlington told Temple[11] that, when the new Dutch ambassador to London, Johan Boreel, himself a Zeelander, had gleefully reported the prince's reception in Middelburg to the king, Charles was very reserved, fearing as he did that 'the suspicion of cognizance might hinder your negotiations' (in Holland). And that suspicion, Temple had been expressly instructed to dispel.[12] Clearly Zeeland did not count for much with the English government. That was made clear also in the decision, taken at about that time, to transfer the Scottish staple from Veere to Dordt. The prince had twice written to Charles[13] to plead against this measure, which would reduce his income as Marquis of Veere and detract from his general prestige in Zeeland; Boreel had done his best as well,[14] but all in vain.

One can only say that the English government showed a true insight into the power structure of the Republic when it decided to throw its weight behind the States of Holland. These were prepared to render some return, provided only the other states accepted the Harmony. And the English government accordingly let it be known that it would be wiser for the prince to content himself with little than to risk the loss of everything.[15] The Dowager was the first to heed that piece of prosaic advice, and the prince was not slow to follow suit. A policy of submission did not really suit the young man's temperament, but in the hard school of De Witt's guardianship he had learned to hide his ambitions and to restrain the outbursts of his passion. In the spring of 1669, he accordingly resolved to accept the Harmony.

Temple was said to have let slip out, while 'feverish and drunk', that, in his view, the prince was still no more than a boy, and that his behaviour in Zeeland had been unwise. Can we believe the ambassador's vehement denial that he had at any time spoken so disrespectfully of his own king's nephew?[16] I am inclined to think that the intemperate utterance can very well be reconciled with the admiration for the young man which Temple expressed on other occasions. The prince was still a boy and the political tradition in which he had been reared had taught him a number of most unfortunate attitudes, which he was only just beginning to overcome – inasmuch as he was able to do so. He was not really responsible, as we saw, for the Zeeland escapade, though the foolish appointment of Odijk was his own idea. That man immediately dragged the prince's name into unwholesome quarrels about the allocation of offices. It is true that up to a point this was inevitable. The Orange party, no less than the States party, was a clique, or a collection of cliques, and after a victory it invariably counted on greater rewards than it was in anyone's power to dispense. Yet one cannot help feeling that Pieter De Huybert, who as early as October complained bitterly of the wrong done to his sons and of broken promises to himself, was treated with far less than generosity.[17] Moreover, in March 1669, the loyal Justus De Huybert complained to Huygens that the joyful entry of His Highness, which ought to have made Zeeland an example to the other provinces, had on the contrary – 'alas, alas, poor province of Zeeland!'

– so badly shaken the province during the past few months, that it was in danger of complete collapse. The prince's prestige was bound to suffer as a result, 'even though, young man that he is, he has been misled into the belief that he would come out of it unscathed'.[18] As in the Buat affair, William was clearly determined to stick to his close friends, among whom ill-famed and unpatriotic elements abounded. The wilfulness that characterized his conduct on this occasion – De Huybert was wrong to consider it a result of his youth – was to be part of him all his life, and so was a degree of moral indifference in the choice of his instruments.

More remarkable is the fact that so early in his career, and in the face of strong prejudice from those in his immediate circle, William had enough sense to recognize the power of the States of Holland, and that he was able to keep his self-assertive character sufficiently in check to reach an understanding with them. If William III had been nothing but a party fanatic, relying solely on the commonalty and the preachers and ignoring the reality of national life in the manner of the court nobility, Dutch history might indeed have been faced with a catastrophe (we shall look at the dangers in a moment). As it was, the young man surprised everyone who came in contact with him with the maturity of his judgement, his great will-power, and his self-command.[19] These were the qualities that enabled him, not at once, but after overcoming his inner reluctance with every new shock, to arrive at that reconciliation with the Holland regent class which alone could ensure him an important place in the history of the nation. His grandmother had set him the example, but how fiercely had he stood up to her as late as 1666! He certainly owed a great deal to the events of that year. The Buat affair had been a salutary warning, and so had the purge of his court, and quite particularly his closer contact with De Witt. Not that the Child of State had been completely transformed by his education – far from it.

Even with respect to foreign support, William's attitude remained largely a matter of tactics. He was not altogether blind to the danger of outraging Dutch opinion,[20] but he had to run some of that risk, for he felt he was not merely a Dutchman, not merely a subject of the States: his princely birth and rank did give him the right to some freedom of action. Thus his acceptance of the Harmony was no more than a ruse, and his contemporaries cherished few illusions as to that. Wicquefort, in a report to the French government, praised the wisdom of the prince's new attitude: 'In that way alone could the prince get his foot into the stirrup.'[21] In other words, there would be no sincere co-operation with the regents until they had revoked the Perpetual Edict – which, as we shall see, they did in 1672.

It was a striking spectacle, this inflexible self-confidence with which an untried young man pressed his claim to political leadership over the acknowledged, able and successful rulers of his early days. To begin with he was convinced that he was entitled to that leadership as his birthright. What resounded in hundreds of pamphlets, in poems of praise, in sermons and orations, what De Witt had, in the name of the States of Holland, obstinately denied in the *Deduction* of 1654[22] and no doubt insisted upon in his lectures – all that was for William an unshakeable dogma. In him lived the quality of his glorious ancestors, and he felt called by God himself to continue their work. The royal rank of his mother added to his self-assurance. The cheers of the crowd, their uncritical confidence were a continual incentive. And soon afterwards came the realization that he was, in fact, a leader of men.

William accepts the Harmony; Holland struggles against the Introduction

But, as we saw, in the meantime, he decided to bow before Holland's demands, early in 1669, and took great pains to persuade his supporters in Zeeland, Friesland and Groningen, who had previously been asked to stand fast against Holland's proposal, to embrace those very proposals, so that Holland might one day be reminded of its promise to co-operate in the prince's 'introduction' to the Council of State. Zeeland presented few difficulties. That province and Holland were still negotiating about the composition of their common high courts of justice; Holland, basing herself on the growth of her population, desired a larger say and, as usual, drove her superiority home to the weaker province, and the prince, by publicly declaring that Zeelanders need not encumber their cause with his interests, helped Zeeland to save face as she now went back on her previous position.[23] By July, the States of Zeeland had passed the necessary resolution and communicated it to Friesland and Groningen, in the expectation that the three would jointly notify their agreement to the States-General.[24] But the northern provinces were not so easily brought round because, as I mentioned earlier,[25] they were afraid that the separation of offices might jeopardize the position of their own Stadholder. Hence it was not until March 1670, that the three provinces advised the States-General of their joint acceptance of the Harmony.

When that happened, the States of Holland at long last faced the necessity of implementing their promise to co-operate in 'the Introduction'. But Holland was not yet ready for that. Now that they had to act, questions arose which had been overlooked before: How precisely was the Introduction to be staged? What precise seat in the Council was the prince to occupy? And, above all, should he be allowed to have full, or advisory voting rights?

When the deputies of Holland informed the States-General that their States wished first to examine all these questions, great murmurings went up in the High-and-Mighty Assembly. Had not Holland herself suggested the entire plan? Did she mean to back out now that everybody else had accommodated themselves to her wishes? Great pressure was exerted upon the President, who happened to be a Hollander, to settle the problem there and then; De Witt was summoned and apparently succeeded in restoring calm.[26] However, in the States of Holland there was still a great and violent commotion before the deputies could be brought round, or rather, before a majority vote could be forced through. The Generality had to wait for two months while the Hollanders fought it out among themselves.

We have seen that the Men of True Liberty had been doubtful about the compromise as early as 1667. Ever since, they had been revelling in the deadlock created by the opposition of the three provinces. Holland's powers of obstruction had all along been unassailable. In addition, circumstances had greatly changed. In particular, the prince's 'intrusion' as First Noble of Zeeland was more than many deputies could stomach. That new office linked him very closely to Zeeland, and in the Council of State, where Zeeland already counted two permanent members (against Holland's three, who were changed every year), the balance of power had been altered to the disadvantage of the leading province. It could not be denied that Holland had taken on an obligation, but the deputies were only prepared to implement their promise in a way least likely to strengthen the prince's position or, for that matter, Zeeland's own ambitions. The advice of the 'member' of the Nobility – indubitably the work of De Witt – with which the discussions were opened, was therefore to grant the prince no more than an advisory vote. That, it was claimed, was fully in accord with the original intention, for on 5 August 1667, it had been decided to bring the prince into the Council for the purpose of 'imbuing' him, in other words, of teaching him how to conduct matters of state. The advice was, moreover, supported with four new arguments. To begin with, the prince 'cannot but show favour to Zeeland, being the first member there'; as a result, Zeeland would, in fact, get three members in the Council of State. Secondly, the prince owned numerous estates in the Generality Lands, concerning which questions were brought before the Council nearly every day. Thirdly, he was 'great and respected' and his vote would therefore carry undue weight. Fourthly: 'he is born of England and allied to many potentates, such as Brandenburg'. Some towns – Dort, Delft and Gorcum among them – were not even willing to grant William an advisory vote; all they were prepared to do was to give him a seat so that he might 'watch and listen'. Rotterdam went further still and wanted to withhold the 'seat' until the prince had cut the ties that bound him to Zeeland.

But Haarlem – no doubt under the influence of Fagel – upheld the view that the agreement of 1667 must be read as stipulating a vote for the prince, and an unqualified one at that – it had never been the intention 'to seat him in the Council as a man of straw or mere decoration, but as a man of birth';[27] moreover, 'it was always deemed desirable that our governors should have ties with great princes, from whom the State can draw advantage'. To win the favour of Charles II through the prince, indeed, that was, as we know, the policy of many, while De Witt and his friends, remembering Frederick Henry, William II and Buat, feared that the Stuart ruler would only try to use the Prince of Orange for his own purposes. We shall see in a moment how the course of international relations lent force to each of these two views in turn, and that Van Beuningen and others in Amsterdam were inclined to side with Fagel rather than with De Witt.

The Haarlem view was endorsed by Amsterdam, and it was this which gave the affair its serious significance. When Haarlem argued forcefully that it could not be held to the Perpetual Edict once the vote was denied the prince; when Delft reproached Haarlem with acting against the best interests of the country and Haarlem retorted angrily; when Rotterdam accused Haarlem of 'perjury' and Haarlem claimed that Councillor Pieter de Groot of Rotterdam (who was summarily dismissed from his post of pensionary of Amsterdam in 1667) was unfit to represent his country as ambassador to France – when all this happened, the Men of True Liberty, whose main aim had been to rally all Hollanders behind the 1667 resolution and who considered the unanimity of Holland the mainspring of the entire state, were deeply aggrieved. And now Amsterdam had decided to instruct its deputies to vote for the prince, thus completely undermining De Witt's position. De Witt still tried to sway the undecided members of Holland by gaining the support of the other provinces. The young prince, for his part, worked no less hard at the same task. Thus he tried to win over Utrecht by appeals to Van Amerongen.[28] In them, he called the opponents of the full vote – his own guardians and educators – 'men of evil intent'. Needless to say, he put pressure on Holland as well; Van Beverning held out high hopes for Gouda (his own town), which were not, however, fulfilled. But Amsterdam was able to carry most of the towns in the Northern Quarter with her and that was enough: the resolution granting the prince a decisive vote was passed on 16 May with a majority of ten to nine.[29]

Even then, De Witt tried to restore unanimity (his instructions made this his duty) and at the same time to whittle down the prince's growing power. In his 'concordance' he accepted the voting decision, but hedged it with new conditions: whenever the Council had to deal with matters involving the prince's relatives (particularly England and Brandenburg)[30] the prince would have to absent himself, nor would he be allowed to vote on matters concerning the Generality lands. De Witt had been careful to obtain the consent of the Amsterdam deputies before he came out with these restrictions. Van Beuningen, who had arrived in the Hague for final discussions about a mission to England, had agreed without much difficulty. But in Amsterdam, various burgomasters, encouraged by Valckenier, had rejected the restrictions without so much as putting them to the town council, and moreover had urged Haarlem to stick to her guns as well. As a result, the concordance was not carried by a unanimous vote, though in the end

Enkhuizen, alone, refused to instruct its deputies to vote for the proposal.

The debate continued deep into the night, with heated tempers. Men had been posted outside the assembly room, to bring news to the prince who was anxiously awaiting the decision at Odijk's house. When it was finally taken, the Grand Pensionary must have been very unhappy about the lack of unanimity and about the fact that the prince now had a decisive vote on most, if not on all, important matters of state. He could, however, content himself with one important gain: the Council had also decided that any decision to appoint the prince to the Captain-Generalship would require the unanimous vote of the Holland Assembly.

The commonalty cheered the prince's promotion, and the States of Holland themselves recognized that, although not yet a major, the prince had, in fact, reached the age of manhood, and that it was therefore time to discharge his governor, Van Ghent, and the education commission.[31] De Witt could, however, console himself with the knowledge that the prince's vote in the Council of State did not pose any serious threat – the Council had lost much of its former sway over the country's political conduct. He was far less happy when the prince also expressed the wish to attend the States-General and when the six provinces supported him with a reference to a clause in the decision to grant the prince a vote, namely that His Highness having been invited to do so was happy to appear in the High and Mighty Assembly. The deputies of Holland were completely taken aback. How ever had these words got into the decision? 'Straight from above,' answered the president, a Frisian, 'pointing heavenwards.'[32] It turned out that a clerk had unthinkingly copied[33] the phrase from the commission of William II, and Holland had an easy task preventing the prince from getting his way by 'a ruse'.[34] Even those Hollanders who had wavered in previous debates, now stood firm, as De Witt noted to his great satisfaction. Temple, too, did not like the prince trying to force the pace – 'this is a country where fruit ripens slowly'.[35]

In fact, the Perpetual Edict was still in force, and the State of Holland still sovereign. The prince, after his introduction called on the deputies to thank them. It happened that those of Amsterdam were out on two successive occasions, and so decided to wait on the prince instead. This they did on the prompting of Burgomaster Vlooswijk, who had special reasons for doing so. His daughter had married one Honiwood, an English captain of horse, whose estate had been seized by the English when Honiwood had continued in the State's service during the war. The Amsterdam deputies had moved heaven and earth to get the estates returned. Kievit, above all, had seized the chance and let it be known that he alone could prevail upon the English, but that he would only do so if his own position were first restored. He was probably right to think that he could count on the support of the English government, but Holland had not the slightest intention of remitting his sentence. De Witt simply maintained that the two cases were quite distinct, and the interested parties had to bow before that judgement. Now, they were hoping for the intercession of the Prince of Orange, whose introduction into the States they had supported if not wholly, at least partly, for that very reason. Hence when they now waited on the prince, a fact that proud men like Bontemantal were quick to resent, compliments had hardly been exchanged before Burgomaster Van Vlooswijk took the prince aside to breach the subject of Honiwood's estate. But the Amsterdam Town Council, which had supported the introduction, did not see matters in that light, and, moreover, disapproved of the whole visit. A few months later, when the regents of Amsterdam, together with the regents of Delft and Rotterdam, dined with De Witt and his father, Liberty and the Perpetual Edict were not forgotten among the numerous toasts.[36]

In principle, nothing had changed, albeit Amsterdam had stood up against De Witt, and albeit she had exerted herself to earn the prince's gratitude. Apart from a wish to please England (I shall return to that matter in a moment) and the personal interest of Burgomaster Vlooswijk, Amsterdam, like De Huybert, was also swayed by envy and resentment of De Witt's dominant position. The Grand Pensionary had now been in office for seventeen long years, and his sway over the assembly of Holland must often have been a thorn in the flesh of powerful Amsterdam. There was much talk of domination by Dort, Delft and Rotterdam, the towns with which the Grand Pensionary was most closely associated,[37] and there was a strong feeling that Amsterdam was entitled to a larger say in the conduct of affairs of state. As a result, Amsterdam, in December 1669, proposed the appointment of a Secretary of State, a new post intended to remove the Grand Pensionary, too heavily burdened as things were, from the conduct of foreign affairs. The man they had in mind was Van Beuningen. De Witt did not openly oppose this plan, a plan that would have completely undermined his position – he simply allowed it to die a natural death. However, the very proposal showed him that for the time being he could no longer count on Amsterdam. The death, in 1664, of De Graeff van Zuid-Polsbroeck, his wife's uncle, had greatly weakened his standing in the town, though he still numbered many friends and supporters among the citizens (e.g. De Graeff's family and Lambert Reynst). Moreover, for a time, he even succeeded in keeping on good terms with Valckenier, who was Amsterdam's up-and-coming great man. No one was more zealous for the cause of Liberty than this burgomaster, who had called Grotius's *Vindica-tion* 'the political catechism of all those who love Liberty'.[38] But Valckenier was an ambitious person, given to intrigues, and any relationship with him was bound to be fraught with difficulties. In his own town, he alienated group after group by his insolence and rude manners; he maintained himself chiefly by the fear he inspired. And now he came out with the remark that he thought Van Beverning a wise man for keeping his distance from the government, 'seeing that things must go wrong with the Grand Pensionary De Witt'. On another occasion he opined that 'the prince must become master in the end'.[39] Valckenier could count on the support of one man with firm political convictions, namely Van Beuningen, the proposed Secretary of State. Not only was Van Beuningen a personal rival of De Witt's but he also held many distinct political views. In particular, he was far less prepared than De Witt to make sacrifices to friendship with France, and argued, quite rightly, that the ties to France had already been severed. He called for retaliatory measures against Colbert's tariff policy (for an embargo on French brandy in particular), and trusted to closer relations with England, in which De Witt, with no less justification, had lost faith, as the best means of warding off the French menace.

England's coolness; Van Beuningen's mission; The Dover plot (1 June 1670)

Neither De Witt nor Van Beuningen realized the full danger in which the Republic now found itself. Rarely in the history of Europe did any country play so fast and loose as France and England had begun to do. The two kings had sworn destruction to the

Republic in their hearts, and were merely playing for time before delivering the fatal blow.

D'Estrades was recalled in 1668, not only because he had failed to prevent the Triple Alliance, but also because he was thought to be too involved with the States. His successor, Pomponne, was given the task of lulling the Dutch to sleep. And indeed, De Witt clung to his conviction that the Triple Alliance need not necessarily undermine friendship with France, whose support he needed now as before. Tiresome negotiations with England, dragging through the years, about 'the perfection of the Triple Alliance', had demonstrated all too clearly how little security had been won in 1668. French encroachments in the southern Netherlands, endorsed at the peace of Aix-la-Chapelle, were so many bases for launching new attacks on Spanish territory, which the disintegrating Spanish empire would be quite unable to repulse, and De Witt was most anxious to gain Pomponne's support for his plan to 'canton' the southern Netherlands, in case of young Carlos's long-expected death. The Grand Pensionary was clearly quite oblivious of the deep and irremediable resentment his 'ingratitude' and 'presumption' had aroused in Louis XIV – and this despite obvious signs of coolness and the fierce tariff struggle.

On the English side, too, there was a disturbing lack of warmth and zeal. In the spring of 1670, this took on alarming forms, when England refused to invite the Emperor to join the Triple Alliance. (The 1668 rapprochement between France and the Emperor had fallen by the wayside, and Lisola was back at his old work.) Moreover, England revived her old dispute with the Republic over the East Indies, and renewed the challenge to the Dutch company's monopoly claims. Now there was the further problem of compensation to English estate owners in Surinam, recently acquired by Zeeland; this became the subject of acrimonious discussions. And it was for the purpose of discovering what precisely the English expected the Republic to do about Surinam, and at the same time, if possible, to cement the bond of friendship, that Van Beuningen was chosen to lead a special mission to London – Johan Boreel was thought to be quite incapable of acting in this matter.[40]

The mission had De Witt's whole-hearted support though he expected far less of it than Van Beuningen did. When the struggle in the States of Holland over the prince's vote had been at its most violent, the Rotterdam delegates had proclaimed that they would do their utmost to prevent Van Beuningen's mission because 'everybody knows that it was only in order to curry favour there that he was advocating the prince's cause so fiercely'.[41] But now that this affair was at last out of the way, there was no harm in giving Van Beuningen his head. Undoubtedly he made great play with his feelings for the prince in the hope of influencing the English all the more. He was further able to offer concessions in the Surinam business[42] (Amsterdam was quite happy to be generous at the expense of Zeeland). For both these reasons, indeed, Temple warmly commended him, and Arlington replied that he would be the more welcome on account of his town's (Amsterdam's) good relations with the prince.[43] But all this was no more than vain protestation. In fact, London took care to guard against[44] Van Beuningen's well-known ability and smooth tongue[45] from the very start.

English policy was now quite set. In complete secrecy – which was even extended to several ministers – Charles II had at long last been able to conclude that alliance with France which he had sought so anxiously for years. The way had been prepared ever since 1669. French support for Charles, now that he openly professed his Catholicism, and a common attack against the Republic, had been two of the main points of the discussions, in which England was represented by Arlington – the champion of Protestantism and the Orange cause and the avowed friend of the Dutch! On 1 June 1670, the treaty was signed at Dover, after mediation by Charles's sister, the Duchess of Orleans.

The treaty laid it down that when, in due course, he saw fit to proclaim his conversion to Roman Catholicism in public, Charles could count on Louis's help against possible resistance at home (the size of the French subsidy had been a matter of much discussion in the preceding correspondence). Charles would also have the full support of Louis when raising claims to Spanish possessions on the death of Carlos II. (Charles had asked for the American colonies and for Ostend, but the precise details had not yet been settled.) By a further article, the two kings agreed, on the grounds of their serious grievances against the States-General, 'who had so often been guilty of black ingratitude against the founders and creators of their Republic and who had even had the impudence to pose as sovereign arbiters over all other potentates', to make war on them jointly (at a date to be chosen by Louis after Charles had proclaimed his conversion). Of the territories wrested from the States-General, the King of England would be satisfied with the island of Walcheren and Sluis with Cadsand.

And seeing that the dissolution of the government of the States-General might result in some damage to the Prince of Orange, nephew of the King of Great Britain, since places, towns and districts belonging to him might be included in the partition, it is hereby agreed and decided that the afore-mentioned Kings will do their utmost that the afore-mentioned Prince may find his advantage in the continuation and the conclusion of this war, as will be fixed hereafter in separate articles.

All that these 'separate articles' laid down, however, was that the provisions for the prince must form no obstacle or delay to the common declaration and pursuit of the war against the Republic.[46] The treaty also contained an article guaranteeing the peace of Aix-la-Chapelle: the King of Great Britain was given the right to maintain that treaty in accordance with the obligations laid down in the Triple Alliance.

Of the entire document, this was perhaps the most hypocritical passage. The Triple Alliance contained a treaty of friendship with the Republic, which Charles was betraying by this new engagement, and as for the peace of Aix-la-Chapelle, i.e. the treaty guaranteeing the integrity of what was left of the Spanish Netherlands, it was indeed a curious way of strengthening that integrity to help France subject the northern Netherlands (not to mention the fact that Charles had promised the main part of the Spanish succession to Louis, on Carlos's death).

Charles had originally intended to declare his conversion to Catholicism as a first step, but Louis, afraid that this might plunge England into chaos and thus interfere with the attack on the Republic, was anxious to declare war first. And that was, in fact, what happened: Charles flinched from challenging his subjects. As a result, he found himself in an exceedingly difficult position – just how difficult may be gathered from the game he was forced to play with Buckingham. That man was too much of a Protestant to be taken into Charles's full confidence, and yet far too influential and ambitious to be left out completely. Charles accordingly sent him to France, ostensibly to negotiate a treaty (which had already been signed) – or rather the treaty minus the article dealing with Charles's conversion to Catholicism. The spectacle of Buckingham, who

thought he was making history, and all of whose earnest negotiations were no more than a farce, is, I believe, unique in the
annals of diplomacy. Yet 'his' treaty, which was signed on 31
December 1671, was not wholly without effect on the subsequent
events. It made the war the main objective of the alliance, and
even specified a date for its inception: the end of April or the
beginning of May 1672 (Louis had already abandoned the original
plan of launching the attack in 1671, because the enlistment of
support from German rulers was taking longer than he had
thought).

The Prince of Orange then, according to the plan of the royal
plotters, was to benefit from a war directed against the power, nay
against the very existence, of the northern Netherlands. That aim
had first been mentioned in a plan which Charles had instructed
Bellings, his Catholic confidant, to draw up in December 1669.
In the final treaty, one sentence from the original plan was omitted,
a sentence that cast a good deal of light on Charles's true intentions.
It explained that the prince was deemed worthy of benefit because
the 'prestige accruing to the said prince and his supporters will
greatly contribute to the success of this war, and will, at the very
least, create so much distrust and division between the Hollanders
that the conquest of their country will be greatly facilitated'.[47]
In a conversation, soon afterwards, between Colbert de Croissy
and Arlington, this point was developed further. 'No doubt,' said
Arlington,[48] 'my king must take to heart anything that concerns
the Prince of Orange, but his principal object in inserting this
article has been to detach the prince and his party from the interests
of the present régime of the States-General and to stir up divisions
among them which will promote our success in the war.'[49] Now,
it was clearly in Charles's best interest to evince as little zeal for the
prince as possible; else Louis (and this is precisely what he was
doing) might argue that all concessions to the prince were in fact
concessions to Charles, and object to the large sums of money his
royal brother was demanding over and above the territorial benefits.
In any case, Charles's true attitude to Orange epitomized the entire
English policy to that House: it served as a lever by which the
Republic could be enfeebled and divided against itself. Moreover,
he also expected William, after having collaborated in the ruin
of the Republic, to offer his services in administering what
remained of it in the interest of England. But these were ambitions

that he preferred not to stress at this stage of his negotiation with Louis – he would to make them known in his own good time.

That neither the prince's 'introduction' nor the grant to him on a 'decisive vote' had made the slightest impression of Charles must now be clear. Van Beuningen's efforts in England were doomed to failure from the start. The only possible remedy would have been direct contact with Parliament, without the king's knowledge, and if need be against his opposition. But to risk that, the ambassador would have to grasp the impending danger to the full, and that he failed to do. He noticed that public opinion was predominantly anti-French, and took that as an assurance that the English government would be unable to sign a separate treaty with France. Arlington was at great pains to deceive him further (precisely because he was afraid of driving him into the arms of the opposition). Buckingham's mission did, however, make Van Beuningen uneasy, and there were other storm signals as well, but he continued to let himself be fobbed off with reassuring explanations. Meanwhile his own negotiations bore no fruit – the English refused to consider the inclusion of the Emperor or to collaborate in the tariff measures against France. Instead, Van Beuningen was showered with complaints about books and medals commemorating the raid on Chatham and the peace of Breda. This looked very much as if the English were trying to pick a quarrel, and it was with great reluctance that De Witt forced through a number of resolutions designed to remedy some of these English grievances.

In August, the real situation was shown up in a flash, when France suddenly occupied the independent duchy of Lorraine, and England continued to evade the (redoubled) demand of the States to strengthen the Triple Alliance by the inclusion of the Emperor. Temple's position had become quite untenable and after he had explained this to his government, he was recalled in September – as a temporary measure, England explained and, in fact, he left Lady Temple behind. In his conversation[50] with De Witt, before departing, Temple maintained it was unthinkable that any crowned head should follow a policy so detrimental to his own honour and safety as the one Charles was now accused of pursuing . . . But De Witt, no doubt, remembered with bitterness Temple's positive assurances at the time of the conclusion of the Triple Alliance, and his worst fears were confirmed when Temple failed to return to the Hague.

Despite all these setbacks, the Republic did not relinquish her efforts to reach an understanding with England and France. France, where old Willem Boreel had died in September 1668, received Pieter de Groot as the new ambassador on 12 September 1670. His whole-hearted belief that the friendship of France was indispensable to the Republic seemed to make him the best man for the job, but the fact that Amsterdam 'hated' him[51] after the unpleasant way in which his pensionaryship had come to an end, did constitute a grave complication. In any case, matters could not be left at attempts to preserve the old alliances (with France in 1662 and with England in 1668) – Spain, helpless Spain, so long disdained by De Witt, had, at last, to be wooed as well. It proved difficult to persuade Van Beverning to serve as an ambassador there, but in December he set out on the journey.

So menacing had the situation become – De Witt, in the Holland Assembly compared it to that of a ship before an approaching storm[52] – that the Republic had begun to look seriously to its defences. The refusal of Amsterdam (which, in practice, meant the intractibility of Valckenier), to help before a tax grievance was remedied, caused the loss of a great deal of precious time. De Witt complained repeatedly to Van Beuningen, who, from far-away London, did his best to make Valckenier see reason. As long as Holland was still bickering, little help could be expected from the other provinces, but even when Amsterdam came round to the majority view just before the end of the year, the defence of the Republic was held up for many further months by Zeeland – a subject to which we shall be returning.

William in England (October 1670–February 1671); Odijk holds up re-armament; De Witt's suspicions

While tension was thus at its height, the Prince of Orange paid his long postponed visit to the English court. In 1669, he had suggested this visit himself several times, and in March 1670, Charles sent him an invitation.[53] At that point, his introduction to the Council of State kept him in the Republic, but in June, the king repeated his offer.[54] The Dowager did not favour the plan, no doubt because she feared that it might add to the suspicions which the States of Holland harboured against the prince;[55] there were, indeed, murmurings that he might start fresh intrigues in England.[56] But the prince was not easily put off from seeking aid from wherever it might come, so much so that he kept up personal contacts with even the French ambassador, who was now no friend of the States. Pomponne assured him in April that the Duchess of Orleans, his aunt, who was then on the point of going to Dover (for a purpose that no outsider could divine), would never forget his interests,[57] and the prince, for his part, informed Pomponne in June that congratulations by Louis on his introduction, which had meanwhile been accomplished, might prove extremely useful. Louis lost no time in instructing his ambassador to convey to the young man his most cordial felicitations, and more than that: the king went on to tell William 'that this honour was but a step to higher promotion, namely to the same authority which his ancestors had so lawfully and meritoriously exercised in the State; that, he, the king, would be pleased to speed him along that path'. This message as the Dowager rightly foresaw, was bound to have the most untoward repercussions.[58]

The prince's hesitation to visit England after the repeated invitation of his uncle was due to other reasons than swayed his grandmother. William was most anxious to dispel the view that the King of England was treating him with disdain by persisting in his refusal to repay the family debt. He told Temple that, by so doing, Charles was making his, William's, friends feel 'how little hee is considered by His Maty, whose countenance will be a great supporte to him in the course of his fortunes heere'.[59] When Temple did not dare to give him any assurances, the prince not only wrote to Sylvius, but also sent his private physician Rumpf across to England to take advice from Lord and Lady Arlington.[60] In addition to discovering the prospects of William's own financial claims, Rumpf was asked to find out what chances Van Beuningen had of success, especially with his negotiations on behalf of the East India Company. If these were poor, then a visit to England was bound to do the prince's name no good; if the king, on the contrary, were inclined to meet Van Beuningen's demands, William would like to share in the credit . . . Arlington professed[61] his profound gratitude for William's confidence in him; in his reply he pointed out that William, as a prince of the blood, might well be expected to ascend to the throne one day and that this was another reason why he should show himself to the English people; he assured him further that his presence might prove helpful in the matter of the debt, but held out little hope for Van Beuningen's negotiations. The wisest thing, therefore, would be to postpone the visit until October, by which time Van Beuningen would certainly have left, and when 'the prince might look forward to a very good reception, which, as he saw it, would make His Highness agreeable to the State and the commonalty of the United Provinces'.

The prince was quick to take the hint and, early in July, he asked De Witt to request the State for the necessary leave. This was readily granted, the more so as several provinces in the States-General still felt he could assist in Van Beuningen's negotiations, and that Van Beuningen should be instructed accordingly. However, De Witt was able to inform Van Beuningen that Holland looked upon the resolution which the States-General finally passed, as a mere compliment to the prince and not as a means of insinuating William 'directly or indirectly into Your Honours' (i.e. Van Beuningen's and Boreel's) negotiations'.[62] The resolution invited the prince 'to use his renown and good offices to dispose the king amicably towards the state and, generally, to insist upon and commend the interest of the state in the best way imaginable'. Had the States been able to catch sight of the prince's instructions to Rumpf or into Temple's correspondence (let alone of the Dover plot) they would certainly not have been so naïve as to think that Charles's connection with Orange would cause the English to make even the slightest concession to Dutch interests – that connection was never more than a lever for turning Dutch party strife to England's best advantage.

In October, Sylvius and Lord Ossory, son of the Duke of Ormonde, who had married a daughter of Beverweert, arrived to fetch the prince. The prince's large train included Zuylestein, his former governor, from whom the States of Holland had been unable to separate William for long, and Beverweert's sons Odijk and Ouwerkerk (all three of them Nassaus with a bend sinister in their shields); his young friend Hans Willem Bentinck, a younker from Overijsel; and old Huygens (now well past seventy) as the financial expert. A number of well-born young men crossed the sea independently.[63] Van Beuningen had not yet taken his leave from England, but the prince avoided his and Boreel's company as much as possible.[64]

The prince remained in England for nearly four months, apparently with success. He managed to obtain some financial satisfaction, although not nearly as much as he had been led to expect. The definite recognition of his precedence over Rupert of the Palatinate proved to the public at home how high was their prince's position in the world. Rupert was hurt and would not meet William but then such unpleasantness was part and parcel of life in the seventeenth century, and William was not unduly perturbed, particularly as the English people made a great show of their respect and interest, with a dinner in the City, doctorates from Oxford and Cambridge, and all-round expressions of admiration for the simplicity, the self-command and the intelligence, of the young man. Arlington was especially cordial[65] – not that this meant very much from a man who had sacrificed his convictions rather than lose his king's favours, and who even now opened his house near Newmarket to Louise de Kérouailles, a tool of the French ambassador, so as to facilitate her liaison with Charles II. At any rate, Arlington came to know the prince at close quarters, for he dined him in London almost every day.[66] But what of Charles?

They formed a remarkable contrast – the urbane, gay, witty, and cynical uncle and his reticent, withdrawn and passionate nephew. Charles's only fixed political principle was his desire 'not to set out upon his travels again'. And it was these very 'travels' that had made him so un-English in character. His love of Catholicism was that of the European imbued with the swelling tide of the Counter-Reformation. Catholicism, to him, was the only fitting religion for people of birth, and especially for kings. Hence, when he unbosomed himself to the prince, he told him that Protestants must be regarded 'as an apostate group, divided among themselves ever since they had seceded'; he asked him to bethink himself lest he allow those Holland blockheads to mislead him. When the prince hurried to report this conversation to Zuylestein, both expressed surprise that the king should have seen fit to entrust so dangerous a secret – his Papist convictions – to so young a man. That, at any rate, is how Bishop Burnet put it much later,[67] saying that he had it from the prince himself. His story is borne out by Colbert de Croissy's report of 4 December to Louis XIV, that Charles was greatly pleased with the gifts of the young Prince of Orange, but that William himself had proved 'so passionate a Hollander and a Protestant that even if Your Majesty had not opposed the communication to him, even partially, of the secret (of Dover) those two reasons alone would have deterred him'.[68]

Charles, in fact, had been most anxious to make his nephew privy to the treaty of Dover.[69] Shortly before William's arrival he had even told the French ambassador that this was his intention – he had meant to hold out the prospect of sovereignty over what would be left of the Republic – and Louis had at once lodged a strong protest.[70]

'A passionate Hollander and a Protestant.' This discovery did not alter Charles's intention to use his nephew and the Orange party as instruments of his own policy. To begin with, neither he nor his intimates had the slightest doubt but that, when it came to the crunch, the prince would never identify himself with the States against what to all of them seemed to be so obviously 'his interest'. In this view they were encouraged by the fact that William, as we have seen and will see again, was not averse to asking for English assistance – at least not while the anti-Dutch tendency of the royal policy was kept a secret from him – and by the continued party hatred and suspicions in the Netherlands.

Back in Holland, De Witt knew nothing of the prince's stand for Protestantism either. Moreover, his own government was most unfortunately impressed by the prince's long stay in England. 'They are convinced,' Wicquefort noted on 29 January 1671,[71] 'that he is serving the state ill and that he is trying to strengthen the understanding between France and England so that those two may work for his elevation.' How far from the truth all this was, and yet how understandable after the Buat affair and in view of the dark clouds the Hague could see gathering on the international horizon! The full perfidy of Charles II was not yet known, but, late in February, Pieter de Groot had learned particulars of Buckingham's negotiations in Paris during the last winter, and the Hague might easily have guessed the rest – if only they could have brought themselves to believe such monstrous news. The English plan, De Groot reported, was not merely to make war upon the Republic, but to undermine its very foundations by overthrowing the constitution.

It has been judged wise to take that course, in order not only to dispel jealousy of, but inspire sympathy towards, the King of England, the better to disrupt the commerce of a state that is monopolizing all trade and dictating to all kingdoms. It is thought that the best way of putting a successful stop to all this is to turn the Republic into a sovereignty and to place it into the hands of the Prince of Orange, who, thus put under an obligation to his protectors, may be expected to serve their interests.[72]

De Groot had been told that the King of England would use a request for the elevation of the prince as motive for breaking with the Republic. 'Not altogether credible – but not to be brushed aside either,' was De Witt's judgement on the report.[73]

The entire summer of 1671 went by and still the bubble had not burst. Louis had not yet drawn his diplomatic net as tight as he wished, and was still busy exhausting his troops in unreal manœuvres and trench work. He himself paid a visit to Dunkirk and to his recent acquisitions in Flanders, ominously near the Dutch frontiers. The tariff war raged on; early in the year, the States finally put an embargo on French brandy, followed by an embargo on 'cool' wines – clearly the Republic was not prepared to take all Colbert's measures lying down. In England itself, Charles had been forced to play a game with his Parliament all spring in order to get hold of money – to that purpose he had paraded his faith in the Triple Alliance. As summer came, the Republic had cause to be anxious about Temple's recall, and anxiety mounted alarmingly when the royal yacht, *Merlin*, came to fetch Lady Temple, and, sailing impudently through De Ruyter's fleet in the Maas estuary, opened fire when the Dutch did not immediately strike their flags. This 'insult' was greatly enlarged upon in England in an effort to rouse opinion and, at the beginning of January 1672, Sir George Downing, the notorious trouble-maker, was fetched from the Treasury and sent over to Holland to demand satisfaction. Even then, the Republic remained uncertain what England was really up to, though no one was by then in any doubt that France was crouching for an attack.

However, as we saw, by the end of 1670, it had already become clear that the Republic would have to re-arm, and by 1671, the navy, under De Ruyter, was ready, and the garrisons of the Rhine fortresses in the districts of Cologne and Cleves had been greatly strengthened – despite the difficulties and delays caused by provincial obstruction.[74] Amsterdam had come round before the end of 1670, and soon afterwards ceased to put obstacles in De Witt's way – Valckenier's party had been decisively beaten in 1671 at the customary February elections of magistrates, burgomasters and aldermen. The various groups in the Old Council (consisting of ex-burgomasters) whose leaders had been wronged or insulted by Valckenier had banded together against him; many regents[75] had, moreover, taken strong exception to the tone Valckenier and his friends had seen fit to adopt towards De Witt. The result was a complete eclipse of Valckenier's sun.[76] Van Beuningen, who had bound his career to Valckenier's leadership, was not given the burgomaster's office. Valckenier himself was appointed a Commissioned Councillor, a three-years' job in the Hague: for a man of his ambitions this was as good as being exiled; in February 1672, he did not even take part in the elections and the candidates of his adversaries were elected unanimously. While the town-hall revolution did not make De Witt master of Amsterdam, it at least freed him of the hateful and unbridled opposition of Valckenier.

But Zeeland continued to place obstacles in the way of the re-armament programme. By February 1671, the province was still withholding consent to the necessary money grants, and this despite every conceivable pressure. The stumbling block was the First Noble and the two vassal towns Veere and Flushing. The whole thing was the doing of Odijk who, according to a reporter[77] was trying to blackmail the States into granting a colonelcy to one of his friends. In any case, De Witt was greatly put out, and when the Prince of Orange returned from England towards the end of February, at about the time of De Groot's letter and the revelations from Paris, De Witt must have regarded him with even deeper suspicion. The prince's conduct, however, was exemplary. He assured De Witt[78] that he had known nothing of Zeeland's obstruction, and that as soon as he was informed of it,[79] he had sent a messenger to Odijk ordering him to join his own vote as First Noble and those of the two Vassal towns to the rest, and that was, in fact, what happened.

The end of this affair might have been expected to lessen De Witt's suspicions of the young prince (though it did not, of course, increase his admiration for the prince's choice of representative as First Noble). We who can read the young man's intimate letters know that, in the conflict between England and the Republic, he took his stand firmly on the Dutch side – as his uncle had been quick to discover. He expressed his uneasiness about Temple's recall to Arlington[80] and also sent the following message to Ossory: 'I hope that the king will not leave us (the *us* is eloquent) in the lurch, and that he will adhere to the treaties he has made with the States.' This was in the summer of 1671; later that year, he wrote to Charles: 'People here have strong doubts as to whether you can be numbered among our friends; for my part, however, I very much hope that you can.'[81] It was almost as if William's journey to England had made him more strongly conscious that he was a Dutchman, and of the need to stand by his country in its hour of danger. And yet, while the crisis was approaching, and while his elevation to the Captain-Generalship remained a bone of contention between the six provinces and Holland and even within Holland herself, William took a step behind De Witt's back, a most questionable step no doubt, and one in which De Witt, had he but known about it, would have found confirmation for his worst fears and a justification of his attempts, even at that juncture, to keep the prince out of office.

Pressure to make William Captain-General; Enkhuizen's proposal (4 Dember 1671); De Witt's opposition

The consensus of opinion in the country was undoubtedly that no stone should be left unturned to reconcile England and that any favours shown to the prince would tend towards that result. De Groot's report that the English government meant to ask for the prince's elevation – which the French ambassador publicly confirmed,[82] no doubt in order to stir up further dissension – merely served to turn De Witt even more resolutely against the idea. 'No foreign meddling' became the watchword of the party of Liberty.[83] But the awful danger of a war with the two mighty kingdoms, and without any strong allies – French diplomacy had seen to that – weighed more heavily with other people. True, Van Amerongen had sent fairly optimistic reports from Berlin of the Elector's intentions; and Van Beverning returned from Madrid with an alliance, but then what help was there from miserable Spain? As early as May, Gelderland proposed that the States-General appoint the prince Captain-General; the prince had visited Arnhem in person to rally his supporters. But Holland succeeded in having the proposal shelved,[84] with an appeal to the Act of Harmony, by which the provinces had agreed not to raise the matter until the prince's twenty-third birthday.

The commonalty, however, was not so readily put off by fine

parliamentary points. More passionately than ever before, they clamoured for the prince's appointment, as the state's only salvation. Talk of English interference was discounted, and the opposition of the States of Holland was generally ascribed to their secret pro-French leanings.[85] Nothing could have been more unfair. Pieter de Groot had sent bitter complaints to De Witt about his experiences at the French court. He even suggested that, in the coming conflict, it might be wise to sue for the support of the Huguenots, a powerful group that was growing more and more desperate as Louis pursued his totalitarian policy. He entered into highly confidential but no more than provisional discussions with Schomberg, a German princeling and general in the French service, who felt his future undermined by the régime's increasing intolerance of non-Catholics. Schomberg, he contended, was the ideal substitute for Field-Marshal Wirtz, who seemed to be thinking of leaving the service of the States. Nothing came of this, for Wirtz stayed on (Schomberg later entered the English service and was made an English duke by King William); but it does show – and there is other evidence as well – that even the staunchest Loevesteiners wanted to maintain the country's independence of France as well as of England, if necessary by an appeal to Protestant sentiment.

Nevertheless, the States' position *vis-à-vis* the Prince of Orange became steadily weaker, not least because of the attitude of that same Wirtz, whom they themselves had brought to the Republic in 1667[86] and who now asked to have the prince placed above him as Captain-General. This, he argued, was the only way out. The entire officers' corps desired it, and only thus could the army's confidence be restored. The public too, as we saw, was of much the same opinion, though the hope that peace with England might thus be preserved was only a partial reason for their attitude. They also felt that things in general would be so much better under Orange[87] that they would willingly have paid their heavy taxes.[88]

In the long run, the Holland regent class, badly shaken, and oppressed by their grave responsibility, could not hold out against such pressure. On 4 December 1671, Enkhuizen laid before the States of Holland the same proposal that Gelderland had unsuccessfully brought up six months earlier.

There was something heroic about the inflexibility with which

De Witt attempted to resist the popular clamour, even in the face of overwhelming danger. He was opposed by his Nobility, otherwise as pro-States as the best: now all five of the members wanted to consent to the proposal, and three of them with great fervour; their pensionary asked them 'modestly' not to decide on so weighty a point without consulting the full assembly, and was, in fact, able to enter the States in the afternoon without any commitment. He warned the Assembly against the proposal with all his might. Just as it had been wrong in 1665 to chose a sick and impotent admiral (Wassenaer of Obdam) and an old and vacillating commander of the army (Johan Maurits), so would it now be wrong to entrust the country's fortunes to 'a young and inexperienced leader'; moreover, the Enkhuizen proposal ran counter to the existing laws and resolutions and he, as Grand Pensionary, felt bound to bring this to the notice of the members. The deputies then decided to put the entire matter to their principals. However, before the question could be considered by the various town councils, it came up before the so-called Great Commission, a delegate assembly of the States of Holland, in which everyone spoke for himself. Eight small towns were not represented on that body, which included the Nobles and the ten larger towns, together with the Commissioned Councillors and the secretary of the Northern Quarter. The latter, as De Witt put it, voted against the laws and against his repeated warnings and arguments; only Dort, Delft, Gouda, Rotterdam, Alkmaar and Hoorn decided to adhere to the Harmony and to send the prince into the field in a purely political capacity, i.e. as one of the States-General's deputies. But as De Witt foresaw clearly, Gouda and Alkmaar would change their minds in the full assembly, and six of the eight small towns, as he knew, would also vote against him.

That Amsterdam, despite Valckenier's defeat, also went over to the opposition, was a fatal blow – the town council decided in favour of the prince's appointment on 16 December. Bontemantel, a great admirer and supporter of the Grand Pensionary, was among those who voted for the resolution because, as he explained, it would serve,

to soothe England and Brandenburg; because the military lean towards the Prince; because it is said that Field Marshal Wirtz prefers to take the field under a Captain-General; because the commonalty are crying out for it; because the six provinces steadily insist on it; because the

Commissioned Councillors of both the Quarters are of the same opinion, and because the principal members of Holland have spoken in its favour. Another deputy added: 'Because it will be agreeable to the ministers of religion.'[89]

The idea that England might be soothed by the elevation of the prince was, as we know, a mere illusion, albeit a widespread one. Boreel, like Van Goch before him, kept sending assurances from London that the nomination would have a wonderful effect.[90] Van Beuningen, who had thought so in 1670, was still of the same opinion,[91] and so was Van Beverning. There was a plan to send a new special mission to England, and nobody wanted to accept that task before the King of England had first been appeased by the prince's elevation. This, at any rate, was the claim of Sylvius,[92] who passed through Holland on his return from a mission to Brandenburg. Downing, too, was in Holland at the time, and his secretary wrote with satisfaction of the general enthusiasm which the prince had encountered during a recent tour. 'We doubt not of a successful issue,' was his view of the Captain-Generalship.[93]

The English would, indeed, have welcomed the appointment, though they did not, of course, have the least intention to call off the impending war. Hence they were careful not to demand the elevation openly – it would have been rather embarrassing to their plans if the Dutch, as was only to be expected, would have granted their request with alacrity.[94] Downing, in whose instructions the prince and his party were not even mentioned, did his utmost to foster fresh quarrels. He assured Arlington that the Orange party was anxious to meet the king on the flag issue[95] but he did not seek contact with them, for all that. What he was out for was to provoke a further rupture and not to heal the old wounds. Arlington, for his part, declared roundly in the Committee of Foreign Affairs: 'Our business is to break with them and yet to lay the breach at their doore.'[96] Downing, anxious to keep on the right side of the Orange party, sent an urgent appeal to Arlington early in January:[97] 'Be good enough that I may receive the king's writ to call me back so that I may retain my credit with the moderate part of the government here, with the army and with the commonalty; with all those I shall, if the occasion offers, be able still to do service to His Majesty.' (He was obviously afraid of being overtaken by the war.)[98]

As for the Captain-Generalship, now that the States of Holland had voted for the resolution, De Witt was left with only a small band of faithful supporters. Dort, Delft and Rotterdam formed its nucleus; Hoorn, Brielle and Monnikendam made up the rest – they were in a minority of six to thirteen. But by his continued appeal to the Act of Harmony, the Grand Pensionary, who had to formulate the decisions of the assembly, was able to argue that the minority was, in fact, upholding a 'law' adopted unanimously, and could not therefore be outvoted. His delaying powers were undiminished, and he used them to the full.

His utter contempt for popular illusions was De Witt's greatest strength, and at the same time his greatest weakness. It was surpassed only by his contempt for those regents cowardly enough to give way before it.

'The adherents of the Lord Prince of Orange,' he wrote to De Groot on 10 December,[99] 'and also many good patriots whom the Lord God has not seen fit to endow with sufficient constancy and courage,'[100] argue openly that the state, left to itself, cannot resist the power of France and that all there is left to the Republic is either to fall victim to France, or else 'to throw ourselves into the arms of England' at the cost of appointing the prince Captain-General. 'I confess freely,' De Witt went on, 'that I regard this cure to be worse than the ill.' He was no doubt thinking of that liberty which previous Princes of Orange had attacked, and could not conceive that regents and Hollanders should now be willing to 'lay the foundation of their own slavery'.[101] Moreover, he was convinced (as the context of his letter clearly proves) that conceding the prince's appointment was tantamount to surrendering to England the independence of his country. He instructed De Groot once more to set out to the French government (when presenting Louis with a letter from the States-General, in which they humbly inquired what might be the cause of his displeasure) that French policy could only serve to turn the Republic into an English vassal state. De Witt had clearly not yet abandoned the hope that this prospect might make the French see reason.

This, too, as we know, was an illusion, and De Witt himself soon came to realize that a mere refusal to elevate the prince was no solution to his domestic difficulties. In the confidential letters De Groot wrote to him, we can see what leading Men of True Liberty were feeling at that time. De Groot's first reaction had been as sharp as De Witt's own: any concession to the prince would merely encourage England and France to make fresh demands and hence 'to subvert our entire government'. Moreover, little confidence could be placed in 'a chief commander of twenty-two years' (the prince was, in fact, no more than twenty-one!). 'Let us rather trust in God, who had never abandoned us.' But a fortnight later, De Groot had changed his tune. Conversations with French ministers had proved most disappointing. De Groot had come to appreciate that France had dropped all the old objections to the Prince of Orange. On the contrary, they now counted on getting control of the state by first elevating and then corrupting the prince. When Louis himself, soon afterwards, replied to the letter from the States-General in the haughtiest manner, and with threats, De Groot wrote to inform De Witt that, in his view, the nomination would have to be borne if it would help to reconcile Charles. It was dangerous, no doubt, to allow oneself to be pressed in that way, but the prince could not be kept down in any case, and so it was best to put a good face on his promotion . . .[102]

Holland had already made a start with the drafting of an instruction. This was in accordance with the resolution of Amsterdam and, by itself, in keeping with the Harmony. De Witt could not therefore oppose it, the less so as the States had laid it down that, in the instruction, the Harmony was to be respected.[103] The discussion now centred on the various articles of the instruction, and the argument was fierce. Dort, Delft and Rotterdam were drawn up against Haarlem and Leyden, the former demanding greater restrictions, and the latter the greatest possible freedom of movement for the future Captain-General. When the instruction was finally agreed, it was more in the spirit of the advocates of restriction than in that of the prince's friends. Not only was the incompatibility of the military office with the Stadholderate expressly laid down – together with the ruling that the future Captain-General would have to swear an oath on this – but it was also stipulated that the nominee might not draw pay from, or serve under, a foreign ruler, and that his official actions were subject to the approval of the Delegates of the States-General. The prince's youth was a complete justification of this stipulation; what proved a most unfortunate clause, however, was the withholding of the right of patents (the raising of levies) from him (the regents clearly remembered how his father had abused this privilege). Instead, and in accordance with the rules laid down by the Great Assembly in 1651 under the fresh impression of the attack on Amsterdam, every province was to make separate arrangements for the raising of levies in its own territory. As soon as the instruction had been confirmed unanimously by the other provinces, the Assembly was ready to agree to the appointment of the prince to the Captain-Generalship for one campaign.[104]

The readiness with which the prince's friends fell in with the instruction did not dispose De Witt to greater mildness: 'They think that once he has got the appointment, their man can ride roughshod over the restrictions . . .'[105] But the prince himself proved less tractable than his friends. William let it be known that he could not accept such conditions and, as a result, Holland met with strong opposition in the Generality. The prince certainly had reason on his side. It was dangerous, and it was unfair, to ask him to risk his entire reputation on the fortunes of one campaign (and of one with such unfavourable prospects at that!)[106] After all the tiresome discussions between her own members, Holland now faced the additional burden of protracted negotiations with the six provinces.

William's secret offer to Charles II (January 1672)

At that very time, with the Orange side beating furiously against the dam of the new resolution by Holland, and even while Downing was rudely presenting the Hague with his most humilating demands, William addressed himself to Charles II, using the good offices of Sylvius who, as we saw,[107] happened to be travelling through the Republic. William authorized[108] him to make the following declaration:

Unless His Majesty be too closely bound to France, he may never find a better opportunity for obtaining from the States whatever he wish, and should His Majesty be willing to let me know his desires, I am confident that, so long as they are not directly hostile to the foundations of this Republic, I shall be able to obtain them for him in spite of Mr. Grand Pensionary De Witt and his cabal, who will thereby be worsted, while I and my friends, in whom His Majesty can place his trust, will be placed at the helm; once his Majesty has had his wish, he will, moreover, be able to count on this state for all time. I have no doubt that His Majesty will believe that, so long as I have any authority in this state, I shall be utterly devoted to H.M.'s interests, in so far as my honour and the faith which I owe to this country can allow me, being well assured that His Majesty would not wish it otherwise. – N.N.

[Sylvius] will also explain to His Majesty that no member of the government has any knowledge of this matter, and that I pray H.M. to keep it secret; I assure H.M. that I shall deal cautiously with his reply, whatever it may be, and that, in all this, I have no other aim than the interests of His Majesty.

It will be observed that William never questioned the validity of the republican constitution or his own obligations towards the state. Yet what a dangerous game he was playing nevertheless! What he was, in fact, proposing was the overthrow of the governing party with the help of his foreign connections and at the cost of his country's submission to the English rival.

'Whatever the king might wish.' The chief bone of contention at the time was the English demand for satisfaction in the *Merlin* affair and for a general promise that the Dutch would in future strike the flag, and this not as a mere sign of respect, but as a recognition of the king's command of the sea. The Orangists, taking heart from Boreel's optimistic letters (he kept repeating that once the flag incident and the prince's appointment had been settled, England was ready to talk peace) refused to appreciate the difference, but De Witt, who saw very clearly that the English government was using the flag incident as a mere pretext for hiding the alliance with France from their own people, continued to make a clear distinction between homage to a royal ally (which was permissible) and the acceptance of claims which might impede the country's freedom of the sea (which must be resisted to the utmost).[109] The States-General themselves were quick to reject the humiliating demand that Van Ghent, the commander who, the English alleged, had insulted the *Merlin*, should be punished; Boreel, who had hinted that such punishment might be meted out, was reprimanded.[110] The negotiations (if that term applied) had been transferred to London in February, for Downing had once again left the Netherlands in a hurry – in far too great a hurry for the English government, whose game might thus have been given away. Charles now used the negotiations, and his conversations with Boreel, to mention East India grievances, and to demand the payment of a tribute for permission to fish off the Scottish coast.

And it was at this crucial stage that William had seen fit to come out with his offer to Charles. Buat's intrigue had been worse only inasmuch as it came at a time when England had already declared war on the Republic, though the Republic had not then been threatened by France as well. No doubt the ominous international situation offered some excuse for William's behaviour; but it should be noted, first, that the States took a far more courageous stand in the face of these difficulties, and second, that his motives were mixed, to say the very least: he was anxious to hasten his appointment as Captain-General, and also to wrest the conduct of affairs of state from De Witt's hands. De Witt, though ignorant of William's personal intervention, had no illusions as to the ambitions of William's party. We have seen that he looked upon the elevation of Orange as a means of opening the door to Charles, and looking at the events in retrospect, no one can claim that he was wrong.

Fortunately for the country and for William's own reputation, Charles scorned the offer – William's reservations, few though they were, proved unacceptable to England. Charles *was* too closely bound to France; he *did* want to overthrow the foundations of the Republic; he intended to use William only when there was no state left to claim his loyalty. And so, when he replied, just over a month later, by which time William had already been appointed Captain-General (we shall see below on what conditions), he began his letter with congratulations, and went on to say: 'I have made no hurry to reply to what you laid before me through Sylvius, because I do not believe that you will be able to do what you wish to take upon yourself. It is enough that you have been able to promote your own affair so well; I must go on with mine in the public and customary way, as you will see from the documents I have handed to the States' ambassador here.' – Charles's cavalier tones were not likely to find an echo in William's proud heart – the king was quite wrong to believe that the prince would sit back humbly until England was ready to beckon him.

Captain-General on restrictive conditions (25 February 1672); Charles II not reconciled

The prince was the less amenable to such treatment as he had meanwhile been appointed Captain-General, albeit after swearing an oath that he would not seek or accept the Stadholdership. De Witt had an understandable fear that the prince would misuse this office and turn it to the advantage of his English connection, but, in the event, the Captain-Generalship appeased William's ambition and strengthened his sense of national responsibility.

Despite the prince's objections and the renewed opposition of the six provinces, Holland had decided to insist on the conditions laid down on 19 January.[111] De Witt then had a conversation with William lasting for two hours but leading to no compromise. Worse, Haarlem and Leyden reproached the prince for spoiling his own cause.[112] Soon afterwards, however, the Orangist towns in Holland grew restless again and set up the cry that Holland must yield 'lest the Republic be ruined'.[113] The winter passed, and the campaigning season was fast approaching – a French attack might be expected at any moment, and there had still been no single-minded attempt to strengthen the army, for the six provinces had persisted in withholding their consent before Holland gave way. Holland had pleaded in vain, on more than one occasion, that recruiting was a matter of priority[114] – her case, and hence the Republic's strength, were sacrificed to Orange party bias. Political disunity had yet another untoward consequence, and this time both parties were to blame. Wirtz's authority as commander, which had not been too strong from the outset, was undermined further by the suggestion that William should be placed above him. Meanwhile, the two parties in Holland, and the various provinces, carried on interminable discussions about 'temperaments', 'expedients', or 'conciliations'.[115] At last, De Witt, urged to do so by his friends, made another attempt to come to terms with the prince. This time Amsterdam cooperated fully with the Dort group (if I may call it that). The February election had brought De Witt's great friend Lambertus Reynst into the burgomasters' office, together with Hendrik Hooft, who despite his Arminian leanings, was far less reliable. De Witt also worked on the prince and the six provinces through Fagel (whom De Witt had helped to the post of greffier to the States-General after he ceased being Pensionary of Haarlem in 1670) and Van Beverning. The complicated discussions were crowned with success and, on 25 February, the Generality resolved to appoint William III Captain-General *for the duration of one campaign*. Holland's conditions of 19 January were thus accepted in full, but Holland now agreed that, on reaching the age stipulated in the Act of Harmony, the prince would be appointed Captain-General *for life*.

A few days later, William dined the Holland deputies. There was an enormous crowd of curious spectators. The Grand Pensionary must have sat down to the meal with very mixed feelings:

had he had his way, this darling of the people cheering outside, this nephew of Charles II, would never have been placed into high office. De Witt had been forced to choose the lesser of two evils, but he had, at least, done his utmost to preserve the Act of Harmony, and to ensure that his triumphant host, whom he distrusted so deeply, was hemmed in on all sides.[116] Even so, he must have had grave doubts as to the reliability of these curbs.

The commonalty was exuberant. 'Throughout the country, the people were overjoyed. They felt as courageous as lions, and said that one man would count for six.' The Hague lawyer who wrote this sentence, though no friend of De Witt, added ironically:[117] 'That lumpish people has no understanding of Liberty, nor even knows what it means.' The poets played innumerable variations of the heroic theme,[118] and the Exchange reacted favourably as well.[119] The dominant note was relief that the obstinate regents of Holland had at last done what was needful to reconcile the King of England. As one poet put it:

> No drummer roll can rouse our heart,
> As William's glorious fame;
> 'Gainst England's dagger and fierce dart
> We shelter in his name.[120]

That shelter, however, proved to be a mere illusion. The simple-minded Boreel, though he knew about the Anglo-French negotiations (the final arrangements were made that February), and though he had time and again to listen to the king's petty complaints about Dutch medals, paintings and books glorifying the raid on Chatham (the painting he particularly objected to was hung in the town hall of Dort and showed a triumphant Cornelis de Witt against the background of a burning port), could still write that the king and the Duke of York were 'highly pleased' with William's appointment.[121] Meerman, however, a Leyden regent and confidant of De Witt, who, in March, went on the long-overdue special mission to England, reported at once that 'from now on there is nothing for it but to see to vigorous defences at sea and on shore'. De Witt was delighted to receive this 'honest warning'.[122] Boreel, meanwhile, was still harping on the possibility of persuading Charles to preserve the peace by the offer of a large sum of money. De Witt was greatly irritated: Boreel's silly talk had been damping the zeal of the provinces all along; a month was lost because it pleased Overijsel and Gelderland to discuss his pleas. Only after Meerman's report did they consent to rearm the land forces, which nobody would need more badly than they did!

Pieter de Groot had been warning his country that no good was to be expected of France, that England was indissolubly bound to France, and that all the Republic could do in these circumstances was to rearm with all speed and to look for new allies. On 25 February, the States gave him permission to leave France, but illness prevented him from departing before 25 March. In England, the miserable spectacle of long-suffering Dutch negotiators trying to pacify a deliberate trouble-seeker had meanwhile continued unabated. But on 23 March, the English government ordered an unprovoked attack upon the heavily laden Dutch merchant fleet as it approached the Isle of Wight from the Mediterranean – a repetition, therefore, of the method used in 1665. Once again, the attack was boldly repulsed. Charles's endeavour to arouse his people against the old rival over the flag issue had not been unsuccessful, but his position was weak all the same. His government was divided from public opinion by too wide a gulf: the alliance with France was unpopular, and Charles's indirect attempt to help the Catholics with a royal declaration of 'indulgence' had caused a great deal of Protestant suspicion. Even before the storm finally broke, the government was unable to meet all its financial commitments.

After the attack on its merchant fleet, the States at once took steps. A few days later, England issued a declaration of war which amounted to a tissue of false grievances and accusations. The French declaration of war on 6 April was a very different matter: it merely mentioned the king's displeasure at the behaviour of the States and added that his glory could no longer suffer to be besmirched in that way.

The fleet prepares; Sole Bay (7 June); Defective land defences; The French-Münster attack

How did the Republic prepare to meet the sudden onslaught?

Her only ally was Spain. In 1671, Van Beuningen had gone to Brussels, and in the spring of 1672, Cornelis de Witt had met Monterey in the same city, to put the finishing touches to a mutual assistance pact. In addition, there was the hope of persuading the Elector of Brandenburg to side with the Republic: Van Amerongen, a zealous Orange noble from Utrecht, had concluded a treaty with him. The Emperor, too, was showing signs of friendship: the example of the other Hapsburg power, Spain, had made an impression in Vienna, and Lisola was doing his utmost to loosen the Emperor's ties with France. On the other hand, it was certain that the Archbishop of Cologne would not only allow the French to pass through his territory (including the district of Liège) but that he would give them active support. The States had tried to stir up the citizens against him, but their troops under Bampfield had been forced to evacuate the bishopric in December 1671. It was feared that matters would take a like course in Münster, where Bernhard von Galen was bound to seize the opportunity of the French attack, though, in the event, he made no move until May.

Luckily, the Dutch navy was in fine fettle – or else a successful landing by the Anglo-French forces coupled to an attack on land might speedily have spelled the end of the Republic.

Public opinion in the Republic was outraged by the unprovoked attack on the Smyrna fleet, and Charles's treachery was lampooned in a number of 'bluebooks'. Several writers professed themselves amazed[123] that he, who had been so severely chastised at God's hand, should have dared again to conjure up the vengeance of heaven, and for French gold at that; he was reminded of his father's death on the scaffold, both in high-flown poetic phrases, and with vulgar abuse. The Orange party could hardly persist in its pro-English attitude, now that it had been so spectacularly slighted by its English patron. More than one pamphleteer observed bitterly that the prince's elevation to the Captain-Generalship had failed to produce the desired effect. 'Do you mean to tell me,' asked the peasant in *Samenspraeck* on hearing of the attack on the Smyrna fleet, 'that the Englishman has again thrust out his thief's hand to seize our ships? And there I was thinking that all would be well now that the prince is become a General.'[124]

In May, the navy put out to sea – or at least that part of it under the control of the Holland Boards of Admiralty. De Ruyter was in command, with Cornelis de Witt acting as Deputy of the States-General – his lifeguard in the livery of Holland and other ceremonial pomp drew a great deal of critical attention. And on the day he set sail, his own town witnessed a spectacle that gave him a foretaste of what awaited his family: a number of citizens, 'assisted by the mob', invaded the town hall, dragged out the painting of the raid on Chatham (which England had mentioned in her declaration of war), hacked it to pieces, cut out the head of Cornelis de Witt, and nailed it to the gallows.[125]

Cornelis was undeterred. A number of leading Amsterdamers had joined the navy, and also recruited and equipped a number of men at their own expense. The English preferred not to join battle on that occasion, and on 7 June De Ruyter put to sea once more and courageously attacked the vastly superior English fleet with its French auxiliaries at Sole Bay. Though he was unable to defeat them completely, he had, in any case, averted the threat of an English landing. Immediately afterwards, the hard-pressed States were forced to divert part of the navy to the defence of the hinterland. Cornelis de Witt himself had to leave the fleet for health reasons.

The Republic fared much worse on land, where the weakness of the federal system made itself felt to the full. Holland could only assert her strength at sea, so much so, in fact, that De Witt had been able to persuade the reluctant States-General to entrust naval matters to a Secret Commission, thus greatly strengthening the Republic's power to strike in unison.[126] Even so, Zeeland had refused to let its squadron sail out with the rest in May (and Friesland still lacked the necessary funds), with the result that the chance of engaging the English before the French could join them, was missed. On land, the Grand Pensionary and Holland had their hands tied even more firmly. Here the Council of State had the first say, and Holland's influence could only make itself felt when the enemy was knocking at the door. Then, despite its heavy debts and taxes, in spite of unrest and panic, the province could still conjure up enough money to oversubscribe its quota to the Generality of 58 per cent. But, as we saw, until well into 1672, the struggle round the Captain-Generalship, and Orangist hopes that England's neutrality or even England's assistance might still be obtained, continued to act as dampers on all defensive preparations. Only in March was unanimity reached, and could the work proceed apace.

Strong personalities in the various States assemblies now asserted themselves: not only Cornelis de Witt and Vivien, who belonged to the closest circle round the Grand Pensionary, but also

Hop, the independent pensionary of Amsterdam, Van Beverning, who became president of the Deputies on the Field – a sensible choice, because no mutual suspicion impeded his collaboration with the young Captain-General, and many others as well.

But it was late, much too late. It proved exceedingly difficult to recruit enough troops in so short a time. Holland passed resolutions to arm its own peasants, to send out the town guards, to enlist the citizens. They were called upon not only to defend their own province, but were sent to man fortresses in Brabant and even to the Ijsel region where the battle was expected to rage most fiercely. But what the Republic really needed was the help of professional soldiers, and these were chiefly found in Germany, where several rulers had entered into agreements with the French, and the rest had raised their price considerably. Even so, it proved possible to scratch together a few regiments, albeit their spirit and that of the Dutch soldiery, so long neglected, left much to be desired.[127] The commanders complained of the poor quality of their officers, and there was a general lack of confidence. Fortress-works were in a pitiable state, and incoming reports all made alarming reading. The gunpowder in Crèvecoeur and Engelen near Bois-le-duc dated back to 1629, when Frederick Henry had conquered the town. In the Ijsel towns and the Rhine fortresses, which were expected to bear the brunt of the first onslaught, the gun-mountings were defective, walls were about to collapse on the suburbs built immediately beneath them, and there was an acute shortage of ammunition. Only Maastricht was well-prepared, and there a large force had been assembled in the hope of holding up the French for a considerable time. Strategists at the time were wont to place far too great reliance in fortresses and hence to tie down much too large a part of the army in them. Much was also expected from the advance defence posts along the Rhine.[128] And if the French should pass these obstacles, it was intended to hold them on the Ijsel where feverish work was now in progress. Unfortunately, just when it was finished, the Ijsel defences lost much of their importance: an unusually dry summer had caused the water level to drop so low that the river could now be forded in several spots, and things were little better with the Rhine, below the Waal. Moreover, the army, or rather what remained of it outside the many garrisons, was far too weak to man these positions.

And when the French came rushing in, they smashed the outer

defences like so many bits of cardboard. On 19 May, the entire French expeditionary force, one hundred thousand strong, led by the greatest commanders of the time, Condé and Turenne, was drawn up before Maastricht. They decided to encircle the town, and to send the bulk of the force on to the Rhine and thence to invade the Republic. Orsoy, Rhineberk and Bury capitulated. Wesel held out for four days, Emmerik was evacuated, and the garrison of Rees was compelled to surrender by the citizens within. In Rhineberk treachery was coupled to cowardice – the commander's right-hand man was an Irish Papist. When the garrison was allowed to retire to Maastricht, most of the men ran off on the way, and the officers were arrested on arrival and ear-marked for court martial. The other captured garrisons were not released for six weeks, and then only against ransom. In Wesel, the most important fortress of all – 'the entire garrison, even including the commanders, were herded together like so much cattle and driven into the church by the southern door, between a double row of distinguished French officers seated in Spanish chairs'. Here, the two thousand or so officers and men 'ran about in utter confusion, each looking for a place to rest his head'.[129] The news of these and similar surrenders was not likely to encourage those still holding the Ijsel.

On 1 June, Münster troops invaded Overijsel, where, as in 1665, they quickly occupied the whole of Twente. The road to the Ijsel now lay open before Münster, while the main French force veered westward to fall upon the Betuwe across the Rhine. Montbas, a Frenchman in the States' service who had married a sister of Pieter de Groot, abandoned his post, but Wirtz was able to repair the damage in good time. On 12 June, the French nevertheless effected a crossing near the Tolhuis. It now looked very much as if they would make a further crossing below Arnhem, to attack the rear of the main force drawn up on the Ijsel under the Prince of Orange to face the expected attack from Münster-Cologne. That self-same day, the Deputies in the Field decided 'hastily' to 'split up' the army on the Ijsel.

Van Beverning, one of the Deputies, though not – as De Witt testified before the States of Holland – 'one of the timorous',[130] had all the while been sending the gloomiest reports about the untenability of the Ijsel front and the morale of the troops, but the Grand Pensionary had continued to insist on holding the line. In the assembly of Holland, he had contrasted the 'resolute bearing' of the Prince of Orange with the pessimism of Wirtz, and as late as 4 June the States still proposed to insist in the States-General that the Ijsel defences must be held. However, meeting at Arnhem soon afterwards, the Deputies in the Field and special delegates from the States-General (including Hop and Fagel) advised, under the fresh impact of the disastrous news from the Rhine, that the Deputies should be given a free hand, and, on the grounds that 'war could not be conducted from a distance',[131] the States, on 7 June, granted them freedom of action in conjunction with the Captain-General. But by then that freedom could no longer be exercised. The army now counted 22,000 men, in addition to the thousand or so citizen soldiers and armed peasants from Holland and Utrecht, who merely added to the general confusion. But even the regular soldiers, as the Deputies discovered, lacked the courage of resistance, and were 'liable to fright and terror'. Nijmegen and Zutfen were panic-stricken and riot-torn. The decision to withdraw was taken not a moment too soon, but the way it was implemented was particularly inept.

It will be remembered that according to the instruction to William III, the real command of the army did not rest with him, but with the Deputies, whose 'patents' were, moreover, still vested in their respected provincial States. The withdrawal decision now showed how disastrous this arrangement really was – for only the Deputies' provincialism could have explained their resolve to leave a number of regiments from Gelderland, Overijsel, Friesland and Groningen behind when they ordered the general withdrawal from the Ijsel towns in the full knowledge that, once the front-line was broken, these towns could not possibly hold out against the enemy.[132] A mere 9,000 of the 22,000 followed their Captain-General and the Deputies to the west. We do not know what the prince may have thought of that waste of manpower; in any case, the matter was outside his competence. What is therefore all the more surprising is that Van Beverning did not apparently see fit to lodge a protest.[133]

De Witt, on the other hand, realized full well what was at stake, and urged that the bulk of the army be brought to Holland. It might be tempting to look upon the Grand Pensionary's view as just another expression of provincialism. In fact, De Witt based his wish not only on the fact that Holland had more than fulfilled her obligation to the Union, but also on the realization that the other provinces could only be saved 'through the strength with which Holland might later contribute to their recovery'.[134] If need be, he was prepared to abandon parts of Holland as well and to withdraw his defending force to Amsterdam, which was in a particularly strong position. 'From that place, as from the heart,' all the members 'could be assisted with might and main, and the enemy's claim to the country disputed to the last man, with Batavian tenacity.'[135] De Witt's view was strategically sound, and it was tragic that, had he not been swayed by his distrust of Orange, he might well have found a staunch supporter in an independent Captain-General; for in fact now, as so often, the interests of Holland and those of the Union were at one.

He had, moreover, clear justification for his strategy because, in the past few months, Holland had prepared for a last-ditch stand by looking into, and actually ordering, the flooding of various parts of her territory. That these measures could protect Holland alone was not the fault of the province. In the spring, the Hollanders had done what they could to reach an arrangement with Utrecht on establishing a line of defence from the Grebbe Sluice to Amersfoort, which would have included the whole of that province, or failing that, a line running from Naarden, Vecht, Vaartse Rhine, and past Utrecht town.[136] This had been rejected, as De Witt put it, on 'wholly erroneous foundations of jealousy'.

By the time the retreating Ijsel army reached Utrecht on 15 June, the defence of that town seemed a hopeless proposition. Yet, quite unexpectedly, Van Beverning and William III were still willing to hold it. The States of the province and the town magistrates did what they could, but the town militia, fearing a siege, had begun to close the gates against William's troops. They did so in a moment of panic, but the story had a most depressing effect on the mood of the States-General (who, this time, lacked the wisdom of refraining from attempts to conduct the war 'from a distance'). In any case, the town was unwilling to have its suburbs razed, a condition on which the prince was insisting. After a few days of indescribable confusion, the States-General issued an express order to continue the retreat, revoking it almost immediately, but too late. And so the army withdrew behind the Holland water line. That 13,000 men had been squandered on the Ijsel towns when Utrecht was left without a garrison struck the citizens as a bitter injustice. But it was certainly a salutary decision. The new positions were occupied on 18 June.

Even then, the situation remained precarious, for not only was the army demoralized and far too weak, but it was weeks before the inundation plan could be fully implemented, and this despite the preparations I have mentioned. The army command was unfamiliar with conditions in the polderland, the authorities in near-by towns gave little help, their citizens kept panicking, the peasants more than once offered armed resistance, blocking the dykes, or draining the water at night. If the French had continued their advance in the wake of the retiring States army, they would certainly have been able to enter Holland in force. But the invaders' perspective, too, was clouded by superstitious fear of the fortresses, and while the Münster troops were able to take the Overijsel towns within a few days, the French were wasting precious days on the capture of fortresses on the Ijsel, Rhine and Waal. On 27 June, Louis XIV himself appeared at Zeist, the French headquarters near Utrecht. Peace negotiations had already been opened, and he was waiting confidently for the surrender.

Distress of Holland; Attempted assassination of De Witt; Jacob van der Graeff

The calamities in the east had made a shattering impression on Holland, which was only increased by the sudden influx of well-to-do refugees with as many chests and trunks as they could manage. De Witt's own courage did not fail, but as he warned the States, fear and defection all round 'will spoil all our chances'. In the States-General, the deputies of Holland declared[137] that 'the military position was not nearly as grave as the lack of courage'. On 21 June, De Witt expressed similar feelings in a letter to Vivien: 'I see our greatest misfortune not in the power or progress of the enemy, but in the general insurrection, the disobedience and reluctance of our citizens and peasants, by which the strength of authority is sapped and action everywhere held up.'[138]

Excitement, fear, rage — all of these were understandable reactions to the discovery that the fortresses had been sorely neglected and that the army, too, was in exceedingly poor shape. And what a spectacle of miserable confusion was the collapse of Overijsel and Gelderland, with the magistrates and garrison commanders laying the blame at one another's door everywhere.[139] In Arnhem and Doesburg, just as in Wesel, the soldiers (and also the unfortunate peasant auxiliaries from Holland) were locked up in the churches, while the local militia was left free – in accordance with an agreement between the burgomasters and the enemy. Though Deventer had been declared an imperial city when the Town Council first entered into negotiations with the Bishop of Münster, its garrison feared no better than those of Arnhem and Doesburg and, warned by the example, the garrison of Zwolle took to their heels. Two younkers from Overijsel (one of them a Bentinck) acted as spokesmen of the Bishop, and soon afterwards the entire nobility (with only a few exceptions) signed an ignominious truce, in which the collapse of the Republic was taken for granted. In both provinces, 'Papists' had begun to come to the fore. Kampen capitulated after weeks of vain efforts to obtain ammunition from the Generality magazine, and later from Amsterdam. Its garrison, for one, had been anxious to make a bold stand, and the magistrates and citizens at first rejected any idea of capitulation. But in the end they, too, had been forced to surrender, the more so as 'the womenfolk' and 'the mob', here, as elsewhere, had been loud in their clamourings for an 'accord'.

As a result of a party struggle that divided the whole country, the commonalty turned a blind eye to cowardice among the citizens and soldiery, and blamed every defeat on the 'treacherous' regents, and the regents of Holland in particular. The fact that the nobles of Overijsel and Gelderland, most of them active supporters of the prince, had been far more directly implicated in the disaster was conveniently forgotten[140] – indeed, the regents were pilloried for hampering the prince's powers of resistance and for their tolerance of Papists and Arminians (against whom the clergy had been inveighing all along). The wildest rumours went the rounds. Ammunition had been sent up the Rhine, not for the Dutch fortresses, but for the French magazine at Neuse; the loyal governor of Wesel, who wanted to prevent this betrayal, had been dismissed and replaced by a traitor.[141] The land army had been neglected and the navy prepared so that Orange might suffer defeat and Cornelis de Witt score a triumph.[142] Another report had it that when the three Presidents of the High Council (of Justice), the Court (of Justice), and the Chamber of Accounts of Holland, had called upon the Grand Pensionary to ask what they should do, 'he merely shrugged his shoulders and said that a good and speedy accommodation with the enemy might be the best way out'.[143] And this of a man who, with 'Batavian constancy', was doing his utmost and who, if necessary, was prepared to hold out in a remote corner of the country!

Alas, he had now become the focus of popular discontent. The most courageous and indefatigable patriot, the builder of the navy, the man who had done more than anyone to improve and strengthen the land defence, the originator of the system of alliances that was soon to bring salvation, had become a butt for street brawlers and topers. His leadership was utterly scorned, and he was called the arch-traitor. Malicious grumbling was soon to turn into vicious roaring[144] – a turn of events that cannot but fill the modern observer with profound disgust. The very people whose poets had exclaimed that they would fight like lions under the prince as captain, that one of them would be worth six of the foe, ran away as soon as the enemy knocked at their gate. The castle of Loevestein was deserted by the Rotterdam guards on a flimsy pretext. In Gorcum, in Schoonhoven, the towns nearest to the enemy fire, and in several eastern towns, the citizens fell over one another in their anxiety to surrender. The peasants in the inundated areas merely took up arms to protect their meadows against their own soldiers. But safe behind the line, their like clamoured and blustered against the regents, the scapegoats who now had to take all the blame.

On 21 June, four young men on an evening walk along the Vijverberg noticed that the light was still burning in the assembly room of the States of Holland. One of them piped up: 'The States are still at it, and the Grand Pensionary must be with them. The sooner that scoundrel is out of the way the better for us all.' And then they waited. When De Witt appeared, one of the four heroes knocked the torch out of his hands and together they fell upon the Grand Pensionary who, though he defended himself bravely, collapsed with knife wounds in his side and shoulder. The assailants left him for dead, but De Witt was tough and, though he had to keep to his bed for a few weeks, eventually recovered. Of the four young miscreants, one was caught the same day. He turned out to be the younger son of Councillor Van der Graeff, a noted Orangist. He confessed and mentioned the names of the three others: one was his own brother. All three managed to lie low until the danger had passed with the downfall of De Witt's régime.

Borrebagh, who had delivered the first blow, was a postmaster. He was not even dismissed from office. But meanwhile the Court of Holland, under pressure from the indignant States, was forced to make an example of young De Graeff. On 29 June, he was sentenced for the crime of *laesa majestas*, and beheaded that self-same day.

The attack itself, which was almost unique in the annals of Dutch history,[145] no less than public reaction to it, showed quite unmistakably how badly disordered the Republic was. Young Jacob van der Graeff was probably not the worst of the four. Immediately after his execution, a little blue book was published. It bore the title *The Struggle of Jacob*, and gave a detailed account of the last days of his life. Its author was possibly Pastor Simonides who, with Pastor Vollenhovius, had administered to him in prison and on the scaffold. The pamphlet was soon in everyone's hands; it was re-printed repeatedly and for years remained edifying reading for the Reformed congregation.[146] And certainly his last days as they are here sketched out have a moving quality – a struggle ending in the victorious certainty of salvation and joy in death. We are told that, after a few days of weeping and groaning, the unhappy boy recovered his poise. He comforted the pastors who had come to comfort him. He sang duets with the jailer. He admonished his compatriots to refrain from cursing, the cause of God's wrath. On the scaffold, a miracle happened. The hangman felt that this was not an ordinary job. He bungled, and afterwards could not clean the blood from his sword. The dead man's head was bathed in a halo of light.

But the religious symbols of the narrative thinly disguised the underlying party passion and hatred against the victim of Van der Graeff's attack. It *was* admitted that he had asked for De Witt's pardon, and that he *had* received it. But his 'repentance' had only been in respect of the general sinfulness he shared with the rest of mankind, not of his cowardly murder attempt, which was not mentioned by a single word. We can understand the bitterness with which one of De Witt's supporters wrote a few months later, that the author of that pamphlet about 'Van der Graeff's saint-like repentance on the gallows, shared a grave responsibility for the death of the two brothers De Witt'.[147] In the prevailing mood, thousands were prepared to accept Van der Graeff as a martyr and to see in his 'godliness' one more proof of the wickedness of his victim, so much so that a special order had to be made proscribing public prayers for the condemned man (this was also mentioned in the pamphlet).[148] Rioting broke out in several towns, and quite a show of military force was needed in order to proceed with the execution in the Hague. Van der Graeff's sentence was, in fact, the last show of strength by a dying régime.

De Groot's mission to Louis XIV (26 June); Amsterdam's bravery

De Witt's report to Vivien[149] had been incomplete – 'our greatest evil' was not only the rebelliousness of the citizens, but also the weakness of those in authority. The Town Councils in Overijsel and Gelderland had not been the only ones to fail in their duty – things were greatly remiss in Holland as well. As early as 13 June, Burgersdijk, the pensionary of Leyden, proposed the sending of an embassy to England. When Amsterdam protested, Gorkum retorted that it was easy for Amsterdam to strike an attitude – she would be swallowed up last of all. Gorkum at any rate supported Leyden's proposal, and by the 15th, the States-General had decided to send missions to both kings. Like Amsterdam, De Witt had been against the resolution, and so had Fagel, the greffier of the States-General. But now that De Witt was laid up and Vivien had to lead the States of Holland, it was felt that the situation had grown so desperate that negotiations with France must be tried, come what may.

The embassy to Louis XIV was made up of Pieter de Groot, Johan van Ghent and Nassau-Odijk. On the night of 22 June, they arrived in ransacked Keppel, on the Old Ijsel near Doesburg; early next morning, they were joined by Louvois and Pomponne, who refused to state the French terms but merely asked the Dutch delegates to consider 'in what state their affairs already were, and how much worse they would soon become'. Louis was treating all the territories he had conquered as his by right and must be paid compensation for them, in addition to a large war indemnity; moreover, these terms did not in any way prejudice those of his allies. This, in short, was the message with which Pieter de Groot returned to the States of Holland on 25 June.

He told the States that it would be possible to recover the occupied parts of the sovereign provinces against cession of the entire Generality Lands, and suggested that this was the only way out – protracting the negotiations might lead to complete ruin, whereas a quick decision might yet preserve the States government, the territorial integrity of the seven provinces, and the Protestant régime.

At that moment, the French had already occupied Utrecht and Naarden; Muiden was still being held against all expectations, but might be expected to fall as well. All the 'posts' on the 'waterline' were holding, albeit only just, and at various points the water level was still very low, or else the water was being drained off by the irate peasantry. There was an acute shortage of arms and ammunition, and the defence works along the line were in need of much improvement. The peasants commandeered for that task were intractable with fright and suspicion, while the citizens of Delft, the Hague and elsewhere refused to man the seemingly untenable 'posts' near Gorkum and Gouda. Troops had to be used to prevent the country-folk from tampering further with the inundations; in the towns, and quite especially in Rotterdam, unrest was mounting ominously. The French could be expected to break the line at any moment; small towns, such as Gorkum and Schoonhoven felt the dagger at their throats; Gouda and Leyden feared it would be their turn next and knew that with them the whole of south Holland would fall; only Dort, now an island fortress, might hold out somewhat longer; and so might Amsterdam, cut off from the mainland by the inundations together with the Haarlemmermeer and the Zuiderzee. However, once Kampen surrendered on 23 June, there was the added danger that the enemy might use the Zuiderzee for launching a naval attack. Panic reigned supreme at Medemblik.

These were the circumstances in which the States of Holland examined De Groot's offer on 25 June.[150]

One by one the members, 'opining' in the customary order, ranged themselves behind it; the fifth member, Leyden, wanted to go even further and leave De Groot unbound by any conditions. 'They would not have given this advice had they not regarded the situation as desperate.' Leyden insisted that the full assembly put the proposal before the Generality (across the Binnenhof) there and then. But then Amsterdam spoke up, and her voice was far less shaken. Her deputies declared – in the person of Pensionary Hop – that they could not possibly agree to such a resolution without consulting their masters. They exhorted the members to take courage and to reflect that they, as deputies, were not competent to surrender the whole country. And the deputies seemed to heed this sound bit of advice – if Amsterdam held out, no one else was prepared to take responsibility for so grave a step, although Gorkum, Edam and Medemblik 'lamented that there was no salvation now that the posts could no longer be defended'. Alkmaar, moreover, sided boldly with Amsterdam. However, when the question was raised for a second time, almost all the leading members insisted that Amsterdam fall in with the wishes of the majority. Leyden called hotly on the deputies not to let Amsterdam ride roughshod over them – unanimity might be the normal rule but in an emergency like the present one that rule would have to go by default. 'Not all towns are as easy to defend as Amsterdam, and Leyden does not mean to be ruined for Amsterdam's sake alone.' Alkmaar immediately countered that 'they would rather be beaten to death by the enemy than by the citizens'.

The citizens indeed! It was impossible to conceal the crisis from them, now that the deputies of all the eighteen voting towns had returned from the Hague for consultations. In various places, crowds collected in front of the town hall, while those inside were discussing peace or continued resistance, and although many citizens were no less war-weary than their regents, most were filled with violent hatred of the French. De Groot's life was threatened when he came home to Rotterdam, and even those town councils that had remained staunch throughout were widely distrusted.

Thus in Amsterdam, a civic guard noted in his diary, as if he knew all about it, that twenty of the thirty-six councillors were for 'surrender' and that the rest had brought them to see reason only by the threat of calling in the commonalty. His story had no substance whatsoever in fact. There *were* 'many arguments for and against' in the council, and there *were* those who feared that they might lose 'state, town and possessions', and who therefore pressed for a truce even if that meant handing over one-sixth of the inhabitants' possessions (this, at least, is what Bontemantel, a member, who attended the debate, wrote of the proceedings).[151] One of the councillors, Roch, muttered under his breath: 'Better half an egg than an empty shell' – Amsterdam could not hold out by herself when all other towns were lost. But these faint-hearted men no more formed the majority than did the group who wanted to break off all negotiations there and then. Valckenier, whose vigorous personality asserted itself in moments like these, Hasselaer, the town sheriff, Alderman Bontemantel, and men like burgomaster Van de Poll (Van Beuningen was again away at Brussels), expatiated on the natural strength of the town, recalled Copenhagen, which thirteen years earlier had survived alone when the entire Kingdom of Denmark had fallen[152] and which had been the centre of national resurgence; and held out the hope that the increase in France's power might move other rulers to spring to Holland's assistance: 'God has a thousand means of redressing the state in its distress.' For these reasons, no offer at all must be made. But, quite obviously, that struck the majority as far too unrealistic. The resolution they accepted in the end[153] began with a plain statement that the French demands were unacceptable and that they would 'rather sacrifice their goods and their blood'. Instead, Amsterdam offered to buy a truce with a very large sum of money, on condition that no further demands would be made on her by France's allies and that these would be full 'freedom of religion and government'.[154]

This was the instruction with which the Amsterdam deputies came back to the States on 27 June. But the panic-stricken deputies had taken a decision in their absence: the States-General must be asked to give De Groot full powers of negotiation without further ado. The entire assembly of Holland, with the exception of those towns still consulting their masters, and of Enkhuizen, which refused her vote, marched across the Binnehof to their High Mightinesses. Groningen, of course, was absent (the town was at the moment putting up a brave defence against Münster); Utrecht declared she had no vote in the present matter (the entire province was in the hands of the enemy); Gelderland and Overijsel for all that they were in the same situation, gave their consent; Zeeland and Friesland declared they had no instruction from their principals; the Frisian president of the week refused to 'conclude', and when Utrecht and Zeeland would not take his place, a member of the Holland Nobility, Maesdam by name, stepped into the breach. Fagel, the greffier, also refused to sign the resolution.

Was it a valid resolution? It had, in any case, been taken in the most irregular fashion. Yet it was with this imperfect document in his pocket that De Groot left early next morning, urged on by the pensionaries of Leyden and Gouda,[155] and with a promise that they would send him the 'extension' (the final text).[156] De Groot interrupted his journey at army headquarters near Bodegraven to inform Van Beverning and the prince of his mission. Van Beverning declared that he would have been loath to carry such a message, and the prince said much the same thing,[157] though he at once wrote to the States for permission to ask the French for a *sauvegarde* of his own possessions. Other owners of estates did the same, and the requests were all granted. Still, the prince's attitude formed a somewhat shabby contrast to the bold stand of Amsterdam (and soon afterwards of Zeeland).[158]

De Groot met his fellow deputies at Rhenen; Van Ghent declared himself ready to support him; Odijk, on the contrary, whose province, as De Groot had to admit, had abstained from voting, kept aloof as much as he could. On 28 June, De Groot told Louvois and Pomponne that he and his colleagues had been granted unlimited powers to conclude a peace, 'on condition, however, that the sovereignty of each of the respective provinces would in all respects be restored and preserved'.[59] In practice, therefore, he had not been given full powers – even in the absence of Amsterdam, Leyden's advice had not been heeded. Fortunately, the French king was so far above himself by now (and was, moreover, taking an unconscionable time in launching his attack upon Holland) that he demanded far more than De Groot and Van Ghent could grant on the strength of their instruction. In addition to the Generality lands, Louis now had laid claim to the Betuwe, which was in the possession of Gelderland, and to Delfzijl, in the province of Groningen, and demanded that the Republic revoke all trading legislations unfavourable to France, give a promise to enter into negotiations about the East India Company, and grant equal rights to Roman Catholics in all parts of the Republic, which ran counter to De Groot's instructions. All this in addition to any demands England (and Münster) might care to press. The ambassador argued in vain, and eventually returned to report his failure to the States of Holland, before whom he appeared on 1 July.

Here the Amsterdam deputies had lodged a vigorous protest against the taking of so weighty a decision in their absence. Feelings at the meeting – on 27 June – had run very high,[160] and Hop had used most undiplomatic language. He had accused the other members of 'selling their sovereignty and liberty', adding that, whereas Amsterdam could face the commonalty without shame, those who had surrendered before a single shot was fired, might well tremble for their lives. He was told, with equal anger, that the situation was desperate, that *nothing* could be saved once the French army succeeded in breaching the line which, as anyone with even a modicum of sense could tell, was liable to crack at any moment. Most of the small towns of north Holland were quick to agree, and Burgersdijk, the pensionary of Leyden, even proposed that the States consider the possibility of separate provincial negotiations in case the present proposals led to a dead end. The news from the front, he claimed, grew more desperate with every moment (he had just received a letter from his burgomaster, Van Leeuwen, to the effect that the French were about to force the post on the New Bridge before making straight for Leyden and the Hague); Holland would just have to stew in her own juice. The result of his speech was unexpected: Dort and Delft now joined Amsterdam and Alkmaar rather than be party to an irreparable breach of the Union.

In comparing the attitudes of the various towns, it is important to remember their respective geographical situations. Thus while Leyden and Gouda were immediately threatened, Amsterdam was relatively safe. And now that the enemy was at the gate, every town and province looked to its own safety first. The sense of national unity which was needed to conceive and implement plans like De Witt's – to withdraw into an impregnable corner and thence spring back upon the enemy – did not prevail with most other regents, particularly when their own towns were under heavy pressure. Zeeland, Friesland, and Groningen, which opposed De Groot's mission, did so in the certainty that, like Amsterdam, they were capable of defending their own territory.

The States of Zeeland, hurriedly informed of Holland's panic, sent an exceptionally vigorous protest to the Generality on 29 June.[161] However, Zeeland's dislike of De Groot's negotiations took a most curious form. In their anxiety, the regents had decided to consult the commonalty, and in Middelburg, more than a hundred of 'the most respectable citizens' together with the guilds, elected eight delegates to hold discussions with the town council. They learned from Van Borssele van der Hooge, just back from the Hague, that the Hollanders were no longer capable of defending themselves and were about to capitulate to France. He made no mention of Amsterdam's opposition, and held out no hope from the Prince of Orange, who was himself negotiating a *sauvegarde*.

According to Van Borssele, Middelburg had but two alternatives: to join Holland in submitting to France, or else reach agreement with England. France struck him as by far the better bet of the two. The citizens, however, declared after some deliberation that they would rather sacrifice their goods and blood for their liberty and religion; that they would have no part in any agreements the other provinces might enter into with France; that the assistance of the Prince of Orange must be sought – at the moment, the citizens of Veere had already compelled their government to proclaim him Stadholder! – and that if bow to someone they must, they 'would sooner choose to join with England seeking, under her protection, to obtain what safeguards they could for their religion and liberty'.[162]

These and similar provincial sentiments, however understandable, threatened to undermine what unity there remained. Only a broad political front could overcome them, and that front could only be presented by men who had outgrown their own narrow provincial horizons. One of these was De Witt; another was the Prince of Orange; a man like Van Beverning, too, had held office far beyond his native Gouda; Fagel, likewise, was now Greffier of the States-General first and a Haarlemer second. The De Huyberts of Zeeland were men of a similar calibre. In its protest, Zeeland now blew the anti-Papist trumpet for all it was worth, but its notes were anything but the simple provincial blasts of the Middelburgers.[163] In Holland, De Witt's proposal to make Amsterdam the seat of government was discussed once again on 27 June; it is significant that, whereas but a fortnight earlier, it had been well received by the deputies who represented Holland in the Generality,[164] now only Dort and Delft supported the plan.

Leyden, which was so anxious to reach a compromise with France, even at the risk of breaking the Union, was also loud in its support of Orange. It now contended[165] that the stipulation in the Perpetual Edict that the prince submit to the judgement of 'the political government' was bound to lead to confusion, and that 'the unfortunate movements' of the army were clear evidence of just that. There was a good deal of truth in this argument, but it did little to cool angry tempers when Burgersdijk, furious at the tone adopted by Hop, and blaming Amsterdam for thinking only of its own defence, introduced his proposal to abolish these restrictions with wild assertions that by ignoring Leyden's warnings, the States had brought the country to its present impasse, shocking and angering the neighbouring provinces. The Leyden proposals[166] were, of course, laid before the principals, and on 1 July, the day De Groot returned from his negotiations, they came up for discussion again.

By then, domestic disagreements were precipitating a major crisis: the Perpetual Edict was being assailed on all sides, and the States could not at once concentrate their attention on De Groot's message. Before I look more closely at this crisis, I must, however, just mention that there was never any question of an acceptance of the French demands by the States of Holland. Van Borssele, in his address to the Middelburgers, had not only forgotten Amsterdam and done injustice to the Prince of Orange, but had given an altogether oversimplified picture of the policy pursued by the majority in the States of Holland. When all is said and done, Pieter de Groot had not been given *carte blanche*; indeed, he had been handed conditions that had prevented a 'capitulation' and now that they were faced with the question of relaxing these conditions, the majority, and among them 'the most considerable towns', with the exception of Leyden, reacted with indignation. They said, as Fagel reported that same day to the prince,[167] that they would much rather be killed by the sword. Fagel himself declared that he would 'much rather, if it were possible, die ten times than become a miserable slave of France and bequeath to posterity the public ruin of soul and body, and these sentiments I convey to anyone I meet'.

The people act; Events in Dort and Rotterdam; The Perpetual Edict dissolved, William III Stadholder of Holland (4 July 1672)

Still, there had been cause enough for thinking that the regents of Holland had steered the country towards surrender, and what was worse, surrender to France, and citizens were not in a mood meekly to submit to the principle that 'the Lord God has pleased to endow the magistracy with judgement' and the people with 'the glory of obedience'.[168] And the regents of Holland were never the ones to submit their judgements to the popular will, as Zeeland had done. No wonder then that when the storm broke, it took such violent forms and that, though it was by no means the Loevestein regents who had been for a surrender or the prince-men who had called for resistance, the popular movement should have sought its salvation with Orange.

Rioting was rife everywhere. In Amsterdam, on 27 June, even old Johan Maurits was molested in the streets, and called a traitor. But the citizens, in their companies, had so far stood up to the mob which was incensed by the spectacle of the well-to-do taking their belongings to safety on boats and carriages. The cry now went up that the burgomasters were plotting to surrender the town, and that they had coined the slogan: 'Rather French than prince.' The people began to clamour for control of the town garrison and possession of the keys to the gates.

In Dort, there had been formal discussions between citizens and regents about the defence of the town, but on the 28 June, when the talks were resumed, 'some of the leading citizens'[169] no longer left it at polite arguments, but poured out into the streets. The Orangists seized the opportunity to ask for the revocation of the Perpetual Edict, and the regents were besieged in their houses with demands that the prince be elected Stadholder. Driven into the town hall under pressure, the members declared that some of them would forthwith wait upon the prince.

When the deputation left, it included town councillors together with representatives of the civic guard and the guilds and a host of 'landworkers and hotheads'.[170] The official delegates were so overcome by fear that they implored the young Captain-General, who objected that he could not possibly leave the army, to save their town from massacre and, on 22 June (the same day that Jacob van der Graeff was executed in the Hague) William arrived in Dort. He, no less than his pale-faced hosts, was bound by oath to adhere to the Perpetual Edict, and the regents thought that they could appease the populace simply by dining and wining their darling in *De Pauw*. But the people thought otherwise. In the presence of the prince, the civic guards, their pikes couched and the muzzles of their musquets pointed into the burgomaster's coach, challenged their leaders to appoint the prince Stadholder there and then. 'Gentlemen, I pity you,' said the prince. Back in *De Pauw*, a document was drafted, by which the town council rejected the Perpetual Edict and declared the prince to be Stadholder as far as it lay in the power of the town of Dort so to appoint him; at the same time the document absolved His Highness from the oath never to accept the Stadholdership – the presence of two pastors was intended to add force to that absolution, on the strength of we know not what theological law. All members of the Dort council signed the act; Cornelis de Witt, still ill in bed after his return from the fleet, did so only after much pleading by his wife, who crossed out the letters V C (*vi coactus*) with which the obstinate man had wanted to attest to his unaltered conviction.

In Rotterdam, meanwhile, the misguided populace tried to prevent the Commissioned Councillors from embarking for the theatre of war. Only with the help of a cavalry company that happened to be passing through (on 17 June), could the Commissioners continue with their task, but the uproar continued. The citizens, in their company formation, had gone out to build entrenchments round the town. First, they had compelled the government to let them do that useless labour, soon afterwards they were grumbling that it was too heavy. Their political attitude may be gathered from a message which Leonard van Naarssen, one of the most peaceful and respectable men among them, took to Burgomaster Gaalt on 25 June: he offered to put to sea and look for the Duke of York, the commander-in-chief of the English fleet, if only the town authorized him to announce the appointment of the prince to the Stadholdership, and to negotiate a peace; he was bound to be successful, since all the king desired was the protection of His Highness . . . The burgomaster then warned the zealous patriot that his plan was both 'criminal' and 'ludicrous'.[171]

Van Naarssen slunk away, but next day a number of his friends made their way into the town hall and asked the councillors for an oath that the town would not be surrendered behind the citizens' backs; and, after much talk, the council did as they were asked. Their authority was greatly undermined by the fact that Orangists among them were working hand in glove with the disorderly elements outside. Republican members, too, had by then come to realize that the Perpetual Edict was doomed, but found themselves between the upper and the nether millstones: they felt bound by their oath of 1667, and could not offer their resignation either – no regent ever resigned. Thus when Sonmans tried to tender his resignation and even withdrew from the town, his fellow members did not feel free to absolve him from his councillor's oath, least of all in this crisis: it was and remained his bounden duty to assist the council with his advice and vote. So highly did they, and many others, think of their responsibility.

All the more did the fury of the trembling multitudes rebound upon their heads. Their patriotic decision of the 25th went unheard, and next evening, when Pieter de Groot and his fellow deputies returned from the States of Holland, they were greeted with wild scenes. De Groot, in particular, was jeered: he had a clubfoot and, what was much worse, he was Montbas's brother-in-law, and there were many threats to his life. In the morning, he lodged a strong protest with the council, and demanded the arrest of some of the ringleaders. An example now might still work wonders on the rest. The council was full of promises, and pressed De Groot to ignore the insults and to continue with his work for peace; even the Orangists, who soon afterwards made common cause with the mob, did not dare to ask that his full powers to negotiate be withdrawn – and that was the main point at issue.

On 29 June, the news from Dort brought the rioters out into the streets once again. It all began with a group of civic guards. They deserted their trenchwork, assembled in the big church square, and challenged everyone leaving morning service (it was a Wednesday, but in those anxious times extra services were held daily) with the question: 'Are you pro-States or pro-prince?' A bookseller by the name of Borstius, son of a pastor who, instead of treating his congregation to edifying words, used 'to stir them up against the lawful authorities', now took the lead. A large mob surged towards the council house, and, fencing himself in against the vast crowd with walking sticks and bits of rope, the bookseller asked them to declare for the Prince of Orange as Stadholder and against the Perpetual Edict. When he was greeted with loud and repeated roars of *yes!*, the civic captains and lieutenants, accompanied by Leonard van Naarssen, called upon the burgomasters, pleading that they were acting under pressure, and urging that the council be summoned to prevent worse. And the council duly assented that very evening.

Burgomaster Pesser, loath to go back on his oath, decided to go to the Hague in person, there to obtain the assistance of the States. Since a coach would have drawn too much attention, he left quietly on foot and had already crossed the Koolweg Gate, when he was seen and brought back by the people. Amid taunts and jeers, he had to affirm that he was an Orangist, to swing his hat and shout *vivat Orange*, and with many kicks and blows and threats of worse to come, he was taken to the chief watch. The captain then locked him up in the cellar of the town hall, while upstairs the council, mortally frightened, and with captains and lieutenants walking in and out, swore and unswore anything that was demanded of them.

Next day, a deputation from Rotterdam went to the prince's headquarters at Bodegraven. One determined burgomaster – it was Vroesen, whose story I have broadly followed – saw to it that His Highness learnt of the compulsion under which the decision had been taken. Van Naarssen, who had come along with a number of civic guardsmen, shouted to the prince over the heads of the regents that the Perpetual Edict had been annulled; the prince simply nodded in reply. On the way back home, violent quarrels broke out among the motley crew of Rotterdamers, and the outspoken burgomaster thought it better to part company with them at Gouda and to go on to the Hague rather than return to Rotterdam.[172]

Yet Rotterdam was by no means satisfied. People were beginning to realize that their independent decision to make the prince Stadholder did not really get them anywhere. On 1 July, Van Naarssen, with two Orangist councillors, called once more at the burgomasters' chamber to tell the gentlemen 'that the citizens were beginning to murmur again'; they now desired the town to propose in the States of Holland that the prince be charged with the Stadholdership over the entire province. Naturally, the burgomasters and the councillors as well had 'once again to dance to the pipes of the mutineers'. That same afternoon, a deputation set out for the Hague to propose to the States the revocation of what had been intended to be a perpetual arrangement. Pesser, released the day before, was present, and who could more forcibly testify than he that all their lives were at stake.

Sedition had meanwhile spread over all Holland. Gouda and Delft were invaded by armed peasant bands. In Delft, the civic guards looked on from their water line, in Gouda, they offered resistance. The peasants were, in fact, far less concerned with rumours of surrender than with the inundation of their fields, but they, too, clamoured for the elevation of the prince. At Amsterdam, the rabble emerged from their slums, the women like so many termagants, shouted at a burgomaster who was about to board the mail coach for the Hague, that he was going to sell his country. That they did no worse, was only due to the fact that the civic guard still stood behind the regents and continued to maintain the public peace.

On 1 July, nevertheless, the day on which De Groot reported, the States of Holland had to listen to gloomy stories of sedition from Dort, Rotterdam, Delft, Gouda, and even Haarlem. And, to top it all, there were the deputies from Rotterdam, sent that same afternoon, with the 'complaint' that their council had been forced to promise the citizens to lay before the assembly the demand for the elevation of His Highness.

By the Perpetual Edict, such a demand could neither be made nor heeded. The States were in a great quandary. Burgersdijk, of Leyden, now the acting Grand Pensionary (in the absence of De Witt and of Vivien, who had gone home to deal with the riots) and speaking for the Nobility, suggested that all members should be given permission to propose whatever was needful to the salvation of the country; next, that they should release one another from the oath to adhere to the Perpetual Edict. Many deputies found this a hard pill to swallow; Haarlem, on the other hand, argued that their deputies' lives would not be worth a candle if they returned empty-handed. In the end it was decided that they should absolve one another from the oath, and, after consulting their principals, return in two days' time to vote on the prince's elevation.

The regents knew that they were beaten. In Amsterdam, Valckenier even proposed to leave the Perpetual Edict unchanged and to appoint the prince Count of Holland, but this came to nothing since people and regents alike had no wish to restore a monarchical system. The unhappy associations were still too fresh in their memory. And so Amsterdam town council unanimously revoked the five-year-old Edict, and it was Amsterdam which, on the evening of 3 July, a Sunday, proposed to elevate the prince to the Stadholdership. No voice was raised against this resolution, but several towns (Haarlem, Leyden, Gouda, Alkmaar, Schoonhoven, Purmerend) did show some reluctance in granting the Stadholder the annual right to select magistrates; in other words, they would not go back on the decision of 1651. But the Rotterdamers and other deputies warned that 'doing things by halves would only serve to incense the commonalty further'.[173]

And so it came about that, in the early hours of 4 July, William III was appointed Stadholder 'with the same prerogatives as his noble ancestors', and a deputation of eleven, drawn from the Nobility and the principal towns, was nominated to take the solemn news to the prince. Leyden's proposal that, in his capacity of Captain-General, the prince should also receive the right to raise levies had already been accepted by the States of Holland; moreover, the States of Zeeland appointed him Stadholder, as well.

Van Beuningen persuades the States of Holland to break off the negotiations with France (7 July)

It was not until late that same Monday, 4 July, that the States of Holland could give their attention to De Groot's report about his negotiations with the French.[174]

Again he was facing men who, a week earlier, had sent him on his mission in such a panic. If they now changed their tune – as Fagel had predicted on 1 July that they would[175] – it was because the French had proved utterly unreasonable. Leyden and Gouda were even now prepared to submit, and Gouda, in particular, took the gloomiest view of the defensibility of Goejanverwellesluis, a defence post just outside the town, and of the reliability of her citizens. Leyden, too, in a broad survey of her countless miseries, laid great stress on the widespread unrest, and Rotterdam agreed that the citizens were doing more harm than good, and that a host of militiamen had deserted their posts after reviling the government.[176] Even so, Rotterdam, for one, agreed that the conditions handed to De Groot were the maximum concessions anyone could reasonably be expected to make – the French demand for the surrender of so many towns and districts, and for the admission of Catholics into the government, which, as Haarlem put it 'forces us to live with the knife permanently on our throats', was utterly intolerable, and it was 'far better to die sword in hand'. The Nobility, Dort, Delft, and a number of smaller towns, all echoed these sentiments, with the result that, as we saw, the mood of the States was changed radically.

The time factor, too, played a part in this process. On 24, 25 and 26 June, a French break-through looked imminent, but the French had failed to seize their opportunity: Louis and his court had remained at Zeist, waiting for the States to come to him cap in hand. As a result, Holland was given a breathing space which she turned to good account. 'Matters,' as Haarlem put it, 'have been improving; the defences have been strengthened, the water has risen, the army is in better shape, and there is hope of outside assistance.' And though Leyden took the opposite view, the majority concurred with Haarlem.

And so the French demands were rejected, and the discussion now centred on the question whether negotiations should be continued nevertheless or broken off completely if politely. Amsterdam was for a break, and the sooner the better. At this point the meeting decided to consult the new Stadholder.

On 6 July[177] the discussions were resumed, but it was not until the next day that the scales came down heavily on the side of Amsterdam. Before that happened, De Groot, who still counted on being sent back to the French king, had asked that Van Beuningen be requested to accompany him. All the leading members assented, but when Van Beuningen himself took the floor he was able to change their mind. He called De Groot's entire mission a terrible mistake – far more had been promised than it was possible to give. The offer of the Generality Lands was bound to alienate the country's only ally, Spain, for the Spanish Netherlands were being placed in an impossible position. Moreover, no such offer should ever have been made without the co-operation of the Prince of Orange; Zeeland had been right to protest,[178] and the commonalty would rise up in arms. Let France, therefore, try to conquer by force and face the consequences. The Emperor, Spain, and the German rulers could not remain indifferent in the face of this aggression, and, above all, there was the chance that England would break with her French ally. De Groot must not go back, because he was suspected by the commonalty (one can imagine how the rest of the assembly flinched on hearing these forthright remarks). The members had voted in a panic and must now repair the damage. When Van Beuningen had done, the remaining members 'opined' with him, and decided unanimously to break off the negotiations. De Groot would go back, but merely to tell the French that their conditions were 'intolerably severe'.[179] Amsterdam was unwilling to make even this concession, for by sending De Groot at all the assembly was bound to give offence to the commonalty, but the others were adamant. For the rest, Van Beuningen had his way.

It was not only his eloquence which explains his success, nor Amsterdam's prestige. What counted for even more was that he spoke with the authority of an expert on international affairs, and that he enjoyed the confidence of the prince. He had come straight from the young man's headquarters, where he had joined in talks with Arlington and Buckingham, the English envoys, and it was clearly England alone that could now persuade the French to moderate their demands.

Arlington and Buckingham cheered by the people (4 July); The prince resists their bait (5 July)

On Monday, 4 July, Arlington and Buckingham landed at Maassluis on their way to Louis XIV's camp.

Could the Dutch really derive any comfort from this mission? Not if the reports that had reached the States of Holland from England were correct in any way. The special embassy sent following the resolution of 15 June (Halewijn from Dort and Dijkveld from Utrecht) had not been admitted to any negotiations – although, for fear of public opinion in England, they had not been allowed to depart either. It was embarrassing for the English that their French ally was making such rapid progress, when they themselves had no military conquests to their credit. Even so, they gave the envoys to understand that they were counting not only on the salute of the flag and a heavy tribute for fishing rights, but also on Sluis, Flushing and Brielle (in pledge) and on a hereditary position for the prince or on the right to appoint guardians during his minority. When the States received this news on 3 July, they must have wondered whether their hopes in the English envoys were not utterly misplaced. Indeed, the envoys might well be on their way to cause further mischief not only by arranging the partition of the Dutch state with the French king, but also by inflaming Dutch public opinion. This became obvious the moment they set foot on Dutch soil. One of the chief organizers of the Orangist movement in Rotterdam rowed out to take them the glad tidings of the prince's elevation,[180] and when they entered Maassluis, they were welcomed and feasted by the citizens as if they had come as saviours. The civic guard was drawn up, there were toasts all round, gun salutes, a guard of honour all the way to the Hague, to enthusiastic shouts of: 'God bless the King of England and the prince, and the Devil take the States!' The English themselves could hardly believe their eyes and ears. A member of the English suite, describing it all to a friend, expressed the fear that he might be taken for a braggart. 'Their hatred to them (the States) is growne soe great that wee want only an English regiment to reduce the whole country, soe forward they seeme to throw themselves into the armes of England.' The Prince of Orange, he went on, could only save the country by placing himself under the protection of England, and Arlington and Buckingham were both firmly convinced that he would do just that.

The moment had clearly arrived for implementing what had been so plainly intended by England in signing the treaty of Dover:[181] to use the Orange connection as a means of crippling the Republic. The signs could not have been more favourable. The people's mood was such that the prince, had he been so minded, could readily have played the traitor's part in which his uncle had cast him.

Learning from the English envoys that, on their way to the French headquarters at Zeist, they meant to call at the prince's headquarters at Bodegraven, the States-General authorized William to negotiate with them, and, as we saw, sent Van Beuningen and Van Beverning to assist him in this task. No towns, fortresses or men-of-war were to be ceded; nor would the Republic agree to an annual tribute for fishery rights, although talks on the last point might be continued. This the English envoys were told by Van Beuningen, who accompanied them from the Hague to Bodegraven. It was not much to their liking, but they still felt that they could drive a wedge between the prince and the States – one of their chief objectives.

The prince, they felt sure, would make few difficulties about handing over a mere handful of towns and villages. They had seen the Dutch fleet lying at anchor in the river Maas and had noticed how depleted the crew was, now that so many of the sailors had been drafted to the inland defences. 'If the Prince of Orange could be persuaded to send in the Dutch fleete to the Duke (of York),' Buckingham wrote just before leaving the Hague, 'and deliver up some townes into our hands, it would bee in my opinion not only the best way for us, but also the surest for him to finde his accounte in this businesse.'

That same evening, the two envoys had their first conversation with William – alone. When he reproached them about England's conduct of the war, they assured him, in strict confidence, that the king was determined that William should not be the loser by England's success. This was a telling retort – at least by their lights – and they were astounded to find that the prince did not see it their way. To begin with, he was unwilling to concede that England's victory was as certain as the gentlemen asserted. He said that help from Brandenburg, from the Emperor, and from Spain, would compel the French to withdraw. He went on to speak, as Van Beverning had done before him, and would indefatigably continue to do, of the dangers to which England exposed herself by supporting the French invasion of the Republic. (Dijkveld, who had come back to the Netherlands with the English envoys, had informed the Hague that Louis's quick successes were creating grave disquiet in England.)[182]

He was authorized, the prince told his visitors straight away, to negotiate an association between the two countries, and expected England to press France for a favourable peace. He expatiated on the extravagant nature of the French demands: 'They (the Dutch) would dye a thousand deaths rather than submit to them.' The English replied that they would do their best, but 'to make our termes goe downe the more easily', they asked that the towns England herself desired were to be given her 'as a pledge only'. The prince rejected this idea out of hand; the States would not hear of it, and he could not in all conscience advise them to do otherwise: 'Wee desired him to bethinke himself well not only to remove the warre out of his country but to establish to himselfe a soverainty over it, wherein both the kings would secure him from abroad and at home from all dangers. Hee replied hee liked better the condiçon of statholder which they had given him and that hee beleived himselfe obliged in conscience and honour not to prefer his interest before his obligation.'

Simple words – but noble because William III truly meant them, and courageous too, because he spoke them in times so critical, that the cynical courtier who recorded them for posterity could not believe that the prince was not bound to 'bethink himself'. At that stage, Van Beunigen and Van Beverning were introduced into the talks (the prince had to promise not to mention the offer of the sovereignty), and Van Beuningen, in particular, dwelled at length on the error of English policy. The envoys had expected just that from him, but were completely taken aback when they found that the prince, too, continued to stand his ground, and this despite the fact that, as they could clearly observe, his entire court was of quite a different opinion. 'Whether wee would or noe wee heard them wishing there were a dozen of the States hanged soe the countrey had peace and the prince were Soveraigne of it.'

Van Beuningen must have found the prince's stand most heartening, and it was with a good conscience that he returned to the States of Holland next day to advise them against further negotiations with France. No doubt he was deceived about the goodwill of Arlington and Buckingham, when he claimed that they would press the French to restrict their demands to Maastricht and the Rhenish towns[183] – if that was indeed their intention, they must have been sorely disappointed by the French response.

England looks to Zeeland; The negotiations continued; Treaty of Heeswijk; The envoys return (25 July 1672)

Whether there had been misunderstandings at Bodegraven, or whether Van Beuningen had deliberately painted too rosy a picture in the Hague, no one can say today.[184] What is certain, however, is that the English envoys, on their way to Utrecht and the French headquarters, had by no means relinquished the hope that the prince 'would yet listen to reason'. He, for his part, was confident that Charles himself was more likely to heed his pleas than the envoys, and accordingly he sent Van Reede, the son of Van Renswoude, on a private mission to England, ostensibly to inform Charles of the elevation, since Arlington and Buckingham had held out no hopes for a mission 'in favour of a peace on the pretended grounds of honour and conscience'.

At Zeist, the two English envoys now met Lord Halifax, who had previously gone there via Bruges, so that he might assess the mood in Zeeland. They had good reason to hope for help from that quarter, for, in late June, Odijk had invited his brother-in-law, Arlington, to a meeting in Sluis with a view to discussing the future of the province. Halifax had accordingly been instructed to sound Odijk as to the willingness of Zeeland to place herself under the protection of England. The Foreign Committee was aware that France might frown on this meeting, but consoled itself with the thought that, after all, 'Zeeland is our share'. Even so, Halifax was asked to be circumspect. At the same time, England instructed Sylvius, that notorious conspirator, to go to Zeeland as well, there to prod Odijk, 'his old friend', into action, and 'to undertake anything that may invite & encourage ye busying of ye Zeeland towns'.[185] Sylvius was to get more detailed instructions from Arlington, and the king himself intended to have a talk with him – such was the interest Charles attached to the mission of Sir Gabriel – Sylvius had meantime been knighted.

And what Halifax reported from Zeist, could only strengthen the impression that the Republic was ripe for the plucking – if only the Prince of Orange would lend a hand. Halifax brought back a 'formal resolution' by the Middelburg commonalty[186] that 'they would rather fall into the hands of the English than of the French'. That was hopeful news, indeed, the more so as the French had just decided, rather than force the Holland water line, to throw the weight of their army against Den Bosch: nothing but the approach of the hated French was more inclined to swing the province behind England.

In reality, the Zeeland project turned out to be something of a fiasco. To begin with, Sylvius got little encouragement from his talks with Odijk. 'I do not see that Odijk has either the credit or the power to form any scheme that would correspond with the king's intentions.'[187] Not that Sylvius looked upon the affair as hopeless; on the contrary, he urged Charles to make Zeeland an open offer of his protection, with guarantees to her religion and trade. If only Boreel in England, and Odijk and his friends in Zeeland were thus approached, the 'prince's servants and who lean towards England' were bound to bring the work to a successful conclusion.

And the English government continued to work in that direction. While Sylvius joined the envoys at French headquarters, other agents were sent to keep the Zeeland intrigue on the boil. Their leader, one Hartopp, relied on information from 'Deacon' Fletcher, an Englishman in Middelburg, who was very popular there and, moreover, on intimate terms with Buysero, the young secretary of Flushing and the son of the greffier to the prince's council. They had long consultations with a number of sympathetic regents, and were able to persuade some of them – including Fannius, who had previously been De Witt's confidant in Zeeland – to propose to the States that they open negotiations with the king's representatives then in Bruges. But the States refused to listen, and Odijk himself opposed the motion, although somewhat feebly.[188] Two obstacles proved insurmountable – as the English had already been warned by their friends. One was the presence of the States navy under De Ruyter off Schoneveld: weakened though it was, it would never willingly allow England to subject Zeeland. Secondly, there was the fear of the Orange party that the interests of the prince – of the Stadholder, to whom they had just sworn an allegiance – might be damaged by submission to England.[189]

In other words, Zeeland behaved much as Holland: she made her attitude dependent upon that of the prince, and partly feeling among the commonalty being what it was, had the prince only behaved as England expected, Charles would have surely had his way.

But after their journey through frantic Holland, and what with the hopeful tidings from Halifax before them, the English envoys had to acknowledge that William was quite unwilling to protect his own 'best interests'. At the same time, the French had scored so many resounding victories, and were in so jubilant a mood, that the envoys saw little chance of persuading Louis and his ministers to temper any of their demands. England's cause was obviously served better by sticking to her French ally at all costs, and then have part of the crippled Republic for the mere asking.

And so, on 9 July, the envoys sent three messengers (Sylvius was one of them) to the prince, with a renewed request for his co-operation, and a more precise offer of a reward for his services: the prince was asked to sign a declaration (drafted by Arlington in person)[190] that he would urge the States to accept what conditions the two kings might think fair and just, whereupon he might count on becoming sovereign over what was left of the Republic. In particular, all the 'cautionary' towns pledged to the King of England by the peace treaty, would become his sovereign possession for all time. Arlington, moreover, remembering the prince's unexpected qualms at Bodegraven, had included an unctuous sentence to the effect that the prince was in all conscience convinced that he could in no other way restore peace to his unhappy country, and that he would subsequently, as God had decreed, govern it in peace. In a covering letter,[191] the envoys assured the prince that they had done what they could for him but that, in the absence of a favourable response, they would be forced to advise Charles to take 'far different measures'.

And William did not yield. While one of his three visitors left for England to report that the prince was 'not yet' ready to listen,[192] William himself wrote to the envoys[193] expressing his surprise that they had not told him anything about their promised efforts to get the French to moderate their demands, and that his three visitors had only tried to convince him that the Republic must submit to whatever unspecified conditions would be imposed upon her; he must therefore request a precise stipulation of these conditions. According to Wicquefort[194] the door was still wide open at this stage. Thus, when the prince informed the three messengers that he had just taken the oath, and that they had come too late, whereupon Sylvius had ventured to remind him of the oath he had taken less than six months ago never to accept the Stadholdership, William swallowed the insult, and merely said he would see if the States were prepared to release him from that second oath as well. He added that he was not rejecting the offers of the two kings outright, that, indeed, he was very grateful for their goodness.

A week later, Syvlius brought him a letter from the English envoys written from Bokstel, the new French headquarters. One day earlier, on 16 July, they had fulfilled their real mission by signing a new Franco-English treaty[195] at near-by Heeswijk. In it, the two kings pledged themselves not to make peace except by common consent. Louis merely reiterated all his unacceptable demands, and the English raised theirs to include a large war indemnity and a claim to Walcheren, Sluis and Cadzand, Goeree and Voorne; they also demanded sovereignty for the prince of what would be left of the Republic. This treaty, and these demands, Sir Gabriel now handed to the prince, together with a letter from the envoys warning against all further attempts to foster dissent between the two kings.

Having composed this new ultimatum, the envoys made for Antwerp, where they hinted to Monterey that, were he to break with the Republic, he might be allowed to keep all the towns in the Generality his troops had occupied. If, however, he continued to help the Dutch, now that their cause was lost, he would merely be digging his own grave . . . It was at this stage (on 20 July) that Sylvius reported back to them, and what he had to say was not at all hopeful.

Sylvius had met the prince at Schoonhoven. William had been most reluctant to open, let alone reply to, the envoys' letter, unless

Van Beverning, Van Beuningen and Van Amerongen, the deputies of the States, were present as well. In the end, he glanced at the contents and expressed his bitter disappointment at the harsh demands: those of the French were extravagant, those of the English impossible. Never would Flushing submit to foreign rule, and the most the Republic might be prevailed upon to do was to offer Brielle, Sluis and Cadzand in pledge. He had expected far milder conditions and perhaps a recommendation to the States-General that he should be given the sovereignty.[196]

Arlington and Buckingham, who had all along felt certain that the prince would fall in with their plans, shrank from returning home without a peace. And so they decided to send the indefatigable Sylvius to French headquarters at Bokstel, with the suggestion that both parties should drop some of their demands. But the French were in no mood to make even the slightest concession. The fortress of Crèvecoeur had been taken the day before and Bommel had surrendered that very morning. Louis felt that, in these circumstances, there was no need at all to curry favour with the prince. If he had any proposal to make, let him send someone to London or Paris. Louis was about to return home; the English envoys, in his opinion, could do no better than do likewise.

The envoys had meanwhile been joined by two visitors from Holland. One of these was Van Beuningen, who tried once again to convince them that it was in England's best interests to side with the Republic against France. He warned them that his country, rather than face partition, would seek salvation under a single master, namely France. However, Arlington and Buckingham, who were certain that Zeeland was about to submit to them, brushed this warning aside. At table, Van Beuningen greatly irritated them by asserting that England could not exist for three years once Holland had been ruined.[197]

The other visitor had been sent by William. He was the young Rhinegrave, Charles Florentine van Salm, son of the governor of Maastricht, and to the annoyance of many people[198] one of William's closest confidants. He now bore the message that the prince was not seeking the sovereignty, but that he would readily accept it if it was offered him by the people. Let the envoys but tell Van Beuningen that this was what King Charles would like to happen, and it would come to pass. (We saw that William said much the same thing to Sylvius.) Arlington now pretended that, though this request was purely to the prince's advantage, England would nevertheless be prepared to make some minor territorial concessions. In the event, these turned out to be so insignificant that Van Salm could merely shrug his shoulders. He promised to put the matter before the prince and return with William's answer post haste. In spite of Louis's advice that they should go home, the English envoys decided to wait a few days for Van Salm's return. Their patience was rewarded with a letter from the Rhinegrave, 'with two lines of compliments from the prince, but without a word about affairs'. At this, the two envoys were 'greatly surprised'.

After mulling matters over for another day, they sent Sylvius back to the prince with a report of French intransigence and the announcement that they themselves were returning to England. The States might direct their answer to London, or Paris, or to both. It must have been on 28 July, when Sylvius called upon the prince with this message.

Campaign of slander; Rotterdam council in difficulties; William's intervention (7–10 July)

After Sylvius's first visit, Van Beuningen had already told the States to be prepared for disappointment. Even so, the treaty of Heeswijk must have been a crushing blow to them.

Luckily, panic had somewhat subsided, now that there was no longer the threat of an immediate French break-through. On 12 July, after Van Beuningen's first warning, Leyden had pressed for an agreement at all costs, on the grounds that there was a shortage of supplies and that things in general had come to an intolerable pass.[199] Now there was another danger: the prince's elevation notwithstanding, the commonalty remained in a state of turmoil and threatened the security of the state from within. The regents had bowed before the storm, but had not broken its force – the masses now clamoured for the dismissal of all those traitors who had been ready to surrender the country to the French, and of all those friends of the Arminians and the Papists who had made life difficult for the orthodox. Slanders rose from a whisper into a roar, and the attack which had previously been focused on the Perpetual Edict now raged even more violently against unpopular regents, indeed, against all regents, and the entire social system. And the alarmed regents of Holland and Zeeland came to realize that salvation could only come from William, the prince who had been raised to his high position by that same wild crowd and who alone had the power to calm their excited mood.

Events in Rotterdam were a case in point. A few days after the prince's elevation, the Rev. Borstius published a pamphlet entitled *Verscheyde consideratiën*,[200] which repeated all the distortions and lies rife at the time and which, moreover, was but one of a host of scurrilous broadsheets. It began with a historical review. After the death of William II, 'Liberty' had come to stand for greater freedom for Arminians, Socinians and other erring spirits, and for lesser freedom for the Reformed Church. Declared enemies of the church had been appointed as political delegates to the church councils or consistories.[201] The Act of Seclusion had been forced upon a reluctant Cromwell. Maarten Harpertszoon Tromp, the Orangist, had been killed in 1653 by a bullet from his own fleet, and so had his son. 'Rather France than prince,' had been the watchword of the States party. De Witt's Turenne plan of 1665 had been tantamount to handing the country over to Louis XIV. The English attack on the Dutch merchant fleet in the Vlie had been as heroic as the Dutch raid on Chatham; the English would have been as entitled to present their admiral with a gold cup, as the States were when they so honoured De Ruyter. Nor was the writer content to leave it at belittling De Witt's political achievements. He went on to hint that the Grand Pensionary was in possession of secret funds, which he spent as he pleased, and that he had deposited a fortune in the Bank of Venice. Buat's death was laid at the door of Paets, one of De Witt's chief supporters in Rotterdam.

The writer became even more vitriolic when he turned his attention to the war. England, he claimed, was being presented as a blackguard for declaring war on the Republic when, in fact, the Republic herself had provoked the collapse of the Triple Alliance. To prove this point, he repeated a story that Charles II had previously dished up in his final talks with Boreel – to the latter's utter astonishment – namely that Montbas had gone to Paris with Pieter de Groot for the express purpose of persuading Louis XIV to launch a common attack on England. Louis, generous man that he was, had revealed this scheme to Charles II; hence the latter's bitterness. Borstius admitted that Boreel had denied the truth of this accusation, but only because he had not been let into the secret. France, refusing to be bluffed with the threat of a useless

navy then drew up with her army merely to take what had previously been 'sold' to her (by the same men who were provoking
her; but then Borstius wrote for people who did not greatly bother
about logic). The defence works were in such poor shape because
the deputies of the States had taken bribes and then closed their
eyes to the defects. The commander of Wesel had been ousted
by a scoundrel.[202] The envoys sent to England (Halewijn and
Dijkveld) had not been authorized to make Charles any serious
proposals, so that His Majesty had been right in saying: 'I see that
the Hollanders are still as proud as ever.' (It will be remembered[203]
that the English government had kept the ambassadors at bay, but
had tried to hide this fact from their own people. We shall see in a
moment that Borstius's story about the ambassadors' 'misde-
meanour' came straight from the English propaganda machine.)
Even so, Charles II (whose generosity apparently knew no bounds)
had sent ambassadors to Holland (in fact, they had merely passed
through on their way to Louis XIV with whom they were about to
arrange the partition of the Republic) and, moreover, with full
powers to negotiate. 'The ambassadors themselves made no secret
of this fact, but those of Holland brushed them off with empty
compliments. What further proof is needed that they would
rather sell Holland to France than restore His Highness and choose
the side of England?'

The reader might wonder why I have given so much prominence
to so low and unworthy an attack. I have, in fact, omitted Borstius's
further references to French gold, and to godless burgomasters
worse than heathens and Turks, but I feel that to convey a true
picture of the prevailing atmosphere, it is not enough to drop
general remarks about 'dirty pamphlets' and 'disgraceful insinuations', as so many historians have done. My synopsis will have made
it clear that there was method in the slanderers' apparent madness –
just how much method the reader may gather from the riots which
broke out in Rotterdam when pamphlets of this type began to
pour into the streets.

We have seen how an Englishman, 'beloved of the commonalty',
supported the intrigues of Hartopp and Buysero in Middelburg. In
Rotterdam, another Englishman played an even more prominent
part in fostering popular discontent. Thus on the evening of 7
July, when Leonard van Naarssen, as representative of the commonalty, accompanied by several captains of the militia and 'a large

number of raving women', called at the house of Burgomaster Vroesen, he was delivering a declaration by the English merchant, Reeve of Rotterdam. In it, Reeve declared that he had dined with Arlington and Buckingham and that he had heard from their own mouths that, whereas the Dutch ambassadors had come to England empty-handed,[204] the English envoys had been authorized to negotiate a peace there and then. Reeve offered to go after them and beg them to return. To all of which, Burgomaster Vroesen rightly retorted 'that it was a sad thing to see that good citizens have been so misled'.

But Naarssen had come to air other grievances as well – the commonalty was demanding that the council rid itself forthwith of 'suspect' members, and that a number of 'esteemed' citizens be henceforth admitted to all dicussions bearing on the English negotiations. Next morning, when the council was about to send a delegation to the Hague in order to lay Naarssen's demands before the States, an excited crowd broke in and insisted, first that the delegates be changed, and next (to the consternation of Leonard van Naarssen, for Borstius's brother-in-law, William Bastiaans, had seized the leadership from him) that a list of eight demands be adopted forthwith. These included the immediate recall of the regular deputies to the States and their replacement by named substitutes acceptable to the citizens; full information about all negotiations with France and England; the speedy conclusion of a peace treaty with the latter, 'for which purpose ambassadors from England are at present in this country'; and the detention and expulsion from government service of nine suspect members and of their descendants until the fourth generations. The council realized that resistance would be useless, and Burgomasters Pesser and Vroesen, with two other councillors (the rest, including De Groot, were absent) surrendered their persons to two militia captains and were shut up in the aldermen's chamber.

It was all done in a jovial fashion. There was a splendid repast in which the burgomasters were joined by the captains and by friends. There was, however, an anxious moment, when the citizens confiscated a letter addressed to Vroesen, and immediately searched it for what they were sure would be 'treasonable' remarks. When the contents proved to be completely innocuous (the letter was a request from a cousin in Oudewater for hospitality to relatives fleeing from the French) the citizens rather sheepishly tried to seal up the letter again and handed it over. Vroesen, to guard himself against possible calumnies, had the contents recorded by a notary, one of the guards waiting outside with burning torches, and had the document witnessed by some of the officers.[205]

But the citizens were not always so reasonable. Some regents were roundly abused in the streets and even threatened with knives. Some of 'the mob' broke into their houses; others were repulsed by the civic guards. States deputies who crossed the town with orders for De Ruyter, were forced to reveal their highly confidential papers.

On 9 July, in the midst of all the excitement, Kievit, the refugee of 1666, suddenly turned up aboard a yacht belonging to the States of Zeeland. In a call 'to all faithful patriots',[206] he proclaimed the justice of his cause, and protested his love of Orange and of peace. On his arrival, he had been uncertain whether he could enter the town of his birth openly or would have to take refuge with the prince, but when his supporters, with whom he had kept in contact throughout his exile, came out to meet him in force, and when the civic guard fired a salute in honour of his homecoming, Sir John Kievit set foot on Dutch soil amid great cheering, wavings of hats and shouts of *Vivat Orange*.

Meanwhile, the prince had decided to heed the States' request and to do what he could to restore calm in the towns and also in the countryside, where the peasants continued to resist conscription and to hamper the work of inundation. On 8 July, the prince issued a very outspoken manifesto in which he not only threatened disturbers of the peace with dire punishment, but also expressed his clear conviction that no regent of Holland had been guilty of treason or underhand dealings with the enemy, but that each one of them had performed his duty as befitted 'a true and honest regent'. And when the deputies sent by the citizens of Rotterdam arrived at Bodegraven, proud of their great achievement, the prince dealt with them 'rather masterfully'. That, at least, was how Van Beuningen put it in a letter to his colleagues in Rotterdam, in which he was also pleased to suggest that it was he who had persuaded His Highness to adopt so stern a tone. Van Beuningen, moreover, drafted the letter which the prince himself sent to Rotterdam by the hand of a trumpeter, and in which William openly sided with the town council. When the trumpeter arrived on 10 July, the people at first called him an impostor and the letter a falsification, and there were wild scenes everywhere. De Groot, in particular, was repeatedly threatened and abused.[207] It was only when the delegates themselves returned with a severe admonishment to the people, on paper, to obey their magistrates and to let him, the prince, wield his office without let or hindrance, or else incur his indignation, that quiet came to prevail at long last.

Change in the Prince's attitude towards the regents; Charges against De Groot (20–23); Letter to De Witt (22); Cornelis de Witt accused (26 July); Developments in Zeeland; The popular movement

But were the regents really safe? Those of Rotterdam, and particularly the ones whom the people suspected, were so grateful to William that they sent three of their number back to Bodegraven with warm expressions of their appreciation and an invitation to the prince to visit their town in person, so that he might help to consolidate the return to law and order. Van Beverning gave them a most sympathetic hearing. He seemed most incensed at 'the impudence of Kievit's arrival' – Kievit, whom the Rotterdam regents had meanwhile assured that they would not oppose any favour the prince might care to show him! Van Beverning added that though he had heard His Highness speak of the Kievit and Van der Horst affair 'in a way that showed he felt they had been dealt with very unjustly',[208] now that His Highness had become Stadholder he would not want to support anyone against the law of which he himself had become the head; nor could he believe that His Highness would keep himself in power through mob violence and by giving offence to respectable people. However, next morning, when the Rotterdamers called on Van Beverning again, after he had spoken to the prince (who was still too busy to receive the deputation), they found him 'a good deal more reserved', and their eventual meeting with the prince himself proved a great disappointment. He interviewed them while on horseback, about to ride off to Schoonhoven. As Burgomaster Vroesen tried to open the conversation with a solemn address, the prince caused his horse to prance about so that the three delegates had to keep jumping out of the way. Moreover, the prince kept his head covered, when the three delegates had just seen him lifting his hat to a clerical deputation. And Vroesen had hardly delivered his address when the prince

put spurs to his horse, and called over his shoulder: 'I have informed your honours time and again that I cannot come; I simply
cannot come!'

Quite clearly, during the days following his elevation, other
influences had made themselves felt with the prince. This also
appeared in his attitude that same day – 15 July – when the States
of Holland asked him to sign a placard against seditious actions.
He refused point blank to let this placard go out over his name;
the disorders could not be stopped by such methods. He suggested
instead that a 'distinguished commission' visit the towns, but when
he was urged to accompany that commission himself, he declared
(and with some justification) that he lacked the time. His change
of attitude became even more obvious on 20 July, when he appeared before the States-General to communicate the new Anglo-
French demands and was invited to express his own opinions about
them.

He refused to do so, unless a number of persons were first asked
to leave the assembly. This was an unprecedented act of interference with the liberties of the sovereign States, and the deputies
of Holland, the only ones with the courage to protest, expressed
the fear 'that this might create further commotion'.[209] However,
when the subject was brought up in the States of Holland that
same afternoon, the Nobility proposed that the prince should have
his wish, and also that the exclusion should be kept secret 'so that
the persons concerned should not be exposed to scandal and mal-
treatment by the people'. Most of the members, Amsterdam among
them, refused to accept this proposal, and it was decided to request
the prince not to express his opinion before the full assembly, but
before the Commission of the Triple Alliance (a kind of Secret
Commission created in 1668). In the end, the prince did speak in
the full assembly, but only because the person he had had in mind
all along had absented himself of his own free will. But now
Haarlem declared itself dissatisfied – His Highness had spoken of
suspect persons in the High and Mighty Assembly: these must not
be allowed to return and should be punished. His Highness was
begged to name them, so that the law might take its course.
William then informed a representative of the States that the person
he had objected to was De Groot. Even then, he refused at first
to press charges, but merely hinted that De Groot had offered
France far more than he had been empowered to do. Although

Haarlem felt this was enough evidence to charge De Groot, the States of Holland considered the accusation far too vague to vilify a man who had done no more than his duty.

De Groot, however, did not await further developments. That same day, he took his family to Antwerp, thus avoiding violence but inviting slander. In a letter to the States, he complained bitterly of the ingratitude of his fellow countrymen; but it takes little imagination to realize that his escape merely served to add fuel to the fire of anti-Loevestein discontent.

A letter which William III saw fit to address to De Witt on 22 July had much the same effect. Ten days earlier, the Grand Pensionary, still recovering from his wounds, had asked the prince to clear his name of the slanders that the pamphleteers and others were pouring out against him, and in particular, of the allegation that he had embezzled public funds (the *Verscheyde Consideratiën* was not the only pamphlet to assert this),[210] and that he had neglected the army. On the first point he had obtained a public, if somewhat weak, refutation from the Commissioned Councillors, who declared that they knew of no secret funds that had been provided for him. And when William, too, gave his answer nine days later, he merely recalled the slanders to which he himself and his house had been exposed, and added that the pressure of his activities was such that he could not examine the charges in detail, but felt certain that the careful records which De Witt himself had undoubtedly kept must speak for themselves. It was anything but a glowing testimonial, and De Witt's enemies must have read it with the greatest of glee. 'On receiving this answer, Jan slunk away with a long face,'[211] one of them wrote jubilantly.

A few days later, Cornelis de Witt was seized in Dort and transported to the Hague (an extremely high-handed action by the Court of Holland which, in normal circumstances, would not easily have run the risk of stepping into the legal preserves of a voting town). Cornelis had been arrested on a deposition of an ill-reputed wretch, the barber William Tichelaar, who claimed that, in his capacity of *Ruwaard* (Governor) of Putten, Cornelis had tried to suborn him into a plot for assassinating the prince. The whole thing was, of course, nothing but a trumped-up charge, but Tichelaar had approached the prince and it was William himself who took the accusation before the court. The judges fell over one another in their zeal to earn the prince's gratitude, and at the same time to wash off some of the blood of Buat and of Van der Graeff. And so they seized upon the palpable lies of a notorious scoundrel, now basking in his sudden importance and patriotic fervour, and made ready to ruin a great man.

A man like Cornelis de Witt! But then, as far as Orangist fanatics were concerned, his valour at sea counted against rather than for him. We have seen how they were wont to diminish the glory of Chatham. Surely, a pamphleteer wrote, he had only fought the English out of hatred against the prince![212] In any case, the barber's charge must now be made to stick at any price.

As if to add weight to the slander, the Grand Pensionary of Zeeland addressed another protest to the States of Holland against the negotiations with France.[213] While Zeeland's protest of 29 June had been admirable, the new message was not only unnecessary but highly dangerous to boot: Holland was informed that Zeeland had never been willing to join in surrender; that she would never grant freedom to the Papists, who were being everywhere encouraged to flaunt their presence; that Zeeland would rather suffer the perils of the sword than charge herself with guilt, and so on. During discussions of this document in the States of Holland, Delft made the very just remark[214] 'that the Zeelanders contribute words rather than works, that they are deficient in everything, in raising levies, in reserves, in militia and naval equipment; that their protest has no other intention than sheer ostentation and the wish to whitewash themselves'. And indeed, these Zeeland petitioners were being harassed by their people. Early in July, the peasants of Walcheren had forced one of the gates of Middelburg, and with the help of local sympathizers, had done a lot of damage in the town. Their motive had been neither pure love of Orange nor pure hatred of France – in fact, when the representatives of the merchants and of the guilds called on the prince soon afterwards, with proposals for various reforms, all of these were directed against oligarchic abuses. Hatred of the regents, was also the cause of other riots in Zeeland – especially in Zierikzee, and later in Flushing,[215] whence a faithful supporter sent the prince an anguished appeal for help – and in Holland, as well.

Every now and again, the pamphleteers, too, spoke out against the regent régime as such. 'Liberty is our own priceless possession,' wrote a Rotterdamer, 'we alone elect those in authority over us, and from our midst.' But, he went on to say, for some time now 'they have been imagining that their power comes from themselves and that our Liberty is their exclusive property'.[216] In various towns, reform programmes were drawn up and either secretly distributed or pasted up, or even, as in Rotterdam, with great commotion handed by the local government officers to the magistracy. The citizens were quite suddenly full of grievances against their regents. 'A group of arrogant louts and libertines, who cannot read their own handwriting, has been pushed into office,' ran one Amsterdam complaint, or request,[217] as it was called, which was handed to William III on the occasion of his visit in mid-August.

The idea that the citizens might find their remedy in voting 'better' men into office did not seem to occur to most of them. Instead, they looked to the prince, and the first thing they expected of him was that, like his ancestors, he would play a part in the appointment of magistrates. Their deepest grievance was that all the important local government posts – at Delft, at Leyden, at Amsterdam – were being 'sold to the unfit',[218] i.e. to the non-Reformed – for the unruly middle and lower classes felt strongly bound to the church. This was also reflected in a host of articles against political supervision of the church councils – that great nightmare of the Reformed clergy. The 'unfit' also included the servants of the regents, most of whom were foreigners. They (the Mofs, a popular term of abuse for the Germans) 'know how to beg, how to stand about cap in hand, and have an iron cheek – that is precisely why they can ride roughshod over the common citizens'.[219] We must go back to the old charters, said the civic guard in *Wachtpraetje*, to the time when the civic guard played a part in the town's affairs; everyone's home must have a charter-book by the side of the Bible.[220]

The new movement was characteristically devoid of any constructive ideas; a further weakness was its dependence upon the mob. It was the mob which everywhere led the revolt, and the reluctance of the armed burghers to stop the excesses caused alarm in the town councils. Try as they might, with the help of militia officers, to guide popular discontent into more legitimate channels, the excesses could no longer be stopped. In fact, the burghers themselves included a number of violent men whose actions ran counter to their fellows' respect for order and authority.[221] Thus the arrests of leading citizens in Rotterdam, including

Justus de Huybert, was generally deplored even by some of the leading Orangists.[222]

William's secret negotiations; The seven points (end of July); Charles's letters (22 July and 10 August)

Nevertheless the rebels, encouraged as they felt by the support of the young Stadholder, soon grew more violent still. We saw that his attitude altered quite suddenly, and we must now look for the reasons that motivated the change.

Clearly, William was not swayed by any great love of the democratic, or anti-oligarchic, aims of the burghers, nor did he sympathize with their desire to reform the prevailing abuses of civic life. All along, his attention had been riveted on quite other matters: on foreign policy and on resistance to Louis XIV. What he needed, above all, was political power, and inasmuch as the 'mutineers' were willing and were able to help him towards that aim, he was not inclined to frown upon their actions. Not that William was hypocritical when he originally promised support to the regents;[223] he simply shared the views and prejudices of Dutch society in his day, and believed that the regents were the natural wielders of authority. But then England began to tighten the noose round his country, and when she did, William was forced to look anew at his domestic troubles as well.

We saw that, on 5 July, on the occasion of his first encounter with Arlington and Buckingham, he declined the offer of sovereignty outright. He must still have hoped that, what with France's rapid victories and the potential threat these posed to England, Charles would be anxious to achieve a tolerable peace. On 12 July, he was cured of that illusion by Sylvius and his two companions. What now? We saw that he immediately changed his attitude towards the States régime. It was not that he longed for the crown as such – he was enough of a realist to see that as Stadholder he could wield more genuine power than as king – after all, he had his uncle's example before him – and he realized that a royal title was not only unusual in Holland but frowned upon as well.[224] If, however, that was all that stood in the way of peace, he was willing to consider the matter. After the treaty of Heeswijk, the situation became still more serious, and William told Sylvius that he might now be prepared to accept the crown if the English were adamant on that point. He also sent his personal envoy, the young Rhinegrave, to Antwerp with the same message.

Meanwhile he felt the need to lay his views about the Anglo-French demands before the States-General. We saw that, after making some difficulties, he eventually offered them his advice on 20 July. He told them[225] that the letter from Arlington and Buckingham contained not one paragraph that he found acceptable. They ought rather to let themselves be hacked to pieces than accept such terms. Moreover, the idea that he should be offered the crown had been proposed by his enemies, not by his friends.

As we saw, on 12 July, after Van Beuningen had returned with bad news from Bodegraven, Leyden struck up her usual defeatist tune. Now that the terms of the treaty of Heeswijk were revealed, there was cause for alarm indeed! And yet when the prince made his forthright announcement there was no one to refuse his lead. Van Beuningen and the other envoys proposed to tell France that her conditions were quite unacceptable; the States agreed unanimously not to break off negotiations with England; and Leyden herself called on the assembly to heed the advice of the Prince of Orange, possibly because, like the rest of the members, she had just witnessed the ominous outburst of the prince against Pieter de Groot.

In the coming weeks, the prince went a good deal further in following the English on the dangerous path of private negotiations. All his hopes were now centred on a personal favour from Charles II. Had not Van Beuningen declared before the States assembly that the harsh terms were the work of the king's ministers, not of the king himself?[226] And it was on this slender hope that the States authorized the prince to persuade Charles not to ratify the treaty of Heeswijk.

This resolution was not passed until 10 August,[227] and we know[228] that Sylvius had called on the prince with the message that he should now address his own proposals to London and Paris, in late July. And it was certainly without consulting Van Beuningen or Van Beverning, whom he had involved so ostentatiously in his plans until then, that William had made these proposals. In any case, he was now acting on his own responsibility and although the conditions with which the States-General had presented him on 5 July were not revoked by the resolution of 10 August, the seven

articles Sylvius took away with him completely ignored the States'
restrictions. These articles were:

(1) The English flag to be saluted at all times. (2) One hundred
thousand pounds annually to be paid for the fishing permit. (3)
Surinam to be ceded. (4) Four hundred thousand pounds to be paid
as a war indemnity. (5) The town of Sluis to be given in pledge.
(6) The sovereignty over the seven provinces to be bestowed
upon the prince. (7) All this on condition that H.M. make peace
with the Republic and desist from giving France any further
support.

Not until some years after the death of William III was this
document made known to the world, and when it was, the enemies
of the House of Orange were quick to denounce it as a serious blot
on William's memory. Modern historiographers,[229] though unable
to suppress a note of regret and criticism, have gone out of their
way to blame William's action on the harsh circumstances in which
he found himself, and to explain that the sovereignty clause was
not dictated by William's personal ambition, but by his desire to
detach England from France. No doubt they are right, yet it
cannot be denied that the memory of William III would be fairer,
had he left it at his proud refusal to Arlington and Buckingham
of 5 and 6 July, or his courageous words in the States-General
of 20 July. No doubt, circumstances were critical enough to justify
any concession that promised to cut the tie between England and
France. Just as Pieter de Groot was entitled to present the threat
of an imminent French break-through as a justification for his
advice, so also could William plead before of circumstances in
mitigation of his attitude in late July, the more so as his offer cut
less deeply into the fabric of the Dutch state than De Groot's
compromise would have done. But it remains a fact that, on 5 July,
the States-General had expressly refused to pay a tribute for fishery
rights or to make territorial concessions. Moreover, it must be
remembered that, had Charles agreed to William's articles, the
prince would have become sovereign by the grace of his uncle.
And so, much as Louis's arrogant refusal to accept De Groot's
offer proved a national blessing, Charles's mistaken reading of the
situation helped to save the Republic and the House of Orange –
for the second time[230] – from the dire consequences of William III's
personal diplomacy.

For Charles II was not satisfied with William's offer. He continued to address his young nephew in tones of paternal condescension and superior wisdom. On 22 July, he sent Van Reede with two letters to the prince, which William probably received before dispatching Sylvius with the seven points. One of Charles's letters was meant for public consumption (we shall hear more about it), the other was strictly personal.[231] In it, the king warned his nephew against the counsel of his advisers (Van Beverning and Van Beuningen), and begged him to place his trust in his loving uncle, who made 'little doute by the blessing of God of establishing you in that power there, which your forefathers alwaies aimed at,[232] and I hope your ambission is not lesse, for being my nephew'. Soon afterwards, he sent Dr Rumpf with a reply to William's seven points,[233] which, he felt, fell far short of what he had expected. Moreover, his nephew was wrong in thinking that he could drive a wedge between England and France. 'Bethinke yourself well,' the kindly uncle continued, 'what will become of you, when the warr shall be ended, if I have not a footing in that country to stand by you against the designes and machinations of those that shall finde themselves throwne out of the government, to which they have been so long accustumed.' Nothing could have expressed more eloquently what William's 'sovereignty' would have meant in fact.

Alas, even Charles's rejection of the seven points, which was received in mid-August, did not put a final stop to William's dangerous intercourse with his uncle. Worse still, his secret activities forced him to be on his guard against the very regents of Holland to whom he had drawn so close for a moment. Now he turned on them the suspicions and resentment of the commonalty, for only thus could he be certain of facing them with the *fait accompli* of his assumption of sovereign power.

Opposition moves; Differences of opinion about the fleet (5–14 August); Anti-Orangist pamphlets; De Witt's resignation

His fear of States resistance was only too well founded. True, Wicquefort mocked at the slavish attitude of these heroes of Liberty, true also that on 8 August, the Council of Ancients in Dort – the town of the De Witts! – 'having observed in all the members a particular love and affection for His Highness and all those of his blood', saw fit to call on the States of Holland to provide the prince with a guard of halberdiers, and to beg him to take a wife as soon as possible.[234] True also that the burghers of Rotterdam showed an unseemly zeal in welcoming Kievit into their midst. However, when Haarlem turned so viciously against De Groot, the assembly refused to victimize a man who, they argued, had done no more than follow the instructions of them all. Even Amsterdam, which had disapproved of De Groot's mission and did not like him personally, now endorsed this stand.

Even Amsterdam, I say, for Amsterdam, on the whole, felt most kindly towards the prince. On 8 July, in a survey of the town's defences, the town council assured His Highness that they looked upon him 'as one on whom God Almighty has bestowed the neeful qualities to repair the country's sad plight by his wise conduct'.[235] And this was more sincerely meant than Dort's effusion of loyalty. In Amsterdam, as we know, many regents still shared the illusion that it was possible, and, indeed, good policy, to influence England through 'the interests' of the Prince of Orange. On 17 July, Hooft called on William with a message from the town council. If the situation was such that only a treaty could save the day, and if the prince deemed it 'necessary to have higher dignities conferred upon his person and to have his authority augmented, the town of Amsterdam was ready to contribute its vote in all good conscience'.[236] It seems unlikely, however, that when Amsterdam spoke of 'higher dignities' she was thinking of bestowing the crown on him.[237]

In any case, on 14 July, Amsterdam did not support Dort's original proposal that the prince be given full powers to conclude a peace with England. Amsterdam, in fact, held out against the proposal until 14 August, when the prince visited the town to restore order among the civic guard – or was it merely to show the burghers that he enjoyed the guard's confidence and was therefore master of the city? Be that as it may, the city was now sufficiently impressed to vote with Dort, but failed to budge the States.

At about that time, the prince came into conflict with practically the entire States of Holland – led by Amsterdam herself – on a point of vital interest: the deployment of the navy.

On 5 August, the States of Holland were informed that the East India fleet was safely back in Delfzijl, and immediately decided to ask the States-General that De Ruyter be ordered to escort the precious ships back to Holland. When the prince, as Admiral-General, was asked for his opinion – after the orders to De Ruyter had gone out, as he did not fail to observe[238] – he repeated his earlier advice that De Ruyter should be told 'not to enter into battle recklessly'. – The orders did, in fact, authorize the Admiral to attack the enemy if the latter should have seized the Dutch merchant fleet, provided only that this was deemed practicable by his sailors and soldiers[239] – a qualification which, in the opinion of almost the entire States, left De Ruyter sufficient leeway. They felt that to add the prince's further qualification would only serve to undermine the resolution of De Ruyter himself and his officers who were, in any case, inclined to be over-cautious.[240] The original orders were therefore left unchanged, and this in the face of Gorcum's reminder that should the navy run into trouble as a result of ignoring the advice of His Highness, the commonalty would rise up in a great rage. However, when the matter subsequently came up for discussion in the States-General, and opposition to Holland was rife, the province reluctantly bowed to the majority. De Ruyter received the new signal off Texel, four days after he had sailed out in accordance with the message of 7 July, and continued his voyage, highly disturbed by the sudden change. Meanwhile, the prince had learned that the merchant fleet was safely back, and he wrote from Bodegraven that De Ruyter should be recalled forthwith. Amsterdam and Rotterdam questioned the reliability of the prince's information; Haarlem, on the other hand, argued that the English were about to land on Walcheren, and that the defence of this island was, in any case, more important than that of the Indian cargo. Confusion now reigned supreme in the States of Holland as well as in the States-General. The majority had but one wish – to leave it all to the prince – and although Amsterdam raised objections, this was what was eventually decided. On 17 July, the States-General in the presence of the prince, ordered De Ruyter's immediate return. The new signal only reached the admiral when he had performed his task (without meeting the English navy) and would have returned in any case.

Must we seek the basis of this entire conflict in the fact that Amsterdam and the other Company ports prized their precious cargo more highly than the safety of Zeeland? We know that they did not believe the story of an imminent landing on Walcheren, and, indeed, the rumours proved completely unfounded. But we also know that the prince, despite his protest that 'the salvation of the navy is the salvation of the country', was most anxious to avoid any clash at sea, while there was still hope that his secret negotiation with Charles II would bear fruit.

At any rate, the incident showed clearly how impotent the proud and sovereign States had grown in their confrontation with the new Stadholder. Never before had it been brought home to them quite so plainly that this untried young man had a will of his own – unless it was in his inflexible refusal to come down on the popular movement with a firm hand. And the States of Holland, who had been able to resist Frederick Henry and William II, were unable to stand up to one who enjoyed the support of their own burghers – their abortive attempts to block his path merely strengthened William's resolve to thwart them.

However, as he knew full well, the political views of the Loevestein party were far too deeply ingrained in Dutch society to be eradicated overnight. Suspicion of the prince's English connections had become second nature to De Witt and his followers, and though they were ignorant of the precise details of his negotiations with Sylvius, they had a fair idea of what was happening behind their backs. The very name of Sylvius was steeped in unhappy memories and it was a bitter blow to read glorifications of Buat in all Orangist pamphlets, and a worse blow still to witness Kievit's triumphant return. At the beginning of August, the Stadholder, using his right of pardon, annulled the sentence of 1666, Rotterdam having previously declared that she would not oppose this step. Loevesteiners saw their worst fears confirmed in every new move the prince made. Envy of the noblemen in the prince's suite further intensified their distrust – I have mentioned the Rhinegrave and Van Reede; but there were many others like them.[241] And though the times were unpropitious for active resistance, with sycophants abounding everywhere, there was nevertheless a good deal of murmuring and grumbling, some of it quite open.

In his letter of 1 July, when the prince's elevation was still pending, Fagel had written 'that the present affection towards Your Highness displeases many people, who, however, do not dare to give public utterance to their feelings'. Instead, they belittled his actions, claiming, for instance, that his defence post on the Water Line was the most neglected of them all.[242] Nor was that the worst allegation. Thus a pamphlet which appeared early in July,[243] dwelled at length on a brawl during which some of the men had shouted that the surrender of the Rhine and Ijsel towns was the result of William's plotting with the King of France. Most of the States' party pamphlets – and a good many of these did appear beside the avalanche of Orangist broadsheets – adopted a fairly rational and conciliatory tone; they were chiefly written in defence against all the unsubstantiated slanders that were being repeated everywhere.[244] But some were aggressive rather than defensive, and in these the prince's English relatives were the main butts.

Thus one pamphleteer[245] called Borstius, the author of the *Verscheyde Consideratiën*, a Masaniello, an inciter of the people against their lawful authorities, and went on to give his own views on the historical background to the present conflict. He traced the links between Orange and Stuart to their beginnings; produced lengthy quotations from *Digby's Cabinet*[246] to explain the tortuous course of Frederick Henry's policy, and denounced the marriage of William II: 'We can still taste the dregs of his wedding cup.' This writer left it at that, but another roundly accused the prince of treason. His tirade bore the title: *Hollants venesoen in Engelandt gebacken, en geopent voor de Liefhebbers van het Vaderlant* (Dutch venison cooked in England and served up to the Patriots),[247] and alleged that William had begun to plot with Charles during his visit to England eighteen months ago. It was then that the prince had been 'filled with the hope that he might rule over the free provinces', on condition that he accepted his sovereignty from Charles against a pledge of Dutch towns. The entire war had been a sham (Orangist pamphleteers made the same claim but the culprits were, of course, different). The navy had admittedly played its part well, but only because William had been forced to leave De Witt in command. Even so, William had been able to frustrate De Ruyter's original plan by using his influence over the Frisians and the Zeelanders (who, as we know, put to sea when it was too late).[248] William himself had made haste to evacuate all the regions promised to Louis. Now he was doing what he could to deliver Holland over to England. After reading this, one is not surprised to find that an Orangist pamphleteer[249] should have pilloried 'the heirs of Barnevelt' for scoffing that 'now this brat of a boy has been made Captain-General over the army, it is almost as if the country had been ceded to Brandenburg and to England'. And one begins to wonder how much credence must be given to the testimony of Baron de W. (probably a south-Netherlander), who, on or about 10 August, sent a report to Arlington of an alleged conversation between himself and De Witt.

On 4 August, De Witt, now recovered from his wounds, had appeared before the States of Holland to offer his resignation in a most dignified and measured address. The misfortunes to which the state had succumbed despite all the preparations – he contended[250] – had caused the commonalty in their consternation to 'adopt a sinister view of the actions of their regents' in which he had so large a share that he could not, 'in all consciousness judge otherwise but that the continuation of his service as Grand Pensionary would do disservice to the common cause'. The Nobility thereupon advised the States to 'bow to the times' – De Witt's faithful service was no longer needed. The resignation was accepted and he was allowed to retire without a stain on his character, and was given a seat in the High Council of Justice. At that moment, Cornelis had already been locked up in the Gevangenpoort, 'in Buat's room' as a hostile pamphleteer remarked triumphantly.[251] The ridiculous slander that he had had to leave the fleet because of a violent quarrel with De Ruyter (they were said to have come to blows) was meant to blacken him in the eyes of those who were not yet prepared to count his fight against the English as a crime, but De Ruyter – a man of unimpeachable integrity and moral courage, furnished Johan de Witt with a letter openly nailing that lie, and moreover, stating that Cornelis had never shown less zeal against the French than he had towards the English. The slanderers, who did not yet feel the time had come to allege that De Ruyter, too, had sold himself to the French, merely scoffed that the style of the letter betrayed the hand of Long John De Witt.[252]

And what did Baron de W.[253] have to say about the mood and thoughts of the late Grand Pensionary when he called on him a week later? De Witt, he claimed, had attributed the salvation of the country – the inexplicable interruption of the French advance – to God's merciful intervention. He was clearly hoping that the tide against him would turn as soon as the people realized that this whole war had been planned during the prince's journey to England and during his subsequent talks with the Elector of Brandenburg. De Witt, the Baron concluded, still had friends enough in the government who were merely lying low; the prince would meet with stiff opposition and be in grave danger as long as these men were left in office.

Though the Baron was clearly well-informed, it is difficult to believe that De Witt should have spoken so freely before a complete stranger. But there is nothing incredible about the report of his distrust of the prince, or about his hopes for a better future. It is a sad fact that this true patriot should have continued to misjudge the prince to the end.[254] But then he had seen enough of the way in which the Orange-Stuart connection and the English subversion of anti-States elements had consistently poisoned the political atmosphere in his beloved country. Hence he was bound to be filled with distrust, and this attitude, in turn, explains the bitterness and the hatred with which the victorious Orange party set about the elimination of what few Loevesteiners were still left in office.

Charles II's letter to the prince published (15); Massacre of the De Witts (20 August)

Thus, even after the disappointing experience with Arlington and Buckingham, the Orangist campaign of slander, of whitewashing England and of inciting the mob to violence proceeded apace, and this with the clear intention of coercing the regents into 'changing the law'.

For that was what the entire campaign amounted to. Now, rigid though the constitution was – it barely permitted the resignation of a regent[255] – it left one loophole: the States had the right to empower the Stadholder to replace all officials of the sovereign town councils; the precedent had been set up in 1618, under Maurice.

In the new circumstances, however, such a step was fraught with grave dangers. Early in August, Van Amerongen informed the prince that Amsterdam was in a state of 'far greater confusion than three weeks ago';[256] only William's personal intervention could now save the situation. Yet when William visited Amsterdam soon afterwards, his presence in the city did not, and was, moreover, not meant to, strengthen the position of a city council that had done so much both for the prince and for the country as a whole.

In July, the author of *Den Grooten en Witten Duyvel* (The Great White Devil) who was not, as the title of his pamphlet might suggest, another cheap lampooner but, for all his fierceness,[257] a man of some culture and political understanding, still contended that, since the Prince of Orange had been able to give a clear lead to the better type of regent, there was no longer any need to punish the guilty ones, and hence for causing a violent commotion. In August, however, the same writer argued[258] that the prince had been precipitate in issuing his circular of 8 July. The regents had committed a long list of crimes (mostly unsubstantiated insinuations),[259] and while it was all very well to try to pacify the commonalty, the prince had after all been raised to the Stadholdership on a wave of popular discontent, so that there was a 'fair chance' that further good might come if discontent were left to run its course.

These were the kind of promptings to which the prince's suite now lent a ready ear. Was Van Beverning still trying to restrain the prince from entering into a compromising alliance with 'the mob' against the regents? Anti-States pamphleteers accused him of just that and depicted him as an evil influence, an accomplice of De Witt,[260] now the chief butt of popular discontent. The prince's lukewarm reply to De Witt's letter of 12 July was seized as a licence to utter the vilest slanders.[261] The glorification of Jacob van de Graeff came very near to a glorification of the attempted murder, and there were open calls for a more successful repetition. None was more treacherous than the *Missive van den Koninck van Vrankrijk aen den Raedpensionaris De Witt* (Letter by the King of France to Grand Pensionary De Witt),[262] which showed Louis XIV giving final instructions to his 'henchman' before returning to Paris towards the end of July. Louis congratulates De Witt on the rejection of the resolution of 22 July (the impeachment of Pieter de Groot); he is confident that De Witt will continue to spread confusion, especially with the help of Van Beverning, who is being kept informed of all French intentions and who is acting as a go-between. The expressions of dismay at De Witt's attempted assassination and of relief at his survival which followed, were so many invitations to fresh murder attempts.

It was in this atmosphere that a letter from the King of England to the Prince of Orange burst on the public on 15 August – the letter which the prince had received through Van Reede, before the end of July.[263] On 29 July, William had communicated its contents to Fagel, asking him to deal with them as he deemed fit. The Greffier laid the document before the States-General, who ordered him to return it to His Highness with their thanks.[264] However,

Haarlem – the same town that had called for the prosecution of Pieter de Groot; and is it unfair to add: Fagel's own town? – insisted on having it read out in the States of Holland as well. While it is not clear who was responsible for making the contents public,[265] whoever did so must have had the permission of both the prince and of Fagel.

The publication of Charles's letter was a shameless party manœuvre. Wicquefort wrote[266] that those responsible 'could have had no other intention than to bring the men at the helm into ill repute and to expose them to popular fury, with what dire consequences we shall learn anon'. Not that those responsible desired or even foresaw the massacre of the De Witts. But there is no doubt that by playing on the hatred and suspicion of the commonalty, they were doing their utmost to undermine the position of the regents of Holland, and that – to this end – they saw fit to dish up the enemy's propaganda lies. This fact alone made them responsible for one of the saddest incidents in all Dutch history.

For Charles's letter was full of accusations against the Loevestein party, which was falsely blamed for the entire war; Charles's continued desire to weaken the Republic by inflaming party passion was, moreover, clearly reflected in his praise of the commonalty for having effected the elevation of his nephew and in the mendacious promise that he would use his influence with the French king[267] on behalf of the prince and the Netherlands (how vague!), once 'affairs were brought in such a state that it will be no longer in the power of this violent faction, or of another equally malicious one, to dissolve and make fruitless what has been affected so far'.[268]

The people knew all about the letter even before it was published – Haarlem had probably let the cat out of the bag – and a Rotterdam pamphleteer summarized its contents as follows: that the king regarded his nephew as a son, that he had no grudge against him or against the 'good' inhabitants of this country, but only against the Loevestein faction. 'Should the commonalty ever get wind of this, and these gentlemen yet remain as obstinate as ever and refuse to resign their offices', then, indeed, they would have cause to feel sorry for themselves. And the author ended with a gleeful warning to the Loevestein regents: 'Uncle, you have lost your stick.'[269]

Meanwhile, excitement about the fate of Cornelis de Witt was mounting in the Hague. On 14 August, there was a rumour that the prisoner had been allowed to escape, and a riot was only just averted. Henceforth, the civic guard kept watch over the Gevangenpoort. Cornelis was expected to be sentenced any day and 'the quiet citizens' anticipated plunder and arson in case of an acquittal. 'The Councillors will have a rough time, however clear their conscience.'[270] According to Van der Goes, a Catholic and no friend of the Loevestein party, the Councillors were bound to acquit the prisoner, for they were clearly afraid to extort the truth from him by torture. In fact, the gentlemen proved him wrong, for though no damaging fact was brought to light against Cornelis – unless his reluctance to put his signature to the revocation of the Perpetual Edict be so considered – he was put on the rack on 19 August. His innocence was proof even against that: the torturers were unable to draw a confession from him, and the law required no less. The panic-stricken judges were undeterred. Next morning, they passed a sentence by which the *Ruwaard* was deprived of his office and condemned to exile – albeit they could not lay a single crime at his door.

That same day, a Saturday, the mob broke loose. Johan de Witt, undaunted as ever, went to the Gevangenpoort to fetch his brother home. Tichelaar had meanwhile been set free and now harangued the crowd that his own release was clear evidence that he had been wrongly accused, and that the *Ruwaard* had, in fact, tried to suborn him into a plot for assassinating the prince. Cornelis ought to have been sentenced to death, and his lenient treatment was proof that his judges had been Loevesteiners one and all. This argument was taken up by the mob, who shouted that the law had been broken. At first, they merely intended to hold the two brothers until the prince might be prevailed upon to appear in person, but a few firebrands called for summary justice. For hours, until late in the afternoon, the citizens, now drawn up in their companies, kept the square round the Gevangenpoort occupied, while the cowardly authorities, Commissioned Councillors and magistrates alike, were afraid to use the troops and, in the end, even ordered them to withdraw. Kievit and his brother-in-law Tromp were in the Hague watching it all with great pleasure. Their names and those of Van der Horst, Buat and Van der Graeff, resounded everywhere. At about five o'clock, the heavy doors of the prison were forced by musket shots and the two brothers dragged out and cruelly murdered. Their naked bodies were hung from the gallows and mutilated past recognition. A brisk trade was done in their severed parts.

The murder itself was committed by a small band of hotheads and villains – many of the crowd who witnessed the deed were filled with horror and indignation. Great, indeed, was the number and vigorous the tone of the pamphlets that expressed such sentiments.[271] The entire regent class, whose fearful passivity had made the horror possible, was profoundly shocked at what they now described as 'the execrable fact'. But the crowd which had all day long allowed the bullies and fire-eaters to cajole them and who, after the deed, had cheered Kievit and Tromp so enthusiastically as, marching in their companies, they had passed them by outside an inn, had lost all respect for law and order – fear of war, party passion, love of Orange, even religious zeal, had all combined to release the normal social brakes.

In the towns of Holland, the murder served as a signal for a general attack on the regents, and a witch-hunt for 'traitors' in every quarter. The pamphleteers shed what inhibitions they may still have had, as the mob indulged in what can only be called a savage dance of glee round the violated corpses. Perhaps the most shocking aspect of the whole affair was the way in which the clerical party greeted the murders.[272] Thus, when Pastor Simonides, now released 'from the yoke that he had borne so unwillingly', next day preached a sermon on the assassination, he called it a judgement of God. Revenge for Buat and Van der Graeff – that, too, was uppermost in the minds of all the firebrands.

And inseparably linked to their jubilation was the thought of England, of Protestant England, the land of Charles II, who loved the Prince of Orange as his son, who had just declared that he was waging war for the sole purpose of putting an end to the intolerable presumption of the Loevesteiners. To that false Messiah, that enemy of the Dutch people, the foolish crowd had sacrificed two men who had so faithfully stood up to him in the nation's best interest. The hearts of the late Grand Pensionary and the late Deputy at Sea were cut out and sold to England.[273] A rhymer summed up the popular hatred of the victims in the following lines:

> Orange they stifled,
> While Britain they scorned.[274]

As for the future, another versifier prophesied:

> Viva Oranje is now our shout,
> And who will not join us will feel our knout.[275]

In the absence of any official action against the criminals, the regents felt the ground giving way beneath their feet; their self-confidence already undermined by the collusion between the Stadholder and the popular movement, was now shattered by the prince's apparent unwillingness to apply the law in its full severity.

Intimidation; The resolution of 27 August; The 'change of the law'; Pieter de Groot's mission examined

William III used the murder and the consternation it aroused to further his own ends with cold-blooded lack of scruple. In this he enjoyed the support of Fagel, who but two days earlier had been appointed Grand Pensionary on William's recommendation, and who, on assuming office, spoke of his admiration for his unfortunate predecessor.[276] As soon as William learned about the crime, he told a States deputy that he saw no possibility of proceeding with vigour, seeing that the crime had been committed 'by the leading citizens'.[277] Again, when the Amsterdam city council, profoundly agitated, sent him a political lampoon pasted up in the Exchange and threatening to do as the Hague had done unless 'respectable merchants' were appointed as councillors, and a tribute were paid to the faithful Stadholder, 'so that he may be lord and servant no longer', the prince listened 'with little attention', pleaded lack of personal authority and the inability to deploy soldiers, and advised the city fathers to come to terms with the chief malcontents.[278]

In Rotterdam, where the position of the government was notoriously weak, the mob went into action straight away. The Sabbath was barely over, when the civic guards wrested control of the town from the impotent burgomasters. The captains then summoned the city council and handed the helpless assembly – some of whom were known to have had dealings with 'the traitors' and felt their last hour had struck – a document to be signed by twelve specified members. Needless to say, Vroesen and Pesser were included among the twelve. The signatories were expected to declare that they were resigning for the sake of peace and quiet, and to request the Stadholder to appoint their successors from a list proposed by the citizens. During the entire discussion – with the councillors not mentioned on the list of twelve wisely refraining from any expression of opinion – the mob outside kept howling that if the meeting lasted much longer they would come to fetch noses and ears as the people of the Hague had done on Saturday. Resistance was clearly useless. The captains and some of the citizens had meanwhile drafted a long list of suitable persons to which the remaining regents now added further names, until there were three times as many candidates as there were vacancies. The list was submitted to the prince who let his choice be known by 25 August, thus lending his authority to the demands of the mob. Kievit headed his list; Leonard van Naarssen and Willem Bastiaans were two of his other choices.

Dort, Leyden, Delft and even Orangist Haarlem, all witnessed commotion among the civic guard; in other towns, the main threat came from the peasantry. On 26 August, Fagel thought it was time that the States of Holland granted the prince a general authorization for 'changing the law'. The proprieties, he felt, must be observed even now, and the first move would clearly have to come from the Commissioned Councillors. These men, who had behaved so feebly on the 20th, now declared they felt apprehensive about the adjournment of the States assembly; as Councillors, they were now responsible for maintaining order and they did not feel equal to the task. They accordingly advised the States to ask the prince to intercede with the commonalty, at the same time authorizing him 'to persuade those regents who were most offensive to the public to take their leave from the government'.[279] The new Grand Pensionary reported that he had consulted His Highness, who had, however, been unwilling to commit himself (was that necessary when events at Rotterdam spoke so plainly?); he was ready to do what the States judged best – (except taking vigorous action against the rioters) – meanwhile, he was of the opinion that many of the accused regents were quite innocent.[280] Even so, it took some persuading before the States were prepared to place themselves so unconditionally into His Highness's hands. In particular, Fagel had to threaten them in the friendliest manner that 'it was far better to forgo a mere formality than allow the commonalty to impose order'. And so, on 27 August, it was resolved to authorize the prince, in all towns where 'difference' or 'murmuration' was rife, to attempt, at the request of the town government, *of the citizens, or even on his own initiative*, to persuade the people that their displeasure was groundless and, in case he failed therein, 'to persuade, direct, or if need be force the regents in question to resign from the government without suffering any injury, the prince being requested to take them under his protection'.[281]

And now the ball started rolling in earnest. Town after town called for the prince's intervention, and a host of regents were dismissed and replaced by others. Sometimes this was done under the pressure of a genuine popular outburst, as in Rotterdam. At Gouda, however, the council took the momentous decision after nothing more untoward had happened than that unknown persons had pushed a list of unpopular regents under a burgomaster's door. Still, it would be wrong to think that the commonalty got the better of authority throughout the land – wherever the town council was united, it generally carried enough prestige to maintain itself. In most places, however, the council was packed not only with frightened men but also with self-seekers who looked to the prince to further their petty ambitions.

This is, for instance, what happened in Amsterdam, as Bontemantel's records show only too clearly.[282] According to him, there had been no need at all to appeal to the prince against the lampoon of 23 August, which was merely the work of a few agitators. The main problem in Amsterdam was not so much the mob as Valckenier, who was taking revenge for his defeat of eighteen months ago. Then, in early September, Van Beverning came back, and he was quick to surmount his initial reluctance against employing the mob. 'This favourite of His Highness,' as Bontemantel later discovered, informed one of his relatives, Burgomaster Hooft, that the prince would not be satisfied until the whole council had resigned, and that the council had better be warned by the example of the Hague. In the streets, meanwhile, the mob indulged in a few bouts of shouting and stone-throwing, and Burgomaster Van de Poll was wrongly decried as a traitor who had wanted to surrender the town at the end of June. But on the whole, the city remained peaceful and there was no pressure on the burgomasters to act as they did when, on 5 September, they proposed to offer their collective resignation to His Highness. The pensionary, Hop (whose bold conduct in the States on 25 and 27 June will be remembered), refused 'after long and excited nay, tearful speeches' to transmit this message; his colleagues' cowardice was too patent for him: 'I cannot understand why the members are acting in this way . . . seeing that the citizens still respect their authority, there is no possible justification for surrendering the government.' The report adds that 'he was so overcome with emotion that he became speechless'.

It was only after this ignominious resolution had been taken that the citizens became agitated. Moreover, those who flocked to the town hall as representatives of the commonalty were so unrepresentative of the latter that even the prince ignored them – from the list of recommendations they drew up, he picked only one for the sixteen vacancies he had created. More, a countermovement was got up: several civic companies joined forces to draw up petitions for the retention of dismissed members. There were indignant rumours that the entire change of officials had been the work of Valckenier – all those dismissed from office were precisely the men who had voted against him in February 1671.

A bitter Placard[283] dealing with the dismissal of the Amsterdam magistracy, alleged that Van de Poll had been removed simply 'because he had protested against the surrender of the country'. Several others were mentioned in much the same vein. On the other hand, we might point out that one man who, on 26 June, had exclaimed: 'Better half an egg than an empty shell,'[284] was still a councillor when the rest was no longer there.

Nor does this remark apply to Amsterdam alone – the new régime could not have survived strict scrutiny of all its representatives' behaviour in June. We saw[285] how Rotterdam Council, at the height of the first commotion, forgot all party bias when it came to persuading Pieter de Groot not to give up his mission. Or take Leyden. Here the malcontents among the citizens[286] were loud in their protest against 'those among the magistracy who were of the Arminian and Loevestein faction and rather French than prince' and who 'were therefore the chief reason why Pieter de Groot had been sent to the King of France', adding all sorts of particulars of which we knew that they were completely untrue. Moreover, as we also know, it was not the Loevestein party, but Pensionary Burgersdijk who, in the critical days of June, had been a leader among the defeatists. Well, Burgersdijk, too, had survived the change. Pieter de Groot's mission had helped to stir up the commonalty. But then the touchstone had been peace with France, while now it was blind obedience to the Prince of Orange.

Blind obedience not so much to what he was thought to stand for, as for what he himself deemed best. To that end, he allowed those regents who stayed at their post (everywhere the majority, and sometimes the large majority), together with the newly appointed men (few of whom were on the side of the people) to govern the towns no less freely than the regents had done before them. Haarlem was a case in point. Here the civic guard and burgher committees had compelled the council to resign with threats of violence, and then sent for orders from their beloved Stadholder, in the confident expectation that he would back their truly revolutionary, provisional government. But William took quite a different view of the regents of Haarlem than he did of those from Rotterdam. The former had always served him loyally in the States assembly, and so the joy of the burghers was of short duration. The entire Haarlem regency was restored with only one exception. Nor did the citizens of towns in which the regents were replaced have much greater cause for celebration. Sometimes the new members (as, for instance, Kievit and his comrades in Rotterdam) turned out to be thoroughly corrupt. Those who had democratic hopes in the new régime were quickly disappointed – they received little sympathy from William. Now that he had succeeded in making the change of régime, the gulf between the oligarchy and the man in the street was still as large as ever it had been.

REFERENCES

1. *Briefwisseling van Huygens*, VI, p. 235.
2. The words 'plot' and 'surprised' are used in a vehemently anti-Orangist pamphlet entitled *Zeeuwse vreugde* etc., Knuttel 9675, p. 28. The view that the regents were divided in their sentiments, but did not dare to show them, was expressed in an anonymous letter to the Dowager, Aitzema, XIV, 510 f.; cf. Aitzema's own comment: p. 522 f.
3. *Zeeuwse vreugde* etc., p. 26.
4. XIV, 523.
5. *Zeeuwse vreugde* etc., p. 16.

6. XIV, 522.
7. *Brieven aan De Witt*, III, p. 440 f.
8. *Brieven aan De Witt*, II, p. 418.
9. *Resolutiën van Consideratie*, p. 827.
10. Japikse, *Prins Willem III*, I, p. 146: Courtenay, *Life of Temple*, II, p. 393.
11. *Arlington's Letters*, I, p. 350.
12. Acting on Temple's report, the Foreign Committee decided that the King should 'take no notice of what has yet passed from those of Zealand to ye Pr of Orange'; and Temple was instructed to repeat his assertion that neither the English government nor Boreel had had any knowledge of the plan; Goodison.
13. On 18 April and on 30 August 1668: S.P.F., Holland; Goodison.
14. Boreel to Lauderdale, 13 September 1668: B.M., Add. Mss., 22878; Goodison.
15. *Arlington's Letters*, I, p. 360. – Dr. Japikse (*Prins Willem III*, I, p. 149) writes: 'Temple, impressed by the strong Orangist movement and the person of the Prince, asked for support of William's appointment as Captain- and Admiral-General, but the proposal was rejected in London.' This claim is based on the minutes of the Committee of Foreign Affairs on 23 and 25 October and on 10 November OS: Temple's own letter proposing the scheme is missing. The minutes say that Temple had devised the scheme 'from his owne reasonings; tho' he found severall of ye States of that mind. That ye Prince himselfe . . . (illegible) would not be contrary to it'. (According to Goodison.) I am inclined to think that Temple's proposition involved support for the Harmony Project, as a means of speeding up the Prince's appointment. There is no evidence of 'a strong Orangist movement' nor does it appear that Temple contrived his plan 'impressed by the Prince's personality'.
16. On 27 October 1668, to Arlington; Goodison.
17. See his letters, in *Correspondentie van Willem III en H. W. Bentinck*, II², p. 9 ff. P. de H. reminded the Prince of his faithful services against all 'reproaches, nay threats of others' and moreover at a time when virtually everyone else had abandoned him (the P.), while he 'as becomes people of quality and honour' had never haggled over his services.
18. *Briefwisseling van Huygens*, VI, p. 245.
19. See Japikse, *Prins Willem III*, pp. 116 seq., 152 seq.
20. See his assurances in 1667, mentioned on p. 264. Dr. Japikse takes these, rather too readily, as the expression of William's deepest conviction: *Prins Willem III*, I, p. 137.
21. Lefèvre-Pontalis, *op. cit.*, II, p. 85.

22. Chap. 1, Part II: 'That in a free Republic no one has any right to high dignities by virtue of his birth, etc.': p. 46.

23. This fact was remarked upon in newsletters from the Republic on 29 March, 16 April, 4 June, and in a letter from Temple of 17 May 1669: S.P.F., Holland and Newsletters, Holland; Goodison.

24. *Correspondentie van Willem III en H. W. Bentinck*, II², 17, note 1.

25. On p. 280.

26. Bontemantel, *Resolutiën Raad*, cited by C. G. Smit, *Notulen gehouden ter vergadering der Staten van Holland in 1670 door Hans Bontemantel*, p. XVIII. My account of the subsequent events in the Holland States is based on Bontemantel's minutes as edited by Dr. Smit.

27. C. G. Smit, *op. cit.*, p. 53.

28. *Corr. van Willem III en van Bentinck*, II², pp. 22 seq.

29. In a detailed account of the Prince's position since 1668 (composed on 24 June 1670 by request of Arlington; Goodison), Temple wrote that Amsterdam decided the issue by bribing Schoonhoven. Bontemantel's minutes prove decisively that this story is false. When the votes were taken for the first time, on 19 April, Schoonhoven had already been one of the five towns to vote in favour of a decisive 'voice' (Amsterdam, Haarlem, Leyden, Enkhuizen and Schoonhoven).

30. C. G. Smit, *op. cit.*, pp. 118, 123.

31. Wagenaar, *Vaderlandsche Historie*, XIII, p. 432.

32. Van Boetselaer van Asperen to De Witt, 7 June 1670: *Brieven van De Witt*, II, p. 506.

33. Wicquefort, *Histoire des Provinces-Unies*, IV, p. 141.

34. *Brieven van De Witt*, IV, p. 48.

35. Temple to Arlington, 17 June 1670: S.P.F., Holland, 186; Goodison.

36. C. G. Smit, *op. cit.*, pp. 145, 167.

37. So Temple suggested in his report of 24 June 1670 (see note 29). In a letter of 24 December 1669 to Arlington, *Works*, II, p. 91, he spoke of *Leyden*, Dort and Rotterdam – Leyden was clearly a mistake.

38. According to L. Reynst, 2 September 1667: *Brieven aan De Witt*, II, p. 417.

39. Bontemantel, *De regeeringe van Amsterdam*, ed. Kernkamp, II, p. 157.

40. Lefevre-Pontalis, *op. cit.*, II, p. 33.

41. Newsletter (French), 23 May 1670: Newsletters, Holland, p. 53; Goodison. According to Bontemantel's minutes (C. G. Smit, *op. cit.*, 136) Rotterdam claimed that it would be 'ridiculous' to send

Van Beuningen or anyone else, while there was constant disagreement.

42. Temple to Arlington, 16 May 1670; S.P.F., Holland, 186; Goodison.

43. 16 May OS 1670, *Arlington's Letters*, I, p. 434.

44. *Ibid.*

45. Somewhat later – on 6 June 1670 – Temple again described Van Beuningen as a 'fort honneste homme, one that putts all the good of his countrey' in the alliance with England 'and who upon the Prince's occasions will deserve the good-will of our Courte'. However, he 'is not alwaies so willing to heare as to be hearde, and out of the abundance of his reasoning is apt sometimes to reason a man to death'; to Arlington, S.P.F., Holland, 186; Goodison. The same observation was made by others; thus Lionne wrote to the French ambassador in England (Colbert de Croissy): 'C'est un grand hâbleur et pressant dans ses raisonnements' (Mignet, *Négociations relatives à la succession d'Espagne*, III, 182).

46. Mignet, *op. cit.*, III, p. 187 ff.

47. Mignet, *op. cit.*, III, p. 122.

48. *Ibid.*, p. 128.

49. Charles himself said something of the kind to the ambassador, when he told him 'that that stipulation would raise no difficulties, that he only had it inserted to let the Prince know that he does not abandon him and to stir up dissension among the States': *ibid.*

50. *Works*, II, p. 164.

51. *Brieven aan De Witt*, II, p. 486.

52. C. G. Smit, *Bontemantel's notulen . . . 1670*, p. 200.

53. *Arlington's Letters*, I, p. 430.

54. *Ibid.*, p. 435.

55. Temple wrote that she 'very little favors his journey into England, and whether her opinions will advantage his affaires heere I cannot say': 21 April 1670, S.P.F., Holland, p. 186; Goodison.

56. Newsletter of 11 April 1670: 'Les intrigues qu'il fera hors du païs luy feroit aussy perdre des amys': Newsletters, Holland, p. 53; Goodison.

57. Newsletter of 11 April 1670: Pomponne 'a fait assurer M. le Prince que Madame aura des ordres particuliers pour luy dont il aura sujet d'estre satisfait'; Newsletters, Holland, 53; Goodison. In his history, Wicquefort added that the ambassador promised the Prince a change in his fortunes and an inevitable change in the state as a result of these decisions. A remark like this, made in the light of later events, hardly inspires confidence. The more guarded newsletter of 11 April 1670, on the other hand, is absolutely trustworthy.

58. Newsletter of 10 July 1670; Newsletters, Holland, p. 53; Goodison.
59. Temple to Arlington, 17 June 1670, S.P.F., Holland, p. 186; Goodison.
60. *Correspondentie van Willem III en H. W. Bentinck*, II, p. 26.
61. Report by Rumpf, p. 28 ff.
62. *Brieven van De Witt*, IV, p. 93.
63. L. Sylvius, *Historiën onzes tijds* (sequel to Aitzema; Aitzema had died in 1669), I, p. 133, mentions Brederode, Obdam, Van Zuylestein, two Barons van Gent, Van Valkenburg. According to a note by Wicquefort (*Histoire*, IV, p. 122) many of the 'volontaires' returned home when the Prince tarried beyond expectation.
64. Not so much to avoid giving offence to the Hague, as Japikse supposes (*Prins Willem III*, I, p. 167) as to avoid compromising himself by the inevitable failure of the negotiations.
65. *Arlington's Letters*, II, p. 312.
66. Barbour, *op. cit.*, pp. 170 seq.
67. *History of his own times* (ed. O. Airy), I, p. 495.
68. Dalrymple, *Memoirs of Great Britain and Ireland* (1773), II, p. 79; this contains the earliest abstracts from the correspondence of the French ambassadors in England with Louis XIV.
69. The article in the treaty, that the stipulation about the Prince ought not to hamper Charles's declaration of war on the Republic, was found in a 'separate article' and not in the treaty proper. The only explanation for this is that the English must have feared the bad impression this article would make on the Prince and his confidants. On 24 April 1670, Colbert de Croissy wrote: 'Ils ont dit que cet adjousté (?) destruieroit entièrement le bon effet de cette stipulation': B.M., Basquet Transcripts (copies of French diplomatic correspondence from England), pp. 3, 124; Goodison.
70. Dalrymple, *op. cit.*, II, p. 49.
71. *Histoire*, IV, footnote p. 122.
72. *Brieven aan De Witt*, II, p. 542 seq.
73. *Brieven aan De Witt*, IV, p. 161.
74. See p. 316.
75. Bontemantel, *Regeering van Amsterdam*, II, p. 157.
76. *Ibid.*, II, p. 168.
77. On 6 and 17 February 1671: Newsletter, Holland, p. 54; Goodison.
78. *Brieven van De Witt*, IV, p. 160.
79. According to the writer of the newsletters mentioned in note 77, by the Dowager.
80. 'J'ay esté marri d'apprendre par la lettre que vous avez pris la peine de m'escrire que Sa Majesté a rapellé M. Temple; j'ay peur que cela n'est un mechant signe': S.P.F., Holland, p. 187; Goodison.

81. *Correspondentie van Willem III en H. W. Bentinck*, III, p. 37 and insertion p. 39.

82. Newsletter of 13 January 1671; Newsletters, Holland, p. 54; Goodison.

83. 'Depuis que l'on est icy prévenu de l'opinion que l'Angleterre a voulu stipuler quelque chose à l'avantage de M. le Prince d'-Orange, la Hollande s'en esloigne tout à fait, et c'est la raison pourquoy l'on envoya ordre à M. Boreel, il y a quelque temps, que si les Ministres de l'Angleterre prétendoient stipuler quoique ce soit à l'occasion de la plus estroitte alliance, il eust à déclarer que l'on n'en feroit rien': Newsletters, Holland, p. 54: 12 June 1671; Goodison.

84. The reason why this fact was not recorded in the States resolutions, and why so many historians are unaware of it; there are, however, several (incorrect) allusions in Van der Goes' *Briefwisseling*. Japikse supposes that Gelderland did not broach the matter until November (*Prins Willem III*, I, p. 174). My particulars are taken from Newsletters, Holland, p. 54; Goodison.

85. *Briefwisseling van de gebr. Van der Goes*, II, p. 289, 321.

86. *op. cit.*, II, p. 304.

87. 'There are some who think that matters will not be mended, until the Prince have the credit': *op. cit.*, II, p. 263.

88. De Witt himself mentioned this fact in his summary of the 'spacious and fallacious arguments' by the Prince's advocates: *Brieven*, IV, p. 178.

89. Resolutiën Raad, in *Brieven van De Witt*, IV, p. 217 note.

90. *Brieven aan De Witt*, II, p. 595.

91. Lefèvre-Pontalis, *op. cit.*, II, p. 105.

92. 'L'on ne doute pourtant point que l'on trouve quelque expédient pour achever cette affaire à la satisfaction de son Altesse, Mssrs Les Etats espérant par ce moyen-là de faire cognoistre au Roy qu'ils sont disposez à luy donner toute sorte de satisfaction sur ses demandes, n'y ayant personne qui aye voulu accepter l'Ambassade qu'ils destinent pour l'Angleterre sans que ceste affaire ne soit auparavant achevée': S.P.F., Holland, p. 188: 19 January 1672; Goodison; cf. Newsletters, Holland, p. 55: 22 January; *ibid*.

93. In Goodison.

94. In the letter to William mentioned on p. 335, Charles explained that his inactivity was due to his fear that open pressure might damage William's prospects; an obvious insincerity.

95. This claim is corroborated by De Witt: *Brieven*, IV, p. 179; Boreel pressed the matter persistently.

96. Barbour, *op. cit.*, p. 182.

97. S. P. F., Holland, p. 188: received 19 January OS 1672; Goodison.
98. Keith Feiling, *op. cit.*, p. 340.
99. *Brieven van De Witt*, IV, p. 177.
100. He thus made a clear distinction between the Orangists and those of the States party who had taken fright.
101. *Brieven aan De Witt*, IV, p. 219.
102. *Brieven aan De Witt*, II, 551, p. 582.
103. 'With proper precautions for the preservations of the Country's safety and freedom, and especially with the insertion of the precautions laid down to that end in the Act of Harmony of 31 May 1670 and approved in the Generality by agreement of the Provinces'; *Resolutiën Holland*, 1671, p. 735: 12 December.
104. *Resolutiën Holland*, 1672, p. 87.
105. *Brieven van De Witt*, IV, p. 183.
106. Some Loevesteiners did, in fact, count on that. Thus on 14 January, A. van der Goes told his brother about a burgomaster who openly said something of the kind: *Briefwisseling Van der Goes*, II, p. 333.
107. See p. 330.
108. The instruction to Sylvius with covering letters (all undated) to Charles II and Arlington in *Correspondentie van Willem III en van H. W. Bentinck*, 40. Dr. Japikse supposes that it must have been issued some time in January. With the help of Sylvius' letter (see p. 330), we can be more precise: the instruction was issued shortly after 19 January.
109. *Notulen van Hop en Vivien*, p. 21; cf. *Secrete Resolutiën Holland*, pp. 227 seq. The offer was that the Dutch fleet would strike the flag before even a single English ship (more than the commitment stipulated at the peace of Breda), but on condition only that England would lend assistance against France in accordance with the Triple Alliance, and with the explicit stipulation that this concession was in no way to infringe the freedom of the seas. Leyden wanted to delete this last passage! (*Notulen Hop en Vivien, loc. cit.*). – Mary Trevelyan's assertion that Boreel was instructed to concede all demands on the point of the flag (*William III and the Defence of Holland*, 98) is entirely unfounded.
110. *Notulen van Hop en Vivien*, 44.
111. See p. 333.
112. Wicquefort, *Zeeoorlogen*, II, p. 79. See also Japikse, *Prins Willem III*, I, p. 177.
113. Leyden declared that she had never meant to be unbending: *Notulen van Hop en Vivien*, p. 22.
114. A fact stressed in August 1672 in the very well-informed pro-States pamphlet *Naukeurige bedenkingen van 't voornaemste dat dese*

noch onlangs so bloeyende staet is overghekomen (Kn. 10386): p. 20.

115. *Brieven van De Witt*, IV, p. 256.

116. Japikse uses the term 'petty', when describing De Witt's opposition to the appointment: *Prins Willem III*, I, p. 178. Inevitably so, for to him Loevestein stubbornness was the prime motive. This factor was certainly not absent. But Japikse (like most later historians) underrates De Witt's legitimate fear that, because of William's English connections, his appointment might increase the danger from outside. Thus Japikse fails to mention P. de Groot's disclosures about the secret treaty between England and France and its designs for the Prince; these, however, must have greatly influenced De Witt's attitude. Japikse calls the instruction to Sylvius (p. 333) 'an exuberant, unbalanced effusion' (*op. cit.*, 177). Certainly not! I hope that I have been able to show that this document was completely in the tradition of the Orange party.

117. *Briefwisseling Van der Goes*, II, p. 343. This comment was really occasioned by a false rumour, a fortnight before the actual event occurred.

118. For instance in the sonnet, *Den Batavier op het aenvaerden van het K. schap-G.* (Kn. 9964).

119. *Briefwisseling Van der Goes*, II, p. 343: the shares of the O.I.C. had fallen from 420 to 398, but rose again to the former level. This, of course, meant that people no longer feared a war with England.

120. J. Vollenhove, *D'Orangeboom herlevende in* etc.; Knuttel 9968.

121. *Notulen Hop en Vivien*, p. 47.

122. *Brieven van De Witt*, IV, p. 261.

123. For instance in *'t Samenspraeck tusschen . . . over het verraderlijck bedrijf der Engelsche aen de Smirnaes en Spaensche vloot*, Knuttel 9975 and in *Geveynsde vrundschap* etc. (a poem containing a cry for vengeance against Charles II), Knuttel 9978.

124. In *Eenvoudig burgerpraatje over een boekje Consideratiën* etc. (Knuttel 10014) the clergyman says: 'I, too, like thousands of others in our country had hoped that now [that the Prince has been appointed C.-G.] England would keep her covenant and support us against the French.'

125. P. Valkenier, *'t Verwerd Europa*, I, p. 677.

126. De Jonge, *Geschiedenis van het Nederl. zeewezen*, III[1], 68.

127. A striking account of the malpractices and abuses in the army is found in *Zeemans Praetje*. . . ., Knuttel 10236.

128. The author of *Naukeurige bedenkingen*. . ., Knuttel 10386, argues forcibly that it would have been far better to evacuate most of them and reinforce one or two of the others.

129. *Bondigh en waerachtigh verhael van het voornaemste voorgevallen aan*

den Rhijn etc. *naeukeurigh opgesocht en beschreeven van een oogh, en oorgetuyg* etc., Kn. 10045; 5.

130. *Notulen Hop en Vivien*, p. 53.

131. Sypesteyn and De Bordes, *De Verdediging van Nederland in 1672*, appendix IV, p. 115.

132. Louvois wrote on 20 June: 'Chaque province redemande ce qu'elle paye pour l'employer à sa defense'; quoted by Mary Trevelyan, *William III and the Defence of Holland*, p. 172. Similarly, the Commissioned Councillors of Holland (27 June) found that 'the allies (the other provinces) having withdrawn the militia to the frontiers, they as good as surrendered the towns': *Notulen Hop en Vivien*, p. 151.

133. In *Naukeurige bedenkingen* (Kn. 10386, 26) he was sharply reproached for this.

134. *Brieven van De Witt*, IV, p. 353: 10 June, to Van Beverning.

135. *Ibid.*, p. 350: 9 June to Van Beverning. In a vigorous speech to the Holland States, De Witt recalled the fact that Denmark had been reduced to Copenhagen, whence she had been fully restored (in 1659, when De Ruyter came to her assistance against Sweden). *Notulen Hop en Vivien*, p. 102: 8 June.

136. Sypesteyn and De Bordes, *op. cit.*, II, p. ff.

137. Cant, Fagel and Slingelandt: *Notulen Hop en Vivien*, p. 106: 11 June.

138. *Brieven van De Witt*, IV, p. 389.

139. Full particulars in L. Sylvius, *Historiën onzes tijds*. Originally in the form of pamphlets.

140. Pro-States pamphleteers made accusations as well, but these went largely unheard.

141. *Den grooten en witten duyvel*, Kn. 10319.

142. Thus claimed S. Tucker from Rotterdam on 28 June: *Zeeoorlogen*, II, p. 140.

143. L. Sylvius, *Historiën onzes tijds*, I (1685), p. 314. This story is based on *D'ontroerde Leeuw* (by G. Gribius? 1672/3?), p. 26. A similar story is found in Wicquefort, *Mémoires*, 207: Fagel is its hero; the obvious lies on p. 206 may serve as a measure for the trustworthiness of this version.

144. Sylvius, *loc. cit.*, explains that, at the time, the little blue books against the brothers De Witt 'were flying about the country in hosts'.

145. Another case was the conspiracy by Oldenbarnevelt's sons to murder Maurice.

146. I have in my possession a 'revised and improved third edition by Marcus Doornick'; Knuttel 10458 f. mentions two third editions but not this one. – It is a poem with a commentary in prose.

147. *Den oprechten Patriot*, etc., Kn. 10498.
148. In another remarkable passage Jacob relates how, walking some days earlier along the Rijswijk road, he was affected by the sight of the Westland churches: the idea crossed his mind that 'with this false and treacherous war the light of God's candle in there might well be extinguished and soon be replaced by superstitious rites'.
149. See p. 345.
150. Mainly based on the account in *Notulen Hop en Vivien*, p. 127 ff.
151. See Resolutiën Raed, III, and Civ. en Mil. Regheeringhe, II G.A.
152. See also De Witt's speech in the States: note 135.
153. By a majority. Judging from Bontemantel's account, those who wanted to break off the negotiations voted against the resolution; in other words, no one dared to advocate negotiations based on the French proposal in the end.
154. Resolutiën Raed (official), G.A., Amsterdam. – Bontemantel notes that as far as he knew the second part of the resolution was never communicated to the States assembly – understandably so in view of subsequent events.
155. *Lettres de P. de Groot à A. de Wicquefort*, p. 324 (letter of 3 April 1674).
156. *Notulen Hop en Vivien*, p. 139: these minutes bear out De Groot's report on the attitude of the two pensionaries.
157. *Lettres de P. Groot, loc. cit.*
158. The letter containing the Prince's request was published by Wagenaar (*Vad. Historie*, XIV, p. 61). It was not only to serve as a weapon in the party struggle eighty years afterwards, but cast doubt on the Prince's intentions at the time.
159. According to the Holland resolution, 26 June: *Secr. Res. Holland*, p. 263.
160. In addition to *Notulen Hop en Vivien*, we also have a letter from Burgersdijk in Kluit, *Hollandsche Staatsregering*, III, p. 536 ff.
161. L. Sylvius, *Historën onzes Tijds*, p. 324.
162. The whole story of Sylvius, *op. cit.*, I, p. 325-327.
163. Likewise the pastors of Walcheren, who decided on 4 July to urge their States to a vigorous policy: see Van Schelven, *Stemmen des tijds*, p. 158.
164. See note 135.
165. On 29 June; Leyden and Haarlem had previously raised the subject on 20 June.
166. *Res. Holland* in Kluit, *op. cit.*, p. 534. That many members agreed with the Leyden proposals can be inferred from what Burgersdijk wrote on 29 June: that he was pressed to leave out the offensive introduction, which had no bearing upon the matter.

167. *Corresp. van Willem III en H.W.B.*, p. 58.
168. *Openhertigh discours . . . tusschen een reghent, capiteyn en coopman;* Knuttel 9125, 1665.
169. Valkenier, *op. cit.*, p. 677.
170. *Hop en Vivien*, p. 161.
171. *Waaragtig verhaal van de muiterij binnen de stad Rotterdam.* This curious pamphlet was published anonymously in 1785. It is described as an eye-witness account and, in fact, has the mark of authenticity. As appears from a comment on p. 58, the work was composed before 1677 (the writer refers to an occurrence in that year as 'afterwards'); in any case it is based on contemporary notes. The intention of the story is to show that the revolt was the work of a small group of ambitious persons.
172. The manner in which the *Waaragtig verhaal* describes his journey to the Hague strongly suggests the authorship of Adriaan Vroessen. See *op. cit.*, pp. 86–93.
173. *Hop en Vivien*, p. 168.
174. The following after *Hop en Vivien*, p. 172–178.
175. See p. 356.
176. *Waaragtig verhaal* etc., 50 ff. The discussions from *Hop en Vivien.*
177. *Ibid.*, 186 ff; 7 July: pp. 191–196.
178. Voices in Zeeland had begun to demand that those who had gone to the French king must now be brought to book: Van Schelven, *op. cit.*
179. *Secr. Res. Holland*, III, p. 267.
180. These and the following particulars from English reports, in *Zeeoorlogen*, II, pp. 144 ff. and 148 ff.
181. See p. 317.
182. See also the dismay of Sidney Godolphin, Charles's agent in the French army. Godolphin, however, concluded that England ought not to declare herself satisfied with *less!* Mary Trevelyan, *op. cit.*, p. 247.
183. *Secr. Res. Holland*, III, p. 267.
184. Fruin thinks that Arlington and Buckingham expressed peaceful sentiments during their visit (*V.G.*, IV, p. 349) and so does Wicquefort (*Mémoires* etc., p. 230) who jeers at Van Beuningen's gullibility. To my mind, this view does not tally with the account by A. and B. themselves, published in 1919 by Colenbrander in *Zeeoorlogen.*
185. Newsletters, Holland, p. 177 (For. Entry Book, For. Comm.; 11 June OS 1672); Goodison. See Mary Trevelyan, *op. cit.*, p. 248.
186. See p. 354.
187. Sylvius to Arlington, Middelburg, July; Goodison.

188. Goodison, *op. cit.*; reporting Hartopp. Odijk had clearly received a warning from the Prince.

189. Baron de W. (see p. 390), who on 17 August sent messages to Arlington from Middelburg about the possibility of an invasion and about discussions with a pro-English Zeeland regent ('he would not, he sayes, for the world betray his countrey, but he is of opinion this is to serve it' . . .), alleged that the same people who remained inactive because of that fear, nevertheless believed that the Prince had committed himself to deliver up the island to the King of England, and that his greatest difficulty was how to do it 'handsomely', without showing his hand: *Zeeoorlogen*, II, p. 178.

190. *Zeeoorlogen*, II, p. 161.

191. *Corresp. van W. III en H. W. B.*, p. 65.

192. *Zeeoorlogen*, II, p. XXV.

193. *Corresp. van W. III en H. W. B.*, p. 66.

194. *Histoire*, IV, p. 447.

195. L. Sylvius, *op. cit.*, p. 372.

196. The claim of Wicquefort (*Histoire*, IV, p. 454 ff.) that the Prince threatened to throw the letters into the fire (a fire in July?) seems doubtful.

197. *Zeeoorlogen*, II, p. 165.

198. Wicquefort, *Histoire*, IV, p. 502.

199. *Hop en Vivien*, p. 210.

200. Kn. 10224.

201. For the tension between regents and ministers of religion see p. 186 f. The grievances of the church were stressed in a host of anti-States pamphlets in 1672.

202. See p. 346.

203. See p. 364.

204. Reported in: *Extract notarieel uyt seeckere missive van een Raetsheer des Konincks van Engelandt*; Kn. 10140.

205. A different version of this story is given by *Verhaal van 't voornaamste (Nauwkeurige bedenkingen)*, p. 17.

206. Kn. 10149; also in Sylvius, Valkenier, etc.

207. *D'ontdeckte Ambassade van De Groot*, etc.; Kn. 10466. My account of events in Rotterdam is mainly based on *Waaragtig Verhaal*.

208. In the text: 'had *not* been dealt with', clearly a printer's error: *Waaragtig Verhaal*, p. 155.

209. *Hop en Vivien*, p. 223. See also Wicquefort, *Mémoires*, p. 246.

210. De Witt specifically mentioned the *Waerschouwinge aen alle edelmoedige ende getrouwe inwoonders van Nederlandt;* Kn. 10346.

211. *De vastgekuypte Loevesteynsche ton aan duygen. . .* , Kn. 10429; written after the murder.

212. *Wederleggingsgedicht van het lasterschrift genaemt 'Verhael van 't voornaemste tgene desen Staet sedert eenige jaren is overgekomen'*; Kn. 1038.
213. Sylvius, *op. cit.*, p. 327. Dated the Hague, 21 July '72.
214. *Hop en Vivien*, p. 230.
215. *Corresp. Willem III en H. W. B.*, p. 87.
216. *Een brief uyt Rdam v. d. 10den July* etc.; Kn. 10153. See also *Bootsmans praet voor boetsmans recht*; Kn. 10236.
217. *Request van de Amsterdamse borgerye aen Z.H., P.v.O.* etc.; Kn. 10213.
218. *Ibid.*
219. Kn. 10565.
220. Cf. the story of a Brussels deacon who wanted the charter used as a school primer: *The Netherlands in the 17th Century*, II, p. 289.
221. Thus the author of *Een brief uyt Rdam* etc. (Kn. 10153) claimed that 'this work has been done by distinguished gentlemen, Captains of the commonalty, the most powerful merchants and prominent burghers', etc.
222. See for instance *Bedenckingen over hergeene door de borgeren van Hollant is teweegh gebracht, in het avancement van S.H., den P. v. O., en verdedigingh tegens soodanige welcke de borgeryen beschuldigen alsof sy hadden begaan Crimen laesae majestatis;* Kn. 10266: 'The arrest of the Magistrates has been a folly of some burghers, but it was done out of love for their country and out of suspicion.' – *Eenvoudigh schuytpraetje t. en Haegenaer en een R'dammer* (Kn. 10473) denies the rumour that Borstius' brother-in-law, Bastaens, had bribed sailors and common women to turn rebellious, and also the allegation that burgomaster Pesser, who was kept prisoner in the guards room under the Town hall, was insulted by the captain of the civic guard. This incident, however, has been noted too often to be doubted.
223. Referring to the circular letter of 8 July, Burgomaster Vroesen observed dryly: 'The designs of the court at that time had not apparently advanced to that state of maturity in which His Highness could dare to decline this request'; *Waaragtig Verhaal*, p. 128.
224. It is difficult to untangle William's real intentions in this matter; the account of Bishop Burnet (*History of his own times*), though full of inadmissible speculations, is corroborated in its essentials by an observation in a contemporary letter from Baron de W.: *Zeeoorlogen*, II, p. 175.
225. *Hop en Vivien*, p. 226.
226. *Ibid.*, p. 228 ff.
227. *Resolutiën Holland*, p. 867.

228. See p. 372.

229. The correspondence between William III and Charles II, including the 7 points, was first published in Burman's revised edition of Costerus' *Historisch Verhaal*, 1736. Burman's original documents were discovered by Schotel in 1866 and published in *Bijdragen voor Vad. Gesch.* in corrected form. The original edition is found in Japikse's *Corr. van W. III en H. W. B.*, 1932, after some additions by Colenbrander in *Zeeoorlogen*, 1919. Their authenticity was disputed at first, but admitted by Fruin (just before Schotel's discovery). Fruin defends William's offer: *V.G.*, IV, whereas Japikse is highly critical of it (*Prins Willem III*, I).

230. See p. 335.

231. *Corr. van W. III en H. W. B.*, p. 74.

232. Dr. Japikse adds: 'as the English King saw it!' (*Prins Willem III*, I, p. 235). But Charles II was in a position to know about William II's ambitions. Dr. J. also thinks that W. III did *not* publish *this* letter (see p. 393) 'evidently because it was a family letter', and also because Charles had 'dealt too liberally with the Dutch sovereignty'. But the passages I quote in the text show that there were other reasons to prevent William from making the letter public. In any case, it was written in English and hence meant to be kept secret, while the other letter was in French and clearly served a propaganda purpose.

233. *Corr. W. III en H.W.B.*, p. 86.

234. *Resolutiën Holland*, 13 August 1672.

235. Wagenaar, *Amsterdam*, I, p. 632.

236. *Ibid.*, p. 633.

237. Burnet makes this claim in *History of his own times*. But the suggestion by Baron de W. that many were opposed to the sovereignty has the ring of truth; *Zeeoorlogen*, II, p. 175 ff.

238. *Hop en Vivien*, p. 252.

239. *Secret Resolutiën Holland*, p. 284.

240. *Hop en Vivien*, p. 255.

241. According to *Deductie, tweede deel v.d. Gr. W. Duyvel*, Kn. 10383, many were anxious 'lest we shall be enslaved by the nobility'.

242. *Corr. W. III en H.W.B.*, p. 58; see Index under Meerman.

243. *Brief uyt 's Gravenhage* etc., 8 July 1672; Kn. 10281.

244. The best example is *Naukeurige bedenkingen van 't voornaemste dat deze noch onlangs soo bloiyende Staet is overgekomen;* Kn. 10386. It was apparently written just before the murder of the De Witts. The writer, who was very knowledgeable about affairs of state, was probably a regent.

245. *Het onbevleckte Wit . . . tegens zeecker Libel genaemt 'Consideratiën';* Kn. 10231.

246. See p. 36, note 73.
247. Kn. 10606. The author was probably Joachim Oudam, a well-known Rotterdam Remonstrant and poet. Dr. Japikse (*Prins Willem III*, I, p. 215, note 1) mentions Knuttel 10292 as 'one of the earliest pamphlets against the Prince'. I doubt, however, whether this reading of that pamphlet, *Den politiquen mantel opgeligt in 't Princen Leger*, is justified.
248. See p. 340.
249. *Ontknoopinghe van den valstrick van S.H. den Heere P.v.O. voor hem geleydt van sijner jeugt af...*; Kn. 10354.
250. L. Sylvius, *op. cit.*, p. 396, quoting *Resolutiën Holland*.
251. *Een Sociniaense consultatie* etc.; the author added: 'Buat's blood cries out for vengeance'; Kn. 10341.
252. Kn. 10387. The author was quite right, incidentally: the letter was, in fact, drafted by De Witt.
253. *Zeeoorlogen*, II, p. 174.
254. See, p. 388.
255. See p. 358 f.
256. *Corr. van W. III en H.W.B.*, p. 85.
257. The subtitle is eloquent: ... *dat den Koninck van Vr. niet door gewelt van wapenen, maer door demalitieuse directie van Jan de Wit, Pensionaris, ende sijne groote complicen, onder 't canon van goude Lowijsen, soo veel steden en sterckten ... onder sijn gehoorsaemheyt heeft bekomen* (That the King of France has subjected so many towns and fortresses not by force of arms, but by the malicious direction of Jan de Wit, Pensionary, and his accomplices under fire of golden Louis); Kn. 10319.
258. *Deductie van den tegenwoordigen toestant van dit Nederlandt; ofte tweede deel van 'den Grooten en Witten Duyvel'*; Kn. 10381.
259. Their children, hardly able to talk, already lisp: 'Sooner French than Prince.' The children of a burgomaster of an important town had dropped the remark: 'When the French are here, Papa will be governor.'
260. A shocking example is quoted in the text below. See also *De Geest van J. de Witt a.d. Hr. Van Beverningh*: Kn. 10454. De Witt himself had enough confidence in Van B. to ask him to present to the Prince his letter concerning the slanderous pamphlets; but that was on 12 July, at a time when the Rotterdam regents, too, still trusted Van Beverning.
261. *Briefw. Van der Goes*, II, p. 401.
262. Kn. 10366. See also Kn. 10440: 'To slay is not to sin.'
263. See p. 385 f.
264. *Hop en Vivien*, p. 251, note 1.
265. Cf. Japikse in *Hop en Vivien*, p. 266, note 2. As appears from the

pamphlet mentioned on p. 393, the secret had already been leaked
to the commonalty.

266. See *Verhael van 't voornaemste*, p. 19.

267. In August, William himself must surely have known how little he
could rely on that promise.

268. From the translation as in L. Sylvius, *op. cit.*, 381; the French
original (the confidential covering letter was in English) was
published in 1932 by Japikse, *Corr. W. III en H.W.B.*, p. 71. Cf.
Wicquefort, *Mémoires*, p. 241 (and 319), and Fruin, *V.G.* IV, p.
342. Fruin attributes Wieg's interpretation to 'spite and party
hatred', and in fact, this source is considerably clouded by such
passions. But Fruin's own opinion that Fagel (to whom he ascribes
the publication) 'had no other intention than to foster the people's
delusion that peace with England was inseparable from the
Prince's elevation', rests on a serious misapprehension of the
situation. The pamphlet quoted below (see note 269) offers irre-
futable evidence of this.

269. *Een Sociniaensche consultatie tusschen Jan en Arent; mitsgaders:
Den inhout v.d. laetsten Brief v.d.K.v.E.a.d.P.v.O.*; Kn. 10341.

270. *Briefw. Van der Goes*, II, p. 400.

271. Noteworthy, besides several other poems, was the excessively
bitter *Den oprechte Patriot;* Kn. 10498. The blood of the martyrs,
the writer argued, is the seed of truth, not only in religion, but also
in affairs of state.

272. *Sententie van den generalen Hove van Nederlandt tegens M.C. de
Witt . . . en M. Jan de Witt. . .;* Kn. 10408. Equally characteristic
was their representation of the murders as the execution of a
people's verdict. The De Witts had 'dared to perturb the state of
religion, thus aggrieving God's Church'. The same allegation
occurs in Kn. 10421: 'These white Devils were aiming at God's
Church and His Royal (sic) Highness.'

273. *Zeeoorlogen*, II, p. 186; and *Briefw. Van der Goes*, II, p. 406. There
is some doubt about the authenticity of this story. That many gave
credit to it is significant in itself.

274. *Haeghse Nouvelles de Rarité;* Kn. 10417.

275. *De onvermakelycke wandelingh na den hemel, ofte helen hemelreys van
J. en C. de Witt;* Kn. 10407.

276. *Hop en Vivien*, p. 289.

277. *Ibid.*, p. 288.

278. *Bontemantel's Regeeringe van Amsterdam*, II, p. 182; cf. Kn. 10214;
also Wagenaar, *Amsterdam*, I, p. 637. The date: 23 August.

279. *Hop en Vivien*, p. 296.

280. *Hop en Vivien*, p. 197.

281. *Resolutiën Holland.*

282. *Regeeringe van Amsterdam,* II, p. 194 ff.
283. Kn. 10561.
284. See p. 351.
285. See p. 358.
286. P. Valkenier, *'t Verwerd Europa,* I, p. 742.

Conclusion

William III was in control of the Republic. He had no need to use his powers for concluding an ignominious peace with England. Charles II's rejection of the seven points, brought home by Dr Rumpf in about the middle of August did not, as I have said,[1] cause a rupture in the negotiations. For a while, William III adopted a purely passive stance, but, in September, after receiving long and pressing letters from Sylvius and even from Charles II himself, he sent Van Reede back to England with instructions to repeat the seven-point offer.

Yet this was a policy doomed to failure. Halewijn, when reporting to the States of Holland on his fruitless mission to England, had rightly contended that the English government continued to see its advantage in pursuing the war. As far as they were concerned, England was far away from the battlefield and the ruin of the Republic was but the ruin of a competitor. That was precisely why the prince had been unable to rouse them against France – 'their actions,' Halewijn asserted, 'may be inconsistent, but they all tend towards the destruction of this country.'[2]

Why William III should nevertheless have pursued his work for peace becomes clear when one reads the letters he received from England. Not that the concern for his personal safety, of which both Sylvius (respectfully) and Charles (cordially) assured him, is likely to have weighed heavily with him – especially after the massacre of the De Witts. He knew he could count on his own people now, and brushed aside all English warnings that this tumultuous rabble might one day turn against him. He certainly saw no reason for accepting Sylvius's offer to garrison the 'cautionary' towns with English troops as a protection against domestic enemies. However, the very fact that these and similar offers kept reaching him, even when he himself had sat by with folded arms, must have persuaded him that the English were at last beginning to see things his way.

And indeed, the scales were beginning to turn against Charles. First the Elector of Brandenburg and then the Emperor concluded a treaty of mutual aid with the Republic, and although the new allies were in no hurry to act, the French felt the threat was such that they decided to evacuate Brabant in late August. Moreover, Charles had never expected or desired a protracted war – the longer it went on, the greater the threat from his own commonalty.

Even so, Charles was far from having reached the point where he must break with France, and when it appeared that Van Reede had nothing new to offer, he flew into a great rage. 'His Majesty,' Van Reede himself noted,[3] 'exclaimed bitterly against His Highness, saying he had long noticed that his kindness was despised by his nephew, who made it impossible to render him any further service. And the more excuses I offered the more he fulminated, employing these identical words: "I should have to be an animal, or a madman, to put faith in such idle talk. The whole thing is *a trick* [*trick* in the original. This suggests that the conversation was carried on in English] to hold me up, to gain time."' In the king's court, too, it was generally believed that William's offer was 'born either of ignorance or of malice, and more probably the latter.' No wonder then, that Arlington sent William a warning,[4] through the English envoy, against making contact with the English opposition, which was then showing clear signs that it had had enough of the war.

While the failure of Van Reede's second mission did not change the situation overnight, it introduced a new, and quite unexpected, element into the relationship between William III and Charles II. The prince was no longer the little boy whom Charles could freely use to subvert the Republic. England was beginning to take cognizance of the fact that the prince had a will of his own, and an iron one at that. True, William responded to Charles's angry outbursts with assertions of profound sorrow, saying that nothing mattered more to him than His Majesty's good opinion. He even sent Arlington an assurance that rumours about his alleged contacts with the English opposition were entirely false, that His Majesty had no more devoted servant than himself – a curious remark when we consider that it was addressed to the enemy by one who held the post of Stadholder-cum-Captain-General. However, in the same letter to Arlington, he also showed his teeth. Arlington had hinted to Van Reede that the prince had better remember that, if he continued to be so unyielding, the Dutch people might treat him as they had the De Witts. 'Do not think that your warning alarms me; I am not easily frightened' – was the phrase with which William ended his brief letter. And in his letter to Charles, he remarked that it was not up to him alone 'to give Your Majesty all you desire'.

The English now found themselves in a somewhat ludicrous position: William's repeated refusal of their 'generous' offer was, in fact, jeopardizing England's own safety. The strength this young man was displaying in such seemingly desperate circumstances took them utterly by surprise. We have come to know him from his least engaging side, from the equivocal part he played in Dutch domestic politics. But in his relations with Charles, William showed a degree of fortitude that stamps him a noble figure. It caused him to scorn the easy course that would have helped to turn him into a mere vassal. True, his seven-point offer to Charles was a poor compromise, but the fact remains that in July, he refused to take advantage of the popular uprising and did not impose Charles's terms as he might easily have done. Again, while he did not scruple to turn the internal commotion against his enemies in the regent class, he told the English quite plainly that he was unable to go over the head of the States. To do all that, great strength of character was needed, and this he derived in full measure from the realization that his interests were bound up far more with the Netherlands than with his uncle.

For the country, passing as it was through a dangerous crisis, his stand proved of crucial importance. William III did not bridge the profound party division that had laid the country low, but by immobilizing one of the parties, with however questionable methods, he was able to give the country a new singleness of purpose, the more so as, practical statesman that he was, he enlisted the support of prominent members of the old régime. Perhaps, had he been able to take the wider view, he might have succeeded in reforming the imperfect constitution; as it was, he had his hands full with a pressing crisis, and it must be counted to his great credit that he should have been able to steer the Republic to safety, without even having to make the sacrifice that the seven-point offer would have entailed.

For by inspiring a policy of manful endurance, which would have been beyond the power of a divided people, by firmly defending the coast with the help of De Ruyter (whom he was able to reconcile with Cornelis Tromp), and by striking out as soon as his allies were ready to meet the French army on Dutch territory, he was able to force Charles to climb down. In 1674, the king was compelled, willy-nilly, to sign a separate peace with the Republic, and although the States-General had to pay a heavy indemnity, there was no longer any question of Orange being raised to a sovereign position, of cautionary towns, of a tribute for fishing rights, or of the cession of Surinam.

Uncle and nephew had suddenly changed roles. It was William now who was looked upon as the great antagonist of Louis xiv, as the hero of Protestantism, even in the eyes of the English opposition, and it was with their assistance that he could at long last attempt to make England join the Republic in a common stand against France – the policy of Temple and Van Beuningen. In 1677, Charles still tried to bind his nephew by encouraging him to marry a Stuart princess, Mary, daughter of Charles's brother, the Duke of York. But as it turned out, that marriage merely consolidated the triumph of Orange over Stuart in 1688, when Parliament proclaimed William and Mary King and Queen of England. It was a triumph shared by the entire Dutch Republic, even though, in the end, it had to pay a heavy price – in the wars that raged in the eighteenth century, England was to benefit greatly from the Anglo-Dutch alliance, while the Dutch were to find it a rather mixed blessing.

In any case, William's triumph had the most profound repercussions on Dutch domestic relations. What we have seen of it was far from edifying. The estrangement of Frederick Henry from the States of Holland, William ii's open conflict with them, which but for his early death would very likely have resulted in open French support for the Orange party, the divorce of the Orange court and Orangists in general from the national interest, which continued even after the death of the Princess Royal, the underhand relations of Orangists with the English court – if we recall all this, we cannot find praise enough for the action of William iii when, overriding the young nobles in his retinue and the blind excitement of the crowd, and young though he was, he made common cause with the Dutch state against England. And yet his name would shine even brighter had he not misused his family ties with Charles to destroy regents who had done what they could for the national cause. We know today that his adversaries mistook his attitude in the critical days of 1672. But not only was it impossible for them not to suspect him after the bitter pills they had had to swallow from his father, his mother and his servants – he himself had given them ample opportunity to gnash their teeth in irritation and fury.

At the end of the day, moreover, the close ties which bound Orange to England, strengthened further by the marriage of William III 1677, and again by William IV in 1734, proved fatal to the internal politics of the Republic, and, moreover, placed her in bondage to England, albeit in response to the imminent threat of France. The dynastic element of the alliance, and the intensification of party strife, increasingly paralysed the hand of the Dutch state and led to the total collapse of the old Republic.

If the truth be told, the pamphleteer who, in 1672, claimed that the people were tasting the dregs of William II's wedding cup,[5] took too rosy a view of the future. The 'Patriotic Movement', which many regents joined, was simply a sequel to the commotion of 1672, and although it inaugurated a new period, it paved the way for a dangerous association with Revolutionary France. More than a hundred years later, Van der Capellen tot de Poll, himself a leading patriot, stated that all the calamities of the country were the immediate result of that hapless wedlock.[6] While this view is ingenuous enough to make the modern reader smile, there is no doubt that eighteenth-century political strife cannot be understood without the dynastic background we have been examining. And conversely, the bitterness with which the marriage tie between Orange and Stuart came to be looked upon in the fullness of time, adds to our understanding of the deep significance of this seventeenth-century union.

REFERENCES

1. See p. 385.
2. *Hop en Vivien*, pp. 289 seq.
3. Published by Dr. E. H. Korvezee, in *Bijdr. Vad. Gesch.*, VI, VII, p. 247.
4. This appears from William's reply to Arlington: facsimile in Japikse, *Prins Willem III*, I, p. 238. When Charles himself spoke of the 'many ill intentioned' of whom the Prince should beware (*Bijdr. Vad. Gesch., loc. cit.*), I do not believe (as does Japikse, *op. cit.*, 237) that he was referring to his enemies in England, but to those in Holland, e.g. Van Beuningen.
5. See p. 389.
6. *Aan het volk van Nederland*, 1781.

Genealogical tables

House of Orange

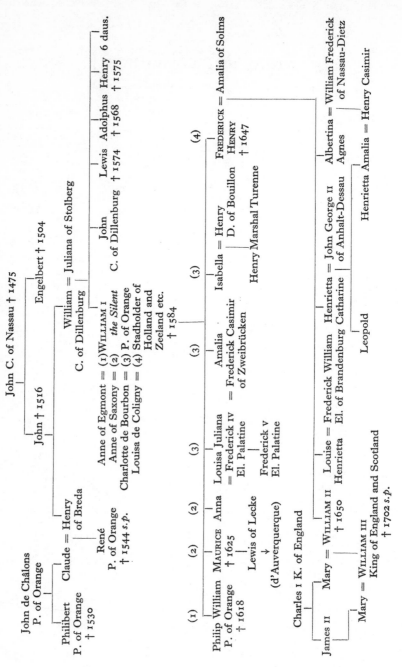

House of Stuart

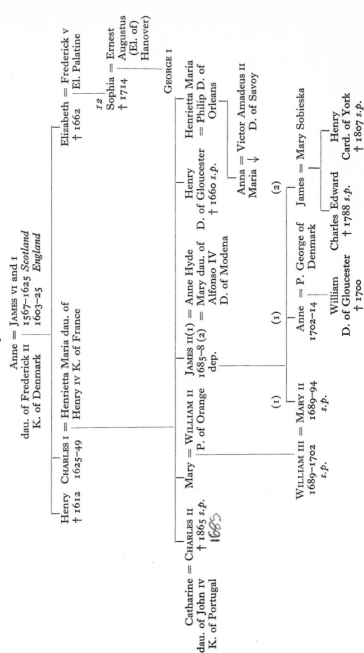

List of abbreviations

A.R.   Algemeen Rijksarchief, The Hague.
B.M.   British Museum, London.
G.A.   Gemeente-Archief, Amsterdam.
P.R.O.   Public Record Office, London.
S.P.F.   State Papers Foreign, P.R.O., London.
Archives   *Archives ou Correspondance inédite de la Maison d'Orange-*
            Nassau, publ. par G. Groen van Prinsterer.
B.V.G.   *Bijdragen voor Vaderlandsche Geschiedenis en Oudheid-*
            kunde.

H.G.   Historisch Genootschap, Utrecht.
B.M.H.G.   *Bijdragen en Mededelingen van het H.G.*
Codex   *Codex Diplomaticus,* H.G.
Kronijk   *Kroniek,* H.G.
W.H.G.   *Werken,* H.G.

Bontemantel, Amsterdam: H. Bontemantel, *De regeeringe van Amsterdam
soo in 't civiel als crimineel en militaire, 1653–1672,* ed. G. W.
Kernkamp; *W.H.G.,* III ser., 7, 8 (I, II), 1897.
Bontemantel, *Notulen . . . 1670:* H. Bontemantel, *Notulen gehouden ter
vergadering der Staten van Holland in 1670,* ed. C. G. Smit; *W.H.G.,*
III ser., p. 67, 1937.
*Briefw. gebr. Van der Goes: Briefwisseling tusschen de gebroeders Van der
Goes,* 1659–1673, ed. C. J. Gonnet; *W.H.G.,* III ser., pp. 10, 11 (I,
II), 1899, 1909.
*Brieven van N. v. Reigersberch: Brieven van Nicholaes van Reigersberch
aan Hugo de Groot,* ed. H. C. Rogge; *W.H.G.,* III ser., p. 15, 1902.
Brieven van De Witt: Brieven aan Johan de Witt, ed. R. Fruin and N.
Japikse; *W.H.G.,* III ser., p. 42, 44 (I, II), 1919, 1922.
Brieven aan De Witt: Brieven van Johan de Witt, ed. R. Fruin, G. W.
Kernamp and N. Japikse; *W.H.G.,* III ser., p. 18, 25, 31, 33 (I/IV),
*Hop en Vivien: Notulen gehouden ter Statenvergadering van Holland door
Hop en Vivien, 1671–1675,* ed. N. Japikse; *W.H.G.,* III ser., p. 19,
1904.

Lettres de P. de Groot: Lettres de Pierre de Groot à Abr. de Wicquefort, 1668–1674, ed. F. J. L. Krämer; *W.H.G.*, III ser., p. 5, 1894.

Knuttel (Kn.): W. P. C. Knuttel, *Catalogus van de Pamfletten-Verzameling berustende in de Koninklijke Bibliotheek*, 1889–1920.

Recueil: Recueil des Instructions données aux ambassadeurs et ministres de France, t. XXI, XXII (Hollande I, II).

R.G.P. Rijks Geschiedkundige Publicatiën.

Briefwisseling Huygens: Briefwisseling van Constantijn Huygens, 1608–1689, ed. J. Worp; R.G.P., 15, 19, 21, 24, 28, 32 (I/VI), 1911–1917.

Corr. W. III en H.W.B.: Correspondentie van Willem III en van Hans Willem Bentinck, eerste graaf van Portland, ed. N. Japikse; R.G.P., K1. ser., pp. 23, 24, 26, 27, 28 (I/V), 1927–1937.

Worp: see *Briefwisseling Huygens.*

Zeeoorlogen: Bescheiden uit vreemde archieven omtrent de Groote Nederlandsche Zeeoorlogen, 1652–1676, ed. H. T. Colenbrander; R.G.P., K1. ser., pp. 18, 19, 1919.

Index

A King and no King, 129

Aitzema, xi, 257; on Henrietta Maria's stay in Netherlands, 11, 13; on the Secret Committee, 21; on Frederick Henry, 22; on execution of Charles I, 46; on English Civil War, 47; on struggle between Holland and William II, 59, 60; on William II's *coup d'état*, 64; on first Anglo-Dutch war, 97, 98, 114; on power of Holland (1656), 130; on education of William III, 175; on second Anglo-Dutch war, 222; on character of William III, 238, 244; on elevation of William III, 239; on trial of Buat, 252, 254, 272; on Perpetual Edict, 271, 272, 302; on William in Zeeland (1668), 302, 303

Aix-la-Chapelle, peace of, 272, 277, 315, 317

Albertina Agnes of Orange, 212, 219, 280

Amalia of Solms, Princess-Dowager, 11, 142, 213, 223, 231, 278; ambitions of, 15, 50, 73, 110, 120; and treaty of Münster, 30; and quarrel over guardianship of William III (1651), 73-7; and relations with exiled Charles II, 101, 133, 134; objection of, to Act of Seclusion, 119-21, 123; opposition of, to William Frederick, 129; and education of William III, 131, 146-7, 163-5, 168-9, 173-5, 185-6, 241-2;

and French occupation of principality of Orange, 139, 175-6, 183, 238; alliance of, with States party, 182-8, 198-9, 229, 230, 236, 240-3; relations of, with Downing, 190, 198; relations of, with Albertina Agnes, 212; relations of, with Arlington, 219; relations of, with Buat, 220, 222, 230; relations of, with Wevelinchoven, 235; William III's antagonism towards, 236, 238, 243, 307; and making of William III a 'Child of the State', 241-3, 255; visits Maastricht (1666), 253; reaction of, to Perpetual Edict, 271; and Act of Harmony, 281-2, 306; and William III in Zeeland (1668), 301-3; declares William III's majority (1668), 303-4; opposes William III's visit to England (1670), 320-1

Amerongen, van, 250, 311, 327, 339, 371, 391

Anjou, 208

Archives de la maison d'Orange, 87

Argyll, Marquis of, 45, 48

Arlington, Earl of, 258, 305, 326; and outbreak of second Anglo-Dutch war, 193; and suggested peace conditions (1665), 204; appointed as Secretary of State, 218; intrigues of, with Buat, 220-1, 228, 231, 243-7, 249, 253, 257, 261; marriage of, to Freule van Beverweert, 226, 238, 281; and peace of Breda, 261-2; and

Witt, Johan de – *continued*
cil of State, 269–72; and Act of
Harmony challenged, 271–2,
278–82, 304; and Triple Alliance
(1668), 272–9, 315, 319–20; and
conflicts over William III's 'introduction', 308–12; Amsterdam's growing resentment of
(1669), 313–14; and Van Beuningen's mission to London, 315–
16, 319, 322; courts friendship
of Spain (1670), 320, 327; fears
of, for safety of Netherlands
(1670–1), 320, 324–7; opposition
of, to William III being made
Captain-General, 327–33, 335;
and acceptance of William III as
Captain-General, 335–7; and
Secret Commission, 340; and
French-Münster attack (1672),
342–5; as focus of popular discontent (1672), 346–9; attempted
assassination of (1672), 347–9,
361; wide experience of, 354–5;
William III's letter to (July

1672), 377, 379, 392; resignation
of, 385, 390; and perennial distrust of William III, 388, 391;
mentioned in States' party pamphlets, 389; massacre of (1672),
391, 393–5, 417, 419
Worcester, battle of, 86, 89

York, James, Duke of, 128, 132,
135, 142, 167, 257; as naval
commander during his exile,
42–3, 81; presence of, at William
II's funeral, 74; in exile at the
Hague, 84–5; in exile at Bruges,
127; marriage of, to Anne Hyde,
148; and Royal African Company, 191–2; and New Netherland, 192; and elevation of
William III, 337, 358, 365; and
marriage of daughter Mary
Stuart to William III, 420

Zuid-Polsbroeck, de Graeff van *see*
Graeff, de
Zuylestein, *see* Nassau-Zuylestein